A PARADE OF LINES

A PARADE OF LINES

PAUL C. HOLMES

ANITA J. LEHMAN

COLLEGE OF SAN MATEO

CANFIELD PRESS

A DEPARTMENT OF

HARPER AND ROW, PUBLISHERS, INC.

SAN FRANCISCO   NEW YORK   EVANSTON   LONDON

A PARADE OF LINES

Standard Book Number: 06–383840–0

Library of Congress Catalog Card Number 70–148573

74 10 9 8 7 6 5 4

Dedicated To

PEACE, BROTHERHOOD, AND LOVE

Also by Holmes & Lehman

KEYS TO UNDERSTANDING: Receiving and Sending
   THE ESSAY 1968
   THE POEM 1969
   DRAMA   1970
   THE SHORT STORY in preparation

Education for freedom must begin by stating facts
and enunciating values, and must go on to develop
appropriate techniques for realizing the values and
for combating those who, for whatever reason, choose
to ignore the facts or deny the values.

Aldous Huxley
Brave New World Revisited

He was made aware of something he hadn't been aware of.

'Learning is discovery.'

*'Even if I am right in my interpretation, if I tell him,
I rob him of the opportunity to discover for himself.'*

Don't Push The River
Barry Stevens

PREFACE

In a world seemingly filled with unending contradictions and monumental problems, young people must be encouraged to believe there is a possibility for change. They also must be shown how they can accomplish these changes in the face of overwhelming obstacles. This book hopes to expose students, through literature and essays, to provocative ideas and problems in a positive manner.

Many people are frozen into a state of limbo unable to act or think rationally because of the sheer magnitude or complexity of life's problems. Some people are so frightened by the future and so discouraged by society's ills that they "drop out" or flee into a fantasy world of drugs. Others foolishly believe that if someone simply recognizes a problem and states it that somehow it will automatically be solved. We believe man's environmental, social, political, and economic dilemmas can be solved; but they will require cool, positive thinking, great courage, and tremendous commitment.

College students often become indifferent and/or discouraged by the ceaseless number of printed lines that are paraded before their eyes. They do not become emotionally involved and consequently they reflect their apathy in written assignments and discussions. This book is purposely designed, with its wide range of pictorial and written materials, to touch every student with at least one idea. These ideas, plus an unhindered interaction between the students, the instructor, and the text, should encourage and facilitate original thinking, writing, and learning. Because we believe that a text of this type should be a jumping off place for further research and exploration, we have not hindered the student's intellectual curiosity with any rigid limits, guidelines, or editorial apparatus. Rather, we view this book as a catalyst which hopefully will facilitate a reaction that might not otherwise occur. It does not proscribe the reaction; it gives the students the freedom to research and define the problem and then come up with his own solutions. The student helps himself to learn how to learn for the rest of his life.

We would like to acknowledge and thank the many associates who have contributed in some way to the development of this book. Fellow faculty members are Helen Berryhill, Jack Gill, Louise Hazelton, and Richard Williamson. Students include Harry Souza, Rose Shirinian, and Curtis Lindskog. We thank James Stockton, designer, and Kenneth Burke, Canfield Press editor, for their work on this book. And, finally, we recognize our families for their cooperation and encouragement: Helen Holmes, Laurie Lehman, and especially the late Jay Lehman, who gave us the title for our book.

Paul C. Holmes
Anita J. Lehman
February, 1970

ART CREDITS

Page 3. *The Kiss:* Augustine Rodin (California Legion of Honor).

Page 4. *The Kiss:* Constantine Brancusi (Philadelphia Museum of Art, the Louise and Walter Arensberg Collection).

Page 24. *Woman Wailing:* Marianna Pineda (used by permission of Marianna Pineda).

Page 30. *The Buffalo Hunter:* Painter unknown (Buell Hammett Memorial Fund, Santa Barbara Museum).

Page 51. *The Gay Quarters of Kyoto:* Japan Edo Period (Museum of Fine Arts, Boston, Gift of Denman Waldo Ross).

Page 56. Photo by Ken Heyman.

Page 61. Photo by Richard A. Estrada.

Page 69. Courtesy of Bay Area Rapid Transit, San Francisco.

Page 79. Photo by P. Buckley, Photo Researchers.

Page 87. Photo by Lynn McLaren, Rapho Guillumette Pictures.

Page 89. Photo by P. Buckley, Photo Researchers.

Page 105. Photo by Richard A. Estrada.

Page 107. *The Riders of the Four Horses:* Albrecht Durer (The Metropolitan Museum of Art, gift of Junius S. Morgan, 1919).

Page 122. Photo by Gene Brown.

Page 136. Photo by Gerhard Gscheidle, Photo Find, S. F.

Page 165. Photo by Van Bucher, Photo Researchers.

Page 171. *The Fall of Icarus:* Pieter Brueghal (Musees Royaux Des Beaux-Arts De Belgique).

Page 181. *The Cry:* Edvard Munch (National Gallery of Art, Washington, D.C.).

Page 185. *Christina's World:* Andrew Wyeth (Collection, The Museum of Modern Art, New York).

Page 221. Photo by Linda Klink, Photo Find, San Francisco.

Page 229. Courtesy of General Motors Acceptance Corporation.

Page 236. Photo by Richard A. Estrada.

Page 259. By permission of Houston Chronicle Publishing Co., Houston, Texas.

Page 262. *The Man With the Hoe:* Jean François Millet (Private collection).

Page 271. Photo by the Equitable Life Insurance Society of the United States.

Page 276. Photo by Lee Reeves.

Page 285. Photo by George W. Martin: DPI.

Page 287. Top: Photo by Howard Harrison, Photo Find, S.F. Bottom: Photo by Michelle Vignes, Photo Find, S.F.

Page 296. Photo by Gerhard Gscheidle, Photo Find, S.F.

Page 303. Photo by Gene Daniels, *Black Star.*

Page 307. *La Familia:* Hose Clemente Orozco (Collection, Museum of Modern Art, New York).

Page 313. Photo by Michelle Vignes, Photo Find, S.F.

Page 328. *The American Gothic:* Wood (The Art Institute of Chicago).

Page 330. By permission of Temple Israel, Tulsa, Oklahoma.

Page 332. *Laocoon* (Courtesy of Vatican Museum).

Page 336. Photo by Gene Brown.

Page 337. *Guernica:* Pablo Picasso (On extended loan to the Museum of Modern Art, New York, from the artist.)

Page 353. Photo by Gene Brown.

Page 365. Photo by David Close.

Page 370. Ken Alexander, San Francisco Examiner.

Page 377. Gray Smith, San Francisco Chronicle.

Page 379. By permission of Planned Parenthood—World Population.

Page 382. Courtesy of San Francisco Bay Area Rapid Transit.

Page 394–95. Photo by James Rose, Sierra Club.

Page 413. Photo by I Burt Shavitz.

Page 417. Drawing by Charles Adams; © 1969 *The New Yorker* Magazine Inc.

Page 424. *The Peaceable Kingdom:* Edward Hicks (Private collection).

Editorial and Design Supervision by Ken Burke

Book Design by James Stockton

Copyediting by Judith Fillmore

Production Manager Christine Schacker

PART I: LINES TO WALK ON

CONTENTS

PART II: LINES TO HANG YOU UP ON

Greed   *Voilence*   *Hate*   *Apathy*

PART III: LINES TO CROSS

Loneliness   *Poverty*   *Injustice*

xii

PART IV: LINES NOT TO CROSS

Militarism   *Overpopulation*   *Pollution*

xiii

A PARADE OF LINES

LOVE

LIFE

COMMUNICATION

LINES TO WALK ON

If I truly love one person, I love all persons, I love the world, I love life. If I can say to somebody else, "I love you," I must be able to say, "I love in you everybody, I love through you the world, I love in you also myself."

Erich Fromm

To love is to have the courage to reach out, to care, to commit oneself to others, to be able to communicate sensitively, to add new dimensions to one's life. To love is to be truly alive.

The Kiss: Augustine Rodin

THY FINGERS MAKE EARLY FLOWERS

Thy fingers make early flowers of all things.
thy hair mostly the hours love:
a smoothness which
sings, saying
(though love be a day)
do not fear, we will go amaying.

thy whitest feet crisply are straying.
Always
thy moist eyes are at kisses playing,
whose strangeness much
says; singing
(though love be a day)
for which girl art thou flowers bringing?

To be thy lips is a sweet thing
and small.
Death, Thee i call rich beyond wishing
if this thou catch,
else missing.
(though love be a day
and life be nothing, it shall not stop kissing).

—e. e. cummings

Reprinted by permission of Harcourt, Brace & World from
e. e. cummings, *Poems: 1923–1954* (New York: Harcourt,
Brace & World, 1951).

The Kiss: Constantine Brancusi.

BOY IN THE SUMMER SUN

By Mark Schorer

Unalloyed, summer had lingered miraculously into late September without a suggestion that autumn was at hand. Leaves and grass were green still, smoke had not yet come into the air, and the lake was calm, almost sapphire blue. Midmornings were hot, like mornings in July. So they walked where the woods were thickest, where the air was always slightly damp, and the cool of night was never quite gone. They did not speak much but went silently along the path, almost shoulder to shoulder, their hands touching, or their arms, as they moved. Now and then the girl spoke, quietly, briefly pointed out a bird, a flower, once a green snake gliding through the grass, and the boy answered with a nod or a monosyllable, his face touched with abstraction and a slight worry. After they came to a place in the wood where they stretched out now with their arms about each other lightly as if the place and this gesture were habitual, they did not speak at all until at last the girl, Rachel, asked suddenly, "Why are you so quiet? Is it Max? Are you angry because he's coming, Will?"

The boy started and looked into her face. "Angry? No, I'm not angry . . . I was just thinking about that lousy job. When I'm out here it's hard to believe that a job like that can be waiting for me when I get back. It's foul."

The girl looked away into the depth of the wood. "Is it, Will?" she asked. "Or is it just that four years of school pretty well spoiled us for anything else? That we never learn there that for most people life finally comes down to work?"

"Maybe that's it."

"Or is it foul, Will? Is it worse that most jobs in the city, in summer?"

"Maybe not. But it's still foul."

They were quiet again, and it seemed a long time later, to him, when Rachel said, "Anyway, I'm glad it isn't Max."

His arms tightened around her shoulders. Then he sat up, his eyes narrowed in the shade, and he asked, "Why should it be?"

She said, "It shouldn't."

He lay down beside her again. He stared up into the lacework of green leaves

Reprinted by permission of Brandt & Brandt from *Story Magazine*, 1965.

arched above them, and at the rare patches of blue sky that the leaves did not cover. Why should it be Max? Or why should she think it might be?

He had been awakened that morning by the ringing telephone, and lay sleepily in bed listening to Rachel's voice talking to someone in a way that did disturb him vaguely then, although now it seemed only mildly irritating that this week end should be intruded upon. "But darling!" her voice had cried over the telephone. "What are you doing here? Come over at once! Mind? Of course not! We'll love it! In two hours? Good!"

When he came to breakfast, she smiled brightly and cried, "Guess who's coming, Will! Max Garey! He got bored and started out early this morning, and just now called from the village. Isn't it grand? Mother's so fond of him—she'll take care of him."

"Does your mother know him? I didn't know she did."

"Oh yes, that last week at school, when she came to help me pack, you know . . ."

"No, I didn't," he said. And now he wondered why she had not told him.

Then Mrs. Harley came out on the porch. "Good morning, Will," she said brightly as she patted her white hair. "Isn't it *nice* that Mr. Garey can come! I'm so fond of Mr. Garey!"

"Yes, isn't it?" Will said into his coffee, and looked across the table into Rachel's eyes, which were shining with pleasure and were quite heedless of the question in his.

"Did you have any work with Mr. Garey, Will? Rachel thought him such a splendid teacher."

"No, I didn't," Will said. "His classes were always filled with girls."

Rachel looked at him quickly. "Now you're being unfair, Will. He's not one of those. Everybody thinks he's a good teacher."

"I'm sorry," he said, and felt suddenly sad, lonely in the bright morning with Rachel across the table from him.

He felt that loneliness again now. "Maybe it is more than the job," he said. "Everything's different since June. I don't know why."

"What do you mean, Will?"

"Just that feeling that everything's breaking up, smashing."

They were quiet then until Rachel said, "I know. I'm different, too. Something's changed in me. There's something sad, some ache . . ."

Will knew that something had changed in her. She was older than she had been in June. There was something about her now that bewildered him, the feeling that she lived without him, an aloofness, a self-sufficiency which was new. She was like a woman, sometimes, putting up with a boy. He had felt it almost every week end, and this and the more general sadness of the summer had darkened otherwise golden hours. And yet there was that in her kisses still, in her sweet arms around him, in her yielding body that belied his feeling. And, with him, there still came from her throat a little moan of pain and passion which he knew no one else had ever heard. And yet, now in the deep cool wood as she lay in his arms, he felt that she had forgotten him beside her.

She spoke at last as with an effort, as if recalling herself from a dream. "You know, Will, after you left school, in that week I stayed on, I saw Max rather often. Then mother met him. She invited him to come up. He was here earlier in the summer. Didn't I tell you?"

"No," he said, his throat contracting. "You must have forgotten."

His sadness knotted in his throat suddenly, intensely, and he remembered then very clearly, almost as if she were saying it again now, something she had said before he left here in June. "Sometimes I wonder if this can last, Will, if it mustn't end. It's been almost too lovely, too complete. We've *realized* each other. We know each other as I think people almost never do. Now it begins to seem a little unreal, perhaps because it's been too lovely, part of this unreal life we're leaving. I wonder if that sometimes happens, Will."

Then he had laughed; but now, as he remembered, his arms tightened around her suddenly, as if from fright, and he leaned down and kissed her. Her lips were quiet, without response. He opened his eyes then to look at her and saw that her eyes were fixed on some remote object in the arch of trees or beyond, some dream, something far from him. He stood up and moved away. "Let's go back," he said, and without waiting for her he started quickly up the path, toward the house.

All the afternoon they lay on the raft, Rachel between them. Max talked, his voice reflective and lazy, mixing with the sun of that afternoon and the endless laziness in the sounds that insects made in the woods and in the long grass along the shore, his voice spinning itself out, pausing now and then to listen to itself, and going on again, with Rachel lying quiet between them, her eyes closed and the oil gleaming on her brown skin. Will's head was turned toward her, his eyes wandering back and forth from her parted lips and her gleaming lashes to the swell of her breasts under her white swimming suit, to her long browned legs and her crossed feet at the end of the raft.

All the time Max's voice went on, the lazy professor's voice. Will could tell as he heard it that it was a voice that always talked and that always had listeners, and yet, now it did not irritate him. He was almost content to lie in the sun with the sensation of burning on his skin, and a soft warm glow of skin absorbing bright sun enough in the afternoon to allay for the moment the morning's inarticulate fears, even though it was Max who was lying stretched out beyond Rachel, who was talking, pausing, talking, sometimes falling silent and no word coming from Rachel or himself, and then starting up again, the voice spinning itself out softly in the afternoon sun, with all the laziness of the afternoon in his slow words.

". . . and so in Donne the central factor is death . . . death, of course . . . he, more than any of the poets, built what he wrote upon what may be called a meta-physic of death . . . death as the great leveler on the one hand, the great destroyer of everything, beauty, love . . . and death as the figure at the gate of Heaven . . . these two, this one . . . the central factor, always present . . ."

They are not long, the days of wine and roses.
    Out of a misty dream
Our path emerges for a while, then closes
    Within a dream.   *Ernest Donson*

His voice was slow, modulated, a little affected, quite soft, and in it, Will knew as he looked at Rachel's face, there was some magic, a magic of wisdom and experience that enthralled her.

Rachel's voice began, slow and soft as if infected by Max's voice, as warm as the sun, and speaking lines that Max doubtless first spoke to her, perhaps—only perhaps—in the classroom:

> "When I dyed last, and, Deare, I dye
>   As often as from thee I goe,
>   Though it be but an houre agoe,
> And Lovers' houres be full eternity,
> I can remember yet, that I
>   Something did say, and something did bestow . . ."

Max laughed. "But darling," he said, "that's still another kind of death, not so serious."

Rachel said nothing. And the sun wove around them its bright and golden web, and the whole world then as they lay there had slipped away and left the three of them stranded together in an unreality of sunlight on burning skin and closed eyelids, and nothing more. And Will, too, felt out of the world of fact, was empty of feeling, as if pure sensation had replaced it. And only slowly did a faint jangling come into his mind, the jangle of Max's word *darling*, like something shaken in a metal box, some harsh sound, or a feeling perhaps, shaking him abruptly from the web. He stirred. He turned. And in turning the web was broken, and he was free of it again, his hand plunged in the cold blue water of the lake and left to dangle there, his eyes turned from Rachel and Max for the moment but seeing nothing in the indeterminable depths of the blue water that gently lapped his hand.

"Not nearly so serious," Max said. "Only a metaphor, a way of speaking . . ."

Will turned toward them again, and now he saw in Rachel's face how serious it was, for she looked suddenly ill, for all the glow of her skin, her face turned away from him and her lips fallen apart, and every line in her face and body taut suddenly, yearning aching suddenly with sharp longing, sharp pain, she quite sick for love. Will's hands closed at his sides and opened again, turned empty to the sun.

"Poetry is full of such conventions, formalized short cuts to express familiar sentiments," Max was saying. "In Donne, of course, there's enough fire, usually, to vitalize them, but in others . . . mere metaphors . . ."

Something in Will's mind snapped, then seemed to shout, *Who cares? For God's sake, who cares?* He was enraged beyond endurance by the man's pompous classroom manner, his easy presence, his way of excluding Will, as if he were alone with Rachel and no one else existed. He hated him, and the very presence of Rachel there made his throat ache with something like the pressure of tears coming. The sun had lost its spell. The buzz of insects on the shore seemed for a moment unbearably loud, and the sun no longer warm, but hot, searing, parching his throat and mouth, blinding him. For now he hated Max, and he knew as he remembered Rachel's voice speaking those lines, that she was lost to him, that he had nothing more for her, that Max had all. And there Max lay, as if he belonged there, had every right to be there, talking and priding himself in his talk, delighting to hear his own words, lecturing there as though Rachel and he were alone in the room, and he, Will, did not exist.

Will's eyes clouded in anger as he stared down into the water disturbed by his hand. He tried not to hear what their low voices said, and only when they were silent did he turn suddenly on the raft again to see how their bodies had moved together, so that their legs touched, and Max's hand lay quite near Rachel's hair. He stood up abruptly, stirring the raft in the water, and then dived deep, swam quickly out and away from them, his arms beating the water in his anger, in a frantic effort to forget the hurt which came from Rachel's willing reception of the man's intolerable arrogance.

He struck out into the lake. The water was cold on his skin, and as he swam, his anger cooled. But when his anger was gone, he felt sad and futile again, swam more slowly, felt helpless and wounded, felt almost weak in the water, so that he grew angry with himself instead and wished that he could hold that other anger. When he turned back and swam slowly toward the shore, only the hurt remained, and he did not go to the raft. There Max's words would still be spinning themselves out in the sunlight, catching Rachel's mind in their spell, catching her heart firmly and her whole mind and life, and holding them there, as if the words were really magic.

He walked up the beach and stretched out on the sand. He lay on his back and looked up into the blue sky, and as he lay there he felt suddenly that this was the last time in his life that he would be doing quite this. All summer he had been coming from the sweltering, grimy city, and in seeing Rachel in the country, in living in her mother's friendly house, in swimming and dancing and drinking and finding cool spots in the woods where the moss was thick and only the trees and birds made sound—in all of this it had seemed that nothing had changed or was ending. And this in spite of the fact that when they parted in June, when they walked for the last time along familiar walks between familiar buildings, they had vaguely felt that an end had come to a period, that a new life was waiting for both of them, and that (Rachel felt) somehow they were therefore ending for one another. But then Max was nothing to him, only a professor whom she liked; so for him nothing really ended.

Now the golden day was unbearable. He turned over on his stomach and put his face in his arms. Almost at once he could feel the sun burning his neck, his back. But it alleviated nothing. There was the dull ache in his chest and throat, the constant feeling that at any moment he would cry out like a child in sobs. It was a pressure in his body that he could not put into thoughts, only the feeling that something was ending, inevitably ending. He thought of his past and it was all gold, all brightness and gold, all magic landscape, all love, all an idyl, all a bright day, and all ending.

He thought he must cry. All his youth was gathered into a knot of pain that choked him, a youth that had been like gold but that pressed against his heart now, dull and heavy. He thought of going back to the city, to the hot office, to the dull and stupid work, sweating over accounts, of the years he had ahead of him in which to slave there. And he knew as he lay in the sand, really *knew*, for the first time, that all of that was no mere interlude, that golden days must end, gold vanish.

He felt a touch on his shoulder, turned, and looked up. It was Rachel, brown in the sun, saying, "Darling, don't be rude."

He sat up. "Am I being rude?"

"Does he bore you?"

"Yes. I don't like him much."

"Well, I'm sorry he came, Will, but I couldn't help it. Come back and try to bear him. He's not bad, you know."

"No?" Will asked as he got up.

She looked at him swiftly, then smiled. "Don't be silly, darling."

"No, *darling*."

"Good."

Then they went up the shore, back to the raft where Max still lay in the lessening glare of the sun.

Then finally he could put up with him no longer. The whole thing, suddenly, was impossible, too foul, too much for him. He sat at the table for a minute more and fought against the impulse to leave. But Mrs. Harley, cooing in a voice that almost made him ill ("But how *interesting*, Mr. Garey. *Do* go on! Do you *really* believe that?") and Max, toying with his fork and smiling with what Will supposed was great "charm" before continuing his monologue, decided him. He looked quickly at Rachel. She sat at the end of the table, opposite her mother. She looked very cool in a white dress, brown throat and arms cool and lovely, her lips slightly parted, her eyes fixed—lost to him.

Then he rose quickly to his feet. "Excuse me, please," he said, and went quickly to the porch, and then outside, down the steps, stumbled down toward the shore under the pines. He sat down in the grass. His fingers fumbled for a cigarette and a match in his pocket. Then he stared out at the water and the new moon hanging close over the opposite shore. In the reeds the frogs sang. From above came the ring of silver on china. He bit hard into his lower lip when he knew suddenly that the salt he tasted was of tears.

Then everything broke, collapsed in him like a sail when the wind dies. He wept as he had not wept since he was a small boy; and there, for a time in the night, he felt that he was a small boy still, alone in the dark and lonely night. He lay on the grass and sobbed, and there was a violence in his weeping as of a body tortured. He smothered the sound in the grass.

But he could not smother the pain in his chest. It was like a live thing in his heart, heavy and pressing, torturing, not relieved by sobs. It came over him in waves of torment, and now it was no longer anything of the mind, but of the body alone, a physical pressure, racking and violent, eruptive and convulsive, as if his very life, well-loved, were ending in the torment.

He did not feel Rachel's hand on his shoulder. It was her voice that recalled him: "Will—darling—please!"

Even then he could not prevent his sobs from coming. It was as if they were something separate from him, separate from his will, as if they had their own life, must come to their own slow end. He felt no shame before her, had no feelings at all, no thoughts, was given over entirely to what seemed wholly a physical act. Then slowly, at last, his shoulders grew quieter. Slowly his breathing quieted. Slowly his eyes dried. And it was over at last. He felt empty, weak, desolate as he turned slowly over on his back to look at her.

The moon was almost in the water. He could see it, touching the opposite shore. The sky was dark, sprinkled with cold stars. These too he saw, blurred and faint, unsteady in the darkness. Beside him knelt Rachel, her white dress a vague lightness, her face above him a vague blur. She spoke again: "Darling, what is it, what's *wrong*?"

He swallowed hard but could not speak. He lay on his back and looked at the blur on her face. His hand reached out and seized hers, held it tightly. Then she lay down beside him suddenly, put her arms around him, and her cheek to his mouth. He sensed the familiar perfume of her hair and moved away from her a little. Now he could see the stars more clearly; their light was brighter, harder, they were steadier in the sky, fixed and remote. Then, although Rachel's arms were around him and her face so close that he could feel her warm breath sweet on his face, he was alone, desolate, empty, alone on the shore under the stars. He did not say this then, nor did he even quite feel it, but he knew it, his body, empty and quiet, knew it—the cold loneliness of the stars even on a summer night. He lay still and looked up. He knew that something momentous had happened, something momentous changed.

"I felt sick," he said at last, though Rachel had not spoken again.

She said nothing for a while, then whispered, "I'm sorry."

"It's all right now."

As if startled by the deadly quiet of his voice, she sat up and looked closely into his face. "*Are* you all right now, Will?"

"Yes, it's all right now." He said it clearly, calmly, his eyes on the distant stars.

"What was it, though?" she asked.

"You know."

"No."

"Yes, you do."

"Not *Max*, Will?"

"What else?"

"Oh, but *darling*—"

"It doesn't matter, Rachel."

"What do you mean—doesn't matter? Do you think—?"

"I know, Rachel. I knew it this morning. But only tonight, suddenly, at the table, when I saw your face while he was talking—it took that long until I really could believe it. But it doesn't matter now."

"You think I love him?"

"You do love him."

Then she did not answer.

"Yesterday I wouldn't have believed that things like this happen. For over a year . . ." He paused. Then, "Nothing will ever be the same again—love, or anything."

"Please, Will. Nothing's happened."

"Everything's happened. Now it's over."

She looked at him closely. Then she said, "I've never heard you talk like that. You're different. Your voice—it's . . ."

"What?"

"You're different. Your voice frightens me. It's so quiet and cold and far away, so different—" She spoke jerkily. "So dead!"

He sat up, leaned back on his elbows. The moon was gone, sunk under the water. The sky was darker, and the stars seemed brighter still, separate, and farther away. Then he lay down again and she beside him. They were both very quiet. Finally she said, "Do you hate me?"

He turned to her. "No," he answered. He watched her face. He saw her eyes sparkling with tears. He said, "What are you crying for?"

"I can't tell you why, I can't say, I don't know. I'm afraid. I do love you, Will. Only now I'm afraid because I do love someone else—more. I don't want to. But I do. It frightens me!"

Now she was no longer older than he. She was a girl again, her woman's poise, given her briefly by this new love, taken from her again by that same love because, in the face of it, she was afraid. She was afraid of its swiftness, of what it might hold, of her own heart, turning. Now he felt older than she, felt that he could tell her something. He said, "I know what it is. It isn't just that we've been in love. We've had such a swell time. I don't know if I can say this, but it's something like this anyway—you weren't just yourself for me, and I wasn't just myself for you. We were both in love with much more than each other. You were all of that life for me, and maybe I was that for you, too. We were that whole life for each other, and we didn't want to lose it, but we couldn't help ourselves, couldn't keep it any longer."

She was crying. She put her face on his shoulder and he felt her tears on his neck. Then he put his arms around her and held her close. But he felt no less alone. And he thought then that this aloneness would never entirely leave him again, but that when he got back to the city next day, after he had been there a while, working in the office, after a week or two or perhaps a whole year, finally anyway, it would have left him somewhat less empty, less deadly calm. Then this day and this summer and all the golden days would have become the dream; and the other life would be real.

"How did your poem go, Rachel? When I last died, and, dear, I die whenever you go from me . . .?"

"Please—don't," she said.

He began to stroke her hair. She was quiet now, no longer crying, held close in his arms. He said, "Maybe it's always like this. Maybe the end of every love is a kind of little death, when you have to put behind more than just the love itself, but all the life, too, in which the love was wrapped. Maybe that's just what living is—a lot of little dyings. I don't know—I can't say it very well. Maybe I don't even know."

For a moment more they sat together and then she said, "We have to go back. They'll wonder . . ."

"All right," he said.

Then, clinging together, helping each other up the slope, they went up to the house, where the lights were, and the sounds of voices, clinging together like children still, under the stars.

What a piece of work is a man! how noble in reason! how infinite in faculty! in form and moving how express and admirable! in action how like an angel! in apprehension how like a god! the beauty of the world! the paragon of animals!

Hamlet
Act II. Sc. ii
William Shakespeare

BUT THE WINTER LASTED TOO LONG

It's still raining,
And cold,
And the fog still covers the coast hills
Most of the day.

I'd hoped we might stay together
Until the summer
When the world would be warm again
And we might find again
Whatever it was that let us love
Each other.

But the winter lasted too long,
Or perhaps,
We just didn't have enough love
To wait for the rain to end.

—Faith Beebe

Reprinted by permission of Faith E. Beebe.

A WREATH FOR MISS TOTTEN

By Hortense Calisher

Children growing up in the country take their images of integrity from the land. The land with its changes is always about them, a pervasive truth, and their midget foregrounds are crisscrossed with minute dramas which are the animalcules of a larger vision. But children who grow in a city where there is nothing greater than the people brimming up out of subways, rivuleting in the streets— these children must take their archetypes where and if they find them.

In P.S. 146, between periods, when the upper grades were shunted through the halls in that important procedure known as "departmental," most of the teachers stood about chatting relievedly in couples; Miss Totten, however, always stood at the door of her "home room," watching us straightforwardly, alone. As, straggling and muffled, we lined past the other teachers, we often caught snatches of upstairs gossip which we later perverted and enlarged; passing before Miss Totten we deflected only that austere look, bent solely on us.

Perhaps with the teachers, as with us, she was neither admired nor loathed but simply ignored. Certainly none of us ever fawned on her as we did on the harshly blonde and blue-eyed Miss Steele, who never wooed us with a smile but slanged us delightfully in the gym, giving out the exercises in a voice like scuffed gravel. Neither did she obsess us in the way of the Misses Comstock, two liverish, stunted women who could have had nothing so vivid about them as our hatred for them. And though all of us had a raffish hunger for metaphor, we never dubbed Miss Totten with a nickname.

Miss Totten's figure, as she sat tall at her desk or strode angularly in front of us rolling down the long maps over the blackboard, had that instantaneous clarity, one metallic step removed from the real, of the daguerreotype. Her clothes partook of this period too—long, saturnine waists and skirts of a stuff identical with that in a good family umbrella. There was one like it in the umbrella stand at home—a high black one with a seamed ivory head. The waists enclosed a vestee of fine but steadfast lace; the skirts grazed narrow boots of that etiolated black leather, venerable with creases, which I knew to be a sign of both respect-

Reprinted by permission of Little, Brown and Company from Hortense Calisher, *In The Absence of Angels* (Boston: Little, Brown and Company, 1951).

ability and foot trouble. But except for the vestee, all of Miss Totten, too, folded neatly to the dark point of her shoes, and separated from these by her truly extraordinary length, her face presided above, a lined, ocher ellipse. Sometimes, on drowsy afternoons, her face floated away altogether and came to rest on the stand at home. Perhaps it was because of this guilty image that I was the only one who noticed Miss Totten's strange preoccupation with Mooley Davis.

Most of us in Miss Totten's room had been together as a group since first grade, but we had not seen Mooley since down in second grade, under the elder and more frightening of the two Comstocks. I had forgotten Mooley completely but when she reappeared I remembered clearly the incident which had given her her name.

That morning, very early in the new term, back in Miss Comstock's, we had lined up on two sides of the classroom for a spelling bee. These were usually a relief to good and bad spellers alike, since they were the only part of our work which resembled a game, and even when one had to miss and sit down there was a kind of dreamy catharsis in watching the tenseness of those still standing. Miss Comstock always rose for these occasions and came forward between the two lines, standing there in an oppressive close-up in which we could watch the terrifying action of the cords in her spindling gray neck and her slight smile as someone was spelled down. As the number of those standing was reduced, the smile grew, exposing the oversize slabs of her teeth, through which the words issued in a voice increasingly unctuous and soft.

On this day the forty of us still shone with the first fall neatness of new clothes, still basked in that delightful anonymity in which neither our names nor our capacities were already part of the dreary foreknowledge of the teacher. The smart and quick had yet to assert themselves with their flying, staccato hands; the uneasy dull, not yet forced into recitations which would make their status clear, still preserved in the small, sinking corners of their hearts a lorn, factitious hope. Both teams were still intact when the word "mule" fell to the lot of a thin colored girl across the room from me, in clothes perky only with starch, her rusty fuzz of hair drawn back in braids so tightly sectioned that her eyes seemed permanently widened.

"Mule," said Miss Comstock, giving out the word. The ranks were still full. She had not yet begun to smile.

The girl looked back at Miss Comstock, soundlessly. All her face seemed drawn backward from the silent, working mouth, as if a strong, pulling hand had taken hold of the braids.

My turn, I calculated, was next. The procedure was to say the word, spell it out and say it again. I repeated it in my mind: Mule. M-u-l-e. Mule.

Miss Comstock waited quite a long time. Then she looked around the class, as if asking them to mark well and early her handling of this first malfeasance.

"What's your name?" she said.

He who desires to see the living God face to face should not seek Him in the empty firmament of his mind, but in human love. *Feodor Dostoevsky*

"Ull-ee." The word came out in a glottal, molasses voice, hardly articulate, the *l*'s scarcely pronounced.

"Lilly?"

The girl nodded.

"Lilly what?"

"Duh—avis."

"Oh, Lilly Davis. Mmmm. Well, spell 'mule,' Lilly." Miss Comstock trilled out the name beautifully.

The tense brown bladder of the girl's face swelled desperately, then broke at the mouth. "Mool," she said, and stopped. "Mmmm—ooo—"

The room tittered. Miss Comstock stepped closer.

"Mule!"

The girl struggled again. "Mool."

This time we were too near Miss Comstock to dare laughter.

Miss Comstock turned to our side. "Who's next?"

I half raised my hand.

"Go on." She wheeled around on Lilly, who was sinking into her seat. "No. Don't sit down."

I lowered my eyelids, hiding Lilly from my sight. "Mule," I said. "M-u-l-e. Mule."

The game continued, words crossing the room uneventfully. Some children survived. Others settled, abashed, into their seats, craning around to watch us. Again the turn came around to Lilly.

Miss Comstock cleared her throat. She had begun to smile.

"Spell it now, Lilly," she said. "Mule."

The long-chinned brown face swung from side to side in an odd writhing movement. Lilly's eyeballs rolled. Then the thick sound from her mouth was lost in the hooting, uncontrollable laughter of the whole class. For there was no doubt about it: the long, coffee-colored face, the whitish glint of the eyeballs, the bucking motion of the head suggested it to us all—a small brown quadruped, horse or mule, crazily stubborn or at bay.

"Quiet!" said Miss Comstock. And we hushed, although she had not spoken loudly. For the word had smirked out from a wide, flat smile and on the stringy neck beneath there was a creeping, pleasurable flush which made it pink as a young girl's.

That was how Mooley Davis got her name, although we had a chance to use it for only a few weeks, in a taunting singsong when she hung up her coat in the morning or as she flicked past the little dustbin of a store where we shed our pennies for nigger babies and tasteless, mottoed hearts. For after a few weeks, when it became clear that her cringing, mucoused talk was getting worse, she was transferred to the "upgraded" class. This group, made up of the mute, the shambling and the oddly tall, some of whom were delivered by bus, was housed in a basement, with a separate entrance which was forbidden us not only by rule but by a lurking distaste of our own.

The year Mooley reappeared in Miss Totten's room, a dispute in the school system had disbanded all the ungraded classes in the city. Here and there in the back seat of a class now there would be some grown-size boy who read haltingly from a primer, fingering the stubble on his slack jaw. Down in 4-A there was a shiny, petted doll of a girl, all crackling hair bow and nimble wheel chair, over whom the teachers shook their heads feelingly, saying, "Bright as a dollar! Imagine!" as if there were something sinister in the fact that useless legs had not impaired the musculature of a mind. And in our class, in harshly clean, faded dresses which were always a little too infantile for her, her spraying ginger hair cut short now and held by a round comb which circled the back of her head like a snaggle-toothed tiara which had slipped, there was this bony, bug-eyed wraith of a girl who raised her hand instead of saying "present!" when Miss Totten said "Lilly Davis?" at roll call, and never spoke at all.

It was Juliet Hoffman who spoke Mooley's nickname first. A jeweler's daughter, Juliet had achieved an eminence even beyond that due her curly profile, embroidered dresses and prancing, leading-lady ways when, the Christmas before, she had brought as her present to teacher a real diamond ring. It had been a modest diamond, to be sure, but undoubtedly real, and set in real gold. Juliet had heralded it for weeks before and we had all seen it—it and the peculiar look on the face of the teacher, a young substitute whom we hardly knew, when she had lifted it from the pile of hankies and fancy note paper on her desk. The teacher, over the syrupy protests of Mrs. Hoffman, had returned the ring, but its sparkle lingered on, iridescent around Juliet's head.

On our way out at three o'clock that first day with Miss Totten, Juliet nudged at me to wait. Obediently, I waited behind her. Twiddling her bunny muff, she minced over to the clothes closet and confronted the new girl.

"I know you," she said. "Mooley Davis, that's who you are!" A couple of the other children hung back to watch. "Aren't you? Aren't you Mooley Davis?"

I remember just how Mooley stood there because of the coat she wore. She just stood there holding her coat against her stomach with both hands. It was a coat of some pale, vague tweed, cut the same length as mine. But it wrapped the wrong way over for a girl and the reverse, wide ones, came all the way down and ended way below the pressing hands.

Where you been?" Juliet flipped us all a knowing grin. "You been in un-graded?"

One of Mooley's shoulders inched up so that it almost touched her ear, but beyond that she did not seem able to move. Her eyes looked at us, wide and fixed. I had the feeling that all of her had retreated far, far back behind the eyes, which, large and light and purposefully empty, had been forced to stay.

My back was to the room but on the suddenly wooden faces of the others I saw Miss Totten's shadow. Then she loomed thinly over Juliet, her arms, which were crossed at her chest, hiding the one V of white in her garments so that she looked like an umbrella tightly furled.

"What's *your* name?" she asked, addressing not so much Juliet as the white muff, which, I noticed now, was slightly soiled.

"Jooly-ette."

"Hmmm. Oh, yes. Juliet Hoffman."

"Jooly-ette, it is." She pouted creamily up at Miss Totten, her glance narrow with the assurance of finger rings to come.

Something flickered in the nexus of yellow wrinkles around Miss Totten's lips. Poling out a bony forefinger, she held it against the muff. "You tell your mother," she said slowly, "that the way she spells it, it's *Juliet*."

Then she dismissed the rest of us but put a delaying hand on Mooley. Turning back to look, I saw that she had knelt down painfully, her skirt hem graying in the floor dust, and, staring absently over Mooley's head, she was buttoning up the wrongly shaped coat.

After a short, avid flurry of speculation we soon lost interest in Mooley and in the routine Miss Totten devised for her. At first, during any kind of oral work, Mooley took her place at the blackboard and wrote down her answers, but later Miss Totten sat her in the front row and gave her a small slate. She grew very quick at answering, particularly in "mental arithmetic" and in the card drills when Miss Totten held up large manila cards with significant locations and dates inscribed in her Palmer script, and we went down the rows, snapping back the answers.

Also, Mooley had acquired a protector in Ruby Green, the other Negro girl in the class—a huge, black girl with an arm-flailing, hee-haw way of talking and a rich contralto singing voice which we had often heard in solo at Assembly. Ruby, boasting of her singing in night clubs on Saturday nights, of a father, who had done time, cowed us all with these pungent inklings of the world on the other side of the dividing line of Amsterdam Avenue, that deep, velvet murk of Harlem which she lit for us with the flash of razors, the honky-tonk beat of the "numbahs" and the plangent wails of the mugged. Once, hearing David Hecker, a doctor's son, declare, "Mooley has a cleft palate, that's what," Ruby wheeled and put a large hand on his shoulder in menacing caress.

"She ain' got no cleff palate, see? She talk sometime, roun' home." She glared at us each in turn with such a pug scowl that we flinched thinking she was going to spit. Ruby giggled. "She got no cause to talk, roun' here. She just don' need to bother." She lifted her hand from David, spinning him backward, and joined arms with the silent Mooley. "Me neither!" she added, and walked Mooley away, flinging back at us her gaudy, syncopated laugh.

Then one day, lolloping home after three, I suddenly remembered my books and tam and above all my homework assignment, left in the pocket of my desk at school. I raced back there. The janitor, grumbling, unlocked the side door at which he had been sweeping and let me in. For the mauve, settling light the long maw of the gym held a rank, uneasy, stillness. I walked up the spiral metal stairs feeling that I thieved on some part of the school's existence not intended for me.

Outside the ambushed quiet of Miss Totten's room I stopped, gathering breath. I heard voices, one surely Miss Totten's dark firm tones, the other no more than an arrested gurgle and pause.

I opened the door slowly. Miss Totten and Mooley raised their heads. It was odd, but although Miss Totten sat as usual at her desk, her hands clasped to one side of her hat, lunch box and the crinkly boa she wore all spring, and although Mooley was at her own desk in front of a spread copy of our thick

---

In nature there's no blemish but the mind; none can be called deformed but the unkind. *William Shakespeare*

---

reader, I felt the distinct, star led guilt of someone who interrupts an embrace.

"Yes?" said Miss Totten. Her eyes had the drugged look of eyes raised suddenly from close work. I fancied that she reddened slightly, like someone accused.

"I left my books."

Miss Totten nodded and sat waiting. I walked down the row to my desk and bent over, fumbling for my things, my haunches awkward under the watchfulness behind me. At the door, with my arms full, I stopped, parroting the formula of dismissal. "Good afternoon, Miss Totten."

"Good afternoon."

I walked home slowly. Miss Totten, when I spoke, had seemed to be watching my mouth, almost with enmity. And in front of Mooley there had been no slate.

In class the next morning, as I collected the homework in my capacity as monitor, I lingered a minute at Mooley's desk, expecting some change, perhaps in her notice of me, but there was none. Her paper was the same as usual, written in a neat script quite legible in itself but in a spidery backhand that just faintly silvered the page, like a communiqué issued out of necessity but begrudged.

Once more I had a glimpse of Miss Totten and Mooley together, on a day when I had joined the slangy, athletic Miss Steele, who was striding capably along in her Ground Grippers on the route I usually took home. Almost at once I had known I was unwelcome, but I trotted desperately in her wake, not knowing how to relieve her of my company. At last a stitch in my side forced me to stop, in front of a corner fishmonger's.

"Folks who want to walk home with me have to step on it!" said Miss Steele. She allotted me one measuring, stone-blue glance and moved on.

Disposed on the bald white window stall of the fish store there was a rigidly mounted eel that looked as if only its stuffing prevented it from growing onward, sinuously, from either impersonal end. Beside it were several tawny shells. A finger would have to avoid the spines on them before being able to touch their rosy, pursed throats. As the pain in my side lessened, I raised my head and saw my own face in the window, egg-shaped and sad. I turned away. Miss Totten and Mooley stood on the corner, their backs to me, waiting to cross. A trolley clanged by, then the street was clear, and Miss Totten, looking down, nodded gently into the black boa and took Mooley by the hand.

As they passed down the hill to St. Nicholas Avenue and disappeared, Mooley's face, smoothed out and grave, seemed to me, enviably, like the serene, guided faces of children seen walking securely under the restful duennaship of nuns.

Then came the first day of Visiting Week, during which, according to convention, the normal school day would be on display but for which we had actually been fortified with rapid-fire recitations which were supposed to erupt from us in sequence—like the somersaults which climax acrobatic acts. On this morning, just before we were called to order, Dr. Piatt, the principal, walked in. He was a gentle man, keeping to his office like a snail, and we had never succeeded in making a bogey of him, although we tried. Today he shepherded a group of mothers and two men, officiously dignified, all of whom he seated on some chairs up front at Miss Totten's left. Then he sat down too, looking upon us benignly, his head cocked a little to one side in a way he had, as if he hearkened to some unseen arbiter who whispered constantly to him of how bad children could be but he benevolently, insistently continued to disagree.

Miss Totten, alone among the teachers, was usually immune to visitors, but today she strode restlessly in front of us, and as she pulled down the maps one of them slipped from her hand and snapped back up with a loud, flapping roar. Fumbling for the roll book, she sat down and began to call the roll, something she usually did without looking at the book, favoring each of us with a warming nod instead.

"Arnold Ames?"

"Pres-unt!"

"Mary Bates?"

"Pres-unt!"

"Wanda Becovic?"

"Pres-unt!"

"Sydney Cohen?"

"Pres-unt!"

"L—Lilly Davis?"

It took us a minute to realize that Mooley had not raised her hand. A light, impatient groan rippled over the class. But Mooley, her face unplifted in its blank, cataleptic stare, was looking at Miss Totten. Miss Totten's own lips moved. There seemed to be a cord between her lips and Mooley's. Mooley's lips moved, opened.

"Pres-unt!" said Mooley.

The class caught its breath, then righted itself under the sweet absent smile of the visitors. With flushed, lowered lids but in a rich full voice, Miss Totten finished calling the roll. Then she rose and came forward with the manila cards. Each time, she held up the name of a State and we answered with its capital city.

Pennsylvania.

"Harrisburg!" said Arnold Ames.

Illinois.

"Springfield!" said Mary Bates.

Arkansas.

"Little Rock!" said Wanda Becovic.

North Dakota.

"Bismark!" said Sidney Cohen.

Idaho.

We were afraid to turn our heads.

Buh . . . Boise!" said Mooley Davis. After this we could hardly wait for the turn to come around to Mooley again. When Miss Totten, using a pointer against the map, indicated that Mooley was to "bound" the state of North Carolina, we focused with such attention that the visitors, grinning at each other, shook their heads at such zest. But Dr. Piatt was looking straight at Miss Totten, his lips parted, his head no longer to one side.

"N-North Cal . . . Callina." Just as the deaf gaze at the speaking, Mooley's eyes never left Miss Totten's. Her voice issued, burred here, choked there, but unmistakably a voice. "Bounded by Virginia on the north . . . Tennessee on the west . . . South Callina on the south . . . and on the east . . . and on the east . . ." She bent her head and gripped her desk with her hands. I gripped my own desk, until I saw that she suffered only from the common failing—she had forgotten. She raised her head.

"And on the east," she said joyously, "and on the east by the Atlannic Ocean."

Later that term Miss Totten died. She had been forty years in the school system, we heard in the eulogy at Assembly. There was no immediate family, and any of us who cared to might pay our respects at the chapel. After this, Mr. Moloney, who usually chose *"Whispering"* for the dismissal march, played something slow and thrumming which forced us to drag our feet until we reached the door.

Of course none of us went to the chapel, nor did we bother to wonder whether Mooley went. Probably she did not. For now that the girl withdrawn for so long behind those rigidly empty eyes had stepped forward into them, they flicked about quite normally, as captious as anyone's.

Once or twice in the days that followed we mentioned Miss Totten, but it was really death that we honored, clicking our tongues like our elders. Passing the umbrella stand at home I sometimes thought of Miss Totten, furled forever in her coffin. Then I forgot her too, along with the rest of the class. After all, this was only reasonable in a class which had achieved Miss Steele.

But memory, after a time, dispenses its own emphasis, making a feuilleton of what we once thought most ponderable, laying its wreath on what we never thought to recall. In the country, the children stumble upon the griffin mask of the mangled pheasant and they learn; they come upon the murderous topknot of the mantis and they surmise. But in the city, although no man looms very large against the sky, he is silhouetted all the more sharply against his fellows. And sometimes the children there, who know so little about the natural world, stumble still upon that unsolicited good which is perhaps only a dislocation in the insensitive rhythm of the natural world. And if they are lucky, memory holds it in waiting. For what they have stumbled upon is their own humanity—their aberration and their glory. That is why I find myself wanting to say aloud to someone: "I remember . . . a Miss Elizabeth Totten."

I want not only to be loved, but to be told that I am loved. The realm of silence is large enough beyond the grave. *George Eliot*

SONNET 18

Shall I compare theee to a summer's day?
Thou art more lovely and more temperate:
Rough winds do shake the darling buds of May,
And summer's lease hath all too short a date:
Sometime too hot the eye of heaven shines,
And often is his gold complexion dimm'd;
And every fair from fair sometime declines,
By chance, or nature's changing course untrimm'd;
But thy eternal summer shall not fade,
Nor lose possession of that fair thou ow'st;*
Nor shall Death brag thou wander'st in his shade,
When in eternal lines to time thou grow'st.
    So long as men can breathe or eyes can see,
    So long lives this, and this gives life to thee.

    —*William Shakespeare*

*Ownest.

BARTER

Life has loveliness to sell,
    All beautiful and splendid things,
Blue waves whitened on a cliff,
    Soaring fire that sways and sings,
Holding wonder like a cup.

Life has loveliness to sell,
    Music like a curve of gold,
Scent of pine trees in the rain,
    Eyes that love you, arms that hold,
And for your spirit's still delight,
Holy thoughts that star the night.

Spend all you have for loveliness,
    Buy it and never count the cost;
For one white singing hour of peace
    Count many a year of strife well lost,
And for a breath of ecstasy
Give all you have been, or could be.

    —*Sara Teasdale*

Reprinted by permission of The Macmillan Company from
Sara Teasdale, *Collected Poems* (New York: The Macmillan Company, 1945).

22

EVELINE

By James Joyce

She sat at the window watching the evening invade the avenue. Her head was leaned against the window curtains and in her nostrils was the odour of dusty cretonne. She was tired.

Few people passed. The man out of the last house passed on his way home; She heard his footsteps clacking along the concrete pavement and afterwards crunching on the cinder path before the new red houses. One time there used to be a field there in which they used to play every evening with other people's children. Then a man from Belfast bought the field and built houses in it—not like their little brown houses but bright brick houses with shining roofs. The children of the avenue used to play together in that field—the Devines, the Waters, the Dunns, little Keogh the cripple, she and her brothers and sisters. Ernest, however, never played: he was too grown up. Her father used often to hunt them in out of the field with his blackthorn stick; but usually little Keogh used to keep *nix* and call out when he saw her father coming. Still they seemed to have been rather happy then. Her father was not so bad then; and besides, her mother was alive. That was a long time ago; she and her brothers and sisters were all grown up her mother was dead. Tizzie Dunn was dead, too, and the waters had gone back to England. Everything changes. Now she was going to go away like the others, to leave her home.

Home! She looked round the room, reviewing all its familiar objects which she had dusted once a week for so many years, wondering where on earth all the dust came from. Perhaps she would never see again those familiar objects from which she had never dreamed of being divided. And yet during all those years she had never found out the name of the priest whose yellowing photograph hung on the wall above the broken harmonium beside the coloured print of the promises made to Blessed Margaret Alacoque. He had been a school friend of her father. Whenever he showed the photograph to a visitor her father used to pass it with a casual word:

"He is in Melbourne now."

Woman Wailing, *by Mariana Pineda*

She had consented to go away, to leave her home. Was that wise? She tried to weigh each side of the question. In her home anyway she had shelter and food; she had those whom she had known all her life about her. Of course she had to work hard, both in the house and at business. What would they say of her in the Stores when they found out that she had run away with a fellow? Say she was a fool, perhaps; and her place would be filled up by advertisement. Miss Gavan would be glad. She had always had an edge on her, especially whenever there were people listening.

"Miss Hill, don't you see these ladies are waiting?"

"Look lively, Miss Hill, please."

She would not cry many tears at leaving the Stores.

But in her new home, in a distant unknown country, it would not be like that. Then she would be married—she, Eveline. People would treat her with respect then. She would not be treated as her mother had been. Even now, though she was over nineteen, she sometimes felt herself in danger of her father's violence. She knew it was that that had given her the palpitations. When they were growing up he had never gone for her, like he used to go for Harry and Ernest, because she was a girl; but latterly he had begun to threaten her and say what he would do to her only for her dead mother's sake. And now she had nobody to protect her. Ernest was dead and Harry, who was in the church decorating business, was nearly always down somewhere in the country. Besides, the invariable squabble for money on Saturday nights had begun to weary her unspeakably. She always gave her entire wages—seven shillings—and Harry always sent up what he could but the trouble was to get any money from her father. He said she used to squander the money, that she had no head, that he wasn't going to give her his hard-earned money to throw about the streets, and much more, for he was usually fairly bad on Saturday night. In the end he would give her the money and ask her had she any intention of buying Sunday's dinner. Then she had to rush out as quickly as she could and do her marketing, holding her black leather purse tightly in her hand as she elbowed her way through the crowds and returning home late under her load of provisions. She had hard work to keep the house together and to see that the two young children who had been left to her charge went to school regularly and got their meals regularly. It was hard work—a hard life—but now that she was about to leave it she did not find it a wholly undesirable life.

She was about to explore another life with Frank. Frank was very kind, manly, open-hearted. She was to go away with him by the night-boat to be his wife and to live with him in Buenos Ayres where he had a home waiting for her. How well she remembered the first time she had seen him; he was lodging in a house on the main road where she used to visit. It seemed a few weeks ago. He was standing at the gate, his peaked cap pushed back on his head and his hair tumbled forward over a face of bronze. Then they had come to know each other. He used to meet her outside the Stores every evening and see her home. He took her to see *The Bohemian Girl* and she felt elated as she sat in an unaccustomed part of the theatre with him. He was awfully fond of music and sang a little. People knew that they were courting and, when he sang about the lass that loves a sailor, she always felt pleasantly confused. He used to call her Poppens out of fun. First of all it had been an excitement for her to have a fellow and then she had begun to like him. He had tales of distant countries. He had started as a deck boy at a pound a month on a ship of the Allan Line going out to Canada. He told her the names of the ships he had been on and the names of the different services. He had sailed through the Straits of Magellan and he told her stories of the terrible Patagonians. He had fallen on his feet in Buenos Ayres, he said, and had come over to the old country just for a holiday. Of course, her father had found out the affair and had forbidden her to have anything to say to him.

"I know these sailor chaps," he said.

One day he had quarrelled with Frank and after that she had to meet her lover secretly.

The evening deepened in the avenue. The white of two letters in her lap grew indistinct. One was to Harry; the other was to her father. Ernest had been her favourite but she liked Harry too. Her father was becoming old lately, she noticed; he would miss her. Sometimes he could be very nice. Not long before, when she had been laid up for a day, he had read her out a ghost story and made toast for her at the fire. Another day, when their mother was alive, they had all gone for a picnic to the Hill of Howth. She remembered her father putting on her mother's bonnet to make the children laugh.

Her time was running out but she continued to sit by the window, leaning her head against the window curtain, inhaling the odour of dusty cretonne. Down far in the avenue she could hear a street organ playing. She knew the air. Strange that it should come that very night to remind her of the promise to her mother, her promise to keep the home together as long as she could. She remembered the last night of her mother's illness; she was again in the close dark room at the other side of the hall and outside she heard a melancholy air of Italy. The organ-player had been ordered to go away and given sixpence. She remembered her father strutting back into the sickroom saying:

"Damned Italians! coming over here!"

As she mused the pitiful vision of her mother's life laid its spell on the very quick of her being—that life of commonplace sacrifices closing in final craziness. She trembled as she heard again her mother's voice saying constantly with foolish insistence:

"Derevaun Seraun! Derevaun Seraun!"

She stood up in a sudden impulse of terror. Escape! She must escape! Frank would save her. He would give her life, perhaps love, too. But she wanted to live. Why should she be unhappy? She had a right to happiness. Frank would take her in his arms, fold her in his arms. He would save her.

She stood among the swaying crowd in the station at the North Wall. He held her hand and she knew that he was speaking to her, saying something about the passage over and over again. The station was full of soldiers with brown baggages. Through the wide doors of the sheds she caught a glimpse of the black mass of the boat, lying in beside the quay wall, with illumined portholes. She answered nothing. She felt her cheek pale and cold and, out of a maze of distress, she prayed to God to direct her, to show her what was her duty. The boat blew a long mournful whistle into the mist. If she went, tomorrow she would be on the sea with Frank, steaming towards Buenos Ayres. Their passage had been booked. Could she still draw back after all he had done for her? Her distress awoke a nausea in her body and she kept moving her lips in silent fervent prayer.

A bell clanged upon her heart. She felt him seize her hand:

"Come!"

All the seas of the world tumbled about her heart. He was drawing her into them: he would drown her. She gripped with both hands at the iron railing.

"Come!"

No! No! No! It was impossible. Her hands clutched the iron in frenzy. Amid the seas she sent a cry of anguish.

"Eveline! Evvy!"

He rushed beyond the barrier and called to her to follow. He was shouted at to go on but he still called to her. She set her white face to him, passive, like a helpless animal. Her eyes gave him no sign of love or farewell or recognition.

ELUSIVE BUTTERFLY

You might wake up some morning,
To the sound of something moving
Past your window in the wind.
And if you're quick enough to rise,
You'll catch the fleeting glimpse
Of someone's fading shadow.

Don't be concerned, it will not harm you.
It's only me pursuing something I'm not sure of.
Across my dream, with nets of wonder,
I chase the bright elusive butterfly of love.

Out on the new horizon,
You may see the floating motion
Of a distant pair of wings.
And if the sleep has left your ears,
You might hear footsteps
Running through an open meadow.

You might have heard my footsteps
Echo softly in the distance
Through the canyons of your mind.
I might have even called your name
As I ran searching after
Something to believe in.

Don't be concerned, it will not harm you.
It's only me pursuing something I'm not sure of.
Across my dream, with nests of wonder,
I chase the bright elusive butterfly of love.

You might have seen me running
Through the long abandoned ruins
Of the dreams you left behind.
If you remember something there
That glided past you followed
Close by heavy breathing,

Don't be concerned, it will not harm you.
It's only me pursuing something I'm not sure of.
Across my dream, with nets of wonder,
I chase the bright elusive butterfly of love.

—*Bob Lind*

Reprinted by permission of Metric Music Company, New York, 1965.

HIGH HORSE'S COURTING

By John G. Neihardt

You know, in the old days, it was not so very easy to get a girl when you wanted to be married. Sometimes it was hard work for a young man and he had to stand a great deal. Say I am a young man and I have seen a girl who looks so beautiful to me that I feel sick when I think of her. I can not just go and tell her about it and then get married if she is willing. I have to be a very sneaky fellow to talk to her at all, and after I have managed to talk to her, that is only the beginning.

Probably for a long time I have been feeling sick about a certain girl because I love her so much, but she will not even look at me, and her parents keep a good watch over her. But I keep feeling worse and worse all the time; so maybe I sneak up to her tepee in the dark and wait until she comes out. Maybe I just wait there all night and don't get any sleep at all and she does not come out. Then I feel sicker than ever about her.

Maybe I hide in the brush by a spring where she sometimes goes to get water, and when she comes by, if nobody is looking, then I jump out and hold her and just make her listen to me. If she likes me too, I can tell that from the way she acts, for she is very bashful and maybe will not say a word or even look at me the first time. So I let her go, and then maybe I sneak around until I can see her father alone, and I tell him how many horses I can give him for his beautiful girl, and by now I am feeling so sick that maybe I would give him all the horses in the world if I had them.

Well, this young man I am telling about was called High Horse, and there was a girl in the village who looked so beautiful to him that he was just sick all over from thinking about her so much and he was getting sicker all the time. The girl was very shy, and her parents thought a great deal of her because they were not young any more and this was the only child they had. So they watched her all day long, and they fixed it so that she would be safe at night too when they were asleep. They thought so much of her that they had made a rawhide bed for her to sleep in, and after they knew that High Horse was sneaking around after her, they took rawhide thongs and tied the girl in bed at night so that

Reprinted by permission of the University of Nebraska Press from John G. Neihardt, *Black Elk Speaks* (Lincoln: The University of Nebraska Press).

The Buffalo Hunter, *Painter: unknown.*

nobody could steal her when they were asleep, for they were not sure but that their girl might really want to be stolen.

Well, after High Horse had been sneaking around a good while and hiding and waiting for the girl and getting sicker all the time, he finally caught her alone and made her talk to him. Then he found out that she liked him maybe a little. Of course this did not make him feel well. It made him sicker than ever, but now he felt brave as a bison bull, and so he went right to her father and said he loved the girl so much that he would give two good horses for her—one of them young and the other one not so very old.

But the old man just waved his hand, meaning for High Horse to go away and quit talking foolishness like that.

High Horse was feeling sicker than ever about it; but there was another young fellow who said he would loan High Horse two ponies and when he got some more horses, why, he could just give them back for the ones he had borrowed.

Then High Horse went back to the old man and said he would give four horses for the girl—two of them young and the other two not hardly old at all. But the old man just waved his hand and would not say anything.

So High Horse sneaked around until he could talk to the girl again, and he asked her to run away with him. He told her he thought he would just fall over and die if she did not. But she said she would not do that; she wanted to be bought like a fine woman. You see she thought a great deal of herself too.

That made High Horse feel so very sick that he could not eat a bite, and he went around with his head hanging down as though he might just fall down and die any time.

Red Deer was another young fellow, and he and High Horse were great comrades, always doing things together. Red Deer saw how High Horse was acting, and he said: "Cousin, what is the matter? Are you sick in the belly? You look as though you were going to die."

Then High Horse told Red Deer how it was, and said he thought he could not stay alive much longer if he could not marry the girl pretty quick.

Red Deer thought awhile about it, and then he said: "Cousin, I have a plan, and if you are man enough to do as I tell you, then everything will be all right. She will not run away with you; her old man will not take four horses; and four horses are all you can get. You must steal her and run away with her. Then afterwhile you can come back and the old man cannot do anything because she will be your woman. Prabably she wants you to steal her anyway."

So they planned what High Horse had to do, and he said he loved the girl so much that he was man enough to do anything Red Deer or anybody else could think up.

So this is what they did.

That night late they sneaked up to the girl's tepee and waited until it sounded inside as though the old man and the old woman and the girl were sound asleep. Then High Horse crawled under the tepee with a knife. He had to cut the raw-hide thongs first, and then Red Deer, who was pulling up the stakes around that side of the tepee, was going to help drag the girl outside and gag her. After that, High Horse could put her across his pony in front of him and hurry out of there and be happy all the rest of his life.

When High Horse had crawled inside, he felt so nervous that he could hear his heart drumming, and it seemed so loud he felt sure that it would 'waken the old folks. But it did not, and afterwhile he began cutting the thongs. Every time he cut one it made a pop and nearly scared him to death. But he was getting along all right and all the thongs were cut down as far as the girl's thighs, when he became so nervous that his knife slipped and stuck the girl. She gave a big, loud yell. Then the old folks jumped up and yelled too. By this time High Horse was outside, and he and Red Deer were running away like antelope. The old man and some other people chased the young men but they got away in the dark and nobody knew who it was.

You are a child of the universe, no less than the trees and stars; you have a right to be here. . . . Therefore be at peace with God, whatever you conceive Him to be, . . . and keep peace with your soul. With all its sham, drudgery and broken dreams, it is still a beautiful world. . . . *Desiderata*

Well, if you ever wanted a beautiful girl you will know how sick High Horse was now. It was very bad how he felt, and it looked as though he would starve even if he did not drop dead sometime.

Red Deer kept thinking about this, and after a few days he went to High Horse and said: "Cousin, take courage! I have another plan, and I am sure, if you are man enough, we can steal her this time." And High Horse said: "I am man enough to do anything anybody can think up, if I can only get that girl."

So this is what they did.

They went away from the village alone, and Red Deer made High Horse strip naked. Then he painted High Horse solid white all over, and after that he painted black stripes all over the white and put black rings around High Horse's eyes. High Horse looked terrible. He looked so terrible that when Red Deer was through painting and took a good look at what he had done, he said it scared even him a little.

"Now," said Red Deer, "if you get caught again, everybody will be so scared they will think you are a bad spirit and will be afraid to chase you."

So when the night was getting old and everybody was sound asleep, they sneaked back to the girl's tepee. High Horse crawled in with his knife, as before, and Red Deer waited outside, ready to drag the girl out and gag her when High Horse had all the throngs cut.

High Horse crept up by the girl's bed and began cutting at the thongs. But he kept thinking, "If they see me they will shoot me because I look so terrible." The girl was restless and kept squirming around in bed, and when a thong was cut, it popped. So High Horse worked very slowly and carefully.

But he must have made some noise, for suddenly the old woman awoke and said to her old man, "Old Man, wake up! There is somebody in this tepee!" But the old man was sleepy and didn't want to be bothered. He said: "Of course there is somebody in this tepee. Go to sleep and don't bother me." Then he snored some more.

But High Horse was so scared by now that he lay very still and as flat to the ground as he could. Now, you see, he had not been sleeping very well for a long time because he was so sick about the girl. And while he was lying there waiting for the old woman to snore, he just forgot everything, even how beautiful the girl was. Red Deer, who was lying outside ready to do his part, wondered and wondered what had happened in there, but he did not dare call out to High Horse.

Afterwhile the day began to break and Red Deer had to leave with the two ponies he had staked there for his comrade and girl, or somebody would see him.

So he left.

Now when it was getting light in the tepee, the girl awoke and the first thing she saw was a terrible animal, all white with black stripes on it, lying asleep beside her bed. So she screamed, and then the old woman screamed and the old man yelled. High Horse jumped up, scared almost to death, and he nearly knocked the tepee down getting out of there.

People were coming running from all over the village with guns and bows and axes, and everybody was yelling.

By now, High Horse was running so fast that he hardly touched the ground at all, and he looked so terrible that the people fled from him and let him run.

Some braves wanted to shoot at him, but the others said he might be some sacred being and it would bring bad trouble to kill him.

High Horse made for the river that was near, and in among the brush he found a hollow tree and dived into it. Afterwhile some braves came there and he could hear them saying that it was some bad spirit that had come out of the water and gone back in again.

That morning the people were ordered to break camp and move away from there. So they did, while High Horse was hiding in his hollow tree.

Now Red Deer had been watching all this from his own tepee and trying to look as though he were as much surprised and scared as all the others. So when the camp moved, he sneaked back to where he had seen his comrade disappear. When he was down there in the brush, he called, and High Horse answered, because he knew his friend's voice. They washed off the paint from High Horse and sat down on the river bank to talk about their troubles.

High Horse said he never would go back to the village as long as he lived and he did not care what happened to him now. He said he was going to go on the war-path all by himself. Red Deer said: "No, cousin, you are not going on the war-path alone, because I am going with you."

So Red Deer got everything ready, and at night they started out on the war-path all alone. After several days they came to a Crow camp just about sundown, and when it was dark they sneaked up to where the Crow horses were grazing, killed the horse guard, who was not thinking about enemies because he thought all the Dakotas were far away, and drove off about a hundred horses.

They got a big start because all the Crow horses stampeded and it was probably morning before the Crow warriors could catch any horses to ride. Red Deer and High Horse fled with their herd three days and nights before they reached the village of their people. Then they drove the whole herd right into the village and up in front of the girl's tepee. The old man was there, and High Horse called out to him and asked if he thought maybe that would be enough horses for his girl. The old man did not wave him away that time. It was not the horses that he wanted. What he wanted was a son who was a real man and good for something.

So High Horse got his girl after all, and I think he deserved her.

"WHY DO I LOVE" YOU, SIR?

"Why do I love" You, Sir?
Because—
The Wind does not require the Grass
To answer—Wherefore when He pass
She cannot keep Her place.

Because He knows—and
Do not You—
And We know not—
Enough for Us
The Wisdom it be so—

The Lightning—never asked an Eye
Wherefore it shut—when He was by—
Because He knows it cannot speak—
And reasons not contained—
—Of Talk—

There be—preferred by Daintier Folk—
The Sunrise—Sir—compelleth Me—
Because He's Sunrise—and I see—
Therefore—Then—
I love Thee—

—*Emily Dickinson*

Reprinted by permission of Little, Brown and Company
from Thomas H. Johnson, ed., *The Complete Poems of Emily
Dickinson* (Boston: Little, Brown and Company, 1957).

THE SCULPTOR'S FUNERAL

By Willa Cather

A group of the townspeople stood on the station siding of a little Kansas town, awaiting the coming of the night train, which was already twenty minutes overdue. The snow had fallen thick over everything; in the pale starlight the line of bluffs across the wide, white meadows south of the town made soft, smoke-coloured curves against the clear sky. The men on the siding stood first on one foot and then on the other, their hands thrust deep into their trousers pockets, their overcoats open, their shoulders screwed up with the cold; and they glanced from time to time toward the southeast, where the railroad track wound along the river shore. They conversed in low tones and moved about restlessly, seeming uncertain as to what was expected of them. There was but one of the company who looked as though he knew exactly why he was there; and he kept conspicuously apart; walking to the far end of the platform, returning to the station door, then pacing up the track again, his chin sunk in the high collar of his overcoat, his burly shoulders drooping forward, his gait heavy and dogged. Presently he was approached by a tall, spare, grizzled man clad in a faded Grand Army suit, who shuffled out from the group and advanced with a certain deference, craning his neck forward until his back made the angle of a jack-knife three-quarters open.

"I reckon she's a-goin' to be pretty late again to-night, Jim," he remarked in a squeaky falsetto. "S'pose it's the snow?"

"I don't know," responded the other man with a shade of annoyance, speaking from out an astonishing cataract of red beard that grew fiercely and thickly in all directions.

The spare man shifted the quill toothpick he was chewing to the other side of his mouth. "It ain't likely that anybody from the East will come with the corpse, I s'pose," he went on reflectively.

"I don't know," responded the other, more curtly than before.

"It's too bad he didn't belong to some lodge or other. I like an order funeral myself. They seem more appropriate for people of some reputation," the spare

Reprinted by permission of The University of Nebraska Press from Willa Cather, *Collected Short Fiction 1892–1912* (Lincoln: The University of Nebraska Press, 1965), pp. 173–185.

If a man does not keep pace with his companions, perhaps it is because he hears a different drummer. Let him step to the music which he hears, however measured or far away.   *Henry David Thoreau*

man continued, with an ingratiating concession in his shrill voice, as he carefully placed his toothpick in his vest pocket. He always carried the flag at the G.A.R. funerals in the town.

The heavy man turned on his heel, without replying, and walked up the siding. The spare man shuffled back to the uneasy group, "Jim's ez full ez a tick, ez ushel," he commented commiseratingly.

Just then a distant whistle sounded, and there was a shuffling of feet on the platform. A number of lanky boys of all ages appeared as suddenly and slimily as eels wakened by the crack of thunder; some came from the waiting-room, where they had been warming themselves by the red stove, or half asleep on the slat benches; others uncoiled themselves from baggage trucks or slid out of express wagons. Two clambered down from the driver's seat of a hearse that stood backed up against the siding. They straightened their stooping shoulders and lifted their heads, and a flash of momentary animation kindled their dull eyes at that cold, vibrant scream, the world-wide call for men. It stirred them like the note of a trumpet; just as it had often stirred the man who was coming home to-night, in his boyhood.

The night express shot, red as a rocket, from out the eastward marsh lands and wound along the river shore under the long lines of shivering poplars that sentinelled the meadows, the escaping steam hanging in grey masses against the pale sky and blotting out the Milky Way. In a moment the red glare from the headlight streamed up the snow-covered track before the siding and glittered on the wet, black rails. The burly man with the dishevelled red beard walked swiftly up the platform toward the approaching train, uncovering his head as he went. The group of men behind him hesitated, glanced questioningly at one another, and awkwardly followed his example. The train stopped, and the crowd shuffled up to the express car just as the door was thrown open, the spare man in the G.A.R. suit thrusting his head forward with curiosity. The express messenger appeared in the doorway, accompanied by a young man in a long ulster and travelling cap.

"Are Mr. Merrick's friends here?" inquired the young man.

The group on the platform swayed and shuffled uneasily. Philip Phelps, the banker, responded with dignity: "We have come to take charge of the body. Mr. Merrick's father is very feeble and can't be about."

"Send the agent out here," growled the express messenger, "and tell the operator to lend a hand."

The coffin was got out of its rough box and down on the snowy platform. The townspeople drew back enough to make room for it and then formed a close semicircle about it, looking curiously at the palm leaf which lay across the black cover. No one said anything. The baggage man stood by his truck, waiting to get at the trunks. The engine panted heavily, and the fireman dodged in and out among the wheels with his yellow torch and long oil-can, snapping the spindle boxes. The young Bostonian, one of the dead sculptor's pupils who had come with the body, looked about him helplessly. He turned to the banker, the only one of that black, uneasy, stoop-shouldered group who seemed enough of an individual to be addressed.

"None of Mr. Merrick's brothers are here?" he asked uncertainly.

The man with the red beard for the first time stepped up and joined the group. "No, they have not come yet; the family is scattered. The body will be taken directly to the house." He stooped and took hold of one of the handles of the coffin.

"Take the long hill road up, Thompson, it will be easier on the horses," called the liveryman as the undertaker snapped the door of the hearse and prepared to mount to the driver's seat.

Laird, the red-bearded lawyer, turned again to the stranger: "We didn't know whether there would be any one with him or not." he explained. "It's a long walk, so you'd better go up in the hack." He pointed to a single battered conveyance, but the young man replied stiffly: "Thank you, but I think I will go up with the hearse. If you don't object," turning to the undertaker, "I'll ride with you."

They clambered up over the wheels and drove off in the starlight up the long, white hill toward the town. The lamps in the still village were shining from under the low, snow-burdened roofs; and beyond, on every side, the plains reached out into emptiness, peaceful and wide as the soft sky itself, and wrapped in a tangible, white silence.

When the hearse backed up to a wooden sidewalk before a naked, weather-beaten frame house, the same composite, ill-defined group that had stood upon the station siding was huddled about the gate. The front yard was an icy swamp, and a couple of warped planks, extending from the sidewalk to the door, made a sort of rickety footbridge. The gate hung on one hinge, and was opened wide with difficulty. Steavens, the young stranger, noticed that something black was tied to the knob of the front door.

The grating sound made by the casket, as it was drawn from the hearse, was answered by a scream from the house; the front door was wrenched open, and a tall, corpulent woman rushed out bareheaded into the snow and flung herself upon the coffin, shrieking: "My boy, my boy! And this is how you've come home to me!"

As Steavens turned away and closed his eyes with a shudder of unutterable repulsion, another woman, also tall, but flat and angular, dressed entirely in black, darted out of the house and caught Mrs. Merrick by the shoulders, crying sharply: "Come, come, mother; you musn't go on like this!" Her tone changed to one of obsequious solemnity as she turned to the banker: "The parlour is ready, Mr. Phelps."

The bearers carried the coffin along the narrow boards, while the undertaker ran ahead with the coffin-rests. They bore it into a large, unheated room that smelled of dampness and disuse and furniture polish, and set it down under a hanging lamp ornamented with jingling glass prisms and before a "Rogers group" of John Alden and Priscilla, wreathed with smilax. Henry Steavens stared about him with the sickening conviction that there had been some horrible mistake, and that he had somehow arrived at the wrong destination. He looked painfully about over the clover-green Brussels, the fat plush upholstery; among the hand-painted china plaques and panels, and vases, for some mark of identification, for something that might once conceivably have belonged to Harvey Merrick. It was not until he recognized his friend in the crayon portrait of a little boy in kilts and curls hanging above the piano, that he felt willing to let any of these people approach the coffin.

"Take the lid off, Mr. Thompson; let me see my boy's face," wailed the elder woman between her sobs. This time Steavens looked fearfully, almost beseechingly into her face, red and swollen under its masses of strong, black, shiny hair. He flushed, dropped his eyes, and then, almost incredulously, looked again. There was a kind of power about her face—a kind of brutal handsome-ness, even, but it was scarred and furrowed by violence, and so coloured and coarsened by fiercer passions that grief seemed never to have laid a gentle finger there. The long nose was distended and knobbed at the end, and there were deep lines on either side of it; her heavy, black brows almost met across her forehead, her teeth were large and square, and set far apart—teeth that could tear. She filled the room; the men were obliterated, seemed tossed about like twigs in an angry water, and even Steavens felt himself being drawn into the whirlpool.

The daughter—the tall, raw-boned woman in crêpe, with a mourning comb in her hair which curiously lengthened her long face—sat stiffly upon the sofa, her hands, conspicuous for their large knuckles, folded in her lap, her mouth and eyes drawn down, solemnly awaiting the opening of the coffin. Near the door stood a mulatto woman, evidently a servant in the house, with a timid bearing and an emaciated face pitifully sad and gentle. She was weeping silently, the corner of her calico apron lifted to her eyes, occasionally suppressing a long, quivering sob. Steavens walked over and stood beside her.

Feeble steps were heard on the stairs, and an old man, tall and frail, odorous of pipe smoke, with shaggy, unkept grey hair and a dingy beard, tobacco stained about the mouth, entered uncertainly. He went slowly up to the coffin and stood rolling a blue cotton handkerchief between his hands, seemed so pained and embarrassed by his wife's orgy of grief that he had no consciousness of anything else.

"There, there, Annie, dear, don't take on so," he quavered timidly, putting out a shaking hand and awkwardly patting her elbow. She turned with a cry, and sank upon his shoulder with such violence that he tottered a little. He did not even glance toward the coffin, but continued to look at her with a dull, frightened, appealing expression, as a spaniel looks at the whip. His sunken cheeks slowly reddened and burned with miserable shame. When his wife rushed from the room, her daughter strode after her with set lips. The servant stole up to the coffin, bent over it for a moment, and then slipped away to the kitchen, leaving Steavens, the lawyer and the father to themselves. The old man stood trembling and looking down at his dead son's face. The sculptor's splendid head seemed even more noble in its rigid stillness than in life. The dark hair had crept down upon the wide forehead; the face seemed strangely long, but in it there was not that beautiful and chaste repose which we expect to find in the faces of the dead. The brows were so drawn that there were two deep lines above the beaked nose, and the chin was thrust forward defiantly. It was as though the strain of life had been so sharp and bitter that death could not at once wholly relax the tension and smooth the countenance into perfect peace—as though he were still guarding something precious and holy, which might even yet be wrested from him.

The old man's lips were working under his stained beard. He turned to the lawyer with timid deference: "Phelps and the rest are comin' back to set up with Harve, ain't they?" he asked. "Thank 'ee, Jim, thank 'ee." He brushed the hair gently from his son's forehead. "He was a good boy, Jim; always a good boy. He was ez gentle ez a child and the kindest of 'em all—only we didn't none of us ever onderstand him." The tears trickled slowly down his beard and dropped upon the sculptor's coat.

"Martin, Martin. Oh, Martin! come here," his wife wailed from the top of the stairs. The old man started timorously: "Yes, Annie, I'm coming." He turned away, hesitated, stood for a moment in miserable indecision; then reached back and patted the dead man's hair softly, and stumbled from the room.

"Poor old man, I didn't think he had any tears left. Seems as if his eyes would have gone dry long ago. At his age nothing cuts very deep," remarked the lawyer.

Something in his tone made Steavens glance up. While the mother had been in the room, the young man had scarcely seen anyone else; but now, from the moment he first glanced into Jim Laird's florid face and blood-shot eyes, he knew that he had found what he had been heartsick at not finding before—the feeling, the understanding, that must exist in some one, even here.

The man was red as his beard, with features swollen and blurred by dissipation, and a hot, blazing blue eye. His face was strained—that of a man who is controlling himself with difficulty—and he kept plucking at his beard with a sort of fierce resentment. Steavens, sitting by the window, watched him turn down the glaring lamp, still its jangling pendants with an angry gesture, and then stand with his hands locked behind him, staring down into the master's face. He could not help wondering what link there could have been between the porcelain vessel and so sooty a lump of potter's clay.

From the kitchen an uproar was sounding; when the dining-room door opened, the import of it was clear. The mother was abusing the maid for having forgotten to make the dressing for the chicken salad which had been prepared for the watchers. Steavens had never heard anything in the least like it; it was injured, emotional, dramatic abuse, unique and masterly in its excruciating cruelty, as violent and unrestrained as had been her grief of twenty minutes before. With a shudder of disgust the lawyer went into the dining-room and closed the door into the kitchen.

"Poor Roxy's getting it now," he remarked when he came back. "The Merricks took her out of the poor-house years ago, and if her loyalty would let her, I guess the poor old thing could tell tales that would curdle your blood. She's the mulatto woman who was standing in here a while ago, with her apron to her eyes. The old woman is a fury; there never was anybody like her for demonstrative piety and ingenious cruelty. She made Harvey's life a hell for him when he lived at home; he was so sick ashamed of it. I never could see how he kept himself so sweet."

"He was wonderful," said Steavens slowly, "wonderful; but until to-night I have never known how wonderful."

"That is the true and eternal wonder of it, anyway; that it can come even from such a dung heap as this," the lawyer cried, with a sweeping gesture which seemed to indicate much more than the four walls within which they stood.

"I think I'll see whether I can get a little air. The room is so close I am beginning to feel rather faint," murmured Steavens, struggling with one of the windows. The sash was stuck, however, and would not yield, so he sat down dejectedly and began pulling at his collar. The lawyer came over, loosened the sash with one blow of his red fist and sent the window up a few inches. Steavens thanked him, but the nausea which had been gradually climbing into his throat for the last half hour left him with but one desire—a desperate feeling that he must get away from this place with what was left of Harvey Merrick. Oh, he comprehended well enough now the quiet bitterness of the smile that he had seen so often on his master's lips!

He remembered that once, when Merrick returned from a visit home, he brought with him a singularly feeling and suggestive bas-relief of a thin, faded old woman, sitting and sewing something pinned to her knee; while a full-lipped, full-blooded little urchin, his trousers held up by a single gallus, stood beside her, impatiently twitching her gown to call her attention to a butterfly he had caught. Steavens, impressed by the tender and delicate modelling of the thin, tired face, had asked him if it were his mother. He remembered the dull flush that had burned up in the sculptor's face.

The lawyer was sitting in a rocking-chair beside the coffin, his head thrown back and his eyes closed. Steavens looked at him earnestly, puzzled at the line of the chin, and wondering why a man should conceal a feature of such distinction under that disfiguring shock of beard. Suddenly, as though he felt the young sculptor's keen glance, he opened his eyes.

"Was he always a good deal of an oyster?" he asked abruptly. "He was terribly shy as a boy."

"Yes, he was an oyster, since you put it so," rejoined Steavens. "Although he could be very fond of people, he always gave one the impression of being detached. He disliked violent emotion; he was reflective, and rather distrustful of himself—except, of course, as regarded his work. He was sure-footed enough there. He distrusted men pretty thoroughly and women even more, yet somehow without believing ill of them. He was determined, indeed, to believe the best, but he seemed afraid to investigate."

"A burnt dog dreads the fire," said the lawyer grimly, and closed his eyes.

Steavens went on and on, reconstructing that whole miserable boyhood. All this raw, biting ugliness had been the portion of the man whose tastes were refined beyond the limits of the reasonable—whose mind was an exhaustless gallery of beautiful impressions, and so sensitive that the mere shadow of a poplar leaf flickering against a sunny wall would be etched and held there forever. Surely, if ever a man had the magic word in his finger tips, it was Merrick. Whatever he touched, he revealed its holiest secrets, liberated it from enchantment and restored it to its pristine loveliness, like the Arabian prince who fought the enchantress spell for spell. Upon whatever he had come in contact with, he had left a beautiful record of the experience—a sort of ethereal signature; a scent, a sound, a colour that was his own.

Steavens understood now the real tragedy of his master's life; neither love nor wine, as many had conjectured; but a blow which had fallen earlier and cut deeper than these could have done—a shame not his, and yet so inescapably his, to hide in his heart from his very boyhood. And without—the frontier warfare; the yearning of a boy, cast ashore upon a desert of newness and ugliness and sordidness, for all that is chastened and old, and noble with traditions.

At eleven o'clock the tall, flat woman in black crêpe entered and announced that the watchers were arriving, and asked them "to step into the dining-room." As Steavens rose, the lawyer said dryly: "You go on—it'll be a good experience for you, doubtless; as for me, I'm not equal to that crowd to-night; I've had twenty years of them."

As Steavens closed the door after him he glanced back at the lawyer, sitting by the coffin in the dim light, with his chin resting on his hand.

The same misty group that had stood before the door of the express car shuffled into the dining room. In the light of the kerosene lamp they separated and became individuals. The minister, a pale, feeble-looking man with white hair and blond chin-whiskers, took his seat beside a small side table and placed his Bible upon it. The Grand Army man sat down behind the stove and tilted his chair back comfortably against the wall, fishing his quill toothpick from his waistcoat pocket. The two bankers, Phelps and Elder, sat off in a corner behind the dinner-table, where they could finish their discussion of the new usury law and its effect on chattel security loans. The real estate agent, an old man with a smiling, hypocritical face, soon joined them. The coal and lumber dealer and the cattle shipper sat on opposite sides of the hard coal-burner, their feet on the nickel-work. Steavens took a book from his pocket and began to read. The talk around him ranged through various topics of local interest while the house was quieting down. When it was clear that the members of the family were in bed, the Grand Army man hitched his shoulders and, untangling his long legs, caught his heels on the rounds of his chair.

"S'pose there'll be a will, Phelps?" he queried in his weak falsetto.

The banker laughed disagreeably and began trimming his nails with a pearl-handled pocket-knife.

"There'll scarcely be any need for one, will there?" he queried in his turn.

The restless Grand Army man shifted his position again, getting his knees still nearer his chin. "Why, the ole man says Harve's done right well lately," he chirped.

The other banker spoke up. "I reckon he means by that Harve ain't asked him to mortgage any more farms lately, so as he could go on with his education."

"Seems like my mind don't reach back to a time when Harve wasn't bein' edycated," tittered the Grand Army man.

There was a general chuckle. The minister took out his handkerchief and blew his nose sonorously. Banker Phelps closed his knife with a snap. "It's too bad the old man's sons didn't turn out better," he remarked with reflective authority. "They never hung together. He spent money enough on Harve to stock a dozen cattle-farms and he might as well have poured it into Sand Creek. If Harve had stayed at home and helped nurse what little they had, and gone into stock on the old man's bottom farm, they might all have been well fixed. But the old man had to trust everything to tenants and was cheated right and left."

"Harve never could have handled stock none," interposed the cattleman. "He hadn't it in him to be sharp. Do you remember when he bought Sander's mules for eight-year-olds, when everybody in town knew that Sander's father-in-law give 'em to his wife for a wedding present eighteen years before, an' they was full-grown mules then."

Everyone chuckled, and the Grand Army man rubbed his knees with a spasm of childish delight.

"Harve never was much account for anything practical, and he shore was never fond of work," began the coal and lumber dealer. "I mind the last time he was home; the day he left, when the old man was out to the barn helpin' his hand hitch up to take Harve to the train, and Cal Moots was patchin' up the fence, Harve, he come out on the step and sings out, in his lady-like voice: 'Cal Moots, Cal Moots! please come cord my trunk.'"

"That's Harve for you," approved the Grand Army man gleefully. "I kin hear him howlin' yet when he was a big feller in long pants and his mother used to whale him with a rawhide in the barn for lettin' the cows git foundered in the cornfield when he was drivin' 'em home from pasture. He killed a cow of mine that-a-way onct—a pure Jersey and the best milker I had, an' the ole man had to put up for her. Harve, he was watchin' the sun set acrost the marshes when the anamile got away; he argued that sunset was oncommon fine."

"Where the old man made his mistake was in sending the boy East to school," said Phelps, stroking his goatee and speaking in a deliberate, judicial tone. "There was where he got his head full of trapesing to Paris and all such folly. What Harve needed, of all people, was a course in some first-class Kansas City business college."

The letters were swimming before Steavens's eyes. Was it possible that these men did not understand, that the palm on the coffin meant nothing to them? The very name of their town would have remained forever buried in the postal guide had it not been now and again mentioned in the world in connection with Harvey Merrick's. He remembered what his master had said to him on the day of his death, after the congestion of both lungs had shut off any probability of recovery, and the sculptor had asked his pupil to send his body home. "It's not a pleasant place to be lying while the world is moving and doing and bettering," he had said with a feeble smile, "but it rather seems as though we ought to go back to the place we came from in the end. The townspeople will come in for a look at me; and after they have had their say I shan't have much to fear from the judgment of God. The wings of the Victory, in there"—with a weak gesture toward his studio—"will not shelter me."

The cattleman took up the comment. "Forty's young for a Merrick to cash in; they usually hang on pretty well. Probably he helped it along with whisky."

"His mother's people were not long lived, and Harvey never had a robust constitution," said the minister mildly. He would have liked to say more. He had been the boy's Sunday-school teacher, and had been fond of him; but he felt that he was not in a position to speak. His own sons had turned out badly, and it was not a year since one of them had made his last trip home in the express car, shot in a gambling-house in the Black Hills.

"Nevertheless, there is no disputin' that Harve frequently looked upon the wine when it was red, also variegated, and it shore made an oncommon fool of him," moralized the cattleman.

Just then the door leading into the parlour rattled loudly, and everyone started involuntarily, looking relieved when only Jim Laird came out. His red face was convulsed with anger, and the Grand Army man ducked his head when he saw the spark in his blue, blood-shot eye. They were all afraid of Jim; he was a drunkard, but he could twist the law to suit his client's needs as no other man in all western Kansas could do; and there were many who tried. The lawyer closed the door gently behind him, leaned back against it and folded his arms, cocking his head a little to one side. When he assumed this attitude in the court-room, ears were always pricked up, as it usually foretold a flood of withering sarcasm.

"I've been with you gentlemen before," he began in a dry, even tone, "when you've sat by the coffins of boys born and raised in this town; and, if I remember rightly, you were never any too well satisfied when you checked them up. What's the matter, anyhow? Why is it that reputable young men are as scarce as millionaires in Sand City? It might almost seem to a stranger that there was some way something the matter with your progressive town. Why did Ruben Sayer, the brightest young lawyer you ever turned out, after he had come home from the university as straight as a die, take to drinking and forge a check and shoot himself? Why did Bill Merrit's son die of the shakes in a saloon in Omaha? Why was Mr. Thomas's son, here, shot in a gambling-house? Why did young Adams burn his mill to beat the insurance companies and go to the pen?"

The lawyer paused and unfolded his arms, laying one clenched fist quietly on the table. "I'll tell you why. Because you drummed nothing but money and knavery into their ears from the time they wore knickerbockers; because you carped away at them as you've been carping here to-night, holding our friends Phelps and Elder up to them for their models, as our grandfathers held up George Washington and John Adams. But the boys, worse luck, were young, and raw at the business you put them to; and how could they match coppers with such artists as Phelps and Elder? You wanted them to be successful rascals; they were only unsuccessful ones—that's all the difference. There was only one boy ever raised in this borderland between ruffianism and civilization, who didn't come to grief, and you hated Harvey Merrick more for winning out than you hated all the other boys who got under the wheels. Lord, Lord, how you did hate him! Phelps, here, is fond of saying that he could buy and sell us all out any time he's a mind to; but he knew Harve wouldn't have given a tinker's damn for his bank and all his cattle-farms put together; and a lack of appreciation, that way, goes hard with Phelps.

"Old Nimrod, here, thinks Harve drank too much; and this from such as Nimrod and me!

"Brother Elder says Harve was too free with the old man's money—fell short in filial consideration, maybe. Well, we can all remember the very tone in which brother Elder swore his own father was a liar, in the county court; and we all know that the old man came out of that partnership with his son as bare as a sheared lamb. But maybe I'm getting personal, and I'd better be driving ahead at what I want to say."

The lawyer paused a moment, squared his heavy shoulders, and went on: "Harvey Merrick and I went to school together, back East. We were dead in earnest, and we wanted you all to be proud of us some day. We meant to be great men. Even I, and I haven't lost my sense of humour, gentlemen, I meant to be a great man. I came back here to practise, and I found you didn't in the least want me to be a great man. You wanted me to be a shrewd lawyer—oh, yes! Our veteran here wanted me to get him an increase of pension, because he had dyspepsia; Phelps wanted a new county survey that would put the widow Wilson's little bottom farm inside his south line; Elder wanted to lend money at 5 per cent a month, and get it collected; old Stark here wanted to wheedle old women up in Vermont into investing their annuities in real estate mortgages that are not worth the paper they are written on. Oh, you needed me hard enough, and you'll go on needing me; and that's why I'm not afraid to plug the truth home to you this once.

"Well, I came back here and became the damned shyster you wanted me to be. You pretend to have some sort of respect for me; and yet you'll stand up and throw mud at Harvey Merrick, whose soul you couldn't dirty and whose hands you couldn't tie. Oh, you're a discriminating lot of Christians! There have been times when the sight of Harvey's name in some Eastern paper has made me hang my head like a whipped dog; and, again, times when I liked to think of him off there in the world, away from all this hog-wallow, doing his great work and climbing the big, clean up-grade he'd set for himself.

"And we? Now that we've fought and lied and sweated and stolen, and hated as only the disappointed strugglers in a bitter, dead little Western town know how to do, what have we got to show for it? Harvey Merrick wouldn't have given one sunset over your marshes for all you've got put together, and you know it. It's not for me to say why, in the inscrutable wisdom of God, a genius should ever have been called from this place of hatred and bitter waters; but I want this Boston man to know that the drivel he's been hearing here to-night is the only tribute any truly great man could ever have from such a lot of sick, side-tracked, burnt-dog, land-poor sharks as the here-present financiers of Sand City—upon which town may God have mercy!"

The lawyer thrust out his hand to Steavens as he passed him, caught up his overcoat in the hall, and had left the house before the Grand Army man had had time to lift his ducked head and crane his long neck about at his fellows.

Next day Jim Laird was drunk and unable to attend the funeral services. Steavens called twice at his office, but was compelled to start East without seeing him. He had a presentiment that he would hear from him again, and left his address on the lawyer's table; but if Laird found it, he never acknowledged it. The thing in him that Harvey Merrick had loved must have gone underground with Harvey Merrick's coffin; for it never spoke again, and Jim got the cold he died of driving across the Colorado mountains to defend one of Phelp's sons who had got into trouble out there by cutting government timber.

THE LANDSCAPE OF LOVE

I

Do not believe them. Do not believe what strangers
Or casual tourists, moored a night and day
In some snug, sunny, April-sheltering bay
(Along the coast and guarded from great dangers)
Tattle to friends when ignorant they return.
Love is no lotus-island endlessly
Washed by a summer ocean, no Capri;
But a huge landscape, perilous and stern—

More poplared than the nations to the north,
More bird-beguiled, stream-haunted. But the ground
Shakes underfoot. Incessant thunders sound,
Winds shake the trees, and tides run back and forth
And tempests winter there, and flood and frost
In which too many a voyager is lost.

II

None knows this country save the colonist,
His homestead planted. He alone has seen
The hidden groves unconquerably green,
The secret mountains steepling through the mist.
Each is his own discovery. No chart
Has pointed him past chasm, bog, quicksand,
Earthquake, mirage, into his chosen land—
Only the steadfast compass of the heart.

Turn a deaf ear, then, on the traveler who,
Speaking a foreign tongue, has never stood
Upon love's hills or in a holy wood
Sung incantations; yet, having bought a few
Postcards and trinkets at some cheap bazaar,
Cries, "This and thus the God's dominions are!"

—*Phyllis McGinley*

Reprinted by permission of The Viking Press from Phyllis
McGinley, *Times Three* (New York: The Viking Press, 1959).

45

THE GIRL WHO DANCED

By Mori Ogai

Now the coal is loaded and all is quiet. The passengers have left the lounge and I am alone. Perhaps I can sit here until the cabin boy comes to turn out the lights. Here I can collect my thoughts.

Tomorrow the ship sails. How I dread the voyage back to Japan! We will sail the same route by which I came five years ago, and remembering everything will be painful to me. How I have changed since I left Tokyo! At first I recorded everything that happened to me and I wrote enthusiastic articles to send back to Japan. The most inconsequential things made an impression on me and I was eager to write them down. But now my mind is numb and I can react to nothing. When I left Berlin last month I thought that once I was out to sea I could at least write about the events which drove me to leave Germany. But now I doubt that I can even do that.

I now find people repulsive. While the other passengers on this ship have spent these last twenty days enjoying themselves together I have been avoiding them. I want nothing to do with anyone. But I can at least escape from others; I cannot escape from myself, and I despise myself more than anybody else.

Sometimes I feel that I would like to talk to someone, but who could understand my misery? I feel nothing but the guilt and grief that gnaw at me until I am numb. I neither wish to speak nor hear. I only want to withdraw from everyone. In people I see my own bitter anguish reflected. Every sight is a mirror which reminds me of Alice and thrusts my misery back at me. Every voice haunts me. People have become specters of the woman I betrayed.

But at least I am alone now. I can sit here until the ship sails, while the other passengers are ashore and it is deserted. Perhaps I can even try to make some kind of record of what has happened to me.

Reprinted by permission of Bantam Books from Michael Rheta Martin, ed., *The Language of Love* (New York: Bantam Books, 1964).

My name is Ota Toyotaro. I was very young when my father died. I grew up under strict discipline and studied hard. From my first day of school until I graduated from Law School at Tokyo University I was at the head of my class. And as my reputation grew, people came to expect great things of me. Finally it was recommended by some high university officials that I study in Berlin, which had become the new capital of Europe.

When I left Japan I was sure I would make a name for myself and bring honor to my family. I was arrogant then, and foolishly conceited. I could not fail at anything, I thought.

But Berlin itself undermined my self-confidence. I had imagined it to be a quiet, sober city. But I discovered that it was noisy and colorful, and often when I should have been studying I walked the streets and boulevards to stare at the officers strutting about town, their chests covered with medals. Or I would watch the stylish women promenade along the avenues. And even while I was working over my books, I kept thinking of the splendid buildings in Berlin, and of the fine carriages that passed everywhere, and of the statue of Victory atop the triumphal tower at the Brandenburg Gate. When I should have been concentrating on my work I wanted to be out of doors exploring Berlin.

All the same, I studied hard at first. I learned French and German and attended classes at the University. But I was disappointed, for they offered no courses in politics there and I had to study more law. Gradually it became more difficult for me to discipline myself. While I was in Japan I had obeyed everyone. And driven by the praise of others, I lived a mechanical life of obedient study. But now that I found myself in Berlin, in an uninhibited university atmosphere, I began to tire of memorizing what was in law books and of using the dry details they contained to pass judgment on people I never knew. It occurred to me that my mother, my Japanese professors, all my superiors, had turned me into a human law book.

In my progress reports to my superiors in Japan I grew quarrelsome. I argued that only the spirit of the law mattered. Why should we bother with trivial, tedious data as long as we respected that great abstraction, Justice? And while earlier I answered the most insignificant inquiries with painfully recorded details, I began to ignore the people in Japan who wrote to me for reports and for long accounts of what I was accomplishing in Berlin.

Yet while I was repudiating authority, something still troubled me. I was now annoyed that I had been following a road others had mapped out for me. But I was still afraid of failing to meet their expectations. I now despised them for driving me, but the thought of displeasing them still frightened me. I could not stop oscillating between freedom and subservience. While I was trying to assert myself in Berlin and break free of the tradition that had bound me, I kept thinking of something that happened to me when I set sail from Yokohama. I walked up the gangplank as though I were a shining hero, knowing that some of my superiors were watching me and that my mother was among them. But once the ship got under way I wept like a child. And while I was in Berlin I began to realize that I lacked as much courage as my convictions demanded of me. In Berlin I was afraid to flirt with girls, and I never wished to mingle with the other Japanese students who were studying there and who disliked me for my independent ways.

II

How unsuspecting I was that evening when I first met Alice. I never thought that such an innocent meeting would develop into the tragedy that has ruined me. I did not realize that my own weakness would become my greatest enemy. I was out for an idle walk, and as I turned off the brightly lit square and began walking down the narrow alley where I lived, I looked up at the old tenements and rooming houses, at an old bearded Jew who always stood in front of a cheap hotel, at the staircase that led down to the blacksmith's shop that was buried in a basement. All these sights were growing familiar to me and I loved them. I was ever conscious of being in another country whose traditions contrasted sharply with our own way of life in Japan.

Suddenly, as I passed the cathedral which was not far from my garret, I heard sobs and turned and saw a young girl standing in the archway. Her face was buried in a torn handkerchief. Usually I am timid, but for some reason I approached her. She could not have been more than seventeen. When she realized I was approaching her she started, like a frightened bird ready to fly away.

"Why are you crying?" I asked, amazed at my boldness. I had never before behaved this way with a stranger.

She turned and looked at me. She seemed to realize that I was sincerely interested in what was troubling her. "You look kind," she said. She began to weep again. Her shoulders shook as she sobbed. "Please help me," she broke out suddenly. "I don't know what I'll do if someone doesn't help me."

"What must I do?" I asked.

"My mother," she said, still sobbing. "She'll beat me if I do not obey the theater manager. My father has died and we are penniless. My mother insists."

"I don't quite understand," I said. "Come, quiet down and I'll take you home. You can explain while we walk. But we had better leave. People are staring at us. They'll think I have been annoying you."

So we began walking, and she talked a little. But I could still not understand exactly what her trouble was. Suddenly she looked up at me, then quickened her pace, walking rapidly ahead of me. I followed, not knowing what else to do. At last she entered a tenement, climbed to the fourth floor, and pulled at the rusty knocker on a narrow door.

"Who's there?" called a woman from inside. Her voice was husky and gruff.

"Alice," the girl replied. A gray-haired woman in an old cotton frock and dirty slippers opened the door. The girl beckoned for me to follow her in, but before I could the woman pulled her into the room and slammed the door in my face. I waited, not wanting to go away, yet not certain I should stay. As I waited I heard the girl and the woman arguing. Finally the woman opened the door and asked me in, apologizing half-heartedly for her rudeness.

I found myself standing in a kitchen, cheaply furnished with a small stove and a few utensils. The woman then showed me into the sitting room. Its roof slanted so that on the far side of it a person could not stand. On the mantel were a few books, a photograph album, and a bouquet in a china vase that seemed too expensive for the rest of the room.

Then I looked at Alice, who stood there while I had entered the room. She was beautiful. Her face was pale, but her skin was soft and clear. Her arms and legs looked lithe and graceful. "Please forgive me," she began. "It was thoughtless of me to bring you here. But you seemed so kind. You probably think I'm terrible. My father died yesterday, and tomorrow we are to bury him. But we haven't the money to do so. We thought we could get some help from the theater manager for whom I have danced for two years. But he wants only to take advantage of me." Then she hesitated for a minute, turning her back on me. She lowered her head and her shoulders trembled as she began to cry again. Suddenly she faced me again and said very quickly and uncertainly, "If you will lend us a little money, you will do me a great service." I looked into her eyes. How clearly they expressed her great need and her embarrassment at having to ask a loan of a stranger. To this day I wonder if Alice ever knew the great power of her eyes.

I took my watch out of my pocket and put it on the table. Then I drew three marks out of my purse. "This is all I have," I said. "Make the money do for the time being. Meanwhile I'll send a pawnbroker over and you can see what he will give you for the watch."

She stood there and stared at me, saying nothing. I looked at her for a minute, then gave her my hand to say good-bye. But instead of shaking it, she put both her hands around it, drew it up to her lips and kissed it. I blushed. Her gratitude embarrassed me.

What pernicious force afterwards brought her to my room to thank me? For when she did I set aside my Schopenhauer and Schiller and the two of us talked and laughed all afternoon. And from then on I was to ignore my books oftener than ever. Alice and I fell in love.

Somehow word reached the Japanese embassy that I was dissipating with a troupe of chorus girls. I often went with Alice to the theater where she danced, and one of the Japanese students who also studied at the University must have seen me there and reported it. The authorities in Japan were already displeased with me because I was no longer studying what I had been told to study, so I was not altogether surprised when the ambassador sent for me and told me that I was to return to Japan at once. If I did not obey, he said, my passage would not be paid. I begged him to give me a week in which to decide.

During that week I received word that my mother had died. So now to my indecision was added painful grief and a deep shame, for in behaving as I had I was dishonoring the woman who had put such trust in me. And when I told Alice that I was being ordered back to Japan, she cried hysterically and begged me not to leave. She could not part with me, she said, and life with her mother would be unbearable if she were never to see me again.

My mind was in a turmoil and I could not decide what to do. The week passed but my indecision remained unresolved. Finally I went to see the ambassador, ashamed to tell him that I had not yet made up my mind. But at the embassy I learned that I did not have to leave after all. For Aizawa Kenkichi, an old school friend, had learned of what had happened to me and interceded in my behalf. He was personal secretary to Count Amagata in Tokyo and he had seen my name in the official records, where it was reported that I had resigned my scholarship in Berlin. He spoke with a newspaper editor in Tokyo who consented to have me remain in Berlin and send dispatches back to Japan. While my salary was small, it was enough to pay for my room and board.

When I told Alice that I could remain in Berlin, she insisted that I live with her and her mother. And after she persuaded her mother to allow me to move in with them, she and I settled down to an existence which was a mixture of joy and sorrow.

III

Alice was fifteen when she began dancing professionally at the Victoria Theater. Soon she became one of the best dancers there. But while she put on heavy make-up and beautiful costumes to perform on the stage, she had barely enough food to live. She had become a slave before I ever met her. Between daily rehearsals, evening performances, meager wages and the responsibility of supporting her mother, she had little time for pleasure.

Although she was an uneducated girl, she always enjoyed reading. Before I met her she read cheap novels which she borrowed from lending libraries. But after we met, I began lending her books. She soon developed good taste and even her manner of speaking became polished.

So when we put our resources together and decided to share our lives with one another, I was pleased. Our life was frugal but we were happy. She would leave for rehearsal in the morning and I would go to a dimly lit restaurant to read and write my news dispatches. Wastrels, pensioners, and office clerks who wished to steal a few minutes from their jobs came to the cheap restaurant. Soon I got to know the people there, and I was permitted to sit all day. Halfway through the morning a waitress would bring me a cup of hot coffee to warm me as I clipped newspaper items and pasted together columns of my own. And in the afternoon Alice would come for me after rehearsal, and together we would leave, walking hand in hand down the narrow streets or across the great squares, laughing and dreaming about growing old and rich with each other. How poor we were then, but how happy!

As for study, it was impossible. During the day I had my newspaper work to do, and at night it was impossible to concentrate on my books. I would sit in the parlor at home and write about administration, about political movements, and about new trends in art and literature. I could write about the death of William I and Frederick III, about the crowning of the new emperor and of the rumors that Bismarck would soon retire. But I could not sit and concentrate on my textbooks. I was busy, I was in love, and my life was full of activity.

I remained registered at the University, but I rarely attended lectures. I could neither afford tuition money nor maintain any great interest in my studies. My education was taking a new turn. For although I ignored my studies, I discovered a new way to learn. For in Germany there were now being produced a number of sophisticated newspapers and periodicals. And through them I now had the opportunity to broaden my mind and to think about many things, while as a student I had acquired a vast knowledge in a narrow field. Now that I was a newspaper correspondent, however, my interest was becoming broader and I was discovering how exciting life could be.

Then came the winter of 1888, a terrible northern European winter. Sometimes in the morning I would open the door and see a sparrow, frozen to death in the bitter cold. Back streets like the one we lived on were always clogged with snow and ice. And in spite of the stove we had in our room, the cold penetrated the walls and made us numb and uncomfortable. In the morning we would put on our clothes and feel the dampness of them. One night during that frightful

The Gay Quarters of Kyoto (Japan, Edo period)

winter Alice collapsed on the stage and had to be carried home. And from her mother I learned that she was pregnant. "This on top of everything else," I thought. "What should I do now?"

The next day was a Sunday and Alice did not go to the theater. Although she was not sick enough to stay in bed, she remained by the stove and hardly talked. And I remained with her, brooding and nervously pacing the floor. Late in the morning the postman arrived with a letter for me. It was from Aizawa. He had just arrived in Berlin with Count Amagata, who wished to see me at once about a possible way to exonerate me from my disgrace. I was astonished, and Alice read the expression on my face.

"Is it bad news?" she asked.

"No," I said. "It's from Aizawa. He is here with the Count and wants to see me immediately."

So I was to have an audience with the Count. Alice and her mother were overjoyed. Alice seemed to forget that she was sick. She ran about the room, looking for my best white shirt, choosing a tie for me, helping me dress.

"There," she said, as she straightened my tie, "no one shall think you an ill-dressed man today. Now do not look sullen. I am so proud of you. I wish I could come too." She smiled now and her face was animated. "Just remember, if you are to become rich you must never leave your Alice."

"Rich!" I laughed, trying to look a little brighter. "I care for you, not for money. I am just going to see my old friend, not the Count."

While Alice's mother called a carriage, I put on my soiled overcoat, took my hat, my gloves, and kissed Alice good-bye. And as the carriage drew away I looked back and saw Alice waving to me through the frozen window. I reached the hotel where Aizawa and the Count were staying. I entered and climbed the marble stairs, stepped into the reception room of their apartment, removed my overcoat, and then entered the inner door, feeling uneasy now. I wondered how Aizawa would greet me after all these years and after the disgrace that had all but ruined me with the authorities in Japan.

Aizawa had grown heavier, but he was as pleasant as he had always been. He seemed unconcerned about what had passed with me and never mentioned what I had done. Instead, he led me straight to the Count, who promptly asked me to translate a German document. I was startled. I took the document, left the room, rejoined Aizawa, then went with him to have lunch.

At lunch he asked me a few questions. But he let me do most of the talking. His was a routine life, while mine was full of experiences and seemed to fascinate him. He did not criticize me for what I had done, although he was often surprised at some of the details. But when I expected him to chide me, he only berated my lugubrious ex-colleagues. And finally he said that I had brought things on myself because of my weak will. "It is futile to cry over the past, though," he said. Then he began to praise my ability and scolded me for wasting it on a Bohemian life and on love for a girl.

As it turned out, Count Amagata wanted to hire me as his private secretary. He knew the details of my resignation, yet my past made no difference to him. He needed someone who knew German, and my ability to translate made an impression on him. Aizawa told me that it was up to me to win the Count's confidence. "You must serve him well," Aizawa warned me. "If you fail him you will bring disaster upon yourself. And as for Alice, you had better drop her, no matter how much she loves you. She is not for you, talented as you are."

When he said this to me, I felt like a man in a rudderless ship who sees a mountain in the distance. Aizawa had showed me the way. He had pointed out the mountain for me. But I was still in love with Alice; the mountain was shrouded in clouds and I could neither be sure it was there nor that it was the right destination for me. I could not desert Alice. I was poor, but I was happy with her.

But I could not say these things to Aizawa. Somehow I could not say what I knew I wanted to say. I could not bring myself to say to this man who was trying so hard to help me, "I love this woman and I will not leave her!" And I found myself promising Aizawa that I would end my affair with Alice, although I knew in my heart that I loved her and wanted her.

That evening, after I left Aizawa I walked home. The wind lashed at my face and whipped through my thin overcoat. The cold penetrated to my heart. I was troubled, for I had promised to betray Alice, not really wanting to carry out the promise.

From then on I saw the Count frequently. At first he was aloof with me and said very little. But gradually he opened up, first commenting vaguely about events in Japan, then speaking about people who blundered. And eventually he began to seek my opinion or even ask my advice. Sometimes we would have a laugh together over some matter.

One day, after I had been working for him for about a month, he said to me, "Tomorrow I am going to Russia. I want you to join me." I had been unprepared for this invitation, and although I said I would go I felt uneasy. When I told Alice where I was to go, she did not complain. She only said that she had been to a doctor and had been advised to take a long rest. She had also lost her job, she told me, because she had missed so much work. I gave her enough money to keep her and her mother and went away with the Count.

I worked hard in Moscow. There were a great many translations to be done and my services were constantly needed to act as an interpreter. But while my mind was with my work my heart was with Alice. I became worried about her after I received her first letter. She had fallen asleep as soon as evening came the night after I left Berlin, she told me, and when she awoke she felt exhausted and depressed. She was afraid that she would starve, and she sat alone staring into the lamp, wishing I were with her. Soon after that she sent me another letter which was even more ominous:

> Now I know how much I love you. I was sure I could remain calm while you were gone, but every day I think of you more and more, until my thoughts torment and distract me. I feel my health failing. And mother babbles constantly and her chattering distresses me.
>
> I will do everything I can to keep you in Berlin. But should you return to Japan, perhaps you can take me with you. Mother could remain with relatives in the country. It frightens me to learn that the Count is depending upon you more and more. What is going to happen? Please, you must never leave me. And above all, you must hurry back to Berlin.

Suddenly, after I read this letter, I realized what had happened. Before Aizawa and the Count came to Berlin, I had resigned myself to spending the rest of my life with Alice. Now I saw that I had been tricked. For Aizawa and the Count had appealed to my desire to excel. As the Count appeared to rely on me more and more, he began to suggest that I return to Japan with him. He never mentioned my private affairs, but I began to suspect that Aizawa had told him of my rash promise to leave Alice. And now that he began praising me as my teachers in Japan had praised me earlier, I felt my sense of obligation to him increase. Once again I felt myself becoming a machine, responding to flattery and commands without taking account of my own mind. While I had been living with Alice I felt like a bird who had cut a string which once fastened its legs to the ground. And here I was discovering that I had quit my role as the puppet for a bureaucratic department in Japan only to become a toy in Count Amagata's hands. I was right back where I started, and Alice had realized it before I ever suspected it.

At last we arrived back in Berlin. I left the Count as early as I could and hurried home to see Alice. I sat thinking of her as I rode along the city streets, scarcely noticing that the snow was frozen into grotesque shapes of ice that reflected the morning sun. Finally the carriage stopped, I heard a window open, then a clatter on the stairs. I had not even picked up my suitcase when Alice ran out to the carriage and embraced me.

"I'm so glad you're back!" she cried. "So relieved! If you hadn't come back to me I would have died."

Her greeting, so sincere and loving, had a stabilizing effect on me. While

I was in Moscow I was forever thinking of patriotism and personal ambition. Allegiance to my own country and the old desire to be a success had driven a wedge between Alice and me. But now that she was in my arms, kissing me, pressing her head to my shoulder, rubbing my cold hands, I felt that I would be willing to do nothing that would separate us. Putting my arm around her, I told her never to worry. I could never leave her. She wiped the tears from her face, apologized for weeping—she was so happy she could do nothing else—and taking my hand, she led me up the stairs.

I was surprised when I saw our room. The desk was piled high with lace and white cloth for diapers. "Look," cried Alice, her eyes dancing, "I'm already preparing. I am so happy. He will have black eyes, like your own, I am sure." How she went on, going from corner to corner, showing me this baby frock and that. "When he is born, you shall name him," she said, running up to me and kissing me. "Laugh if you will; but as for me, I can hardly wait."

IV

For two or three days after I came back from Moscow I avoided the Count. I kept telling myself that he was tired and would not want to see me. But I knew that I was afraid to speak with him. One evening he sent a messenger for me. I called on him the next morning and he said he was glad to see me. He congratulated me for having done a splendid job for him in Russia. Then he said he assumed I was going to return to Japan with him. He needed me, he added, and told me that Aizawa had assured him that nothing prevented my returning right away. "In fact," he said, "I should think that after being away so long, you must be anxious to return to Japan."

I knew that if I wanted to refuse, I would have to tell him at that moment that I wished to stay in Berlin. Once I committed myself to Count Amagata there would be no turning back. I thought of Alice and of how I loved her. I thought of her running to meet me at the carriage that cold morning a few days ago, and of the way she jumped about the room like a happy child, talking of the baby we were to have. The thought of leaving her sickened me.

But somehow I could not refuse the Count. I could not tell him that I had lied to Aizawa when I promised to leave Alice. I knew that my decision to go back home with the Count was amoral. I knew that in my weakness I was destroying Alice. I felt my heart pounding and the blood rushing to my face. If I failed to serve the Count, if I failed to cling to him now, I would lose my country and destroy the honor that was attached to my family name. I thought of Berlin, and of the many people there. Once again I thought of the swirl of soldiers and carriages and pretty European women passing up and down the streets of the great European city. Suddenly I was frightened by the thought of being buried in the vast sea of people in a European metropolis. "I will sail whenever you want me to," I told the Count, standing before him as I had stood on the gangplank in Yokohama five years ago when I knew everyone was watching me.

I walked outside and onto the street, knowing that Alice would have to be told. I walked aimlessly, like a blind man, not caring where I went, not looking where I was going. I now recall that I was almost knocked over by a carriage. Then I realized that I was lying on a bench at the zoo, burning with fever. My head felt as though someone were beating it with a mallet. For hours I lay in a stupor, and when I awoke I was shivering. An inch of snow had fallen while I slept, and I was covered with it.

It must have been well after midnight. I tried to stand but my legs were too numb with cold. I rubbed them with my hands until I could finally hobble away. What I recall now about that night is only that the trolley tracks were buried under the snow and that the gas lamps by the Brandenburg Gate threw off an inconstant flicker and wispy shadows danced upon the snow beneath the lights. Running through my mind was the realization that I had committed a horrible crime.

When I reached our house I saw one light lit in our apartment. It was like a lonely star shining in the black sky. Alice was still awake. The snow, as if it were a swooping white heron, suddenly blocked the light from view. Then, as though the wind were playing with it, the light reappeared. I was exhausted. My whole body ached terribly. But I crawled up the stairs somehow, opened the door, went through the kitchen, and saw Alice seated at the desk sewing diapers.

"What happened to you?" she asked. "Just look at you!"

I tried to answer but could not speak. I knew when I looked at her that I appeared miserable. My hat was gone, and I reached up and felt my wet, disheveled hair. Then I looked down at my clothes. They were soaked and torn and stained from slush. My knees trembled, I tried to take hold of a chair, but I slumped to the floor. I must have fainted, for I remember nothing else.

For two weeks I lay, feverish and delirious. I was aware of Alice's presence and knew that she was nursing me. But I did not know that Aizawa had come and told her everything. And as my own health returned I realized how much she had changed. Her body had become thin, her cheeks hollow, her eyes sunken and bloodshot. It was as if all the sickness had left my own body and gone into hers.

One morning, when I was nearly recovered, she looked at me and screamed, "My Toyotaro, how could you deceive me so?" Then she fainted. We put her to bed and she slept. When she woke she said nothing at first. She stared straight ahead and recognized no one, not me nor her mother nor Aizawa, who was also there. Then she began shrieking, pulling her hair, chewing at the blankets. She cried out and shouted my name. Her mother began handing her things to calm her down, but she threw everything aside until finally her mother handed her the diapers on the desk. She became quiet then, stared at the white cloth, pressed it to her face and then wept on them. She was not violent after that, but her mind had given way completely. Aizawa, who had brought food while I was sick, had fed her body but destroyed her mind. Now she was like an infant. The doctor said she was incurably demented. They tried to commit her to the asylum, but she refused to go. Often she would press a diaper to her body, repeatedly look at it, and then weep. Yet, in spite of everything, she rarely left my bedside while I continued my own recovery. And until the day I left her I repeatedly embraced her and cried over her, knowing that each day there was less life in her. At last I left Berlin and started back to Japan.

The Count, Aizawa, and I arranged to provide Alice and the child with a small annuity. I know that Aizawa Kenkichi only wanted to help me, but I shall hate him until I die.

LAW LIKE LOVE

Law, say the gardeners, is the sun,
Law is the one
All gardeners obey
Tomorrow, yesterday, today.

Law is the wisdom of the old
The impotent grandfathers shrilly scold;
The grandchildren put out a treble tongue,
Law is the senses of the young.

Law, says the priest with a priestly look,
Expounding to an unpriestly people,
Law is the words in my priestly book,
Law is my pulpit and my steeple.

Law, says the judge as he looks down his nose,
Speaking clearly and most severely,
Law is as I've told you before,
Law is as you know I suppose,
Law is but let me explain it once more,
Law is The Law.

Yet law-abiding scholars write;
Law is neither wrong nor right,
Law is only crimes
Punished by places and by times,
Law is the clothes men wear
Anytime, anywhere
Law is Good-morning and Good-night.

Others say, Law is our Fate;
Others say, Law is our State;
Others say, others say
Law is no more
Law has gone away.

And always the loud angry crowd
Very angry and very loud
Law is We,
And always the soft idiot softly Me.

If we, dear, know we know no more
Than they about the law,
If I no more than you
Know what we should and should not do
Except that all agree
Gladly or miserably
That the law is
And that all know this,
If therefore thinking it absurd
To identify Law with some other word,
Unlike so many men
I cannot say Law is again,
No more than they can we suppress
The universal wish to guess
Or slip out of our own position
Into an unconcerned condition.
Although I can at least confine
Your vanity and mine
To stating timidly
A timid similarity,
We shall boast anyway:
Like love I say.

Like love we don't know where or why
Like love we can't compel or fly
Like love we often weep
Like love we seldom keep.

—*W. H. Auden*

I AM THE MUSIC YOU MAKE

rain wind light cold cold dark late stem gate bar flame knife garden blue

noise morning son loud art alive net tiger storm lily job tear maker shove

mirror **Moon** work

coast star

deer good

frog **SUN** soul

tunnel I am the music you make book

grave the blue wings of the ocean lift

noose the crying of the black swan world

supper body

beauty I am the friend **SLEEP** stone

fear of your childhood town

heights weave

garden **Birds** It is in my heart to wish you center

taste no sorrow break

climb no pain afraid

will for I am the will of your last being no betrayal skill

look the shudder of the breaking open thing

wing of terrible gates O thou art good laugh

valley I am the cave and the light and wise grow

rule the watch God keeps and kindling three

name when His children go mad a new fire keep

knock force

angel I am the death you seek other

shadow **LIVE** the life you are afraid charm

terror to know soar

quest *behold this eye of blood!* fence

power rise tree knowledge innocence fall hand thorn get father chain spool

law peace turtle grass snow prayer life black deep first tie hit see eye

—*Kenneth Patchen*

Reprinted by permission of New Directions Publishing Corporation from Kenneth Patchen, *Collected Poems* (New York: New Directions Publishing Corporation, 1945).

58

TO KNOW THE PAIN OF BEING A PERSON

By Harry K. Zeller

If you would see life more clearly and express that insight in "the spare and vivid precision of thoroughbred speech," then study poetry, for the poets have been the antenna of the human race, stabbing our spirits broad awake and causing us to know the pain of being a person. So spoke Dr. H. A. Hamilton, a quiet, charming poetry buff; directing his words to one hundred ministers at Oxford last summer.

On the occasion of this diamond jubilee at La Verne College, I would extend this idea to include the teacher, the parent, the patron, the student; I suggest, in fact, that the whole purpose of education must be to equip each of us to face life with such wholeness that

> we confront realities we prefer to evade or usually avoid

> we come to grips with ideas we find disturbingly new or act as though they do not exist

> we "come alive" to insights to which we have been insensitive and concepts to which we are numb

in consequence of which we keep alive the pain of being a person.

This heightened awareness of things as they are brings pleasure as well as pain. The theoretical scientist must be in great agony because he sees so much more clearly than most of us the potential which man now has for instant and total destruction. His, also, must be the greater excitement than most of us feel, for he sees the power which mankind now has to free himself from back-breaking toil, from poverty and hunger, from epi-demics and the giant killers, and finally, from war itself. The sociologist sees more clearly the dilemmas of our common life, both in its togetherness and in its separateness. The psychiatrist sees beneath the surface, where most of us see only through a cloud darkly. Those who see life firm and see it whole span the extremes of the sublime and the ridiculous, sense more sharply the agony and the ecstasy of life, feel both the pleasure and the pain of being a person.

The statisticians tell us that we are headed for a world of color. By 1980 two-thirds, perhaps three-fourths, of the people of the world will be colored. The take-over in world affairs may be something like what has happened in professional sports since the advent of Jackie Robinson. Those of us who are born white and born free don't like to think about this. We'd prefer to live as though it won't happen here. We hate Stokely Carmichael with such a passion that we cannot hear him say that black power and the white backlash will be *the* issue confronting humanity in the next decade, replacing even capitalism *vis-a-vis* communism in the struggle for the loyalties of men. We simply cannot believe that the white man will not always be king and so we try to keep Carmichael from speaking at all.

Ted Sorenson, who returned recently from a trip around the world, reports that every country he visited had racial problems, many of them crucial, and few, if any, are doing much about it. To sense the depth of this struggle is to know the pain of being a person. Fortunately, the more we know of the spirit of some white

Reprinted by permission of City News Publishing Company from *Vital Speeches* March 15, 1967.

people and some Negro people, the more we are committed to continue the struggle for an equitable society. Negro author Ralph Ellison wrote,

> If you can show me how I can cling to that which is real to me while teaching me a way into the larger society, then I will not only drop my defenses and my hostility, but I will sing your praises and I will help you to make the desert bear fruit.

To be tuned in sharply to these extremes in the racial scene is to keep alive the pain of being a person.

The same thing can be said about poverty and human rights. Recently I scanned Paul G. Hoffman's report to the United Nations entitled, "The Rich and Poor in 1966." The contrast has become conventional. The rich are getting richer and the poor, poorer. Two-thirds of the people of the world will be hungry most of their lives. Three million people die each year as they are pushed beyond the rim of starvation. The life span in India is twenty-seven and one-half years for each man, and he will be hungry most of that time. The statistics of an affluent society are likewise patent. It's a crazy world of contrast for those of us whose lives are plush. Most people have more and owe more. The economy is so heated that it needs to be cooled, but money is in short supply. The stock market goes down while the employment index goes up.

Some of the same contradictions are true about human rights. We live in the tradition of the Magna Carta, the Declaration of Independence, the Four Freedoms, and the democratic ideals. I prefer the term "the brotherhood of man," but we are brought up sharply when we realize in how many places and in what multiple ways the dignity of the human spirit is violated

in our time. The more one sees of the world, the more he is made to realize the gap between we and they, between the "haves" and the "have-nots," between the lords and the slaves, the more he becomes aware that human rights can be shibboleth rather than a determination that "the earth shall be fair and all her folk be one."

Shortly before Adlai Stevenson died, he gave the Dag Hammarskjold Lecture at Princeton in which he declared that we face "a world where the fundamental issues of human rights—which have been hidden in closets down the long corridor of history—will be brought out in the open and placed high on the agenda of human affairs." There is nothing new about poverty. The Book says that the poor we have with us always. But what is new is that man now commands the means for a massive attack on poverty and that the poor are no longer willing to accept indigency. It would be so much easier and more comfortable if we could go on

> as if our luxuries were our business and their limitations were their tough luck
>
> as if our freedom was not contingent upon the freedom of other people
>
> as if we could live our life the way we want to and they could live theirs the way they have to

but the whole process of education, whether by the poet with his stinging needle, or the traveler as he sees much compressed in a short time, or education itself as it opens the mind to truth, compels us to come to grips with this disparity. This confrontation keeps alive the pain of being a person.

Moreover, these vast changes are

coming swiftly to a world where the old authorities—on which we used to lean and to which we appealed when the chips were down—have collapsed. Man is cut loose from his ancient moorings and is floundering like all "get-out." The authority parents had with their children is gone. The discipline teachers exercised upon their pupils is past tense. I may think this is bad and you may think it is better, but our opinions merely underscore the condition. The absence of these traditional authority figures has ushered in a slew of problems which are not parochial and which cannot be isolated from the whole warp and woof of life. They are the same in the parsonage on Fifth Street in a little college town named La Verne as they are on the campus of one of the world's great universities at Berkeley.

Religion was once the sphere of absolute authority. You are aware of

---

It is necessary, while in darkness, to know that there is a light somewhere, to know that in oneself, waiting to be found, there is a light.   *James Baldwin*

how much flux there is in concepts which were once so fixed and final. The tremendous Roman Catholic world, for example, may seem to be talking about birth control, but it is really struggling with the problem of authority. I heard David E. Jenkins of Cambridge say this summer that when the Pope finally comes clean on the issue of birth control, the ancient authority which surrounds the papal chair will have melted away. The current issue of a popular magazine considers "The Pope's Unsolvable Problem." He may say, "Don't take the pill," but that command will no longer bankrupt pill manufacturers. He knows that the pill will be taken, with or without permission, but he hesitates to change the Catholic teaching, lest the infallible seem to be fallible.

The dilemma among Protestants may be more subtle, but it is equally great. In separating from his Pope, Martin Luther had to have some infallibility. It was that kind of world. He set up a Book. If my grandmother could find it in the Bible—and she was quite a hunter!—then there was no question about it. The Bible had all the answers. That little book (which is not little, and much more than a book) is a veritable mine of truth, but it is naive to conclude that if you read it, you will know all you need to know to live in today's world. A decade ago we were quite positive in these solutions. We said, with omniscience, Christ is the answer. That simple announcement is greeted now with the inquiry, Yes, but what is the question?

The whole "God is dead" mood is striking at this absolutism, this insistence on guarantees, which has been so characteristic of religious faith. This summer, in one seminar, we spent three weeks dissecting the four major authorities in the "God is dead" sequence. I may not have understood what was written and spoken, or I may not have liked it, but I confess that I found myself in the corner of those who held that, "the God who will take care of everything" is dead, "the God who is always on our side" is dead, "the God who is a stopgap for the incompleteness of our knowledge" is dead, "the God who is my special guardian angel" is dead, and "the God who makes everything come out all right" is dead.

Dietrich Bonhoeffer was trying to say that the time has come in the life of the world when we must no longer be like children, asking God for this, that and these; as though God were some celestial bellhop who answered our beck and call. Bonhoeffer insisted the era of "that kind of magic" had come to an end. The age of spiritual paternalism is past. Man, he held, has come of age. All the conditions essential for the good life are at man's disposal. He must cease asking God for special favors or dispensations. He must now use the gifts available for the welfare and happiness of all humanity.

We used to talk about things and then add God, as though *He* could be found outside his creation. We used to shy away from humanity, especially humanism, as though being human were a condition for which man needed to apologize. We used to think of the world as the domain of the devil and the church as God's special dwelling place. Clearer perceptions into the nature of things, both without and within, have helped us to sense that "the world is now at the place where every blessed thing gives out messages," as Charles Coulson of Wadam College said recently. In our kind of world to ask God for a special revelation may reveal ignorance rather than faith; to petition God to make an exception in our case may imply impertinence rather than devotion.

Only a rigorous restructuring of the faith that is in us can provide the basis for such a way of life. We can no longer ask God to rear back and pull off a miracle or to call down fire from heaven to punish some lunatic Lucifer who threatens to push the button. God is not some greater Man from U.N.C.L.E. Our TV miracle shows hark back to this primitive desire. The pattern persists in the Man from U.N.C.L.E., the Girl from U.N.C.L.E. (next year it is to be the Son of the Man and the Girl from U.N.C.L.E.), the Moon Spinners, Batman, and the Lone Ranger. The motif is always the same, best depicted for me in the Lone Ranger. (That's my era!) He is the messianic man, the god-figure. He comes out of nowhere. He is hidden from view via a mask or a mist. He arrives in the nick of time. He saves us in the dire emergency. He wipes away our tears. He heals our wounds. He disappears in a cloud or a vapor. He will come again next week, next episode, next emergency! When we cannot see that such easy dependence and deliverance is gone, we are like children playing their little games. When the awareness of this new creaturehood finally penetrates, we are overwhelmed with the pain of being a person.

Such is the tumult which has been stirring in my soul, and as I talk with you tonight, I am merely trying to compose it. You may sense some of the mental and spiritual anguish which is mine as I endeavour to grow out of the dependence which has been such an easy and comfortable way of life from childhood until now. It is a torment as well as a triumph to learn that I must not use God, but that I can enjoy him.

Such a pilgrimage has the bitter-sweet urgency of a lad

who turns from home
eagerly but reluctantly
moving past the point of no return
realizing that he is now really on his own

who becomes aware of the awesome magnitude of life vaster and more complex than his wildest dreams confronting questions bigger than life itself knowing the answers he gives will not be complete

who realizes that the future is wide open and unmade
its opportunities breathtaking
its dilemmas increasing
its guarantees evaporating

So shall his knowledge always be incomplete and a safe future forever beyond his grasp.

In such moments of truth we possess the rhapsody and the rigor of life, and we are possessed of the agony and ecstasy of life. In these moments we know and keep alive the pain of being a person.

63

The unexamined life is not worth living. *Socrates*

DO YOU BELIEVE IN LIFE AFTER DEATH?

WHAT DO YOU CALL THIS?

Reprinted by permission of Publisher's Hall Syndicate. © Jules Feiffer.

WE ARE TRANSMITTERS

As we live, we are transmitters of life.
And when we fail to transmit life, life fails to flow
    through us.
That is part of the mystery of sex, it is a flow onwards.
Sexless people transmit nothing.

And if, as we work, we can transmit life into
    our work,
life, still more life rushes into us to compensate,
    to be ready
and we ripple with life through the days.

Even if it is a woman making an apple dumpling,
    or a man a stool,
if life goes into the pudding, good is the pudding
good is the stool,
content is the woman, with fresh life rippling in to her,
content is the man.

Give, and it shall be given unto you
is still the truth about life.
But giving life is not so easy.
It doesn't mean handing it out to some mean fool, or
    letting the living dead eat you up.
It means kindling the life-quality where it was not,
even if it's only in the whiteness of a washed
    pocket-handkerchief.

    —D. H. Lawrence

THE PERSON OF TOMORROW

By Carl R. Rogers

I am fascinated these days by what I am convinced is a most significant phenomenon. I am seeing a New Man emerging. I believe this New Man is the person of tomorrow. I want to talk about him.

I have seen him emerging, partially formed, from encounter groups, sensitivity training, so-called T-groups. I realize that for many years I saw facets of him emerging in the deep relationship of individual psychotherapy. I see him showing his face in the rapidly growing trend toward a humanistic and human psychology. I see him in the new type of student emerging on our campuses, and in campus unrest all over the world—Paris, Czechoslovakia, Japan, Columbia, Berkeley, San Francisco State, Harvard, and many other places. He is not all lovable, he is sometimes frightening, but he is emerging. I see him in the surge toward individualism and self-respect in our black population in and out of the ghettos, and in the racial unrest which runs like a fever through all our cities. I see elements of him in the philosophy of "dropouts" in our generation—the hippies, the "flower people." I see him, strangely enough, in the younger members of industrial management today. I catch what to my older eyes is a confusing glimpse of him in the musicians, the poets, the writers, the composers of this generation—I'll mention the Beatles, and you can add the others. I have a feeling that the mass media—especially television—have helped him to emerge, though on this I am not very clear. But I have named, I think, a number of the areas and trends which perhaps have caused the emergence, and certainly permit us to see, the qualities of this New Man.

Though I am excited and full of anticipation about this person of tomorrow, there are aspects of the situation which are very sobering. I believe the New Man has characteristics which run strongly counter to the orthodoxies, dogmas, forms, and creeds of the major western religions —Catholicism, Protestantism, Judaism. He does not fit at all into traditional industrial management and

Reprinted by permission of the Center for Studies of the Person, La Jolla, California.

organization. He contradicts, in his person, almost every element of traditional schools, colleges, universities. He certainly is not suited to become a part of bureaucratic government. He doesn't fit well into the military. Since our culture has developed all these orthodoxies and forms of present-day life, we have to ask ourselves seriously if this New Man is simply a deviant misfit, or whether he is something more hopeful.

There is another reason for thinking deeply and soberly about him. He is almost the antithesis of the Puritan culture, with its strict beliefs and controls, which founded our country. He is very different from the person admired by the industrial revolution, with that person's ambition and productivity. He is deeply opposite to the Communist culture, with its controls on thought and behavior in the interest of the state. He in no way resembles the medieval man—the man of faith and force, of monasteries and Crusades. He would not be congenial with the man produced by the Roman Empire—the practical, disciplined man. He is also very alien to today's culture in the United States, which emphasizes computerized technology, and the man in uniform—whether military, police, or government inspector.

If, then, he is new in so many ways, if he deviates so deeply from almost all of the gradually developed norms of the past and even the present, is he just a sport in the evolutionary line, soon to die out or be dis-carded? Personally I do not believe so. I believe he is a viable creature. I have the conviction that he is the person of tomorrow, and that perhaps he has a better chance of survival than we do. But this is only my own opinion.

I have talked about him at some length, but I have made no attempt to describe his attitudes, his characteristics, his convictions. I should like to do this very briefly. I would like to say that I know of no one individual to whom all of the following statements would apply. I am also keenly aware that I am describing a minority, probably a small minority, of our present-day population, but I am convinced that it is a growing minority. What follows is a groping, uncertain characterization of what I see as the New Man. Some of his qualities are probably temporary ones, as he struggles to break free from the cocoon of his culture. I shall try to indicate these. Some, I believe, represent the process person he is becoming. Here then are some of his characteristics as I see them.

He has no use for sham, facade, or pretense, whether in interpersonal relationships, in education, in politics, in religion. He values authenticity. He will not put up with double talk. He hates statements such as these: "Cigarette smoking is a romantic, exciting pleasurable, satisfying thing—(and of course it kills many through lung cancer)." Or, "We are following a noble pathway in protecting South Viet Nam and living up to our commitments and treaties—(but in doing so we kill thousands of men, women, and children, many of them completely innocent, others whose only crime is that they have a goal for their country different than ours)." He hates this kind of thing with a passion. He regards the current culture as almost completely hypocritical. I believe that this hatred for phoniness is perhaps the deepest mark of the New Man.

He is opposed to all highly structured, inflexible institutions. He wants organizations to be fluid, changing, adaptive, and *human*. It will be clear from what follows how deep is his dislike for bureaucracy, rigidity, form for form's sake. He simply will not buy these qualities.

He finds educational institutions mostly irrelevant and futile so far as he is concerned. His unrest—in college and high school—arises out of a hundred specific issues, but none of these issues would be important if his school were truly meaningful for him. He sees traditional education as it is—the most rigid, outdated, incompetent institution in our culture.

He wants *his* learning to involve feelings, to involve the *living* of learnings, the *application* of relevant knowledge, a *meaning* in the here and now. Out of these elements he sometimes likes to become involved in a searching for new approximations to the truth, but the pursuit of knowledge purely for its own sake is not characteristic.

Religious institutions are perceived as definitely irrelevant and frequently damaging to human progress. This attitude toward religious institutions does not mean at all that he has no concern for life's mysteries or for the search for ethical and moral values. It seems, in fact, that this person of tomorrow is deeply concerned with living in a moral and ethical way, but the morals are new and shifting, the ethics are relative to the situation, and the one thing that is not tolerated is a discrepancy between verbal standards and the actual living of values.

He is seeking new forms of community, of closeness, of intimacy, of shared purpose. He is seeking new forms of communication in such a community—verbal and nonverbal, feelingful as well as intellectual. He recognizes that he will be living his transient life mostly in temporary relationships and that he must be able to establish closeness quickly. He must also be able to leave these close relationships behind, without excessive conflict or mourning.

He has a distrust of marriage as an institution. A man-woman relationship has deep value for him only when it is a mutually enhancing, growing, flowing relationship. He has little regard for marriage as a ceremony, or for vows of permanence, which prove to be highly impermanent.

He is a searching person, without any neat answers. The only thing he is certain of is that he is uncertain. Sometimes he feels a nostalgic sadness in his uncertain world. He is sharply aware of the fact that he is only a speck of life on a small blue and white planet in an enormous universe. Is there a purpose in this universe? Or only the purpose he creates? He does not know the answer but he is willing to live with this anxious uncertainty.

There is a rhythm in his life between flow and stability, between changingness and structure, between anxiety and temporary security. Stability is only a brief period for the consolidation of learning before moving on to more change. He always exists in this rhythm of process.

He is an open person, open to himself, close to his own feelings. He is also open to and sensitive to the thoughts and feelings of others and to the objective realities of his world. He is a highly aware person.

He is able to communicate with himself much more freely than any previous man. The barriers of repression which shut off so much of man from himself are definitely lower than in preceding generations. Not only is he able to communicate with himself, he is also often able to express his feelings and thoughts to others, whether they are negative and confronting in nature, or positive and loving.

He likes and dislikes, his joys and his sorrows are passionate and are passionately expressed. He is vitally alive.

He is a spontaneous person, willing to risk newness, often willing to risk saying or doing the wild, the far-out thing. His adventuresomeness has an almost Elizabethan quality—*everything* is possible, *anything* can be tried.

Currently he likes to be "turned on"—by many kinds of experiences and by drugs. This dependence on drugs for a consciousness-expanding experience is often being left behind as he discovers that he prefers to be "turned on" by deep and fresh and vital interpersonal experiences, or by meditation.

Currently he often decides to obey those laws which he regards as just and to disobey those which he regards as unjust, taking the consequences of his actions. This is a new phenomenon. We have had a few Thoreaus but we have never had hundreds of people, young and old alike, willing to obey some laws and disobey others on the basis of their own personal moral judgment.

He is active—sometimes violently, intolerantly, and self-righteously active—in the causes in which he believes. Hence he arouses the most extreme and repressive antipathies in those who are frightened by change.

He can see no reason why educational organizations, urban areas, ghetto conditions, racial discrimination, unjust wars, should be allowed to remain unchanged. He has a sustained idealism which is linked to his activism. He does not *hope* that things will be changed in 50 years; he intends to change them *now*.

He has a trust in his own experience and a profound *distrust* of all external authority. Neither pope nor judge nor scholar can convince him of anything which is not borne out by his own experience.

He has a belief in his own potential and in his own direction. This belief extends to his own dreams of the future and his intuitions of the present.

He can cooperate with others with great effectiveness in the pursuit of a goal which he is convinced is valid and meaningful. He never cooperates simply in order to conform or to be a "good fellow."

He has a disregard for material things and material rewards. While he has been accustomed to an affluent life and readily uses all kinds of material things, taking them for granted, he is quite unwilling to accept material rewards or material things if they mean that he must compromise his integrity in order to do so.

He likes to be close to elemental nature; to the sea, the sun, the snow; flowers, animals, and birds; to life, and growth, and death. He rides the waves on his surfboard; he sails the sea in a small craft; he lives with gorillas or lions; he soars down the mountain on his skis.

These are some of the qualities which I see in the New Man, in the man who is emerging as the person of tomorrow. He does not fit at all well into the world of the present. He will have a rough time trying to live in his own way. Yet, if he can retain the qualities I have listed so briefly, if he can create a culture which would nourish and nurture those qualities, then it may be that he holds a great deal of promise for all of us and for our future. In a world marked by incredibly rapid technological change, and by overwhelming psychological sham and pretense, we desperately need both his ability to live as a fluid process, and his uncompromising integrity.

Perhaps some of you in this audience will have resonated to my description because you see in yourself some of these same qualities emerging in you. To the extent that you are becoming this person of tomorrow and endeavoring to sharpen and refine his qualities in a constructive fashion, I wish you well. May you find many enduring satisfactions as you struggle to bring into being, within yourself and in your relationships with others, the best of this New Man.

The person who most considers others is also the one who has the deepest self-acceptance. *Erich Fromm*

ONE

Put your mind
where your eye is
and feel such power
there is
your single clapping hand
meeting mine
to set
the whole aching world
back in joint.

TWO

Catching deeply
the surface of things
I see
and I see beyond
the grass green
shimmering breeze
your hair
sparkling like sun
among the waves
motionless in time
I hear you
the way I hear silence.

—*Jean Pumphrey*

Reprinted by permission of Jean Pumphrey.

HOW COULD ANYTHING THAT FEELS SO BAD BE SO GOOD?

By Richard E. Farson

Maybe it is time to adopt a new strategy in trying to figure out why life today is so difficult, and what can be done about it. Assume that not only are things often not what they seem, they may be just the opposite of what they seem. When it comes to human affairs, everything is paradoxical.

People are discontented these days, for example, not because things are worse than ever, but because things are better than ever. Take marriage. In California there are about six divorces for every ten marriages—even higher in some of the better communities. One must admit that a good deal of discontent is reflected in those statistics. But the explanation so frequently offered—that the institution of marriage is in a state of collapse—simply does not hold. Marriage has never been more popular and desirable than it is now; so appealing in fact, that even those who are in the process of divorce can scarcely wait for the law to allow them to marry again.

The problem is that people have never before entered marriage with the high expectations they now hold.

Throughout history, the family has been a vital unit for survival, starting as a defense system for physical survival, and gradually becoming a unit for economic survival. Now, of course, the family has become a physical and economic liability rather than an asset. Having met, as a society, the basic survival and security needs, people simply don't need each other anymore to fight Indians or spin yarn—or wash dishes or repair electrical plugs for that matter. The bonds of marriage and family life are no longer functional, but affectional. People used to come to love each other because they needed each other. Now it's just the other way around. They need each other because they love each other.

Listening to the complaints of those recently divorced, one seldom hears of brutality and desertion, but usually something like, "We just don't communicate very well," "The educational differences between us were simply too great to overcome," "I felt trapped in the relationship," "He won't let me be *me*," "We don't have much in common anymore." These

Reprinted by permission of Richard E. Farson and the California Institute of the Arts, Los Angeles, California.

complaints are interesting, because they reflect high-order discontent resulting from the failure of marriage to meet the great expectations held for it. Couples now expect—and demand—communication and understanding, shared values and goals, intellectual companionship, full sexual lives, deep romantic love, great moments of intimacy. By and large, marriage today actually does deliver such moments, but as a result couples have gone on to burden the relationship with even greater demands. To some extent it has been the success of marriage that has created the discontent.

The same appears to be true in the civil rights movement. The gains that have been made have led not to satisfaction but to increased tension and dissatisfaction, particularly among those benefiting from such gains. The discontent is higher in the North than the South, higher in cities than in rural areas.

One could go on—the protests of student activists are greater at the better universities. Demands for freedom and democracy and education and individual liberty and free speech are greatest in the nation which leads the world in these respects. The history of revolutions shows that they come *after* reforms have been made, when people are strong enough to have developed a vision of better things.

The disturbing paradox of social change is that improvement brings the need for more improvement in constantly accelerating demands. So, compared to what *used* to be, society is way ahead; compared to what *might* be, it is way behind. Society is enabled to feel that conditions are rotten, because they are actually so good.

Another problem is that everything is temporary, nothing lasts. We have grown up with the idea that in order to develop personal security we need stability, roots, consistency, and familiarity. Yet we live in a world which in every respect is continually changing. Whether we are talking about skyscrapers or family life, scientific facts or religious values, all are highly temporary and becoming even more so. If one were to plot a curve showing the incidence of invention throughout the history of man, one would see that change is not just increasing but actually accelerating. Changes are coming faster and faster —in a sense change has become a way of life. The only people who will live successfully in tomorrow's world are those who can accept and enjoy temporary systems.

Moments, then, are the most we can expect from the things we create and produce. We are beginning to change their basis of evaluation from the permanent usefulness of things to their ability to create moments of positive experience. Yet with nothing to rely upon except change itself, we find ourselves increasingly disturbed and disrupted as a society.

People are also troubled because of the new participative mood that exists today. It's a do-it-yourself society; every layman wants to get into the act. Emerson's "do your own thing" has become the cliché of the times. People no longer accept being passive members. They now want to be active changers.

This participative phenomenon can be seen in every part of contemporary life—on campus, in the church, in the mass media, in the arts, in business and industry, on ghetto streets, in the family. It is succeeding to the point where people are having to abandon their old concepts of elitism. The myths that wisdom, creativity, and competence are rare, difficult to evoke, and highly desired are giving way to a view that they are rather common, relatively easy to elicit, and desired only in situations where they are not too disruptive or difficult to manage.

The problem is that modern man seems unable to redesign his institutions fast enough to accommodate the new demands, the new intelligence, the new abilities of segments of society which, heretofore, have not been taken seriously. Consequently, people are frightened by the black revolution, paralyzed by student activism, and now face what may be even more devastating—the women's rebellion.

As if all this weren't enough, society may also be experiencing a reverse transmission of culture. To put it simply, today's young people probably know more than their elders. Wisdom and culture have always been transmitted from the older generation to the younger. Now, perhaps for the first time in history, there is a reversal of that process. Young people used to want to be like their elders; today it's the other way around.

The old, of course, always learned some things from the young. Fashion and dance, for example, But now they are learning from youth about the nature of society, about world affairs, about human relations, about life. The young have much to teach in matters of taste and judgment, in ethics and morals. They are attending school in greater numbers, staying longer, and learning more than former generations did. All kinds of people—advertising executives, futurists, artists, designers, social scientists—now look to youth as the leading edge of contemporary culture. If McLuhan is right, the young are sensing the world in ways never sensed before, and, consequently, they have developed an approach to life which is very different from that of their elders. Margaret Mead describes the plight of the over-thirty generation

as being similar to that of the alien trying to learn about a foreign culture. It is small wonder then that the institutions in which leadership is entrusted only to the elders (and what institution isn't?) are so unstable.

Society simply has not had these kinds of problems before, and to meet them it will have to adopt strategies for their solution that are as new, and as different, and as paradoxical as are the problems themselves.

Instead of trying to reduce the discontent felt, try to raise the level or quality of the discontent. Perhaps the most that can be hoped for is to have high-order discontent in today's society, discontent about things that really matter. Rather than evaluating programs in terms of how happy they make people, how satisfied those people become, programs must be evaluated in terms of the quality of the discontent they engender. For example, if a consultant wants to assess whether or not an organization is healthy, he doesn't ask, "Is there an absence of complaints?" but rather, "What kinds of complaints are there?" Psychologist Abraham Maslow suggests that we analyze the *quality* of the complaint being registered. In his terms, a low-level grumble would involve, for instance, a complaint about working conditions; a high-level grumble might have to do with matters beyond one's own selfish interests —a concern for fairness in the treatment of another person, for example— while a meta-grumble would have to do with self-actualization needs, such as feeling that one's talents are not being fully utilized, wanting to be in on things, wanting to make a greater contribution.

As an illustration, instead of trying to negotiate only on the low-order complaints of black students having to do with the number of black teachers on a faculty or the lack of soul food in the school cafeteria, efforts should transcend these problems, meet those demands, and go well beyond them by raising the level of discontent so that black students are complaining about the quality of education and demanding a chance to reinvent the whole system. When such complaints are heard, the situation will be much improved, for then *all* men will be able to engage in a joint effort toward a common goal.

Instead of trying to "cool it" in a crisis, use the time of crisis to make major changes and improvements. Many individuals feel that in a crisis the only thing to do is to try to "hang in there," call everything to a halt, try to maintain previous conditions, let it pass, and hope things will return to normal. Instead, they should capitalize on the momentum that is in the developing mood of people during a crisis to energize the changes that must be made. It is analogous to the jujitsu technique of moving with one's opponent and using his momentum to gain the advantage; of course, in correcting social ills *everyone* gains, nobody loses.

Instead of trying to make gradual changes in small increments, make big changes. After all, big changes are relatively easier to make than are small ones. Some people assume that the way to bring about improvements is to make the change small enough so that nobody will notice it. This approach has never worked, and one can't help but wonder why such thinking continues. Everyone knows how to resist small changes; they do it all the time. If, however, the change is big enough, resistance can't be mobilized against it. Management can make a sweeping organizational change, but just let a manager try to change someone's desk from here to there, and see the great difficulty he encounters. All

change is resisted, so the question is how can the changes be made big enough so that they have a chance of succeeding?

Instead of trying to improve people, improve environments. All too often the conclusion is reached that all problems boil down to such people problems as basic attitude differences and personality clashes. And it is believed that work must first be done to change people. But that may not be the best strategy. People, fundamentally, change little in their personalities and attitudes. They can, however, change markedly in their responses to different environments, situations, and conditions.

It is known how to create conditions which will evoke from just about anybody the full range of human behavior; with relative ease, people can be made to lie, cheat, and hurt others. How simple it is to take the nicest kid on the block, send him to Vietnam, and soon have him killing other people. It is comforting also to know that situations can be created in which people become affectionate, honest, helpful, intimate, and cooperative. All this is fairly simple to arrange in the laboratory. The trouble is that society does not have the designs that elicit these aspects in people.

Buckminster Fuller has said that instead of *reforms* society needs new *forms*; e.g., in order to reduce traffic accidents, improve automobiles and highways instead of trying to improve drivers. The same concept should be applied to human relations. There is a need to think in terms of social architecture, and to provide arrangements among people that evoke what they really want to see in themselves. Mankind takes great pains with physical architecture, and is beginning to concern itself with the design of systems in which the human being is a component. But most of these designs are only for safety, efficiency, or productivity. System designs are not made to affect those aspects of life people care most about such as family life, romance, esthetic experiences, and intimate encounter. Social technology as well as physical technology need to be applied in making human arrangements that will transcend anything mankind has yet experienced. People need not be victimized by their environments; they can be fulfilled by them.

Instead of looking to a professional elite for the solution to any social problem, look to the greatest resource available—the very population that has the problem. Many of us tend to have a low opinion of people, those wretched masses who don't understand, don't know what they need or want, who continually make mistakes and foul up their lives, requiring those of us who are professionally trained to come in and correct the situation. But that's not the way it really works. The fact is that some drug addicts are much better able to cure addiction in each other than are psychiatrists; some convicts can run better rehabilitation programs for convicts than do correctional officers; many students tend to learn more

from each other than from many professors; some patients in mental hospitals are better for each other than is the staff. Thousands of self-help organizations are doing a good job, perhaps a better job at problem solving than is the profession that is defined with that problem. People who *have* the problems often have a better understanding of their situation and what must be done to change it. What professionals have to do is learn to cooperate with that resource, to design the conditions which evoke that intelligence.

In this way society can be truly self-determining and self-renewing. The special beauty of this formulation is that it fits the democratic goal of enabling the people to make a society for themselves. Mankind can rely on people as a resource for much more than is possible to imagine. It's really quite difficult to find the ceiling of what people can do for themselves and each other, given the opportunity.

The great frontier today is the exploration of the human potential, man's seemingly limitless ability to adapt, to grow, to invent his own destiny. There is much to learn, but we already know this: the future need not happen to us; we can make it happen.

PESSIMISM AND OPTIMISM

By Albert Schweitzer

To the question whether I am a pessimist or an optimist, I answer that my knowledge is pessimistic, but my willing and hoping are optimistic.

I am pessimistic in that I experience in its full weight what we conceive to be the absence of purpose in the course of world happenings. Only at quite rare moments have I felt really glad to be alive. I could not but feel with a sympathy full of regret all the pain that I saw around me, not only that of men but that of the whole creation. From this community of suffering I have never tried to withdraw myself. It seemed to me a matter of course that we should take our share of the burden of pain which lies upon the world. Even while I was a boy at school it was clear to me that no explanation of the evil in the world could ever satisfy me; all explanations, I felt, ended in sophistries, and at bottom had no other object than to make it possible for men to share in the misery around them, with less keen feelings. That a thinker like Leibnitz could reach the miserable conclusion that though this world is, indeed, not good, it is the best that was possible, I have never been able to understand.

But however much concerned I was at the problem of the misery in the world, I never let myself get lost in broodings over it; I always held firmly to the thought that each one of us can do a little to bring some portion of it to an end. Thus I came gradually to rest content in the knowledge that there is only one thing we can understand about the problem, and that is that each of us has to go his own way, but as one who means to help to bring about deliverance.

In my judgment, too, of the situation in which mankind finds itself at the present time I am pessimistic. I cannot make myself believe that that situation is not so bad as it seems to be, but I am inwardly conscious that we are on a road which, if we continue to tread it, will bring us into "Middle Ages" of a new character. The spiritual and material misery to which mankind of today is delivering itself through its renunciation of thinking and of the ideals which spring therefrom, I picture to myself in its utmost

Reprinted by permission of Holt, Rinehart and Winston from Albert Schweitzer, *Out of My Life and Thought* (New York: Holt, Rinehart and Winston, 1961).

The existentialists' central proclama-
tion is this: No matter how great the
forces victimizing the human being,
man has the capacity to know that
he is being victimized, and thus to
influence in some way how he will
relate to his fate. There is never lost
that kernel of the power to take some
stand, to make some decision, no
matter how minute. This is why they
hold that man's existence consists,
in the last analysis, of his freedom.
Tillich phrased it beautifully in a
recent speech, "Man becomes truly
human only at the moment of decision."   *Rollo May*

compass. And yet I remain optimistic.
One belief of my childhood I have preserved with the certainty that I can
never lose it: belief in truth. I am
confident that the spirit generated by
truth is stronger than the force of circumstances. In my view no other
destiny awaits mankind than that
which, through its mental and spiritual disposition, it prepares for itself.
Therefore I do not believe that it will
have to tread the road to ruin right to
the end.

If men can be found who revolt
against the spirit of thoughtlessness,
and who are personalities sound
enough and profound enough to let
the ideals of ethical progress radiate
from them as a force, there will start
an activity of the spirit which will be
strong enough to evoke a new mental
and spiritual disposition in mankind.

Because I have confidence in the
power of truth and of the spirit, I believe in the future of mankind. Ethical
acceptance of the world contains with-

in itself an optimistic willing and hoping which can never be lost. It is,
therefore, never afraid to face the
dismal reality, and to see it as it really
is.

In my own life anxiety, trouble,
and sorrow have been allotted to me at
times in such abundant measure that
had my nerves not been so strong, I
must have broken down under the
weight. Heavy is the burden of fatigue
and responsibility which has lain upon
me without a break for years. I have
not much of my life for myself, not
even the hours I should like to devote
to my wife and child.

But I have had blessings too: that
I am allowed to work in the service of
mercy; that my work has been successful; that I receive from other people affection and kindness in abun-
dance; that I have loyal helpers, who
identify themselves with my activity;
that I enjoy a health which allows me
to undertake most exhausting work;
that I have a well-balanced tempera-

ment which varies little, and an energy which exerts itself with calmness and deliberation; and, finally, that I can recognize as such whatever happiness falls to my lot, accepting it also as a thing for which some thank offering is due from me.

I feel it deeply that I can work as a free man at a time when an oppressive lack of freedom is the lot of so many, as also that though my immediate work is material, yet I have at the same time opportunities of occupying myself in the sphere of the spiritual and intellectual.

That the circumstances of my life provide in such varied ways favorable conditions for my work, I accept as something of which I would fain prove myself worthy.

How much of the work which I have planned and have in mind shall I be able to complete?

My hair is beginning to turn. My body is beginning to show traces of the exertions I have demanded of it, and of the passage of the years.

I look back with thankfulness to the time when, without needing to husband my strength, I could get through an uninterrupted course of bodily and mental work. With calmness and humility I look forward to the future, so that I may not be unprepared for renunciation if it be required of me. Whether we be workers or sufferers, it is assuredly our duty to conserve our powers, as being men who have won their way through to the peace which passeth all understanding.

Grownups love figures. When you tell them that you have a new friend, they never ask you any questions about essential matters. They never say to you, "What does his voice sound like? What games does he love best? Does he collect butterflies?" Instead, they demand: "How old is he? How many brothers has he? How much does he weigh? How much money does his father make?" Only from these figures do they think they have learned anything about him.

Antoine de Saint-Exupéry

OLD AGE STICKS

old age sticks
up Keep
Off
signs)&

youth yanks them
down(old
age
cries No

Tres)&(pas)
youth laughs
(sing
old age

scolds Forbid
den Stop
Must
n't Don't

&)youth goes
right on
gr
owing old

   —e. e. cummings

"The Peace Corps ruined my Bernie's life."

"I just don't know. We had such plans for him. When he graduated he was interviewed by all the big companies. What offers he had. He and Barbara were going to get married and live in the Monte Carlo Gardens with the rest of their friends. His father and I had all the furniture picked out. It was only two blocks away from here. We could have had coffee and played Scrabble and watched TV every night. But no. Not Bernie. He had to run off half cocked and live in a shack ten thousand miles away. He works in a hospital of all places. And with a degree in It wouldn't be so bad fo but two years. These ki I just don't know." The Washington, D. C. 20

Reprinted by pern

Reprinted by permission of Harcourt, Brace & World from
e. e. cummings, *95 Poems* (New York: Harcourt, Brace &
World, 1958).

I STAND HERE IRONING

By Tillie Olsen

I stand here ironing, and what you asked me moves tormented back and forth with the iron.

"I wish you would manage the time to come in and talk with me about your daughter. I'm sure you can help me understand her. She's a youngster who needs help and whom I'm deeply interested in helping."

"Who needs help?" Even if I came what good would it do? You think because I am her mother I have a key, or that in some way you could use me as a key? She has lived for nineteen years. There is all that life that has happened outside of me, beyond me.

And when is there time to remember, to sift, to weigh, to estimate, to total? I will start and there will be an interruption and I will have to gather it all together again. Or I will become engulfed with all I did or did not do, with what should have been and what cannot be helped.

She was a beautiful baby. The first and only one of our five that was beautiful at birth. You do not guess how new and uneasy her tenancy in her now-loveliness. You did not know her all those years she was thought homely, or see her poring over her baby pictures, making me tell her over and over how beautiful she had been—and would be, I would tell her—and was now, to the seeing eye. But the seeing eyes were few or nonexistent. Including mine.

I nursed her. They feel that's important nowadays. I nursed all the children, but with her, with all the fierce rigidity of first motherhood, I did like the books said. Though her cries battered me to trembling and my breasts ached with swollenness, I waited till the clock decreed.

Why do I put that first? I do not even know if it matters, or if it explains anything.

She was a beautiful baby. She blew shining bubbles of sound. She loved motion, loved light, loved color and music and textures. She would lie on the floor in her blue overalls patting the surface so hard in ecstasy her hands and feet would blur. She was a miracle to me, but when she was eight months old

Reprinted by permission of Delacorte Press from Tillie Olsen, *Tell Me A Riddle* (New York: Delacorte Press, 1961).

I had to leave her daytimes with the woman downstairs to whom she was no miracle at all, for I worked or looked for work and for Emily's father, who "could no longer endure" (he wrote in his good-by note) "sharing want with us."

I was nineteen. It was the pre-relief, pre-WPA world of the depression. I would start running as soon as I got off the streetcar, running up the stairs, the place smelling sour, and awake or asleep to startle awake, when she saw me she would break into a clogged weeping that could not be comforted, a weeping I can yet hear.

After a while I found a job hashing at night so I could be with her days, and it was better. But it came to where I had to bring her to his family and leave her.

It took a long time to raise the money for her fare back. Then she got chicken pox and I had to wait longer. When she finally came, I hardly knew her, walking quick and nervous like her father, looking like her father, thin, and dressed in a shoddy red that yellowed her skin and glared at the pock marks. All the baby loveliness gone.

She was two. Old enough for nursery school they said, and I did not know then what I know now—the fatigue of the long day, and the lacerations of group life in nurseries that are only parking places for children.

Except that it would have made no difference if I had known. It was the only place there was. It was the only way we could be together, the only way I could hold a job.

And even without knowing, I knew. I knew the teacher that was evil because all these years it has curdled into my memory, the little boy hunched in the corner, her rasp, "why aren't you outside, because Alvin hits you? that's no reason, go out coward." I knew Emily hated it even if she did not clutch and implore "don't go Mommy" like the other children, mornings.

She always had a reason why we should stay home. Momma, you look sick. Momma, I feel sick. Momma, the teachers aren't there today, they're sick. Momma, there was a fire there last night. Momma, it's a holiday today, no school, they told me.

But never a direct protest, never rebellion. I think of our others in their three-, four-year-oldness—the explosions, the tempers, the denunciations, the demands—and I feel suddenly ill. I stop the ironing. What in me demanded that goodness in her? And what was the cost, the cost to her of such goodness?

The old man living in the back once said in his gentle way: "You should smile at Emily more when you look at her." What *was* in my face when I looked at her? I loved her. There were all the acts of love.

It was only with the others I remembered what he said, so that it was the

---

The simplest act of life is an act of affirmation; it is the acceptance of one's own and others' lives as the starting point of all thinking.
  Nicola Chiaromonte

---

face of joy, and not of care or tightness or worry I turned to them—but never to Emily. She does not smile easily, let alone almost always as her brothers and sisters do. Her face is closed and somber, but when she wants, how fluid. You must have seen it in her pantomimes, you spoke of her rare gift for comedy on the stage that rouses a laughter out of the audience so dear they applaud and applaud and do not want to let her go.

Where does it come from, that comedy? There was none of it in her when she came back to me that second time, after I had had to send her away again. She had a new daddy now to learn to love, and I think perhaps it was a better time. Except when we left her alone nights, telling ourselves she was old enough.

"Can't you go some other time Mommy, like tomorrow?" she would ask. "Will it be just a little while you'll be gone?"

The time we came back, the front door open, the clock on the floor in the hall. She rigid awake. "It wasn't just a little while. I didn't cry. I called you a little, just three times, and then I went downstairs to open the door so you could come faster. The clock talked loud, I threw it away, it scared me what it talked."

She said the clock talked loud that night I went to the hospital to have Susan. She was delirious with the fever that comes before red measles, but she was fully conscious all the week I was gone and the week after we were home when she could not come near the baby or me.

She did not get well. She stayed skeleton thin, not wanting to eat, and night after night she had nightmares. She would call for me, and I would sleepily call back, "you're all right, darling, go to sleep, it's just a dream," and if she still called, in a sterner voice, "now go to sleep Emily, there's nothing to hurt you." Twice, only twice, when I had to get up for Susan anyhow, I went in to sit with her.

Now when it is too late (as if she would let me hold and comfort her like I do the others) I get up and go to her at her moan or restless stirring. "Are you awake? Can I get you something?" And the answer is always the same: "No, I'm all right, go back to sleep Mother."

They persuaded me at the clinic to send her away to a convalescent home in the country where "she can have the kind of food and care you can't manage for her, and you'll be free to concentrate on the new baby." They still send children to that place. I see pictures on the society page of sleek young women planning affairs to raise money for it, or dancing at the affairs, or decorating Easter eggs or filling Christmas stockings for the children.

They never have a picture of the children so I do not know if they still wear those gigantic red bows and the ravaged looks on the every other Sunday when parents can come to visit "unless otherwise notified"—as we were notified the first six weeks.

Oh it is a handsome place, green lawns and tall trees and fluted flower beds. High up on the balconies of each cottage the children stand, the girls in their red bows and white dresses, the boys in white suits and giant red ties. The parents stand below shrieking up to be heard and the children shriek down to be heard, and between them the invisible wall "Not To Be Contaminated by Parental Germs or Physical Affection."

There was a tiny girl who always stood hand in hand with Emily. Her parents never came. One visit she was gone. "They moved her to Rose Cottage," Emily shouted in explanation. "They don't like you to love anybody here."

She wrote once a week, the labored writing of a seven-year-old. "I am fine. How is the baby. If I write my leter nicly I will have a star. Love." There never was a star. We wrote every other day, letters she could never hold or keep but only hear read—once. "We simply do not have room for children to keep any personal possessions," they patiently explained when we pieced one Sunday's shrieking together to plead how much it would mean to Emily to keep her letters and cards.

Each visit she looked frailer. "She isn't eating," they told us. (They had runny eggs for breakfast or mush with lumps, Emily said later, I'd hold it in my mouth and not swallow. Nothing ever tasted good, just when they had chicken.)

It took us eight months to get her released home, and only the fact that she gained back so little of her seven lost pounds convinced the social worker.

I used to try to hold and love her after she came back, but her body would stay stiff, and after a while she'd push away. She ate little. Food sickened her, and I think much of life too. Oh she had physical lightness and brightness, twinkling by on skates, bouncing like a ball up and down up and down over the jump rope, skimming over the hill; but these were momentary.

She fretted about her appearance, thin and dark and foreign-looking at a time when every little girl was supposed to look or thought she should look a chubby blond replica of Shirley Temple. The doorbell sometimes rang for her, but no one seemed to come and play in the house or be a best friend. Maybe because we moved so much.

There was a boy she loved painfully through two school semesters. Months later she told me how she had taken pennies from my purse to buy him candy. "Licorice was his favorite and I brought him some every day, but he still liked Jennifer better'n me. Why Mommy why?" A question I could never answer.

School was a worry to her. She was not glib or quick in a world where glibness and quickness were easily confused with ability to learn. To her over-worked and exasperated teachers she was an overconscientious "slow learner" who kept trying to catch up and was absent entirely too often.

I let her be absent, though sometimes the illness was imaginary. How different from my now-strictness about attendance with the others, I wasn't working. We had a new baby, I was home anyhow. Sometimes, after Susan grew old enough, I would keep her home from school, too, to have them all together.

Mostly Emily had asthma, and her breathing harsh and labored, would fill the house with a curiously tranquil sound. I would bring the two old dresser mirrors and her boxes of collections to her bed. She would select beads and single earrings, bottle tops and shells, dried flowers and pebbles, old postcards and scraps, all sorts of oddments; then she and Susan would play Kingdom, setting up landscapes and furniture, peopling them with action.

Those were the only times of peaceful companionship between her and Susan. I have edged away from it, that poisonous feeling between them, that terrible balancing of hurts and needs I had to do between the two, and did so badly, those earlier years.

Oh there are conflicts between the others too, each one human, needing, demanding, hurting, taking—but only between Emily and Susan, no, Emily to-ward Susan that corroding resentment. It seems so obvious on the surface, yet it is not obvious. Susan, the second child, Susan, golden and curly haired and chubby, quick and articulate and assured, everything in appearance and manner Emily was not; Susan, not able to resist Emily's precious things, losing or sometimes clumsily breaking them; Susan telling jokes and riddles to company for applause while Emily sat silent (to say to me later: that was *my* riddle, Mother, I told it to Susan); Susan, who for all the five years' difference in age was just a year behind Emily in developing physically.

I am glad for that slow physical development that widened the difference between her and her contemporaries, though she suffered over it. She was too vulnerable for that terrible world of youthful competition, of preening and parading, of constant measuring of yourself against every other, of envy, "If I had that copper hair," or "If I had that skin . . ." She tormented herself enough about not looking like the others, there was enough of the unsureness, the having to be conscious of words before you speak, the constant caring—what are they thinking of me? what kind of an impression am I making—there was enough without having it all magnified unendurably by the merciless physical drives.

Ronnie is calling. He is wet and I change him. It is rare there is such a cry now. That time of motherhood is almost behind me when the ear is not one's own but must always be racked and listening for the child cry, the child call. We sit for a while and I hold him, looking out over the city spread in charcoal with its soft aisles of light. "Shuggily" he breathes. A funny word, a family word, inherited from Emily, invented by her to say comfort.

In this and other ways she leaves her seal, I say aloud. And startle at my saying it. What do I mean? What did I start to gather together, to try and make coherent? I was at the terrible, growing years. War years. I do not remember them well. I was working, there were four smaller ones now, there was not time for her. She had to help be a mother, and housekeeper, and shopper. She had to set her seal. Mornings of crisis and near hysteria trying to get lunches packed, hair combed, coats and shoes found, everyone to school or Child Care on time, the baby ready for transportation. And always the paper scribbled on by a smaller one, the book looked at by Susan then mislaid, the homework not done. Running out to that huge school where she was one, she was lost, she was a drop; suffering over the unpreparedness, stammering and unsure in her classes.

There was so little time left at night after the kids were bedded down. She would struggle over books, always eating (it was in those years she developed her enormous appetite that is legendary in our family) and I would be ironing, or preparing food for the next day, or writing V-mail to Bill, or tending the baby. Sometimes, to make me laugh, or out of her despair, she would imitate happenings or types at school.

I think I said once: "Why don't you do something like this in the school amateur show?" One morning she phoned me at work, hardly understandable through the weeping: "Mother, I did it. I won, I won; they gave me first prize; they clapped and clapped and wouldn't let me go."

Now suddenly she was Somebody, and as imprisoned in her difference as in anonymity.

She began to be asked to perform at other high schools, even in colleges, then at city and state-wide affairs. The first one we went to, I only recognized her that first moment when thin, shy, she almost drowned herself into the curtains. Then: Was this Emily? the control, the command, the convulsing and deadly clowning, the spell, then the roaring, stamping audience, unwilling to let this rare and precious laughter out of their lives.

Afterwards: You ought to do something about her with a gift like that—but without money or knowing how, what does one do? We have left it all to her, and the gift has as often eddied inside, clogged and clotted, as been used and growing.

She is coming. She runs up the stairs two at a time with her light graceful step, and I know she is happy tonight. Whatever it was that occasioned your call did not happen today.

"Aren't you ever going to finish the ironing, Mother? Whistler painted his mother in a rocker. I'd have to paint mine standing over an ironing board." This is one of her communicative nights and she tells me everything and nothing as she fixes herself a plate of food out of the icebox.

She is so lovely. Why did you want me to come in at all? Why were you concerned? She will find her way.

She starts up the stairs to bed. "Don't get me up with the rest in the morning." "But I thought you were having midterms." "Oh, those," she comes back in and says quite lightly, "in a couple of years when we'll all be atom-dead they won't matter a bit."

She has said it before. She believes it. But because I have been dredging the past, and all that compounds a human being is so heavy and meaningful in me, I cannot endure it tonight.

I will never total it all now. I will never come in to say: She was a child seldom smiled at. Her father left me before she was a year old. I worked her first six years when there was work, or I sent her home and to his relatives. There were years she had care she hated. She was dark and thin and foreign-looking in a world where the prestige went to blondness and curly hair and dimples, slow where glibness was prized. She was a child of anxious, not proud, love. We were poor and could not afford for her the soil of easy growth. I was a young mother, I was a distracted mother. There were the other children pushing up, demanding. Her younger sister was all that she was not. She did not like me to touch her. She kept too much in herself, her life was such she had to keep too much in herself. My wisdom came too late. She has much in her and probably nothing will come of it. She is a child of her age, of depression, of war, of fear.

Let her be. So all that is in her will not bloom—but in how many does it? There is still enough left to live by. Only help her to believe—help make it so there is cause for her to believe that she is more than this dress on the ironing board, helpless before the iron.

MY GENERATION

People try to put us down
Just because we get around.
Things they do look awful cold
Hope I die before I get old.

This is my generation, baby.

Why don't you all f-f-f-fade away
Don't try and dig what we all say
I'm not trying to cause a big sensation
I'm just talking 'bout my generation.

This my generation, baby,
My generation.

>   —*Peter Townshend*
>   (for the Who)

Reprinted by permission of Tro-Devon Music, New York,
1965.

A BILL TO MY FATHER

I am typing up bills for a firm to be sent to their clients.
It occurs to me that firms are sending bills to my
    father
Who has that way an identity I do not often realize.
He is a person who buys, owes, and pays,
Not papa like he is to me.
His creditors reproach him for not paying on time
With a bill marked "Please Remit."
I reproach him for never having shown his love
    for me
But only his disapproval.
He has a debt to me too
Although I have long since ceased asking him to
    come across;
He does not know how and so I do without it.
But in this impersonal world of business
He can be communicated with:
With absolute assurance of being paid
The boss writes "Send me my money"
And my father sends it.

Edward Field

Reprinted by permission of Grove Press from Edward Field,
Stand Up, Friend, With Me (New York: Grove Press, 1963).

BARN BUILDING

By Jack Burris

Two weeks ago my father died. Like most deaths, his came as a shock, despite his two years of illness. I flew back to Kansas for the funeral and went through all the proper forms of mourning, even though, it seemed to me, I was performing a mockery. I had lost my father when I was a boy of twelve, and while his body didn't die until nearly fifteen years later, he had never been alive for me again.

I suppose my father's great goal in life was to be a gentleman farmer. Unfortunately he had neither the knowledge nor the money to fulfill such an ambition, and he was forced to divide his life between farming and a multitude of other occupations. When he was twenty he left my grandfather's farm and went to work at a factory in Joplin, Missouri. His job was to paste labels onto cans of corn as they passed by him. Evidently he attacked the cans with fervency usually unknown in such places, for he was soon made a foreman. He met my mother there, and they married the following year. When they had saved enough money they quit their jobs and bought a farm. After two crop failures my father went to work in a lead smelter, where he soon caught lead colic. After he was well again he worked as a janitor, a farm hand, a ditch-digger, a well-digger, a grave-digger, and finally an undertaker's assistant, while at the same time he took care of his farm. He would probably have remained with this last job for the rest of his life if my grandparents—for no particular reason that I can recall—hadn't suddenly died and left their farm and some savings to him. I assume that my father showed the proper amount of respectful grief at the loss of his parents, but I have often wondered if, inside, he didn't feel pleased at the same time. Surely the thought must have crossed his mind that his parents' death, and his possession of another farm and some money, were God's answers to a long period of almost-daily prayers. Perhaps I am wrong.

My parents talked a great deal about their early years on the farm. I'm not sure whether they desired to share experiences with me, or whether they simply had little else to talk about. My mother would sit piled in her rocking chair, looking like a neat bundle of clothing ready for ironing, and read off her memories as though they were items on a grocery list. "That first year was the hardest. I lost the first baby. Your pa got pneumonia. Aunt Ollie came to stay with us a while, and there wasn't even enough sheets for her bed. The bugs were bad that year, too. And the garden burned up."

My father's memories were different, or perhaps it was only that he told them differently. Sitting at the head of the table he seemed to dwarf everything around him, like an adult playing house with children. The main thing I remember about him wasn't his build, however, but his eyes. They were grey, and like grey clouds on the horizon, they always suggested to me an approaching storm. Most of the time I couldn't force myself to look into them, but when he was remembering the past, his eyes seemed to brighten and even to sparkle, as though the sun was shining somewhere beyond the clouds. Then I could stare right into them and could almost see his past recorded there.

"Trouble always comes in threes," my father said. "One year the wolves got our cow, and then all the chickens died off. And then I'll be damned if we didn't lose a whole field of wheat before I could get it in."

The year he remembered better than any other, and told about most often, was the summer the plague of grasshoppers came. "That was the year you was born, Jerry. Your ma had just gotten back on her feet again in time for planting. Things came up good that year, too. Then one day—Sunday, I think—it seemed like it started getting dark awfully early. I went out to look, and I seen these big clouds coming from the south. Only they wasn't clouds, they was grasshoppers. It didn't take no time for them to eat up everything green in sight."

"They even ate the green peaches off the trees," my mother said.

"That was the same year Old Bess died," my father added in afterthought.

Of all the disappointments my parents had in their lives, I surely must have been the biggest one. In the first place, they had planned upon having a large family of at least a dozen children. Farmers still needed a large family at that time. Five miscarriages and I were the results of those plans. To make matters worse, I wasn't even a typical farm boy. Until I was ten I was weak and unhealthy, with lungs which seemed constantly congested. I wasn't strong enough to do even the simplest farm chores; carrying a bucket of slop to the pigs left me coughing and trembling. Instead of being a help to my parents, I was really just another problem, another responsibility which they had to worry about and care for.

My mother gladly accepted that responsibility. She was constantly showing her love for me. She could never pass by me without touching my shoulder, as if to make sure I was there. Whenever I caught a cold she was filled with both panic and delight. I think she would have been happiest if I had become a complete invalid, for then she would have known that I would always be there for her to love and to nurse.

My father was less demonstrative. I always felt that he loved me, but at the same time I felt the responsibility of earning his love. I often forgot to bring in wood for my mother, but I never forgot to be on time to help my father with the milking. At Christmas I would buy her a cheaper present, and then spend most of my money on a gift for him. It wasn't that I loved him more, but rather that I had a greater need for him to show me his love. Usually the harder I tried to please him, the more disappointed in me he became. It was always my fault, of course. I remember once that the rope broke on the well, dropping an almost-new bucket into the water. I wanted to get it out before he came home, and in the attempt I lost the grappling-hook and about fifty feet of rope— and I didn't get the bucket out, either. Another time I fed the chickens some poisoned corn he was saving for crows. I just seemed to have a natural talent for always doing the wrong things.

When I was twelve a tornado hit the farm, destroying the barn, killing all the pigs and chickens and one horse. My father accepted the news calmly enough —of course by this time he had already had a great deal of practice. "Have to get that barn rebuilt," he said. "Can't have a farm without a barn. Need some hogs now, too. I was talking to Pete Dake the other day, and he told me about a couple of hogs his neighbor owns. Won ribbons with them at the Fair. Might pay to look at them, anyway. There's money in prize hogs."

In order to pay for such a dream, my father took a job as a dynamiter in a local coal mine. He did as many of the farm chores as he could before going to work, but this still left a great deal for my mother and me to do. She had to take care of the chickens and cows during the day, plus keeping up with her housework. Sometimes she even had to help in the fields. The hardest part of my job was caring for the two prize hogs my father bought with his first month's salary. To make matters worse, he had read somewhere—I think in a government pamphlet—that pigs had a natural instinct to be clean, and that they were happier and grew faster in clean surroundings. I was ordered to keep their pens as clean as my mother's kitchen. I tried, but it was an impossible task. Every day I spread new straw in the pen and gave the hogs fresh water and food. Every Saturday I shoveled out the mud and manure and sprinkled white sand onto the floor of the pen. It didn't take me long to realize that my father and the government were both wrong, and that pigs had a natural instinct to be dirty.

By spring there was evidence that my father's investment might pay off. Josie, the sow, got unexpectedly fat, and my mother suggested that one day soon I would have some more pigs to care for. I must say that the news didn't exactly fill me with excitement. One thought kept going around and around in my mind, like an arithmetic problem: "If two hogs can make this much mess, how much can two hogs plus several pigs make?" One Sunday, defying God's wrath and his own conscience, my father built a second pen. I tried to help him, but I probably just got in his way. Anyway he let me hang around, maybe to have someone to listen to him talk.

"Got to fix this shed tight, so it'll be dry," he said. "That old pen doesn't keep nothing out. It'll have to do for a while, though. It's big enough for the sow and pigs, and this one ain't. Once those pigs get raised we'll have enough money for a real pen. Have to spend money to make it. Trouble is, you got to have some of the damn stuff before you can spend it in the first place."

As Josie grew in size, so did my father's dreams. He decided that there would be twelve pigs, each of which would bring, in time, one hundred dollars. Half of the money would be spent on lumber for a new barn. The other half was to be put aside for my education. I was to go to an agricultural college in Kansas just as soon as I finished high school. At that time I had dreams of becoming a doctor, but I didn't dare argue with my father.

One rainy morning when I went out to feed the hogs I found Josie standing sick in the middle of her pen. Her eyes were closed, and her head drooped almost to the ground. Slobbers ran down the corners of her mouth. For seconds she would be motionless, and then her body would begin shaking with a series of spasms. She looked so lonely, standing there, like the last boy to be chosen for baseball. I wanted to help her, but I didn't know how. Billy's pen was at least drier, so I finally put her in there with him.

I told my mother about Josie's sickness before I left for school, and she promised to look in on her during the day. That day was the only one in my life when school seemed dull and boring. All I could think about was Josie and thirteen little pigs. I was sure there would be thirteen—one which my father hadn't expected and which he would give to me. With the hundred dollars I could buy a bicycle and still have enough money left over to buy presents for my parents.

When I got home that evening my parents were standing out by the pig pen. I could see Billy and Josie inside, but I couldn't see any baby pigs. "Ain't they born yet?" I asked, but both of my parents just kept looking down at the ground. Finally my father turned to me and laid a hand on my shoulder.

"Did you turn Josie in with Billy?"

"Yes, sir."

"But why? You know I told you they had to be kept apart until after the pigs was born."

I tried to think of a good answer, but there wasn't any. The truth sounded silly right then, even to me.

"Answer me! Why did you do it when I told you not to?"

"She was sick," I said. "She was all alone and she was sick. I had to go to school, and Mama was busy, so I . . ."

There was a sound like the whine of a sleeping dog, and then I saw my mother's hand timidly touch the sleeve of my father's coat. "He didn't mean no wrong, Jess," she said. "He thought he was doing the right thing."

"He disobeyed me, and I guess he'll have to pay for it. Come on in the house, boy."

"Should have had a barn to put her in," my mother said.

"Damn it, I said I'd build a barn and I will. That still ain't no excuse for what he done."

My father turned, then, and walked toward the house, not once hesitating or looking back to see if I were following. My mother touched my hair lightly, like a puff of wind. I still couldn't understand what had happened, or what I had done that was so terribly wrong.

"We'd better go in," she said. "He'll be waiting."

"But what happened? Where are the pigs?"

"Billy ate them. Sometimes they do that. I don't know why."

Billy was laying self-satisfied in a puddle of mud, his puffy eyes almost closed, like a monster which has eaten his fill and is napping until he can eat again. I wanted to see him butchered right then. I wanted to kill him myself, to stick a knife into his fat throat and let the blood run out down my hands and onto the ground.

"But how could he do a thing like that? I kept his pen clean!"

"I tried to get him out," she said. "He just kept dodging me and trying to bite. When they was born I tried to get them away before he seen them, but Josie wouldn't let me even touch them."

"You seen them born?"

"I tried to keep him away. I hit him with rocks, but he didn't pay no more mind than if I wasn't even there. We'd better get on inside. Your pa's waiting, and that only makes him worse."

He was waiting, standing out on the porch and looking in our direction. Even though it was getting dark I could see the black strap in his hand. My mother took my arm and we started toward the house, toward my punishment. Before we got there I had one more question to ask.

"How many of them were there?"

"Only four," she said, "and one of them such a runt he couldn't have lived anyway."

Somehow, at that moment, I managed to find a great deal of comfort in that.

About two months after the incident with the pigs my father decided it was time to rebuild the barn. I don't think we really needed a barn for storage as badly as he needed one to complete his image of what a farm should be. Anyway, he sold Josie and Billy, plus two calves, and used the money to buy enough lumber to start the building. In that first drive of enthusiasm he was able to complete the foundation, frame, and roof. Then he slowed down. When the first supply of lumber was used up, more had to be bought out of his paycheck from the mines. Each week he would buy ten or twelve more boards, and then on Sunday he would add these to the barn. He made progress, but not quickly enough to satisfy him. He worked best when the dream was new, and when something took longer than a few weeks he soon lost interest. That was the case with the barn. He still brought the lumber home each week, but after a couple of months he found that he had too many other things to do on Sunday to spend the time on the barn. "I'll have it finished in time for the hay," he told my mother, "but right now I got to fix up these pens. I been thinking about getting some more hogs. Taste good this winter, when the snow comes."

My father was almost as good as his word. By the time haying was over in late summer, the barn, too, was almost finished. The roof and three walls were completed, and the fourth wall was at least started. Beginning at the roof, he had nailed boards down about five feet of the wall; this was at least enough to cover the loft, so it was possible to store the hay without worry. I'm sure my father really meant to finish that fourth wall before winter. He had the necessary lumber ready, and he had even bought the red paint to cover the building. He just had too many other things to do, and too many outside interruptions.

An accident at the mines caused one interruption. Although my father wasn't hurt in it, ten other men—including two of his friends—were killed. The town of Galena decided to turn one weekend into a period of mourning. On Saturday the stores were to be closed, and then, on Sunday afternoon, funeral services were to be held. My parents planned to go into town early Sunday morning and to spend the day visiting the various families and bodies. They would return home late that evening after the services. I was to stay at home by myself to take care of the farm.

While my parents were dressing that morning, I suddenly got the idea of finishing up the barn by myself. My father had worked on it all of Saturday without accomplishing much; he kept complaining that he didn't have the right tools to work with. At dinner my mother had asked him if he had finished, and he answered, "I wish to hell I'd never even started it." I imagined his surprise when he returned home to find the fourth wall finished and the whole barn covered with a coat of bright red paint. He would say, "Son, that's a damn fine job there. Looks store-bought. How'd you ever manage it by yourself?" And then he would lay his hand against the back of my neck and squeeze gently with his calloused fingers. He had done that once before, when I had caught a fox in my rabbit-trap.

It was hard for me to wait quietly while my parents got ready to leave. I wanted to tell them my plans, and to ask my father a hundred questions about the work on the barn. I tried to rush them as much as I dared, until finally my mother became suspicious and said, "You're sure in a hurry to get rid of us. You got some mischief planned for when we're gone?"

"No. I don't have any plans at all. I thought that if you didn't hurry up you might be late, that's all."

"We'll get there on time. You know your father. If you really want to help you can see if he's ready yet. He's probably out on the porch waiting for me."

He was on the porch, standing there with his hands in his pockets, looking out towards the barn. He seemed very handsome to me right then, and I imagined that he was a great king who was looking out over his kingdom and who was very pleased with what he saw.

"It's a good farm," he said. "All it needs is some hard work."

"Yes, sir," I answered. It seemed a stupid thing to say, but it was difficult to know how to talk to him.

"Have to get you off to college so you can learn to do things right. You'll do okay, soon as you learn some things." He looked up at the sky as if he owned that, too. "Going to be a nice day. Shame to waste it. I wanted to get the barn done. Guess it can't be helped, though. You behave yourself now while we're gone, you hear?"

"Yes, sir. I'll take care of things."

He smiled down at me, and his right hand came slowly out of its pocket. I thought he was going to shake my hand, and I reached up eagerly, but his fingers barely touched mine as they passed me a quarter.

"Save it," he said. "You can buy something nice when you get to town."

My parents finally left. I made myself wait for ten minutes, in case they forgot something and had to come back, and then I gathered my father's tools together and went to the barn. The work didn't look too difficult. Twenty two-by-fours, set about five feet apart, served as the frame for the building. All I had to do was to cut some boards five feet long and nail them to that frame. Since my father had already done the top seven feet, where the hayloft was, I was sure I could finish the job easily enough before sunset.

I measured the first board carefully, making sure to mark it with a straight line as I had seen my father do. "You can't cut a straight line unless you got one marked," he would say. I marked it good and straight, checking it twice with the square. When I started sawing on it, though, it still went crooked. I had the board lying on two saw-horses, and every time I sawed down on one end, the other end would jump up. I had to climb up on top of the board and hold it down with my weight. I got it sawed through all right, finally.

I went ahead and sawed six more boards then, marking them with the first one. It was easier that way then using the ruler all the time. When I tried to nail the boards in place, however, some of them wouldn't fit. The first one I had sawed fit all right, and the next three weren't so far off they couldn't be used, but the final three were about an inch too long. I nailed them up anyway and then sawed them off even with the side of the frame.

It didn't take me too long to realize that there was quite a bit I didn't know about building barns. The longer I worked at it, though, the more I learned. I finally saw that it didn't pay to mark one board with another. I found that it also helps if you sort of hold the board up where it's supposed to go and give it an eye-measuring before you start sawing on it. And I learned not to try to drive a nail in a board too close to the edge. I split six boards before I found that out, but I finally did learn it.

The hardest part was leaving a hole for the window. I knew my father wanted a window on that side so he could shovel the manure out, but I didn't know how to go about building one. It sounded simple enough; all you had to do was leave a hole somewhere along the wall and then put a window in it later. But I couldn't figure out how you went about leaving the right size hole, and where the hole should be, and how you got the rest of the boards to fit right when you were leaving some out. It took me a large slice of the morning to figure out all the answers, and before I realized it, it was already past noon and I hadn't had anything to eat at all that day.

I fixed a sandwich, but it was hard sitting still long enough to eat. I kept seeing the new barn, not as it was right then, but as it would be after I put a coat of paint on it. I imagined my parents looking at it and smiling—not saying a word, but just smiling. And my father would be proud of me, I knew, even though he might not be able to say it out loud.

The clock in the hall struck twice, and I ran back to the barn, for I still had a lot of painting to do before my parents got home. It took me longer than I had planned. The paint didn't seem to go on right, and I was afraid to try thinning it. I had trouble reaching the top part of the barn, too, for even with the ladder I wasn't tall enough. I finally solved that problem by using an old broom for a brush.

By three-thirty I only had one wall about half-way painted. I kept worrying that I wouldn't finish, even though I knew the paint wasn't as smooth as it should have been. By five I was painting close enough to the ground so that I didn't have to use the ladder. In another hour I had finished the wall. I thought about starting on the other walls, but I couldn't get very excited about the idea. I was tired, and besides the paint was almost gone. The important thing, I decided, was that my wall was painted. My parents would just have to imagine how the other three walls would look.

I went to the house and cleaned myself up, and then I sat down on the porch to wait for my parents. It seemed a long wait, but I guess it wasn't really. Finally, just a few minutes before sunset, I saw our old Ford coming down the road.

"I've got a surprise for you," I shouted, not even giving them time to get out of the car.

They climbed out, and my mother embraced me. My father took his hat off and stood studying it, as if he were waiting for something to happen. "You get all the chores done?"

"Yes, sir," I said. I hadn't done them yet, but I knew he'd forgive me for the lie when he saw my surprise. "I want you to see something."

They wouldn't hurry, and I had to keep coming back for them. All the time, though, they did keep trying to guess what the surprise might be, and they didn't even come close. The barn looked beautiful in the sunset, especially my side of it. The red paint reflected and deepened the pink colors from the last light. I turned to them eagerly, wanting to share every moment of their surprise.

"Maybe all the boards ain't ruint," my mother said. "Maybe you could still use them."

"No." He said it as though it were a secret. "No, they're all ruined."

I looked long at my father, trying to find some expression of pleasure on his face, but I couldn't see it too well in the fading light. Suddenly he put his hand on the back of my neck and twisted my face up towards his. I saw his eyes, and then I knew. He slapped me only once, and even the noise seemed soft and far away, like the sound of a fragile dish being snapped in half.

"Jess, he thought he was doing good," my mother said. She tugged at his arm and managed to break his hand loose from my neck. "He was only trying to please you."

My father didn't say anything more. He waved me and my mother aside and walked stiffly toward the house.

"I know you meant well," my mother said, and then she followed him.

I don't remember exactly what I felt right then; I don't believe that at first I felt anything at all. It is always difficult to let go of an accepted truth, and I had accepted my father's love as a truth, a natural obligation which he owed to me and which would always be there, even though at times it might be unspoken. That truth was destroyed, and yet I don't recall any heartbreak or great agony. I felt instead something which I can now only describe as relief. My father didn't love me, but what was more important, I was no longer under any obligation to love him.

I stayed on the farm for five more years, until my mother died. There wasn't much work to do. My father gave up farming and took a job in a factory. We still lived on the farm, I guess because there wasn't any other place we wanted to live. My father and I never argued nor showed particular hatred towards one another, and yet when we talked it was always like the polite, social conversation of two passing strangers. Every day I saw the barn again, and each time I would hear again that sickening sound and feel the burning of his slap. My mother pretended that there was nothing wrong, that we were all happy and served as a family, but it was a lie which, in time, even she had to recognize. Two days after her death I decided to leave the farm, and so I made arrangements to go to an aunt in California. My father drove me to the station, talking all the way about the prices crops were bringing. When we parted he shook my hand, and for the first time I realized that his hair had become completely grey, almost as pale as his eyes.

While I never saw my father again, I did see the farm. It was left to me in his will, and after the funeral I had to find some way of disposing of it. It hadn't changed much, although it hadn't been kept up. The barn was still standing, serving as a grotesque yet fitting monument. There were cracks between the boards wide enough for mice to run through unhampered, and the window, the only intended opening, was just a hole where too-short boards refused to meet.

Standing there alone, I wondered what would have happened if, in reality, I had made the barn as beautiful as I had imagined it in my dreams. Surely my life would have been different. For one thing, I would probably have been a farmer in Kansas instead of a librarian in California. My parents might have been happier, too.

Then, despite my attempts to block it out, a question came to my mind. Why had my father left the barn standing? Surely it must have hurt him to look at it, just as it did me. It had never been used for any practical purpose—not even for storing hay, after that first year. Why hadn't he destroyed it? What had he thought about, living alone all those years? Had he left it standing to remind him of failure and hatred, or had he known regrets, too?

I would never find all the answers, I knew, and it was probably too late even to try. And yet, having once asked the questions, I wished, for a moment, that I were at least able to mourn.

Make the most of yourself, for that is
all there is of you.
Ralph Waldo Emerson

WHY I (DON'T) UNDERSTAND YOU

By Henry Gregor Felsen

Almost every day I get letters from young readers who compliment me on my ability to understand teen-agers. And, almost every day, you complain that the trouble with me as a father is, I don't understand you.

I hope my readers are right. I know you are. For I think I do understand you somewhat as a teen-ager, and I certainly don't understand *you*.

It is important to your welfare and happiness that both of us understand you as an average, Middle Western, suburban teen-age boy. That's the whole point of my work here. But when it comes to understanding the inner, private, special, lifetime *you*— that is *your own* inner, private, special, lifetime task. Your happiness as a human being depends not on how well others seem to understand you, but on how soon and how successfully you discover and understand yourself.

At first thought your complaint of being misunderstood seems a simple problem, the answer to which is more understanding on my part.

Only, that isn't the problem at all.

The most difficult lifelong prob-lem any of us has is learning to tell the difference between *being* misunder-stood, *feeling* misunderstood *and not being able to understand.*

Very often, the hollow teen-age complaint that "My parents don't understand me" can be translated into its real meaning, which is, "My par-ents won't let me have my own way."

Later on in life, this same tune is sung to the words of "My wife doesn't understand me," "My boss doesn't understand me" or (very popular around age twenty) "The world doesn't understand me." And most of the time, the correct translation begins with the words "*I* don't understand . . .''

In all instances the problem is not one of understanding, but of negotia-tion. The cry represents an inability to see any point of view other than one's own, plus an unwillingness to look.

I have heard boys and girls com-plain they were misunderstood at home because their parents wouldn't let them stay out all night, go off on mixed, unchaperoned weekends, drive

Reprinted by permission of Dodd, Mead & Company from Gregor Felsen, *Letters to My Teenage Son* (New York: Dodd, Mead & Company, 1962).

"Then you should say what you mean," the March Hare went on. "I do," Alice hastily replied; "at least—I mean what I say—that's the same thing, you know."

"Not the same thing a bit!" said the Hatter. "Why, you might just as well say that 'I see what I eat' is the same thing as 'I eat what I see!'"

Lewis Carroll

a car without a license, quit school to get married or take a laboring job to support a car, or wouldn't buy them a car, give them all the money they wanted or allow them to smoke or drink.

The reason parents don't allow these things isn't because they don't understand how teen-agers feel, or have forgotten what it is like to be young, but because they do understand, and have not forgotten.

What we are up against here is that the child demands to be "understood" as the person he is at the moment, and the parents' job is to understand him as he is, as he was and as he is going to be. Since the most difficult thing in the world for a child is to see himself ever being or feeling different than he does at the moment, he feels misunderstood. And *feeling*, but not really *being* misunderstood, is a convenient tent for a teen-ager to sulk in, and avoid the truth that would reveal to him his own immaturity—his inability to understand.

If, through some miracle tonight, I could arise in the morning as the most perfect, understanding father in the world, you would continue to feel misunderstood unless there was another miracle, in your room, that enabled you to understand when you were being understood.

The way it is, and was and always will be, there is that private self of yours that no one will ever understand completely, no matter how hard you try to explain yourself. And there is the just-another-human-being you, that is as old as the human race, and so obvious and common that even strangers can identify and understand you at a glance.

That is what I meant when I said I understood you as a teen-ager, but I didn't understand *you*.

For example, I know why you are anxious to own and drive your car. I don't know why you prefer tinkering with a car to playing football.

I know why you are impatient to be a grown man. I don't know what your definition of maturity is.

I know a great many of your opinions. I know hardly any of your thoughts.

I know why you want to stay out late at night with your friends. I don't know what it takes to be your friend.

I know why you are restless in school. I don't know why you like to read and have no head for math.

I know what you want at the moment. I don't know what you long for.

I know why you wear the kind of clothes you do, the way you do. I don't know why you like blue and dislike green.

I know you fall in love. I don't know what there is about a girl that causes you to love her.

I know what kind of boy you seem among other boys. I don't know you.

I understand you. I don't understand *you*.

You know, it is important that I understand you, and it is important that you feel understood, but there is another need that might be just as important. And that is your need, while calling for more understanding, to be misunderstood.

There are times when it is necessary for a teen-ager to feel misunderstood, particularly by his parents. At these times the only thing that infuriates him more than trying to understand him is to prove that you do. Because that makes him go to a lot of trouble to prove that you don't. And one of the most delicate operations of parenthood is to guess correctly the times and ways in which the teen-ager needs to feel misunderstood.

There is, in all of us, a need to feel that we are complex, unique people, and that the emotions we feel are not only new to us, but new emotions. And these highly personal, private emotions and feelings are ruined for us if some other person bleats, "I know just exactly how you feel. I felt just like you when I was your age."

We parents say this with the best of intentions. We say it to relieve tensions, to dispel anxieties and loneliness, to reassure, to show that certain strange and troubling emotions and actions are normal and universal, and to make the child's way through life a little smoother, a little more intelligible, a little more pleasant.

But in trying to be too helpful, too understanding, too kind, too close, too perceptive, too smart and too discerning, we destroy some of life's needed mystery, and diminish the fearful joy of growth.

It is as though an explorer were to imagine himself first on some wild and undiscovered land, then find that not only has someone else been there before him, but that someone else has already pacified the savages, built roads through the jungles, classified the flora and fauna, made the drinking water safe and turned one's dangerous, exciting adventure into a dreary guided tour, and a color slide show of what it "used to be like."

I know when my parents correctly interpreted some obscure mood or troubled action of mine, I often felt cheated rather than assisted. It made me feel that instead of living my own, new, special life, I was merely living theirs over again.

I know I baffled my parents when I rejected their interest in my welfare, and angrily spurned their kindly attempts at advice. But sometimes it is an awful thing to be told on Monday how you are going to feel on Tuesday —then feel that way. It is deadly to hear a parent's voice telling you accurately how you feel about girls, what your thoughts are about finding a place in the world, about your doubts, your dreams, your *day*dreams and even, all too exactly, the nature of your regret at having acted foolishly. Sometimes, when you feel that every step you take is in a parental footstep, you don't even want to walk.

The reason I disobeyed my parents and did foolish things against their advice wasn't because I thought they were wrong about life. It was because I knew, deep down, that they were right. And it was more necessary for me to create my own darkness to stumble around in, than to be led around disaster by their light. And how awful when they made the mistake of letting me know that they *understood*.

I loved my parents, but they were just ordinary people. And it devastated me to think that I was so obvious, so lacking in individuality and complexity, that these ordinary people could troll in my darkest depths with a bent pin, and always come up with a fish.

In some ways, I think it was because my parents were so understanding and knowledgeable that I left home for good when I was sixteen years old. Only among strangers did I feel comfortably inscrutable and unpredictable. I was able to relax only when those who looked into my eyes were unable (I thought) to see a framed portrait of my soul.

I was wrong, of course. That part of me that was myself was never known to my parents, any more than it is known now by my wife, children, friends or even myself. But that part of me that was teen-age, and universal and just plain young human being, was as obvious to my stranger-teachers at the State University of Iowa as it had been to my parents in New York. Not being able to separate my two selves, I went around feeling mysterious, unfathomable and inscrutable, unaware that most of my feelings and "discoveries" were older than the campus, and that most of the other students were thinking and feeling the same way. The reason I felt so comfortably enigmatic and misunderstood was that no one bothered to tell me that I was understood. I thought I was fitting college life to my needs. I never knew that college life had been planned, created and organized to fit mine. The secret of its success was that it never told me so, in so many words.

MAD'S LIFETIME CHART OF ATTITUDES AND BEHAVIOR

WATCHING A DOCUMENTARY ON VIETNAM

Age 7	Age 14	Age 20

Rat-a-tat-a-tat! Give it to 'em good! Kill 'em! Wipe out those Commie rats!

Hey, they're firing that new **XB4 Rocket** . . . the one that can level a **whole town!**

College should defer me until I'm Then, I could enlist in the **Peace** for two years . . . and **Vista** for an two years . . . and by then, I'll be 2

WATCHING A "NEW WAVE" SWEDISH ART FILM

Age 7	Age 14	Age 20

What a dumb movie! Their lips move **one** way . . . and they **talk another!**

Hoo-boy! Here comes the scene where she **takes off all her clothes!**

How **incredibly** symbolic . . . the w the director injects **symbolism** int scene symbolically **devoid** of symb

We feel odd, strange, interesting, frightening, joyful, wonderful and terrible emotions when we are teenagers, and we would rather not be told that someone else is more aware of the turmoil inside us than we are. There is much to discover about the world and ourselves when we are young, and we don't want someone else cheating us of the chance to plant our own flag on new soil, and claiming the area for our own sovereign.

We want what amounts to an equal opportunity to be young, foolish, experimental, wrong, tortured, amazed and overwhelmed; an equal opportunity to learn the bitter from the sweet by tasting, and not being told. Above all, we need to preserve the feeling that, for all our outward resemblance to others, we are special, indecipherable, unique and incomprehensible. We need the security of closed doors between our inner selves and the outer world.

Too much help, too much good advice, too much demonstrated loving understanding, too much guidance, can make us feel emotionally naked and unprotected, and make our lives seem shallow and secondhand. Sometimes the kind of understanding we need most is all the blank "misunderstanding" we can get.

Reprinted by permission of Mad Magazine.

THE SOUND OF SILENCE

Hello darkness my old friend,
I've come to talk with you again,
Because a vision softly creeping,
Left its seeds while I was sleeping
And the vision that was planted in my brain
Still remains within the sound of silence.

In restless dreams I walked alone,
Narrow streets of cobble stone
'Neath the halo of a street lamp,
I turned my collar to the cold and damp
When my eyes were stabbed by the flash of a neon
    light
That split the night, and touched the sound of silence.

And in the naked light I saw
Ten thousand people maybe more,
People talking without speaking,
People hearing without listening,
People writing songs that voices never share
And no one dares disturb the sound of silence.

"Fools!" said I, "You do not know
Silence like a cancer grows.
Hear my words that I might teach you
Take my arms that I might reach you."
But my words like silent raindrops fell
And echoed, in the wells of silence.

And the people bowed and prayed
To the neon God they made,
And the sign flashed out its warning
In the words that it was forming.
And the sign said:
    "The words of the prophets are written
    on the subway walls and tenement halls"
And whispered in the sounds of silence.

    —Paul Simon
    (Simon and Garfunkel)

Reprinted by permission of Charing Cross Music, New York, 1964.

A letter came today. It was from you, but it was not for me. *Faith E. Beebe*

THE WORLD IS WEARIED OF WALLS

The world is wearied of walls—

    Crack off cement,
    Lift down the brick;

    Pry out the nails,
    Pull off the stick;

    Melt through the iron
    With white-hot fire;

    Remove the stones
    Layer by layer—

    Then

    Take the dare
    Of unwalled air.

    —Helen Berryhill

Reprinted by permission of Helen Berryhill.

105

GREED _____

VIOLENCE _____

HATE _____

APATHY _____

LINES TO HANG YOU UP ON

Hate is not the opposite of love;
apathy is . . .
To live in apathy provokes violence . . .
Rollo May

To be unable to love or to show compassion
for someone—a friend, a wife, a husband,
a child, a mother, a father, a neighbor—is
to be one's own opponent, to invite greed,
violence, hate, apathy.

The Riders of the Four Horses: Albrecht Durer.

THE FOUR HORSEMEN

The first be War in tarnished iron clad,
Then Pestilence with mocking lep'rous face.
Upon his heels rides Famine gaunt and glad,
And Death, with a finality most base.
The hid'ous four, do with malignant glee,
Urge on their steeds to trample hapless man,
To grind beneath eight cloven hooves the sea
That preys upon itself when e'er it can.
Yet only do the ghostly horsemen ride,
And only is their scourge felt o'er the lands,
When love of fellow man, both far and wide,
Is lost to greed, and hate, and selfish hands.
So cherish all your friends and mark me well,
For quick to ride are the Four Fiends of Hell.

—Gene Del Tredici

FROM *CHANGED*

I saw a man turned into money:
His head became a bank vault door
in which the wheels were seen to hurry,
the valves were heard to quaintly purr.

The breast was soft as brown purse leather
in which the bones were solid coin.
The bullion heart, held fast forever,
fed stocks and bonds through copper veins . . .

And looking down, I saw, amazed
that the reproductive organs set
in wax and most conspicuously placed,
were nothing more than cancelled checks.

    —George Abbe

Reprinted by permission of William L. Bauhan, Publishers
from George Abbe, *Collected Poems, 1932–1961* (New Hampshire: William L. Bauhan, Publishers, 1961). Copyright ©
1961 by George Abbe.

THE ROCKING-HORSE WINNER

By D. H. Lawrence

There was a woman who was beautiful, who started with all the advantages, yet she had no luck. She married for love, and the love turned to dust. She had bonny children, yet she felt they had been thrust upon her, and she could not love them. They looked at her coldly, as if they were finding fault with her. And hurriedly she felt she must cover up some fault in herself. Yet what it was that she must cover up she never knew. Nevertheless, when her children were present, she always felt the centre of her heart go hard. This troubled her, and in her manner she was all the more gentle and anxious for her children, as if she loved them very much. Only she herself knew that at the centre of her heart was a hard little place that could not feel love, no, not for anybody. Everybody else said of her: "She is such a good mother. She adores her children." Only she herself, and her children themselves, knew it was not so. They read it in each other's eyes.

There were a boy and two little girls. They lived in a pleasant house, with a garden, and they had discreet servants, and felt themselves superior to anyone in the neighbourhood.

Although they lived in style, they felt always an anxiety in the house. There was never enough money. The mother had a small income, and the father had a small income, but not nearly enough for the social position which they had to keep up. The father went into town to some office. But though he had good prospects, these prospects never materialized. There was always the grinding sense of the shortage of money, though the style was always kept up.

At last the mother said: "I will see if I can't make something." But she did not know where to begin. She racked her brains, and tried this thing and the other, but could not find anything successful. The failure made deep lines come into her face. Her children were growing up, they would have to go to school. There must be more money, there must be more money. The father, who was

Reprinted by permission of Laurence Pollinger and the Estate of Mrs. Frieda Lawrence from D. H. Lawrence, *The Complete Short Stories of D. H. Lawrence* (London: William Heinemann, 1961). Also by permission of The Viking Press, New York.

always very handsome and expensive in his tastes, seemed as if he never would be able to do anything worth doing. And the mother, who had a great belief in herself, did not succeed any better, and her tastes were just as expensive.

And so the house came to be haunted by the unspoken phrase: there must be more money! There must be more money! The children could hear it all the time, though nobody said it aloud. They heard it at Christmas, when the expensive and splendid toys filled the nursery. Behind the shining modern rocking-horse, behind the smart doll's-house, a voice would start whispering: "There must be more money! There must be more money!" And the children would stop playing, to listen for a moment. They would look into each other's eyes, to see if they had all heard. And each one saw in the eyes of the other two that they too had heard. "There must be more money! There must be more money!"

It came whispering from the springs of the still-swaying rocking-horse, and even the horse, bending his wooden, champing head, heard it. The big doll, sitting so pink and smirking in her new pram, could hear it quite plainly, and seemed to be smirking all the more self-consciously because of it. The foolish puppy, too, that took the place of the Teddy bear, he was looking so extraordinarily foolish for no other reason but that he heard the secret whisper all over the house: "There must be more money!"

Yet nobody ever said it aloud. The whisper was everywhere, and therefore no one spoke it. Just as no one ever says: "We are breathing!" in spite of the fact that breath is coming and going all the time.

"Mother," said the boy Paul one day, "why don't we keep a car of our own? Why do we always use uncle's, or else a taxi?"

"Because we're the poor members of the family," said the mother.

"But why are we, mother?"

"Well—I suppose," she said slowly and bitterly, "it's because your father has no luck."

The boy was silent for some time.

"Is luck money, mother?" he asked, rather timidly.

"No, Paul. Not quite. It's what causes you to have money."

"Oh!" said Paul vaguely. "I thought when Uncle Oscar said filthy lucker, it meant money."

"Filthy lucre does mean money," said the mother. "But it's lucre, not luck."

"Oh!" said the boy. "Then what is luck, mother?"

"It's what causes you to have money. If you're lucky you have money. That's why it's better to be born lucky than rich. If you're rich, you may lose your money. But if you're lucky, you will always get more money."

"Oh! Will you! And is father not lucky?"

"Very unlucky, I should say," she said bitterly.

The boy watched her with unsure eyes.

"Why?" he asked.

"I don't know. Nobody ever knows why one person is lucky and another unlucky."

"Don't they? Nobody at all? Does nobody know?"

"Perhaps God. But He never tells."

"He ought to, then. And aren't you lucky either, mother?"

"I can't be, if I married an unlucky husband."

"But by yourself, aren't you?"

"I used to think I was, before I married. Now I think I am very unlucky indeed."

"Why?"

"Well—never mind! Perhaps I'm not really," she said.

The child looked at her, to see if she meant it. But he saw, by the lines of her mouth, that she was only trying to hide something from him.

"Well, anyhow," he said stoutly, "I'm a lucky person."

"Why?" said his mother, with a sudden laugh.

He stared at her. He didn't even know why he had said it.

"God told me," he asserted, brazening it out.

"I hope He did, dear!" she said, again with a laugh, but rather bitter.

"He did, mother!"

"Excellent!" said the mother, using one of her husband's exclamations.

The boy saw she did not believe him; or, rather, that she paid no attention to his assertion. This angered him somewhat, and made him want to compel her attention.

He went off by himself, vaguely, in a childish way, seeking for the clue to "luck." Absorbed, taking no heed of other people, he went about with a sort of stealth, seeking inwardly for luck. He wanted luck, he wanted it, he wanted it. When the two girls were playing dolls in the nursery, he would sit on his big rocking-horse, charging madly into space, with a frenzy that made the little girls peer at him uneasily. Wildly the horse careened, the waving dark hair of the boy tossed, his eyes had a strange glare in them. The little girls dared not speak to him.

When he had ridden to the end of his mad little journey, he climbed down and stood in front of his rocking-horse, staring fixedly into its lowered face. Its red mouth was slightly open, its big eye was wide and glassy-bright.

"Now!" he would silently command the snorting steed. "Now, take me to where there is luck! Now take me!"

And he would slash the horse on the neck with the little whip he had asked Uncle Oscar for. He knew the horse could take him to where there was luck, if only he forced it. So he would mount again, and start on his furious ride, hoping at last to get there. He knew he could get there.

"You'll break your horse, Paul!" said the nurse.

"He's always riding like that! I wish he'd leave off!" said his elder sister Joan.

But he only glared down on them in silence. Nurse gave him up. She could make nothing of him. Anyhow he was growing beyond her.

One day his mother and his Uncle Oscar came in when he was on one of his furious rides. He did not speak to them.

"Hallo, you young jockey! Riding a winner?" said his uncle.

"Aren't you growing too big for a rocking-horse? You're not a very little boy any longer, you know," said his mother.

But Paul only gave a blue glare from his big, rather close-set eyes. He would speak to nobody when he was in full tilt. His mother watched him with an anxious expression on her face.

At last he suddenly stopped forcing his horse into the mechanical gallop, and slid down.

"Well, I got there!" he announced fiercely, his blue eyes still flaring, and his sturdy long legs straddling apart.

"Where did you get to?" asked his mother.

"Where I wanted to go," he flared back at her.

"That's right, son!" said Uncle Oscar. "Don't you stop till you get there. What's the horse's name?"

"He doesn't have a name," said the boy.

"Gets on without all right?" asked the uncle.

"Well, he has different names. He was called Sansovino last week."

"Sansovino, eh? Won the Ascot. How did you know his name?"

"He always talks about horse races with Bassett," said Joan.

The uncle was delighted to find that his small nephew was posted with all the racing news. Bassett, the young gardener, who had been wounded in the left foot in the war and had got his present job through Oscar Cresswell, whose batman he had been, was a perfect blade of the "turf." He lived in the racing events, and the small boy lived with him.

Oscar Cresswell got it all from Bassett.

"Master Paul comes and asks me, so I can't do more than tell him, sir," said Bassett, his face terribly serious, as if he were speaking of religious matters.

"And does he ever put anything on a horse he fancies?"

"Well—I don't want to give him away—he's a young sport, a fine sport, sir. Would you mind asking him yourself? He sort of takes a pleasure in it, and perhaps he'd feel I was giving him away, sir, if you don't mind."

Bassett was serious as a church.

The uncle went back to his nephew, and took him off for a ride in the car.

"Say, Paul, old man, do you ever put anything on a horse?" the uncle asked.

The boy watched the handsome man closely.

"Why, do you think I oughtn't to?" he parried.

"Not a bit of it! I thought perhaps you might give me a tip for the Lincoln."

The car sped on into the country, going down to Uncle Oscar's place in Hampshire.

"Honour bright?" said the nephew.

"Honour bright, son!" said the uncle.

"Well, then, Daffodil."

"Daffodil! I doubt it, sonny. What about Mirza?"

"I only know the winner," said the boy. "That's Daffodil."

"Daffodil, eh?"

There was a pause. Daffodil was an obscure horse comparatively.

"Uncle!"

"Yes, son?"

"You won't let it go any further, will you? I promised Bassett."

"Bassett be damned, old man! What's he got to do with it?"

"We're partners. We've been partners from the first. Uncle, he lent me my first five shillings, which I lost. I promised him, honour bright, it was only between me and him; only you gave me that ten-shilling note I started winning with, so I thought you were lucky. You won't let it go any further, will you?"

The boy gazed at his uncle from those big, hot, blue eyes, set rather close together. The uncle stirred and laughed uneasily.

"Right you are, son! I'll keep your tip private. Daffodil, eh? How much are you putting on him?"

"All except twenty pounds," said the boy. "I keep that in reserve."

The uncle thought it a good joke.

"You keep twenty pounds in reserve, do you, you young romancer? What are you betting, then?"

"I'm betting three hundred," said the boy gravely. "But it's between you and me, Uncle Oscar! Honour bright?"

The uncle burst into a roar of laughter.

"It's between you and me all right, you young Nat Gould," he said, laughing. "But where's your three hundred?"

"Bassett keeps it for me. We're partners."

"You are, are you! And what is Bassett putting on Daffodil?"

"He won't go quite as high as I do, I expect. Perhaps he'll go a hundred and fifty."

"What, pennies?" laughed the uncle.

"Pounds," said the child, with a surprised look at his uncle. "Bassett keeps a bigger reserve than I do."

Between wonder and amusement Uncle Oscar was silent. He pursued the matter no further, but he determined to take his nephew with him to the Lincoln races.

"Now, son," he said, "I'm putting twenty on Mirza, and I'll put five for you on any horse you fancy. What's your pick?"

"Daffodil, uncle."

"No, not the fiver on Daffodil!"

"I should if it was my own fiver," said the child.

"Good! Good! Right you are! A fiver for me and a fiver for you on Daffodil."

The child had never been to a race meeting before, and his eyes were blue fire. He pursed his mouth tight, and watched. A Frenchman just in front had put his money on Lancelot. Wild with excitement, he flayed his arms up and down, yelling "Lancelot! Lancelot!" in his French accent.

Daffodil came in first, Lancelot second, Mirza third. The child, flushed and with eyes blazing, was curiously serene. His uncle brought him four five-pound notes, four to one.

"What am I to do with these?" he cried, waving them before the boy's eyes.

"I suppose we'll talk to Bassett," said the boy. "I expect I have fifteen hundred now; and twenty in reserve; and this twenty."

His uncle studied him for some moments.

"Look here, son!" he said. "You're not serious about Bassett and that fifteen hundred, are you?"

"Yes, I am. But it's between you and me, uncle. Honour bright!"

"Honour bright all right, son! But I must talk to Bassett."

Oh my friend, why do you, who are a citizen of the great and mighty and wise city of Athens, care so much about the laying up of the greatest amount of money and honor and reputation, and so little about wisdom and truth?

Socrates, on trial

"If you'd like to be a partner, uncle, with Bassett and me, we could all be partners. Only, you'd have to promise, honour bright, uncle, not to let it go beyond us three. Bassett and I are lucky, and you must be lucky, because it was your ten shillings I started winning with. . . ."

Uncle Oscar took both Bassett and Paul into Richmond Park for an afternoon, and there they talked.

"It's like this, you see, sir," Bassett said. "Master Paul would get me talking about racing events, spinning yarns, you know, sir. And he was always keen on knowing if I'd made or if I'd lost. It's about a year since, now, that I put five shillings on Blush of Dawn for him—and we lost. Then the luck turned, with that ten shillings he had from you, that we put on Singhalese. And since that time, it's been pretty steady, all things considering. What do you say, Master Paul?"

"We're all right when we're sure," said Paul. "It's when we're not quite sure that we go down."

"Oh, but we're careful then," said Bassett.

"But when are you sure?" smiled Uncle Oscar.

"It's Master Paul, sir," said Bassett, in a secret, religious voice. "It's as if he had it from heaven. Like Daffodil, now, for the Lincoln. That was as sure as eggs."

"Did you put anything on Daffodil?" asked Oscar Cresswell.

"Yes, sir, I made my bit."

"And my nephew?"

Bassett was obstinately silent, looking at Paul.

"I made twelve hundred, didn't I, Bassett? I told uncle I was putting three hundred on Daffodil."

"That's right," said Bassett, nodding.

"But where's the money?" asked the uncle.

"I keep it safe locked up, sir. Master Paul he can have it any minute he likes to ask for it."

"What, fifteen hundred pounds?"

"And twenty! and forty, that is, with the twenty he made on the course."

"It's amazing!" said the uncle.

"If Master Paul offers you to be partners, sir, I would, if I were you; if you'll excuse me," said Bassett.

Oscar Cresswell thought about it.

"I'll see the money," he said.

They drove home again, and sure enough, Bassett came round to the garden-house with fifteen hundred pounds in notes. The twenty pounds reserve was left with Joe Glee, in the Turf Commission deposit.

"You see, it's all right, uncle, when I'm sure! Then we go strong, for all we're worth. Don't we, Bassett?"

"We do that, Master Paul."

"And when are you sure?" said the uncle, laughing.

"Oh, well, sometimes I'm absolutely sure, like about Daffodil," said the boy; "and sometimes I have an idea; and sometimes I haven't even an idea, have I, Bassett? Then we're careful, because we mostly go down."

"You do, do you! And when you're sure, like about Daffodil, what makes you sure, sonny?"

"Oh, well, I don't know," said the boy uneasily. "I'm sure, you know, uncle; that's all."

"It's as if he had it from heaven, sir," Bassett reiterated.

"I should say so!" said the uncle.

But he became a partner. And when the Leger was coming on, Paul was "sure" about Lively Spark, which was a quite inconsiderable horse. The boy insisted on putting a thousand on the horse. Bassett went for five hundred, and Oscar Cresswell two hundred. Lively Spark came in first, and the betting had been ten to one against him. Paul had made ten thousand.

"You see," he said, "I was absolutely sure of him."

Even Oscar Cresswell had cleared two thousand.

"Look here, son," he said, "this sort of thing makes me nervous."

"It needn't, uncle! Perhaps I shan't be sure again for a long time."

"But what are you going to do with your money?" asked the uncle.

"Of course," said the boy, "I started it for mother. She said she had no luck, because father is unlucky, so I thought if I was lucky, it might stop whispering."

"What might stop whispering?"

"Our house. I hate our house for whispering."

"What does it whisper?"

"Why—why"—the boy fidgeted—"why, I don't know. But it's always short of money, you know, uncle."

"I know it, son, I know it."

"You know people send mother writs, don't you, uncle?"

"I'm afraid I do," said the uncle.

"And then the house whispers, like people laughing at you behind your back. It's awful, that is! I thought if I was lucky . . ."

"You might stop it," added the uncle.

The boy watched him with big blue eyes that had an uncanny cold fire in them, and he said never a word.

"Well, then!" said the uncle. "What are we doing?"

"I shouldn't like mother to know I was lucky," said the boy.

"Why not, son?"

"She'd stop me."

"I don't think she would."

"Oh!"—and the boy writhed in an odd way—"I don't want her to know, uncle."

"All right, son! We'll manage it without her knowing."

They managed it very easily. Paul, at the other's suggestion, handed over five thousand pounds to his uncle, who deposited it with the family lawyer, who was then to inform Paul's mother that a relative had put five thousand pounds into his hands, which sum was to be paid out a thousand pounds at a time, on the mother's birthday, for the next five years.

"So she'll have a birthday present of a thousand pounds for five successive years," said Uncle Oscar. "I hope it won't make it all the harder for her later."

Paul's mother had her birthday in November. The house had been "whispering" worse than ever lately, and, even in spite of his luck, Paul could not bear up against it. He was very anxious to see the effect of the birthday letter, telling his mother about the thousand pounds.

When there were no visitors, Paul now took his meals with his parents, as he was beyond the nursery control. His mother went into town nearly every day. She had discovered that she had an odd knack of sketching furs and dress materials, so she worked secretly in the studio of a friend who was the chief "artist" for the leading drapers. She drew the figures of ladies in furs and ladies in silk and sequins for the newspaper advertisements. This young woman artist earned several thousand pounds a year, but Paul's mother only made several hundreds, and she was again dissatisfied. She so wanted to be first in something, and she did not succeed, even in making sketches for drapery advertisements.

She was down to breakfast on the morning of her birthday. Paul watched her face as she read her letters. He knew the lawyer's letter. As his mother read it, her face hardened and became more expressionless. Then a cold, determined look came on her mouth. She hid the letter under the pile of others, and said not a word about it.

"Didn't you have anything nice in the post for your birthday, mother?" said Paul.

"Quite moderately nice," she said, her voice cold and absent.

She went away to town without saying more.

But in the afternoon Uncle Oscar appeared. He said Paul's mother had had a long interview with the lawyer, asking if the whole five thousand could be advanced at once, as she was in debt.

"What do you think, uncle?" said the boy.

"I leave it to you, son."

"Oh, let her have it, then! We can get some more with the other," said the boy.

"A bird in the hand is worth two in the bush, laddie!" said Uncle Oscar.

"But I'm sure to know for the Grand National; or the Lincolnshire; or else the Derby. I'm sure to know for one of them," said Paul.

So Uncle Oscar signed the agreement, and Paul's mother touched the whole five thousand. Then something very curious happened. The voices in the house suddenly went mad, like a chorus of frogs on a spring evening. There were certain new furnishings, and Paul had a tutor. He was really going to Eton, his father's school, in the following autumn. There were flowers in the winter, and a blossoming of the luxury Paul's mother had been used to. And yet the voices in the house, behind the sprays of mimosa and almond blossom, and from under the piles of iridescent cushions, simply trilled and screamed in a sort of ecstasy: "There must be more money! Oh-h-h, there must be more money. Oh, now, now-w! Now-w-w—there must be more money!—more than ever! More than ever!"

It frightened Paul terribly. He studied away at his Latin and Greek with his tutors. But his intense hours were spent with Bassett. The Grand National had gone by: he had not "known," and had lost a hundred pounds. Summer was at hand. He was in agony for the Lincoln. But even for the Lincoln he didn't "know" and he lost fifty pounds. He became wild-eyed and strange, as if something were going to explode in him.

"Let it alone, son! Don't you bother about it!" urged Uncle Oscar. But it was as if the boy couldn't really hear what his uncle was saying.

"I've got to know for the Derby! I've got to know for the Derby!" the child reiterated, his big blue eyes blazing with a sort of madness.

His mother noticed how overwrought he was.

"You'd better go to the seaside. Wouldn't you like to go now to the seaside, instead of waiting? I think you'd better," she said, looking down at him anxiously, her heart curiously heavy because of him.

But the child lifted his uncanny blue eyes.

"I couldn't possibly go before the Derby, mother!" he said. "I couldn't possibly!"

"Why not?" she said, her voice becoming heavy when she was opposed. "Why not? You can still go from the seaside to see the Derby with your Uncle Oscar, if that's what you wish. No need for you to wait here. Besides, I think you care too much about those races. It's a bad sign. My family has been a gambling family, and you won't know till you grow up how much damage it has done. But it has done damage. I shall have to send Bassett away, and ask Uncle Oscar not to talk racing to you, unless you promise to be reasonable about it; go away to the seaside and forget it. You're all nerves!"

"I'll do what you like, mother, so long as you don't send me away till after the Derby," the boy said.

"Send you away from where? Just from this house?"

"Yes," he said, gazing at her.

"Why, you curious child, what makes you care about this house so much, suddenly? I never knew you loved it."

He gazed at her without speaking. He had a secret within a secret, something he had not divulged, even to Bassett or to his Uncle Oscar.

But his mother, after standing undecided and a little bit sullen for some moments, said:

"Very well, then! Don't go to the seaside till after the Derby, if you don't wish it. But promise me you won't let your nerves go to pieces. Promise you won't think so much about horse racing and events, as you call them!"

"Oh, no," said the boy casually. "I won't think much about them, mother. You needn't worry. I wouldn't worry, mother, if I were you."

"If you were me and I were you," said his mother, "I wonder what we should do!"

"But you know you needn't worry, mother, don't you?" the boy repeated.

"I should be awfully glad to know it," she said wearily.

"Oh, well, you can, you know. I mean, you ought to know you needn't worry," he insisted.

"Ought I? Then I'll see about it," she said.

Paul's secret of secrets was his wooden horse, that which had no name. Since he was emancipated from a nurse and a nursery-governess, he had had his rocking-horse removed to his own bedroom at the top of the house.

"Surely, you're too big for a rocking-horse!" his mother had remonstrated.

"Well, you see, mother, till I can have a real horse, I like to have some sort of animal about," had been his quaint answer.

"Do you feel he keeps you company?" she laughed.

"Oh, yes! He's very good, he always keeps me company, when I'm there," said Paul.

So the horse, rather shabby, stood in an arrested prance in the boy's bedroom.

The Derby was drawing near, and the boy grew more and more tense. He hardly heard what was spoken to him, he was very frail, and his eyes were really uncanny. His mother had sudden seizures of uneasiness about him.

Sometimes, for half-an-hour, she would feel a sudden anxiety about him that was almost anguish. She wanted to rush to him at once, and know he was safe.

Two nights before the Derby, she was at a big party in town, when one of her rushes of anxiety about her boy, her first-born, gripped her heart till she could hardly speak. She fought with the feeling, might and main, for she believed in common sense. But it was too strong. She had to leave the dance and go downstairs to telephone to the country. The children's nursery-governess was terribly surprised and startled at being rung up in the night.

"Are the children all right, Miss Wilmot?"

"Oh, yes, they are quite all right."

"Master Paul? Is he all right?"

"He went to bed as right as a trivet. Shall I run up and look at him?"

"No," said Paul's mother reluctantly. "No! Don't trouble. It's all right. Don't sit up. We shall be home fairly soon." She did not want her son's privacy intruded upon.

"Very good," said the governess.

It was about one o'clock when Paul's mother and father drove up to their house. All was still. Paul's mother went to her room and slipped off her white fur coat. She had told her maid not to wait up for her. She heard her husband downstairs, mixing a whisky-and-soda.

And then, because of the strange anxiety at her heart, she stole upstairs to her son's room. Noiselessly she went along the upper corridor. Was there a faint noise? What was it?

She stood, with arrested muscles, outside his door, listening. There was a strange, heavy, and yet not loud noise. Her heart stood still. It was a soundless noise, yet rushing and powerful. Something huge, in violent, hushed motion. What was it? What in God's name was it? She ought to know. She felt that she knew the noise. She knew what it was.

Yet she could not place it. She couldn't say what it was. And on and on it went, like a madness.

Softly, frozen with anxiety and fear, she turned the door handle.

The room was dark. Yet in the space near the window, she heard and saw something plunging to and fro. She gazed in fear and amazement.

Then suddenly she switched on the light, and saw her son, in his green pyjamas, madly surging on the rocking-horse. The blaze of light suddenly lit him up, as he urged the wooden horse, and lit her up, as she stood, blonde, in her dress of pale green and crystal, in the doorway.

"Paul!" she cried. "Whatever are you doing?"

"It's Malabar!" he screamed, in a powerful, strange voice. "It's Malabar."

His eyes blazed at her for one strange and senseless second, as he ceased urging his wooden horse. Then he fell with a crash to the ground, and she, all her tormented motherhood flooding upon her, rushed to gather him up.

But he was unconscious, and unconscious he remained, with some brain-fever. He talked and tossed, and his mother sat stonily by his side.

"Malabar! It's Malabar! Bassett, Bassett, I know! It's Malabar!"

So the child cried, trying to get up and urge the rocking-horse that gave him his inspiration.

"What does he mean by Malabar?" asked the heart-frozen mother.

"I don't know," said the father stonily.

"What does he mean by Malabar?" she asked her brother Oscar.

"It's one of the horses running for the Derby," was the answer.

And, in spite of himself, Oscar Cresswell spoke to Bassett, and himself put a thousand on Malabar: at fourteen to one.

The third day of the illness was critical: they were waiting for a change. The boy, with his rather long, curly hair, was tossing ceaselessly on the pillow. He neither slept nor regained consciousness, and his eyes were like blue stones. His mother sat, feeling her heart had gone, turned actually into a stone.

In the evening, Oscar Cresswell did not come, but Bassett sent a message, saying could he come up for one moment, just one moment? Paul's mother was very angry at the intrusion, but on second thought she agreed. The boy was the same. Perhaps Bassett might bring him to consciousness.

The gardener, a shortish fellow with a little brown moustache, and sharp little brown eyes, tiptoed into the room, touched his imaginary cap to Paul's mother, and stole to the bedside, staring with glittering, smallish eyes, at the tossing, dying child.

"Master Paul!" he whispered. "Master Paul! Malabar come in first all right, a clean win. I did as you told me. You've made over seventy thousand pounds, you have; you've got over eighty thousand. Malabar came in all right, Master Paul."

"Malabar! Malabar! Did I say Malabar, mother? Did I say Malabar? Do you think I'm lucky, mother? I knew Malabar, didn't I? Over eighty thousand pounds! I call that lucky, don't you mother? Over eighty thousand pounds! I knew, didn't I know I knew? Malabar came in all right. If I ride my horse till I'm sure, then I tell you, Bassett, you can go as high as you like. Did you go for all you were worth, Bassett?"

"I went a thousand on it, Master Paul."

"I never told you, mother, that if I can ride my horse, and get there, then I'm absolutely sure—oh, absolutely! Mother, did I ever tell you? I am lucky."

"No, you never did," said the mother.

But the boy died in the night.

And even as he lay dead, his mother heard her brother's voice saying to her: "My God, Hester, you're eighty-odd thousand to the good and a poor devil of a son to the bad. But, poor devil, poor devil, he's best gone out of a life where he rides his rocking-horse to find a winner."

LA UNITED FRUIT CO.

Cuando sonó la trompeta, estuvo
todo preparado en la tierra,
y Jehová repartió el mundo
a Coca-Cola Inc., Anaconda,
Ford Motors, y otras entidades:
la Compañía Frutera Inc.
se reservó lo más jugoso,
la costa central de mi tierra,
la dulce cintura de América.
Bautizó de nuevo sus tierras
como "Repúblicas Bananas,"
y sobre los muertos dormidos,
sobre los héroes inquietos
que conquistaron la grandeza,
la libertad y las banderas,
estableció la ópera bufa:
enajenó los albedríos,
regaló coronas de César,
desenvainó la envidia, atrajo
la dictadura de las moscas,
moscas Trujillos, moscas Tachos,
moscas Carías, moscas Martínez,
moscas Ubico, moscas húmedas
de sangre humilde y mermelada,
moscas borrachas que zumban
sobre las tumbas populares,
moscas de circo, sabias moscas
entendidas en tiranía.

Entre las moscas sanguinarias
la Frutera desembarca,
arrasando el café y las frutas,
en sus barcos que deslizaron
como bandejas el tesoro
de nuestras tierras sumergidas.

Mientras tanto, por los abismos
azucarados de los puertos,
caían indios sepultados
en el vapor de la mañana:
un cuerpo rueda, una cosa
sin nombre, un número caído,
un racimo de fruta muerta
derramada en el pudridero.

When the trumpets had sounded and all
was in readiness on the face of the earth,
Jehovah divided his universe:
Anacanda, Ford Motors,
Coca-Cola Inc., and similar entities:
the most succulent item of all,
The United Fruit Company Incorporated
reserved for itself: the heartland
and coasts of my country,
the delectable waist of America.
They rechristened their properties:
the "Banana Republics"—
and over the languishing dead,
the uneasy repose of the heroes
who harried that greatness,
their flags and their freedoms,
they established an *opéra bouffe*:
they ravished all enterprise,
awarded the laurels like Caesars,
unleashed all the covetous, and contrived
the tyrannical Reign of the Flies—
Trujillo the fly, and Tacho the fly,
the flies called Carias, Martinez,
Ubico—all of them flies, flies
dank with the blood of their marmalade
vassalage, flies buzzing drunkenly
on the populous middens:
the fly-circus fly and the scholarly
kind, case-hardened in tyranny.

Then in the bloody domain of the flies
The United Fruit Company Incorporated
unloaded with a booty of coffee and fruits
brimming its cargo boats, gliding
like trays with the spoils
of our drowning dominions.

And all the while, somewhere, in the sugary
hells of our seaports,
smothered by gases, an Indian
fell in the morning:
a body spun off, an anonymous
chattel, some numeral tumbling,
a branch with its death running out of it
in the vat of the carrion, fruit laden and foul.

121

—*Pablo Neruda*

Reprinted by permission of Grove Press from Pablo Neruda,
Selected Poems of Pablo Neruda (New York: Grove Press,
1961).

The streets of our country are in turmoil. The universities are filled with students rebelling and rioting. Communists are seeking to destroy our country. Russia is threatening us with her might and the republic is in danger. Yes, danger from within and from without. We need law and order. Yes, without law and order our nation cannot survive. Elect us and we shall restore law and order. *Adolph Hitler*, Hamburg 1932

FOR WHAT
IT'S WORTH

There's something happenin' here.
What it is ain't exactly clear.
There's a man with a gun over there,
Tellin' me I've got to beware.
It's time we stop, children,
What's that sound?
Everybody look what's goin' down.

There's battle lines bein' drawn,
Nobody's right if everybody's wrong.
Young people speakin' their minds,
Gettin' so much resistance from behind.
It's time we stop, children,
What's that sound?
Everybody look what's goin' down.

What a field day for the heat.
A thousand people in the street,
Singin' songs and carryin' signs.
Mostly saying, "Hooray for our side."
It's time we stop, children,
What's that sound?
Everybody look what's goin' down.

Paranoia strikes deep,
Into your life it will creep.
It starts when you're always afraid,
Step out of line, the Man come
And take you away.
You better stop, hey,
What's that sound?
Everybody look what's goin' down.

    —*Stephen Stills*
      (for the Buffalo Springfield)

Reprinted by permission of Cotillion Music, New York, 1966.

The capacity for getting along with our neighbor depends to a large extent on the capacity for getting along with ourselves. The self-respecting individual will try to be as tolerant of his neighbor's shortcomings as he is of his own.

Eric Hoffer

THE WAY MEN LIVE IS A LIE

The way men live is a lie.
I say that I get so goddamned sick
Of all these pigs rooting at each other's asses
To get a bloodstained dollar—Why don't
You stop this senseless horror! this meaningless
Butchery of one another! Why don't *you* at least
Wash *your* hands of it!

There is only one truth in the world:
Until we learn to love our neighbor,
There will be no life for anyone.

The man who says, "I don't believe in war,
But after all somebody must protect us"—
Is obviously a fool—and a liar.
Is this so hard to understand!
That who supports murder, is a murderer?
That who destroys his fellow, destroys himself?

Force cannot be overthrown by force;
To hate any man is to despair of every man;
Evil breeds evil—the rest is a lie!

There is only one power that can save the world—
And that is the power of our love for all men
    everywhere.

—Kenneth Patchen

Reprinted by permission of New Directions Publishing
Corporation from Kenneth Patchen, *Collected Poems* (New
York: New Directions Publishing Corporation, 1945).

DRY SEPTEMBER

By William Faulkner

Through the bloody September twilight, aftermath of sixty-two rainless days, it had gone like a fire in dry grass—the rumor, the story, whatever it was. Something about Miss Minnie Cooper and a Negro. Attacked, insulted, frightened: none of them, gathered in the barber shop on that Saturday evening where the ceiling fan stirred, without freshening it, the vitiated air, sending back upon them, in recurrent surges of stale pomade and lotion, their own stale breath and odors, knew exactly what had happened.

"Except it wasn't Will Mayes," a barber said. He was a man of middle age; a thin, sand-colored man with a mild face, who was shaving a client. "I know Will Mayes. He's a good nigger. And I know Miss Minnie Cooper, too."

"What do you know about her?" a second barber said.

"Who is she?" the client said. "A young girl?"

"No," the barber said. "She's about forty, I reckon. She aint married. That's why I dont believe—"

"Believe, hell!" a hulking youth in a sweat-stained silk shirt said. "Wont you take a white woman's word before a nigger's?"

"I dont believe Will Mayes did it," the barber said. "I know Will Mayes."

"Maybe you know who did it, then. Maybe you already got him out of town, you damn niggerlover."

"I dont believe anybody did anything. I dont believe anything happened. I leave it to you fellows if them ladies that get old without getting married dont have notions that a man cant—"

"Then you are a hell of a white man," the client said. He moved under the cloth. The youth had sprung to his feet.

"You dont?" he said. "Do you accuse a white woman of lying?"

The barber held the razor poised above the half-risen client. He did not look around.

"It's this durn weather," another said. "It's enough to make a man do anything. Even to her."

Nobody laughed. The barber said in his mild, stubborn tone: "I aint accusing nobody of nothing. I just know and you fellows know how a woman that never—"

"You damn niggerlover!" the youth said.

"Shut up, Butch," another said. "We'll get the facts in plenty of time to act."

"Who is? Who's getting them?" the youth said. "Facts, hell! I—"

"You're a fine white man," the client said. "Aint you?" In his frothy beard he looked like a desert rat in the moving pictures. "You tell them, Jack," he said to the youth. "If there aint any white men in this town, you can count on me, even if I aint only a drummer and a stranger."

"That's right boys," the barber said. "Find out the truth first. I know Will Mayes."

"Well, by God!" the youth shouted. "To think that a white man in this town—"

"Shut up, Butch," the second speaker said. "We got plenty of time."

The client sat up. He looked at the speaker. "Do you claim that anything excuses a nigger attacking a white woman? Do you mean to tell me you are a white man and you'll stand for it? You better go back North where you came from. The South dont want your kind here."

"North what?" the second said. "I was born and raised in this town."

"Well, by God!" the youth said. He looked about with a strained, baffled gaze, as if he was trying to remember what it was he wanted to say or to do. He drew his sleeve across his sweating face. "Damn if I'm going to let a white woman—"

"You tell them, Jack," the drummer said. "By God, if they—"

The screen door crashed open. A man stood in the floor, his feet apart and his heavy-set body poised easily. His white shirt was open at the throat; he wore a felt hat. His hot, bold glance swept the group. His name was McLendon. He had commanded troops at the front in France and had been decorated for valor.

"Well," he said, "are you going to sit there and let a black son rape a white woman on the streets of Jefferson?"

Butch sprang up again. The silk of his shirt clung flat to his heavy shoulders. At each armpit was a dark halfmoon. "That's what I been telling them! That's what I—"

"Did it really happen?" a third said. "This aint the first man scare she ever had, like Hawkshaw says. Wasn't there something about a man on the kitchen roof, watching her undress, about a year ago?"

"What?" the client said. "What's that?" The barber had been slowly forcing him back into the chair; he arrested himself reclining, his head lifted, the barber still pressing him down.

Prejudice is the reason of fools.
                                          Voltaire

McLendon whirled on the third speaker. "Happen? What the hell difference does it make? Are you going to let the black sons get away with it until one really does it?"

"That's what I'm telling them!" Butch shouted. He cursed, long and steady, pointless.

"Here, here," a fourth said. "Not so loud. Dont talk so loud."

"Sure," McLendon said; "no talking necessary at all. I've done my talking. Who's with me?" He poised on the balls of his feet, roving his gaze.

The barber held the drummer's face down, the razor poised. "Find out the facts first, boys. I know Willy Mayes. It wasn't him. Let's get the sheriff and do this thing right."

McLendon whirled upon him his furious, rigid face. The barber did not look away. They looked like men of different races. The other barbers had ceased also above their prone clients. "You mean to tell me," McLendon said, "that you'd take a nigger's word before a white woman's? Why, you damn nigger-loving—"

The third speaker rose and grasped McLendon's arm; he too had been a soldier. "Now, now. Let's figure this thing out. Who knows anything about what really happened?"

"Figure out hell!" McLendon jerked his arm free. "All that're with me get up from there. The ones that aint—" He roved his gaze, dragging his sleeve across his face.

Three men rose. The drummer in the chair sat up. "Here," he said, jerking at the cloth about his neck; "get this rag off me. I'm with him. I don't live here, but by God, if our mothers and wives and sisters—" He smeared the cloth over his face and flung it to the floor. McLendon stood in the floor and cursed the others. Another rose and moved toward him. The remainder sat uncomfortable, not looking at one another, then one by one they rose and joined him.

The barber picked the cloth from the floor. He began to fold it neatly. "Boys, dont do that. Will Mayes never done it. I know."

"Come on," McLendon said. He whirled. From his hip pocket protruded the butt of a heavy automatic pistol. They went out. The screen door crashed behind them reverberant in the dead air.

The barber wiped the razor carefully and swiftly, and put it away, and ran to the rear, and took his hat from the wall. "I'll be back as soon as I can," he said to the other barbers. "I cant let—" He went out, running. The two other barbers followed him to the door and caught it on the rebound, leaning out and looking up the street after him. The air was flat and dead. It had a metallic taste at the base of the tongue.

"What can he do?" the first said. The second one was saying "Jees Christ, Jees Christ" under his breath. "I'd just as lief be Will Mayes as Hawk, if he gets McLendon riled."

"Jees Christ, Jees Christ," the second whispered.

"You reckon he really done it to her?" the first said.

II

She was thirty-eight or thirty-nine. She lived in a small frame house with her invalid mother and a thin, sallow, unflagging aunt, where each morning between ten and eleven she would appear on the porch in a lace-trimmed boudoir cap, to sit swinging in the porch swing until noon. After dinner she lay down for a while, until the afternoon began to cool. Then, in one of the three or four new voile dresses which she had each summer, she would go downtown to spend the afternoon in the stores with the other ladies, where they would handle the goods and haggle over the prices in cold, immediate voices, without any intention of buying.

She was of comfortable people—not the best in Jefferson, but good people enough—and she was still on the slender side of ordinary looking, with a bright, faintly haggard manner and dress. When she was young she had had a slender, nervous body and a sort of hard vivacity which had enabled her for a time to ride upon the crest of the town's social life as exemplified by the high school party and church social period of her contemporaries while still children enough to be unclassconscious.

She was the last to realize that she was losing ground; that those among whom she had been a little brighter and louder flame than any other were beginning to learn the pleasure of snobbery—male—and retaliation—female. That was when her face began to wear that bright, haggard look. She still carried it to parties on shadowy porticoes and summer lawns, like a mask or a flag, with that bafflement of furious repudiation of truth in her eyes. One evening at a party she heard a boy and two girls, all schoolmates, talking. She never accepted another invitation.

She watched the girls with whom she had grown up as they married and got homes and children, but no man ever called on her steadily until the children of the other girls had been calling her "aunty" for several years, the while their mothers told them in bright voices about how popular Aunt Minnie had been as a girl. Then the town began to see her driving on Sunday afternoons with the cashier in the bank. He was a widower of about forty—a high-colored man, smelling always faintly of the barber shop or of whisky. He owned the first automobile in town, a red runabout; Minnie had the first motoring bonnet and veil the town ever saw. Then the town began to say: "Poor Minnie." "But she is old enough to take care of herself," others said. That was when she began to ask her old schoolmates that their children call her "cousin" instead of "aunty."

It was twelve years now since she had been relegated into adultery by public opinion, and eight years since the cashier had gone to a Memphis bank, returning for one day each Christmas, which he spent at an annual bachelors' party at a hunting club on the river. From behind their curtains the neighbors would see the party pass, and during the over-the-way Christmas day visiting they would tell her about him, about how well he looked, and how they heard that he was prospering in the city, watching with bright, secret eyes her haggard, bright face. Usually by that hour there would be the scent of whisky on her breath. It was supplied her by a youth, a clerk at the soda fountain: "Sure; I buy it for the old gal. I reckon she's entitled to a little fun."

Her mother kept to her room altogether now; the gaunt aunt ran the house. Against that background Minnie's bright dresses, her idle and empty days, had a quality of furious unreality. She went out in the evenings only with women now, neighbors, to the moving pictures. Each afternoon she dressed in one of the new dresses and went downtown alone, where her young "cousins" were already strolling in the late afternoons with their delicate, silken heads and thin, awkward arms and conscious hips, clinging to one another or shrieking and giggling with paired boys in the soda fountain when she passed and went on along the serried store fronts, in the doors of which the sitting and lounging men did not even follow her with their eyes any more.

The barber went swiftly up the street where the sparse lights, insect-swirled, glared in rigid and violent suspension in the lifeless air. The day had died in a pall of dust; above the darkened square, shrouded by the spent dust, the sky was as clear as the inside of a brass bell. Below the east was a rumor of the twice-waxed moon.

When he overtook them McLendon and three others were getting into a car parked in an alley. McLendon stooped his thick head, peering out beneath the top. "Changed your mind, did you?" he said. "Damn good thing; by God, tomorrow when this town hears about how you talked tonight—"

"Now, now," the other ex-soldier said. "Hawkshaw's all right. Come on, Hawk; jump in."

"Will Mayes never done it, boys," the barber said. "If anybody done it. Why, you all know well as I do there aint any town where they got better niggers than us. And you know how a lady will kind of think things about men when there aint no reason to, and Miss Minnie anyway—"

"Sure, sure," the soldier said. "We're just going to talk to him a little; that's all."

"Talk hell!" Butch said. "When we're through with the—"

"Shut up, for God's sake!" the soldier said. "Do you want everybody in town—"

"Tell them, by God!" McLendon said. "Tell every one of the sons that'll let a white woman—"

"Let's go; let's go: here's the other car." The second car slid squealing out of a cloud of dust at the alley mouth. McLendon started his car and took the lead. Dust lay like fog in the street. The street lights hung nimbused as in water. They drove on out of town.

A rutted lane turned at right angles. Dust hung above it too, and above all the land. The dark bulk of the ice plant, where the Negro Mayes was night watchman, rose against the sky. "Better stop here, hadn't we?" the soldier said. McLendon did not reply. He hurled the car up and slammed to a stop, the head-lights glaring on the blank wall.

"Listen here, boys," the barber said; "if he's here, dont that prove he never done it? Dont it? If it was him, he would run. Dont you see he would?" The second car came up and stopped. McLendon got down; Butch sprang down beside him. "Listen, boys," the barber said.

"Cut the lights off!" McLendon said. The breathless dark rushed down. There was no sound in it save their lungs as they sought air in the parched dust in which for two months they had lived; then the diminishing crunch of McLendon's and Butch's feet, and a moment later McLendon's voice:

"Will! . . . Will!"

Below the east the wan hemorrhage of the moon increased. It heaved above the ridge, silvering the air, the dust, so that they seemed to breathe, live, in a bowl of molten lead. There was no sound of nightbird nor insect, no sound save their breathing and a faint ticking of contracting metal about the cars.

Where their bodies touched one another they seemed to sweat dryly, for no more moisture came. "Christ!" a voice said; "let's get out of here."

But they didn't move until vague noises began to grow out of the darkness ahead; then they got out and waited tensely in the breathless dark. There was another sound: a blow, a hissing expulsion of breath and McLendon cursing in undertone. They stood a moment longer, then they ran forward. They ran in a stumbling clump, as though they were fleeing something. "Kill him, kill the son," a voice whispered. McLendon flung them back.

"Not here," he said. "Get him into the car." "Kill him, kill the black son!" the voice murmured. They dragged the Negro to the car. The barber had waited beside the car. He could feel himself sweating and he knew he was going to be sick at the stomach.

"What is it, captains?" the Negro said. "I aint done nothing. 'Fore God, Mr. John." Someone produced handcuffs. They worked busily about the Negro as though he were a post, quiet, intent, getting in one another's way. He submitted to the handcuffs, looking swiftly and constantly from dim face to dim face. "Who's here, captains?" he said, leaning to peer into the faces until they could feel his breath and smell his sweaty reek. He spoke a name or two. "What you all say I done, Mr. John?"

McLendon jerked the car door open. "Get in!" he said.

The Negro did not move. "What you all going to do with me, Mr. John? I aint done nothing. White folks, captains, I aint done nothing: I swear 'fore God." He called another name.

"Get in!" McLendon said. He struck the Negro. The others expelled their breath in a dry hissing and struck him with random blows and he whirled and cursed them, and swept his manacled hands across their faces and slashed the barber upon the mouth, and the barber struck him also. "Get him in there," McLendon said. They pushed at him. He ceased struggling and got in and sat quietly as the others took their places. He sat between the barber and the soldier, drawing his limbs in so as not to touch them, his eyes going swiftly and constantly from face to face. Butch clung to the running board. The car moved on. The barber nursed his mouth with his handkerchief.

"What's the matter, Hawk?" the soldier said.

"Nothing," the barber said. They regained the highroad and turned away from town. The second car dropped back out of the dust. They went on, gaining speed; the final fringe of houses dropped behind.

"Goddam, he stinks!" the soldier said.

"We'll fix that," the drummer in front beside McLendon said. On the running board Butch cursed into the hot rush of air. The barber leaned suddenly forward and touched McLendon's arm.

"Let me out, John," he said.

"Jump out, niggerlover," McLendon said without turning his head. He drove swiftly. Behind them the sourceless lights of the second car glared in the dust. Presently McLendon turned into a narrow road. It was rutted with disuse. It led back to an abandoned brick kiln—a series of reddish mounds and weed- and vine-choked vats without bottom. It had been used for pasture once, until one day the owner missed one of his mules. Although he prodded carefully in the vats with a long pole, he could not even find the bottom of them.

"John," the barber said.

"Jump out, then," McLendon said, hurling the car along the ruts. Beside the barber the Negro spoke:

"Mr. Henry."

The barber sat forward. The narrow tunnel of the road rushed up and past. Their motion was like an extinct furnace blast: cooler, but utterly dead. The car bounded from rut to rut.

"Mr. Henry," the Negro said.

The barber began to tug furiously at the door. "Look out, there!" the soldier said, but the barber had already kicked the door open and swung onto the running board. The soldier leaned across the Negro and grasped at him, but he had already jumped. The car went on without checking speed.

The impetus hurled him crashing through dust-sheathed weeds, into the ditch. Dust puffed about him, and in a thin, vicious crackling of sapless stems he lay choking and retching until the second car passed and died away. Then he rose and limped on until he reached the highroad and turned toward town, brushing at his clothes with his hands. The moon was higher, riding high and clear of the dust at last, and after a while the town began to glare beneath the dust. He went on, limping. Presently he heard cars and the glow of them grew in the dust behind him and he left the road and crouched again in the weeds until they passed. McLendon's car came last now. There were four people in it and Butch was not on the running board.

They went on; the dust swallowed them; the glare and the sound died away. The dust of them hung for a while, but soon the eternal dust absorbed it again. The barber climbed back onto the road and limped on toward town.

IV

As she dressed for supper on that Saturday evening, her own flesh felt like fever. Her hands trembled among the hooks and eyes, and her eyes had a feverish look, and her hair swirled crisp and crackling under the comb. While she was still dressing the friends called for her and sat while she donned her sheerest underthings and stockings and a new voile dress. "Do you feel strong enough to go out?" they said, their eyes bright too, with a dark glitter. "When you have had time to get over the shock, you must tell us what happened. What he said and did; everything."

In the leafed darkness, as they walked toward the square, she began to breathe deeply, something like a swimmer preparing to dive, until she ceased trembling, the four of them walking slowly because of the terrible heat and out of solicitude for her. But as they neared the square she began to tremble again, walking with her head up, her hands clenched at her sides, their voices about her murmurous, also with that feverish, glittering quality of their eyes.

I know so many people with 20–20 vision who are blind. They have the ability to see, but they never look. Or if they do, they look only through the veil of their own opinions and prejudices. *Alice B. Toklas*

They entered the square, she in the center of the group, fragile in her fresh dress. She was trembling worse. She walked slower and slower, as children eat ice cream, her head up and her eyes bright in the haggard banner of her face, passing the hotel and the coatless drummers in chairs along the curb looking around at her: "That's the one: see? The one in pink in the middle." "Is that her? What did they do with nigger? Did they—?" "Sure. He's all right." "All right, is he?" "Sure. He went on a little trip." Then the drug store, where even the young men lounging in the doorway tipped their hats and followed with their eyes the motion of her hips and legs when she passed.

They went on, passing the lifted hats of the gentlemen, the suddenly ceased voices, deferent, protective. "Do you see?" the friends said. Their voices sounded like long, hovering sighs of hissing exultation. "There's not a Negro on the square. Not one."

They reached the picture show. It was like a miniature fairyland with its lighted lobby and colored lithographs of life caught in its terrible and beautiful mutations. Her lips began to tingle. In the dark, when the picture began, it would be all right; she could hold back the laughing so it would not waste away so fast and so soon. So she hurried on before the turning faces, the undertones of low astonishment, and they took their accustomed places where she could see the aisle against the silver glare and the young men and girls coming in two and two against it.

The lights flicked away; the screen glowed silver, and soon life began to unfold, beautiful and passionate and sad, while still the young men and girls entered, scented and sibilant in the half dark, their paired backs in silhouette delicate and sleek, their slim, quick bodies awkward, divinely young, while beyond them the silver dream accumulated, inevitably on and on. She began to laugh. In trying to suppress it, it made more noise than ever; heads began to turn. Still laughing, her friends raised her and led her out, and she stood at the curb, laughing on a high, sustained note, until the taxi came up and they helped her in.

They removed the pink voile and the sheer underthings and the stockings, and put her to bed, and cracked ice for her temples, and sent for the doctor. He was hard to locate, so they ministered to her with hushed ejaculations, renewing the ice and fanning her. While the ice was fresh and cold she stopped laughing and lay still for a time, moaning only a little. But soon the laughing welled again and her voice rose screaming.

"Shhhhhhhhhhhh! Shhhhhhhhhhhhhhh!" they said, freshening the icepack, smoothing her hair, examining it for gray; "poor girl!" Then to one another: "Do you suppose anything really happened?" their eyes darkly aglitter, secret and passionate. "Shhhhhhhhhh! Poor girl! Poor Minnie!"

v

It was midnight when McLendon drove up to his neat new house. It was trim and fresh as a birdcage and almost as small, with its clean, green-and-white paint. He locked the car and mounted the porch and entered. His wife rose from a chair beside the reading lamp. McLendon stopped in the floor and stared at her until she looked down.

"Look at that clock," he said, lifting his arm, pointing. She stood before him, her face lowered, a magazine in her hands. Her face was pale, strained, and weary-looking. "Haven't I told you about sitting up like this, waiting to see when I come in?"

"John," she said. She laid the magazine down. Poised on the balls of his feet, he glared at her with his hot eyes, his sweating face.

"Didn't I tell you?" He went toward her. She looked up then. He caught her shoulder. She stood passive, looking at him.

"Don't, John. I couldn't sleep . . . The heat; something. Please, John. You're hurting me."

"Didn't I tell you?" He released her and half struck, half flung her across the chair, and she lay there and watched him quietly as he left the room.

He went on through the house, ripping off his shirt, and on the dark, screened porch at the rear he stood and mopped his head and shoulders with the shirt and flung it away. He took the pistol from his hip and laid it on the table beside the bed, and sat on the bed and removed his shoes, and rose and slipped his trousers off. He was sweating again already, and he stooped and hunted furiously for the shirt. At last he found it and wiped his body again, and, with his body pressed against the dusty screen, he stood panting. There was no movement, no sound, not even an insect. The dark world seemed to lie stricken beneath the cold moon and the lidless stars.

CYCLISTS' RAID

By Frank Rooney

Joel Bleeker, owner and operator of the Pendleton Hotel, was adjusting the old redwood clock in the lobby when he heard the sound of motors. At first he thought it might be one of those four-engine planes on the flights from Los Angeles to San Francisco which occasionally got far enough off course to be heard in the valley. And for a moment, braced against the steadily approaching vibrations of the sound, he had the fantastic notion that the plane was going to strike the hotel. He even glanced at his daughter, Cathy, standing a few feet to his right and staring curiously at the street.

Then with his fingers still on the hour hand of the clock he realized that the sound was not something coming down from the air but the high, sputtering racket of many vehicles moving along the ground. Cathy and Bret Timmons, who owned one of the two drugstores in the town, went out onto the veranda but Bleeker stayed by the clock, consulting the railroad watch he pulled from his vest pocket and moving the hour hand on the clock forward a minute and a half. He stepped back deliberately, shut the glass case and looked at the huge brass numbers and the two ornate brass pointers. It was eight minutes after seven, approximately twenty-two minutes until sundown. He put the railroad watch back in his pocket and walked slowly and incuriously through the open doors of the lobby. He was methodical and orderly and the small things he did every day—like setting the clock—were important to him. He was not to be hurried—especially by something as elusively irritating as a sound, however unusual.

There were only three people on the veranda when Bleeker came out of the lobby—his daughter Cathy, Timmons, and Francis LaSalle, co-owner of LaSalle and Fleet, Hardware. They stood together quietly, looking, without appearing to stare, at a long stern column of red motorcycles coming from the south, filling the single main street of the town with the noise of a multitude of pistons and the crackling of exhaust pipes. They could see now that the column was led by a single white motorcycle which when it came abreast of the hotel turned abruptly right and stopped. They saw too that the column without seeming to slow down or to execute any elaborate movement had divided itself into two single files. At the approximate second, having received a signal from their leader, they also turned right and stopped.

The whole flanking action, singularly neat and quite like the various vehicular formations he remembered in the Army, was distasteful to Bleeker. It recalled a little too readily his tenure as a lieutenant colonel overseas in England, France, and finally Germany.

"Mr. Bleeker?"

Bleeker realized the whole troop—no one in the town either then or after that night was ever agreed on the exact number of men in the troop—had dismounted and that the leader was addressing him.

"I'm Bleeker." Although he hadn't intended to, he stepped forward when he spoke, much as he had stepped forward in the years when he commanded a battalion.

"I'm Gar Simpson and this is Troop B of the Angeleno Motorcycle Club," the leader said. He was a tall, spare man and his voice was coldly courteous to the point of mockery. "We expect to bivouac outside your town tonight and we wondered if we might use the facilities of your hotel. Of course, sir, we'll pay."

"There's a washroom downstairs. If you can put up with that—"

"That will be fine, sir. Is the dining room still open?"

"It is."

"Could you take care of twenty men?"

"What about the others?"

"They can be accommodated elsewhere, sir."

Simpson saluted casually and, turning to the men assembled stiffly in front of the hotel, issued a few quiet orders. Quickly and efficiently, the men in the troop parked their motorcycles at the curb. About a third of the group detached itself and came deferentially but steadily up the hotel steps. They passed Bleeker who found himself maneuvered aside and went into the lobby. As they passed him, Bleeker could see the town, and then leaned their heads together as if every individual thought had to be pooled and divided equally among them. He admitted, after some covert study, that the twenty men were really only variations of one, the variations, with few exceptions, being too subtle for him to recognize and differentiate. It was the goggles, he decided, covering that part of the face which is most noteworthy and most needful for identification—the eyes and the mask around the eyes.

Bleeker went into the kitchen, pretending to help but really to be near Cathy. The protective father, he thought ironically, watching his daughter cut pie and lay the various colored wedges on the white blue-bordered plates.

"Well, Daddy, what's the verdict?" Cathy looked extremely grave but he could see that she was amused.

"They're a fine body of men."

"Uh-huh. Have you called the police yet?"

He laughed. "It's a good thing you don't play poker."

Child's play." She slid the last piece of blueberry pie on a plate. "I saw you through the door. You looked like you were ready to crack the Siegfried line —single-handed."

"That man Simpson."

"What about him?"

Tragedy is the difference between what is and what might have been.
Alba Eban Danth

"Why don't you go upstairs and read a book or something?"

"Now, Daddy—you're the only professional here. They're just acting like little tin soldiers out on a spree."

"I wish to God they were made of tin."

"All right. I'll keep away from them. I promise." She made a gesture of crossing her throat with the thin edge of a knife. He leaned over and kissed her forehead, his hand feeling awkward and stern on her back.

After dinner the troop went into the bar, moving with a strange co-ordinated fluency that was both casual and military and sat jealously together in one corner of the room. Bleeker served them pitchers of beer and for the most part they talked quietly together, Simpson at their center, their voices guarded and urgent as if they possessed information which couldn't be disseminated safely among the public.

Bleeker left them after a while and went upstairs to his daughter's room. He wasn't used to being severe with Cathy and he was a little embarrassed by what he had said to her in the kitchen. She was turning the collars of some of his old shirts, using a portable sewing machine he had bought her as a present on her last birthday. As he came in she held one of the shirts comically to the floor lamp and he could see how thin and transparent the material was. Her mother's economy in small things, almost absurd when compared to her limitless generosity in matters of importance, had been one of the family jokes. It gave him an extraordinary sense of pleasure, so pure it was like a sudden inhalation of oxygen, to see that his daughter had not only inherited this tradition but had considered it meaningful enough to carry on. He went down the hall to his own room without saying anything further to her. Cathy was what he himself was in terms which could mean absolutely nothing to anyone else.

He had been in his room for perhaps an hour, working on the hotel accounts and thinking obliquely of the man Simpson, when he heard, faintly and apparently coming from no one direction, the sound of singing. He got up and walked to the windows overlooking the street. Standing there, he thought he could fix the sound farther up the block toward Cunningham's bar. Except for something harsh and mature in the voices it was the kind of singing that might be heard around a Boy Scout campfire, more rhythmic than melodic and more stirring than tuneful. And then he could hear it almost under his feet, coming out of the hotel lobby and making three or four people on the street turn and smile foolishly toward the doors of the veranda.

Oppressed by something sternly joyous in the voices, Bleeker went downstairs to the bar, hearing as he approached the singing become louder and fuller. Outside of Simpson and the twenty men in the troop there were only three townsmen—including LaSalle—in the bar. Simpson, seeing Bleeker in the door, got up and walked over to him, moving him out into the lobby where they could talk.

"I hope the boys aren't disturbing you," he said.

"It's early," Bleeker said.

"In an organization as large and selective as ours it's absolutely necessary to insist on a measure of discipline. And it's equally necessary to allow a certain amount of relaxation."

"The key word is selective, I suppose."

"We have our standards," Simpson said primly.

"May I ask just what the hell your standards are?"

Simpson smiled. "I don't quite understand your irritation, Mr. Bleeker."

"This is an all-year-round thing, isn't it? This club of yours?"

"Yes."

"And you have an all-year-round job with the club?"

"Of course."

"That's my objection, Simpson. Briefly and simply stated, what you're running is a private army." Bleeker tapped the case slung over Simpson's shoulder. "Complete with maps, all sorts of local information, and of course a lobby in Sacramento."

"For a man who has traveled as widely as you have, Mr. Bleeker, you display an uncommon talent for exaggeration."

"As long as you behave yourselves I don't care what you do. This is a small town and we don't have many means of entertainment. We go to bed at a decent hour and I suggest you take that into consideration. However, have your fun. Nobody here has any objection to that."

"And of course we spend our money."

"Yes," Bleeker said. "You spend your money."

He walked away from Simpson and went out onto the veranda. The singing was now both in front and in back of him. Bleeker stood for a moment on the top steps of the veranda looking at the moon, hung like a slightly soiled but luminous pennant in the sky. He was embarrassed by his outburst to Simpson and he couldn't think why he had said such things. Private army. Perhaps, as Simpson had said, he was exaggerating. He was a small-town man and he had always hated the way men surrendered their individuality to attain perfection as a unit. It had been necessary during the war but it wasn't necessary now. Kid stuff—with an element of growing pains.

He walked down the steps and went up the sidewalk toward Cunningham's bar. They were singing there too and he stood outside the big plate-glass window peering in at them and listening to the harsh, pounding voices colored here and there with the sentimentalism of strong beer. Without thinking further he went into the bar. It was dim and cool and alien to his eyes and at first he didn't notice the boy sitting by himself in a booth near the front. When he did, he was surprised—more than surprised, shocked—to see that the boy wasn't wearing his goggles but had placed them on the table by a bottle of Coca-Cola. Impulsively, he walked over to the booth and sat across from the boy.

"This seat taken?"

He had to shout over the noise of the singing. The boy leaned forward over the table and smiled.

"Hope we're not disturbing you."

Bleeker caught the word "disturbing" and shook his head negatively. He pointed to his mouth then to the boy and to the rest of the group. The boy too shook his head. Bleeker could see that he was young, possibly twenty-five, and that he had dark hair cut short and parted neatly at the side. The face was square but delicate, the nose short, the mouth wide. The best thing about the boy, Bleeker decided, were his eyes, brown perhaps or dark gray, set in two distorted ovals of white flesh which contrasted sharply with the heavily tanned skin on the cheeks, forehead and jaws. With his goggles on he would have looked like the rest. Without them he was a pleasant young man, altogether human and approachable.

Bleeker pointed to the Coca-Cola bottle. "You're not drinking."

"Beer makes me sick."

Bleeker got the word "beer" and the humorous gulping motion the boy made. They sat exchanging words and sometimes phrases, illustrated always with a series of clumsy, groping gestures until the singing became less coherent and spirited and ended finally in a few isolated coughs. The men in the troop were moving about individually now, some leaning over the bar and talking in hoarse whispers to the bartender, others walking unsteadily from group to group and detaching themselves immediately to go over to another group, the groups usually two or three men constantly edging away from themselves and colliding with and being held briefly by others. Some simply stood in the center of the room and brayed dolorously at the ceiling.

Several of the troop walked out of the bar and Bleeker could see them standing on the wide sidewalk looking up and down the street—as contemptuous of one another's company as they had been glad of it earlier. Or not so much contemptuous as unwilling to be coerced too easily by any authority outside themselves. Bleeker smiled as he thought of Simpson and the man's talk of discipline.

"They're looking for women," the boy said.

Bleeker had forgotten the boy temporarily and the sudden words spoken in a normal voice startled and confused him. He thought quickly of Cathy—but then Cathy was safe in her room—probably in bed. He took the watch from his vest pocket and looked at it carefully.

"Five minutes after ten," he said.

"Why do they do that?" the boy demanded. "Why do they have to be so damned indecent about things like that? They haven't got the nerve to do anything but stare at waitresses. And then they get a few beers in them and go around pinching and slapping—they—"

Bleeker shivered with embarrassment. He was looking directly into the boy's eyes and seeing the color run under the tears and the jerky pinching movement of the lids as against something injurious and baleful. It was an emotion too rawly infantile to be seen without being hurt by it and he felt both pity and contempt for a man who would allow himself to display such a feeling—without any provocation—so nakedly to a stranger.

"Sorry," the boy said.

He picked up the green goggles and fitted them awkwardly over his eyes. Bleeker stood up and looked toward the center of the room. Several of the men turned their eyes and then moved their heads away without seeming to notice the boy in the booth. Bleeker understood them. This was the one who could be approached. The reason for that was clear too. He didn't belong. Why and wherefore he would probably never know.

He walked out of the bar and started down the street toward the hotel. The night was clear and cool and smelled faintly of the desert, of sand, of heated rock, of the sweetly-sour plants growing without water and even of the sun which burned itself into the earth and never completely withdrew. There were only a few townsmen on the sidewalk wandering up and down, lured by the presence of something unusual in the town and masking, Bleeker thought, a ruthless and menacing curiosity behind a tolerant grin. He shrugged his shoulders distastefully. He was like a cat staring into a shadow the shape of its fears.

He was no more than a hundred feet from the hotel when he heard—or thought he heard—the sound of automatic firing. It was a well-remembered sound but always new and frightening.

Then he saw the motorcycle moving down the middle of the street, the exhaust sputtering loudly against the human resonance of laughter, catcalls, and epithets. He exhaled gently, the pain in his lungs subsiding with his breath. Another motorcycle speeded after the first and he could see four or five machines being wheeled out and the figures of their riders leaping into the air and bringing their weight down on the starting pedals. He was aware too that the lead motorcycles, having traversed the length of the street had turned and were speeding back to the hotel. He had the sensation of moving—even when he stood still— in relation to the objects heading toward each other. He heard the high unendurable sound of metal squeezing metal and saw the front wheel of a motorcycle twist and wobble and its rider roll along the asphalt toward the gutter where he sat up finally and moved his goggled head feebly from side to side.

As Bleeker looked around him he saw the third group of men which had divided earlier from the other two coming out of a bar across the street from Cunningham's, waving their arms in recognizable motions of cheering. The boy who had been thrown from the motorcycle vomited quietly into the gutter. Bleeker walked very fast toward the hotel. When he reached the top step of the veranda, he was caught and jostled by some five or six cyclists running out of the lobby, one of whom fell and was kicked rudely down the steps. Bleeker staggered against one of the pillars and broke a fingernail catching it. He stood there for a moment, fighting his temper, and then went into the lobby.

A table had been overthrown and lay on its top, the wooden legs stiffly and foolishly exposed, its magazines scattered around it, some with their pages spread face down so that the bindings rose along the back. He stepped on glass and realized one of the panes in the lobby door had been smashed. One of the troop walked stupidly out of the bar, his body sagging against the impetus propelling him forward until without actually falling he lay stretched on the floor, beer gushing from his mouth and nose and making a green and yellow pool before it sank into the carpet.

As Bleeker walked toward the bar, thinking of Simpson and of what he could say to him, he saw two men going up the stairs toward the second floor. He ran over to intercept them. Recognizing the authority in his voice, they came obediently down the stairs and walked across the lobby to the veranda, one of them saying over his shoulder, "Okay, pop, okay—keep your lid on." The smile they exchanged enraged him. After they were out of sight he ran swiftly up the stairs, panting a little, and along the hall to his daughter's room.

It was quiet and there was no strip of light beneath the door. He stood listening for a moment with his ear to the panels and then turned toward the stairs.

A man or boy, any of twenty or forty or sixty identical figures, goggled and in khaki, came around the corner of the second-floor corridor and put his hand on the knob of the door nearest the stairs. He squeezed the knob gently and then moved on to the next door, apparently unaware of Bleeker. Bleeker, remembering not to run or shout or knock the man down, walked over to him, took his arm and led him down the stairs, the arm unresisting, even flaccid, in his grip.

Bleeker stood indecisively at the foot of the stairs, watching the man walk automatically away from him. He thought he should go back upstairs and search the hall. And he thought too he had to reach Simpson. Over the noise of the motorcycles moving rapidly up and down the street he heard a crash in the bar, a series of drunken elongated curses, ending abruptly in a small sound like a man's hand laid flatly and sharply on a table.

His head was beginning to ache badly and his stomach to sour under the impact of a slow and steady anger. He walked into the bar and stood staring at Francis LaSalle—LaSalle and Fleet, Hardware—who lay sprawled on the floor, his shoulders touching the brass rail under the bar and his head turned so that his cheek rubbed the black polished wood above the rail. The bartender had his hands below the top of the bar and he was watching Simpson and a half dozen men arranged in a loose semi-circle above and beyond LaSalle.

Bleeker lifted LaSalle, who was a little dazed but not really hurt, and set him on a chair. After he was sure LaSalle was all right he walked up to Simpson.

"Get your men together," he said. "And get them out of here."

Simpson took out a long yellow wallet folded like a book and laid some money on the bar.

"That should take care of the damages," he said. His tongue was a little thick and his mouth didn't quite shut after the words were spoken but Bleeker didn't think he was drunk. Bleeker saw too—or thought he saw—the little cold eyes behind the glasses as bright and as sterile as a painted floor. Bleeker raised his arm slightly and lifted his heels off the floor but Simpson turned abruptly and walked away from him, the men in the troop swaying at his heels like a pack of lolling hounds. Bleeker stood looking foolishly after them. He had expected a fight and his body was still posed for one. He grunted heavily.

"Who hit him?" Bleeker motioned toward LaSalle.

"Damned if I know," the bartender said. "They all look alike to me."

That was true of course. He went into the lobby, hearing LaSalle say, weakly and tearfully, "Goddam them—the bastards." He met Campbell, the deputy sheriff, a tall man with the arms and shoulders of a child beneath a foggy, bloated face.

"Can you do anything?" Bleeker asked. The motorcycles were racing up and down the street, alternately whining and backfiring and one had jumped the curb and was cruising on the sidewalk.

"What do you want me to do?" Campbell demanded. "Put 'em all in jail?"

The motorcycle on the sidewalk speeded up and skidded obliquely into a plate-glass window, the front wheel bucking and climbing the brick base beneath the window. A single large section of glass slipped edge-down to the sidewalk and fell slowly toward the cyclist who, with his feet spread and kicking at the cement, backed clumsily away from it. Bleeker could feel the crash in his teeth.

Now there were other motorcycles on the sidewalk. One of them hit a parked car at the edge of the walk. The rider standing astride his machine beat the window out of the car with his gloved fists. Campbell started down the steps toward him but was driven back by a motorcycle coming from his left. Bleeker could hear the squeal of the tires against the wooden riser at the base of the steps. Campbell's hand was on his gun when Bleeker reached him.

"That's no good," he yelled. "Get the state police. Ask for half a dozen squad cars."

Campbell, angry but somewhat relieved, went up the steps and into the lobby. Bleeker couldn't know how long he stood on the veranda watching the mounting devastation on the streets—the cyclists racing past store windows and hurling, presumably, beer bottles at the glass fronts; the two, working as a team, knocking down weighing machines and signs in front of the motion picture theater; the innumerable mounted men running the angry townspeople, alerted and aroused by the awful sounds of damage to their property, back into their suddenly lighted homes again or up the stairs of his hotel or into niches along the main street, into doorways, and occasionally into the ledges and bays of glassless windows.

He saw Simpson—or rather a figure on the white motorcycle, helmeted and goggled—stationed calmly in the middle of the street under a hanging lamp. Presumably, he had been there for some time but Bleeker hadn't seen him, the many rapid movements on the street making any static object unimportant and even, in a sense, invisible. Bleeker saw him now and he felt again that spasm of anger which was like another life inside his body. He could have strangled Simpson then, slowly and with infinite pride. He knew without any effort of reason that Simpson was making no attempt to control his men but waiting rather for that moment when their minds, subdued but never actually helpless, would again take possession of their bodies.

Bleeker turned suddenly and went back into the lobby as if by that gesture of moving away he could pin his thoughts to Simpson, who, hereafter, would be responsible for them. He walked over to the desk where Timmons and Campbell, the deputy, were talking.

"You've got the authority," Timmons was saying angrily. "Fire over their heads. And if that doesn't stop them—"

Campbell looked uneasily at Bleeker. "Maybe if we could get their leader—"

"Did you get the police?" Bleeker asked.

"They're on their way," Campbell said. He avoided looking at Timmons and continued to stare hopefully and miserably at Bleeker.

"You've had your say," Timmons said abruptly. "Now I'll have mine."

He started for the lobby doors but Campbell, suddenly incensed, grabbed his arm.

"You leave this to me," he said. "You start firing a gun—"

Campbell's mouth dropped and Bleeker, turning his head, saw the two motorcycles coming through the lobby doors. They circled leisurely around for a moment and then one of them shot suddenly toward them, the goggled rider looming enormously above the wide handlebars. They scattered. Bleeker diving behind a pillar and Campbell and Timmons jumping behind the desk. The noise of the two machines assaulted them with as much effect as the sight of the speeding metal itself.

Bleeker didn't know why in the course of watching the two riders he looked into the hall toward the foot of the stairway. Nor did it seem at all unreasonable that when he looked he should see Cathy standing there. Deeply, underneath the outward preoccupation of his mind, he must have been thinking of her. Now there she was. She wore the familiar green robe, belted and pulled in at the waist and beneath its hem he could see the white slippers and the pink edge of her nightgown. Her hair was down and he had the impression her eyes were not quite open although, obviously, they were. She looked, he thought, as if she had waked, frowned at the clock, and come downstairs to scold him for staying up too late. He had no idea what time it was.

He saw—and of course Cathy saw—the motorcycle speeding toward her. He was aware that he screamed at her too. She did take a slight backward step and raise her arms in a pathetic warding gesture toward the inhuman figure on the motorcycle but neither could have changed—in that dwarfed period of time and in that short, unmaneuverable space—the course of their actions.

She lay finally across the lower steps, her body clinging to and equally arching away from the base of the newel post. And there was the sudden, shocking exposure of her flesh, the robe and the gown torn away from the leg as if pushed aside by the blood welling from her thigh. When he reached her there was blood in her hair too and someone—not Cathy—was screaming into his ears.

After a while the doctor came and Cathy, her head bandaged and her leg in splints, could be carried into his office and laid on the couch. Bleeker sat on the edge of the couch, his hand over Cathy's, watching the still white face whose eyes were closed and would not, he knew, open again. The doctor, after his first examination, had looked up quickly and since Bleeker too had been bent over Cathy, their heads had been very close together for a moment. The doctor had assumed, almost immediately, his expression of professional austerity but Bleeker had seen him in that moment when he had been thinking as a man, fortified of course by a doctor's knowledge, and Bleeker had known then that Cathy would die but that there would be also this interval of time.

Bleeker turned from watching Cathy and saw Timmons standing across the room. The man was—or had been—crying but his face wasn't set for it and the tears, points of colorless, sparkling water on his jaws, were unexpectedly delicate against the coarse texture of his skin. Timmons waved a bandaged hand awkwardly and Bleeker remembered, abruptly and jarringly, seeing Timmons diving for the motorcycle which had reversed itself, along with the other, and raced out of the lobby.

There was no sound now either from the street or the lobby. It was incredible, thinking of the racket a moment ago, that there should be this utter quietude, not only the lack of noise but the lack of the vibration of movement. The doctor came and went, coming to bend over Cathy and then going away again. Timmons stayed. Beyond shifting his feet occasionally he didn't move at all but stood patiently across the room, his face toward Cathy and Bleeker but not, Bleeker thought once when he looked up, actually seeing them.

"The police," Bleeker said sometime later.

"They're gone," Timmons said in a hoarse whisper. And then after a while, "They'll get 'em—don't worry."

Bleeker saw that the man blushed helplessly and looked away from him. The police were no good. They would catch Simpson. Simpson would pay damages. And that would be the end of it. Who could identify Cathy's assailant? Not himself, certainly—nor Timmons nor Campbell. They were all alike. They were standardized figures, seeking in each other a willful loss of identity, dividing themselves equally among one another until there was only a single mythical figure, unspeakably sterile and furnishing the norm of hundreds of others. He could not accuse something which didn't actually exist.

He wasn't sure of the exact moment when Cathy died. It might have been when he heard the motorcycle, unbelievably solitary in the quiet night, approaching the town. He knew only that the doctor came for the last time and that there was now a coarse, heavy blanket laid mercifully over Cathy. He stood looking down at the blanket for a moment, whatever he was feeling repressed and delayed inside him, and then went back to the lobby and out onto the veranda. There were a dozen men standing there looking up the street toward the sound of the motorcycle, steadily but slowly coming nearer. He saw that when they glanced at each other their faces were hard and angry but when they looked at him they were respectful and a little abashed.

Bleeker could see from the veranda a number of people moving among the smashed store-fronts, moving, stopping, bending over and then straightening up to move somewhere else, all dressed somewhat extemporaneously and therefore seeming without purpose. What they picked up they put down. What they put down they stared at grimly and then picked up again. They were like a dispossessed minority brutally but lawfully discriminated against. When the motorcycle appeared at the north end of the street they looked at it and then looked away again, dully and seemingly without resentment.

It was only after some moments that they looked up again, this time purposefully, and began to move slowly toward the hotel where the motorcycle had now stopped, the rider standing on the sidewalk, his face raised to the veranda.

No one on the veranda moved until Bleeker, after a visible effort, walked down the steps and stood facing the rider. It was the boy Bleeker had talked to in the bar. The goggles and helmet were hanging at his belt.

"I couldn't stand it any longer," the boy said. "I had to come back."

He looked at Bleeker as if he didn't dare look anywhere else. His face was adolescently shiny and damp, the marks, Bleeker thought, of a proud and articulate fear. He should have been heroic in his willingness to come back to the town after what had been done to it but to Bleeker he was only a dirty little boy returning to a back fence his friends had defaced with pornographic writing and calling attention to the fact that he was afraid to erase the writing but was determined nevertheless to do it. Bleeker was revolted. He hated the boy far more than he could have hated Simpson for bringing this to his attention when he did not want to think of anything or anyone but Cathy.

"I wasn't one of them," the boy said. "You remember, Mr. Bleeker. I wasn't drinking."

This declaration of innocence—this willingness to take blame for acts which he hadn't committed—enraged Bleeker.

"You were one of them," he said.

"Yes. But after tonight—"

"Why didn't you stop them?" Bleeker demanded loudly. He felt the murmur of the townspeople at his back and someone breathed harshly on his neck. "You were one of them. You could have done something. Why in God's name didn't you do it?"

"What could I do?" the boy said. He spread his hands and stepped back as if to appeal to the men beyond Bleeker.

Bleeker couldn't remember, either shortly after or much later, exactly what he did then. If the boy hadn't stepped back like that—if he hadn't raised his hand. . . . Bleeker was in the middle of a group of bodies and he was striking with his fists and being struck. And then he was kneeling on the sidewalk, holding the boy's head in his lap and trying to protect him from the heavy shoes of the men around him. He was crying out, protesting, exhorting, and after a time the men moved away from him and someone helped him carry the boy up the steps and lay him on the veranda. When he looked up finally only Timmons and the doctor were there. Up and down the street there were now only shadows and the diminishing sounds of invisible bodies. The night was still again as abruptly as it had been confounded with noise.

Some time later Timmons and the doctor carried the boy, alive but terribly hurt, into the hotel. Bleeker sat on the top step of the veranda, staring at the moon which had shifted in the sky and was now nearer the mountains in the west. It was not in any sense romantic or inflamed but coldly clear and sane. And the light it sent was cold and sane and lit in himself what he would have liked to hide.

He could have said that having lost Cathy he was not afraid any longer of losing himself. No one would blame him. Cathy's death was his excuse for striking the boy, hammering him to the sidewalk, and stamping on him as he had never believed he could have stamped on any living thing. No one would say he should have lost Cathy lightly—without anger and without that appalling desire to avenge her. It was utterly natural—as natural as a man drinking a few beers and riding a motorcycle insanely through a town like this. Bleeker shuddered. It might have been all right for a man like Timmons who was and would always be incapable of thinking what he—Joel Bleeker—was thinking. It was not—and would never be—all right for him.

Bleeker got up and stood for a moment on the top step of the veranda. He wanted, abruptly and madly, to scream his agony into the night with no more restraint than that of an animal seeing his guts beneath him on the ground. He wanted to smash something—anything—glass, wood, stone—his own body. He could feel his fists going into the boy's flesh. And there was that bloody but living thing on the sidewalk and himself stooping over to shield it.

After a while, aware that he was leaning against one of the wooden pillars supporting the porch and aware too that his flesh was numb from being pressed against it, he straightened up slowly and turned to go back into the hotel.

There would always be time to make his peace with the dead. There was little if any time to make his peace with the living.

ON THE MOVE

The blue jay scuffling in the bushes follows
Some hidden purpose, and the gust of birds
That spurts across the field, the wheeling swallows,
Have nested in the trees and undergrowth.
Seeking their instinct, or their poise, or both,
One moves with an uncertain violence
Under the dust thrown by a baffled sense
Or the dull thunder of approximate words.

On motorcycles, up the road, they come:
Small, black, as flies hanging in heat, the Boys,
Until the distance throws them forth, their hum
Bulges to thunder held by calf and thigh.
In goggles, donned impersonality,
In gleaming jackets trophied with the dust,
They strap in doubt—by hiding it, robust—
And almost hear a meaning in their noise.

Exact conclusion of their hardiness
Has no shape yet, but from known whereabouts
They ride, direction where the tires press.
They scare a flight of birds across the field:
Much that is natural, to the will must yield.
Men manufacture both machine and soul,
And use what they imperfectly control
To dare a future from the taken routes.

It is a part solution, after all.
One is not necessarily discord
On earth; or damned because, half animal,
One lacks direct instinct, because one wakes
Afloat on movement that divides and breaks.
One joins the movement in a valueless world,
Choosing it, till, both hurler and the hurled,
One moves as well, always toward, toward.

A minute holds them, who have come to go:
The self-defined, astride the created will
They burst away; the towns they travel through
Are home for neither bird nor holiness,
For birds and saints complete their purposes.
At worst, one is in motion; and at best,
Reaching no absolute, in which to rest,
One is always nearer by not keeping still.

—*Thom Gunn*

Reprinted by permission of Faber and Faber from Thom
Gunn, *The Sense of Movement* (London: Faber and Faber).

THE DESTRUCTORS

By Graham Greene

I

It was on the eve of August Bank Holiday that the latest recruit became the leader of the Wormsley Common Gang. No one was surprised except Mike, but Mike at the age of nine was surprised by everything. "If you don't shut your mouth," somebody once said to him, "you'll get a frog down it." After that Mike had kept his teeth tightly clamped except when the surprise was too great.

The new recruit had been with the gang since the beginning of the summer holidays, and there were possibilities about his brooding silence that all recognized. He never wasted a word even to tell his name until that was required of him by the rules. When he said "Trevor" it was a statement of fact, not as it would have been with the others a statement of shame or defiance. Nor did anyone laugh except Mike, who finding himself without support and meeting the dark gaze of the newcomer opened his mouth and was quiet again. There was every reason why T., as he was afterwards referred to, should have been an object of mockery—there was his name (and they substituted the initial because otherwise they had no excuse not to laugh at it), the fact that his father, a former architect and present clerk, had "come down in the world" and that his mother considered herself better than the neighbours. What but an odd quality of danger, of the unpredictable, established him in the gang without any ignoble ceremony of initiation?

The gang met every morning in an impromptu car-park, the site of the last bomb of the first blitz. The leader, who was known as Blackie, claimed to have heard it fall, and no one was precise enough in his dates to point out that he would have been one year old and fast asleep on the down platform of Wormsley Common Underground Station. On one side of the car-park leant the first occupied house, number 3, of the shattered Northwood Terrace—literally

Reprinted by permission of The Viking Press from Graham Greene, *21 Stories* (New York: The Viking Press, 1954). Also by permission of International Famous Agency.

leant, for it had suffered from the blast of the bomb and the side walls were supported on wooden struts. A smaller bomb and some incendiaries had fallen beyond, so that the house stuck up like a jagged tooth and carried on the further wall relics of its neighbour, a dado, the remains of a fireplace. T., whose words were almost confined to voting "Yes" or "No" to the plan of operations proposed each day by Blackie, once startled the whole gang by saying broodingly, "Wren built that house, father says."

"Who's Wren?"

"The man who built St. Paul's."

"Who cares?" Blackie said. "It's only old Misery's."

Old Misery—whose real name was Thomas—had once been a builder and decorator. He lived alone in the crippled house, doing for himself: once a week you could see him coming back across the common with bread and vegetables, and once as the boys played in the car-park he put his head over the smashed wall of his garden and looked at them.

"Been to the loo," one of the boys said, for it was common knowledge that since the bombs fell something had gone wrong with the pipes of the house and Old Misery was too mean to spend money on the property. He could do the re-decorating himself at cost price, but he had never learnt plumbing. The loo was a wooden shed at the bottom of the narrow garden with a star-shaped hole in the door: it had escaped the blast which had smashed the house next door and sucked out the window-frames of No. 3.

The next time the gang became aware of Mr. Thomas was more surprising. Blackie, Mike, and a thin yellow boy, who for some reason was called by his surname Summers, met him on the common coming back from the market. Mr. Thomas stopped them. He said glumly, "You belong to the lot that play in the car-park?"

Mike was about to answer when Blackie stopped him. As the leader he had responsibilities. "Suppose we are?" he said ambiguously.

"I got some chocolates," Mr. Thomas said. "Don't like 'em myself. Here you are. Not enough to go round, I don't suppose. There never is," he added with sombre conviction. He handed over three packets of Smarties.

The gang were puzzled and perturbed by this action and tried to explain it away. "Bet someone dropped them and he picked 'em up," somebody suggested.

"Pinched 'em and then got in a bleeding funk," another thought aloud.

"It's a bribe," Summers said. "He wants us to stop bouncing balls on his wall."

"We'll show him we don't take bribes," Blackie said, and they sacrificed the whole morning to the game of bouncing that only Mike was young enough to enjoy. There was no sign from Mr. Thomas.

Next day T. astonished them all. He was late at the rendezvous, and the voting for that day's exploit took place without him. At Blackie's suggestion the gang was to disperse in pairs, take buses at random, and see how many free rides could be snatched from unwary conductors (the operation was to be carried out in pairs to avoid cheating). They were drawing lots for their companions when T. arrived.

"Where you been, T.?" Blackie asked. "You can't vote now. You know the rules."

"I've been *there*," T. said. He looked at the ground, as though he had thoughts to hide.

"Where?"

"At Old Misery's." Mike's mouth opened and then hurriedly closed again with a click. He had remembered the frog.

"At Old Misery's?" Blackie said. There was nothing in the rules against it, but he had a sensation that T. was treading on dangerous ground. He asked hopefully, "Did you break in?"

"No. I rang the bell."

"And what did you say?"

"I said I wanted to see his house."

"What did he do?"

"He showed it me."

"Pinch anything?"

"No."

"What did you do it for then?"

The gang had gathered round: it was as though an impromptu court were about to form and to try some case of deviation. T. said, "It's a beautiful house," and still watching the ground, meeting no one's eyes, he licked his lips first one way, then the other.

"What do you mean, a beautiful house?" Blackie asked with scorn.

"It's got a staircase two hundred years old like a corkscrew. Nothing holds it up."

"What do you mean, nothing holds it up. Does it float?"

"It's to do with opposite forces, Old Misery said."

"What else?"

"There's panelling."

"Like in the Blue Boar?"

"Two hundred years old."

"Is Old Misery two hundred years old?"

Mike laughed suddenly and then was quiet again. The meeting was in a serious mood. For the first time since T. had strolled into the car-park on the first day of the holidays his position was in danger. It only needed a single use of his real name and the gang would be at his heels.

"What did you do it for?" Blackie asked. He was just, he had no jealousy, he was anxious to retain T. in the gang if he could. It was the word "beautiful" that worried him—that belonged to a class world that you could still see parodied at the Wormsley Common Empire by a man wearing a top hat and a monocle, with a haw-haw accent. He was tempted to say, "My dear Trevor, old chap," and unleash his hell hounds. "If you'd broken in," he said sadly—that indeed would have been an exploit worthy of the gang.

"This was better," T. said. "I found out things." He continued to stare at his feet, not meeting anybody's eye, as though he were absorbed in some dream he was unwilling—or ashamed—to share.

"What things?"

"Old Misery's going to be away all tomorrow and Bank Holiday."

Blackie said with relief, "You mean we could break in?"

"And pinch things?" somebody asked.

Blackie said, "Nobody's going to pinch things. Breaking in—that's good enough, isn't it? We don't want any court stuff."

"I don't want to pinch anything," T. said. "I've got a better idea."

"What is it?"

T. raised eyes, as grey and disturbed as the drab August day. "We'll pull it down," he said. "We'll destroy it."

Blackie gave a single hoot of laughter and then, like Mike, fell quiet, daunted by the serious implacable gaze. "What'd the police be doing all the time?" he said.

"They'd never know. We'd do it from inside. I've found a way in." He said with a sort of intensity, "We'd be like worms, don't you see, in an apple. When we came out again there'd be nothing there, no staircase, no panels, nothing but just walls, and then we'd make the walls fall down—somehow."

"We'd go to jug," Blackie said.

"Who's to prove? And anyway we wouldn't have pinched anything." He added without the smallest flicker of glee, "There wouldn't be anything to pinch after we'd finished."

"I've never heard of going to prison for breaking things," Summers said.

"There wouldn't be time," Blackie said. "I've seen housebreakers at work."

"There are twelve of us," T. said. "We'd organize."

"None of us know how—"

"I know," T. said. He looked across at Blackie, "Have you got a better plan?"

"Today," Mike said tactlessly, "we're pinching free rides—"

"Free rides," T. said. "You can stand down, Blackie, if you'd rather. . . ."

"The gang's got to vote."

"Put it up then."

Blackie said uneasily, "It's proposed that tomorrow and Monday we destroy Old Misery's house."

"Here, here," said a fat boy called Joe.

"Who's in favour?"

T. said, "It's carried."

"How do we start?" Summers asked.

"He'll tell you," Blackie said. It was the end of his leadership. He went away to the back of the car-park and began to kick a stone, dribbling it this way and that. There was only one old Morris in the park, for few cars were left there except lorries: without an attendant there was no safety. He took a flying kick at the car and scraped a little paint off the rear mudguard. Beyond, paying no more attention to him than to a stranger, the gang had gathered round T.; Blackie was dimly aware of the fickleness of favour. He thought of going home, of never returning, of letting them all discover the hollowness of T.'s leadership, but suppose after all what T. proposed was possible—nothing like it had ever been done before. The fame of the Wormsley Common car-park gang would surely reach around London. There would be headlines in the papers. Even the grown-up gangs who ran the betting at the all-in wrestling and the barrow-boys would hear with respect of how Old Misery's house had been destroyed. Driven by the pure, simple, and altruistic ambition of fame for the gang, Blackie came back to where T. stood in the shadow of Misery's wall.

T. was giving his orders with decision: it was as though this plan had been with him all his life, pondered through the seasons, now in his fifteenth year crystallized with the pain of puberty. "You," he said to Mike, "bring some big nails, the biggest you can find, and a hammer. Anyone else who can better bring a hammer and a screwdriver. We'll need plenty of them. Chisels too. We can't have too many chisels. Can anybody bring a saw?"

"I can," Mike said.

"Not a child's saw," T. said. "A real saw."

Blackie realized he had raised his hand like any ordinary member of the gang.

"Right, you bring one, Blackie. But now there's a difficulty. We want a hacksaw."

"What's a hacksaw?" someone asked.

"You can get 'em at Woolworth's," Summers said.

The fat boy called Joe said gloomily, "I knew it would end in a collection."

"I'll get one myself," T. said. "I don't want your money. But I can't buy a sledge-hammer."

Blackie said, "They are working on number fifteen. I know where they'll leave their stuff for Bank Holiday."

"Then that's all," T. said. "We meet here at nine sharp."

"I've got to go to church," Mike said.

"Come over the wall and whistle. We'll let you in."

II

On Sunday morning all were punctual except Blackie, even Mike. Mike had had a stroke of luck. His mother felt ill, his father was tired after Saturday night, and he was told to go to church alone with many warnings of what would happen if he strayed. Blackie had had difficulty in smuggling out the saw, and then in finding the sledge-hammer at the back of number 15. He approached the house from a lane at the rear of the garden, for fear of the policeman's beat along the main road. The tired evergreens kept off a stormy sun: another wet Bank Holiday was being prepared over the Atlantic, beginning in swirls of dust under the trees. Blackie climbed the wall into Misery's garden.

There was no sign of anybody anywhere. The loo stood like a tomb in a neglected graveyard. The curtains were drawn. The house slept. Blackie lumbered nearer with the saw and the sledge-hammer. Perhaps after all nobody had turned up: the plan had been a wild invention: they had woken wiser. But when he came close to the back door he could hear a confusion of sound, hardly louder than a hive in swarm: a clickety-clack, a bang bang bang, a scraping, a creaking, a sudden painful crack. He thought, It's true, and whistled.

They opened the back door to him and he came in. He had at once the impression of organization, very different from the old happy-go-lucky ways under his leadership. For a while he wandered up and down stairs looking for T. Nobody addressed him: he had a sense of great urgency, and already he could begin to see the plan. The interior of the house was being carefully demolished without touching the outer walls. Summers with hammer and chisel was ripping out the skirting-boards in the ground floor dining-room: he had already smashed the panels of the door. In the same room Joe was heaving up the parquet blocks, exposing the soft wood floor-boards over the cellar. Coils of wire came out of the damaged skirting and Mike sat happily on the floor, clipping the wires.

On the curved stairs two of the gang were working hard with an inadequate child's saw on the banisters—when they saw Blackie's big saw they signalled for it wordlessly. When he next saw them a quarter of the banisters had been dropped into the hall. He found T. at last in the bathroom—he sat moodily in the least cared-for room in the house, listening to the sounds coming up from below.

"You've really done it," Blackie said with awe. "What's going to happen?"

"We've only just begun," T. said. He looked at the sledge-hammer and gave his instructions. "You stay here and break the bath and the wash-basin. Don't bother about the pipes. They come later."

Mike appeared at the door. "I've finished the wire, T.," he said.

"Good. You've just got to go wandering round now. The kitchen's in the basement. Smash all the china and glass and bottles you can lay hold of. Don't turn on the taps—we don't want a flood—yet. Then go into all the rooms and turn out drawers. If they are locked get one of the others to break them open. Tear up any papers you find and smash all the ornaments. Better take a carving-knife with you from the kitchen. The bedroom's opposite here. Open the pillows and tear up the sheets. That's enough for the moment. And you, Blackie, when you've finished in here crack the plaster in the passage up with your sledge-hammer."

"What are you going to do?" Blackie asked.

"I'm looking for something special," T. said.

It was nearly lunch-time before Blackie had finished and went in search of T. Chaos had advanced. The kitchen was a shambles of broken glass and china. The dining-room was stripped of parquet, the skirting was up, the door had been taken off its hinges, and the destroyers had moved up a floor. Streaks of light came in through the closed shutters where they worked with the seriousness of creators—and destruction after all is a form of creation. A kind of imagination had seen this house as it had now become.

Mike said, "I've got to go home for dinner."

"Who else?" T. asked, but all the others on one excuse or another had brought provisions with them.

They squatted in the ruins of the room and swapped unwanted sandwiches. Half an hour for lunch and they were at work again. By the time Mike returned, they were on the top floor, and by six the superficial damage was completed. The doors were all off, all the skirtings raised, the furniture pillaged and ripped and smashed—no one could have slept in the house except on a bed of broken plaster. T. gave his orders—eight o'clock next morning—and to escape notice they climbed singly over the garden wall, into the car-park. Only Blackie and T. were left; the light had nearly gone, and when they touched a switch, nothing worked—Mike had done his job thoroughly.

"Did you find anything special?" Blackie asked.

T. nodded. "Come over here," he said, "and look." Out of both pockets he drew bundles of pound notes. "Old Misery's savings," he said. "Mike ripped out the mattress, but he missed them."

"What are you going to do? Share them?"

"We aren't thieves," T. said. "Nobody's going to steal anything from this house. I kept these for you and me—a celebration." He knelt down on the floor and counted them out—there were seventy in all. "We'll burn them," he said, "one by one," and taking it in turns they held a note upwards and lit the top corner, so that the flame burnt slowly towards their fingers. The grey ash floated above them and fell on their heads like age. "I'd like to see Old Misery's face when we are through," T. said.

"You hate him a lot?" Blackie asked.

"Of course I don't hate him," T. said. "There'd be no fun if I hated him." The last burning note illuminated his brooding face. "All this hate and love," he said, "it's soft, it's hooey. There's only things, Blackie," and he looked round the room crowded with the unfamiliar shadows of half things, broken things, former things. "I'll race you home, Blackie," he said.

III

Next morning the serious destruction started. Two were missing—Mike and another boy whose parents were off to Southend and Brighton in spite of the slow warm drops that had begun to fall and the rumble of thunder in the estuary like the first guns of the old blitz. "We've got to hurry," T. said.

Summers was restive. "Haven't we done enough?" he said. "I've been given a bob for slot machines. This is like work."

"We've hardly started," T. said. "Why, there's all the floors left, and the stairs. We haven't taken out a single window. You voted like the others. We are going to *destroy* this house. There won't be anything left when we've finished."

They began again on the first floor picking up the top floor-boards next the outer wall, leaving the joists exposed. Then they sawed through the joists and retreated into the hall, as what was left of the floor heeled and sank. They had learnt with practise, and the second floor collapsed more easily. By the evening an odd exhilaration seized them as they looked down the great hollow of the house. They ran risks and made mistakes: when they thought of the windows it was too late to reach them. "Cor," Joe said, and dropped a penny down into the dry rubble-filled well. It cracked and span among the broken glass.

"Why did we start this?" Summers asked with astonishment; T. was already on the ground, digging at the rubble, clearing a space along the outer wall. "Turn on the taps," he said. "It's too dark for anyone to see now, and in the morning it won't matter." The water overtook them on the stairs and fell through the floorless rooms.

It was then they heard Mike's whistle at the back. "Something's wrong," Blackie said. They could hear his urgent breathing as they unlocked the door.

"The bogies?" Summers asked.

"Old Misery," Mike said. "He's on his way." He put his head between his knees and retched. "Ran all the way," he said with pride.

"But why?" T. said. "He told me . . ." He protested with the fury of the child he had never been, "It isn't fair."

"He was down at Southend," Mike said, "and he was on the train coming back. Said it was too cold and wet." He paused and gazed at the water. "My, you've had a storm here. Is the roof leaking?"

"How long will he be?"

"Five minutes. I gave Ma the slip and ran."

"We better clear," Summers said. "We've done enough, anyway."

"Oh, no, we haven't. Anybody could do this—" "this" was the shattered hollowed house with nothing left but the walls. Yet walls could be preserved. Façades were valuable. They could build inside again more beautifully than before. This could again be a home. He said angrily, "We've got to finish. Don't move. Let me think."

"There's no time," a boy said.

"There's got to be a way," T. said. "We couldn't have got thus far . . ."

"We've done a lot," Blackie said.

"No. No, we haven't. Somebody watch the front."

"We can't do any more."

"He may come in at the back."

"Watch the back too." T. began to plead. "Just give me a minute and I'll fix it. I swear I'll fix it." But his authority had gone with his ambiguity. He was only one of the gang. "Please," he said.

"Please," Summers mimicked him, and then suddenly struck home with the fatal name. "Run along home, Trevor."

T. stood with him back to the rubble like a boxer knocked groggy against the ropes. He had no words as his dreams shook and slid. Then Blackie acted before the gang had time to laugh, pushing Summers backward. "I'll watch the front, T.," he said, and cautiously he opened the shutters of the hall. The grey wet common stretched ahead, and the lamps gleamed in the puddles. "Someone's coming, T. No, it's not him. What's your plan, T.?"

"Tell Mike to go out to the loo and hide close beside it. When he hears me whistle he's got to count ten and start to shout."

"Shout what?"

"Oh, 'Help,' anything."

"You hear, Mike," Blackie said. He was the leader again. He took a quick look between the shutters. "He's coming, T."

"Quick, Mike. The loo. Stay here, Blackie, all of you till I yell."

"Where are you going, T.?"

"Don't worry. I'll see to this. I said I would, didn't I?"

Old Misery came limping off the common. He had mud on his shoes and he stopped to scrape them on the pavement's edge. He didn't want to soil his house, which stood jagged and dark between the bomb-sites, saved so narrowly, as he believed, from destruction. Even the fanlight had been left unbroken by the bomb's blast. Somewhere somebody whistled. Old Misery looked sharply round. He didn't trust whistles. A child was shouting: it seemed to come from his own garden. Then a boy ran into the road from the car-park. "Mr. Thomas," he called, "Mr. Thomas."

"What is it?"

"I'm, terribly sorry, Mr. Thomas. One of us got taken short, and we thought you wouldn't mind, and now he can't get out."

"What do you mean, boy?"

"He's got stuck in your loo."

"He'd no business—Haven't I seen you before?"

"You showed me your house."

"So I did. So I did. That doesn't give you the right to—"

"Do hurry, Mr. Thomas. He'll suffocate."

"Nonsense. He can't suffocate. Wait till I put my bag in."

"I'll carry your bag."

"Oh, no, you don't. I carry my own."

"This way, Mr. Thomas."

"I can't get in the garden that way. I've got to go through the house."

"But you *can* get in the garden this way, Mr. Thomas. We often do."

"You often do?" He followed the boy with a scandalized fascination. "When? What right . . ."

"Do you see . . . ? The wall's low."

"I'm not going to climb walls into my own garden. It's absurd."

"This is how we do it. One foot here, one foot there, and over." The boy's face peered down, an arm shot out, and Mr. Thomas found his bag taken and deposited on the other side of the wall.

"Give me back my bag," Mr. Thomas said. From the loo a boy yelled and yelled. "I'll call the police."

"Your bag's all right, Mr. Thomas. Look. One foot there. On your right. Now just above. To your left." Mr. Thomas climbed over his own garden wall. "Here's your bag, Mr. Thomas."

"I'll have the wall built up," Mr. Thomas said, "I'll not have you boys coming over here, using my loo." He stumbled on the path, but the boy caught his elbow and supported him. "Thank you, thank you, my boy," he murmured automatically. Somebody shouted again through the dark. "I'm coming, I'm coming," Mr. Thomas called. He said to the boy beside him, "I'm not unreasonable. Been a boy myself. As long as things are done regular. I don't mind you playing round the place Saturday mornings. Sometimes I like company. Only it's got to be regular. One of you asks leave and I say Yes. Sometimes I'll say No. Won't feel like it. And you come in at the front door and out at the back. No garden walls."

"Do get him out, Mr. Thomas."

"He won't come to any harm in my loo," Mr. Thomas said, stumbling slowly down the garden. "Oh, my rheumatics," he said. "Always get 'em on Bank Holiday. I've got to go careful. There's loose stones here. Give me your hand. Do you know what my horoscope said yesterday? 'Abstain from any dealings in first half of week. Danger of serious crash.' That might be on this path," Mr. Thomas said. "They speak in parables and double meanings." He paused at the door of the loo. "What's the matter in there?" he called. There was no reply.

"Perhaps he's fainted," the boy said.

"Not in my loo. Here, you, come out," Mr. Thomas said, and giving a great jerk at the door he nearly fell on his back when it swung easily open. A hand first supported him and then pushed him hard. His head hit the opposite wall and he sat heavily down. His bag hit his feet. A hand whipped the key out of the lock and the door slammed. "Let me out," he called, and heard the key turn in the lock. "A serious crash," he thought, and felt dithery and confused and old.

A voice spoke to him softly through the star-shaped hole in the door. "Don't worry, Mr. Thomas," it said, "we won't hurt you, not if you stay quiet."

Mr. Thomas put his head between his hands and pondered. He had noticed that there was only one lorry in the car-park, and he felt certain that the driver would not come for it before the morning. Nobody could hear him from the road in front, and the lane at the back was seldom used. Anyone who passed there would be hurrying home and would not pause for what they would certainly take to be drunken cries. And if he did call "Help," who, on a lonely Bank Holiday evening, would have the courage to investigate? Mr. Thomas sat on the loo and pondered with the wisdom of age.

After a while it seemed to him that there were sounds in the silence—they were faint and came from the direction of his house. He stood up and peered through the ventilation-hole—between the cracks in one of the shutters he saw a light, not the light of a lamp, but the wavering light that a candle might give. Then he thought he heard the sound of hammering and scraping and chipping. He thought of burglars—perhaps they had employed the boy as a scout, but why should burglars engage in what sounded more and more like a stealthy form of carpentry? Mr. Thomas let out an experimental yell, but nobody answered. The noise could not even have reached his enemies.

IV

Mike had gone home to bed, but the rest stayed. The question of leadership no longer concerned the gang. With nails, chisels, screwdrivers, anything that was sharp and penetrating they moved around the inner walls worrying at the mortar between the bricks. They started too high, and it was Blackie who hit on the damp course and realized the work could be halved if they weakened the joints immediately above. It was a long, tiring, unamusing job, but at last it was finished. The gutted house stood there balanced on a few inches of mortar between the damp course and the bricks.

There remained the most dangerous task of all, out in the open at the edge of the bomb-site. Summers was sent to watch the road for passers-by, and Mr. Thomas, sitting on the loo, heard clearly now the sound of sawing. It no longer came from his house, and that a little reassured him. He felt less concerned. Perhaps the other noises too had no significance.

A voice spoke to him through the hole. "Mr. Thomas."

"Let me go," Mr. Thomas said sternly.

"Here's a blanket," the voice said, and a long grey sausage was worked through the hole and fell in swathes over Mr. Thomas's head.

"There's nothing personal," the voice said. "We want you to be comfortable tonight."

"Tonight," Mr. Thomas repeated incredulously.

"Catch," the voice said. "Penny buns—we've buttered them, and sausage-rolls. We don't want you to starve, Mr. Thomas."

Mr. Thomas pleaded desperately. "A joke's a joke, boy. Let me out and I won't say a thing. I've got rheumatics. I got to sleep comfortable."

"You wouldn't be comfortable, not in your house, you wouldn't. Not now."

"What do you mean, boy?" but the footsteps receded. There was only the silence of night: no sound of sawing. Mr. Thomas tried one more yell, but he was daunted and rebuked by the silence—a long way off an owl hooted and made away again on its muffled flight through the soundless world.

At seven next morning the driver came to fetch his lorry. He climbed into the seat and tried to start the engine. He was vaguely aware of a voice shouting, but it didn't concern him. At last the engine responded and he backed the lorry until it touched the great wooden shore that supported Mr. Thomas's house. That way he could drive right out and down the street without reversing. The lorry moved forward, was momentarily checked as though something were pulling it from behind, and then went on to the sound of a long rumbling crash. The driver was astonished to see bricks bouncing ahead of him, while stones hit the roof of his cab. He put on his brakes. When he climbed out the whole landscape had suddenly altered. There was no house beside the car-park, only a hill of rubble. He went round and examined the back of his car for damage, and found a rope tied there that was still twisted at the other end round part of a wooden strut.

The driver again became aware of somebody shouting. It came from the wooden erection which was the nearest thing to a house in that desolation of broken brick. The driver climbed the smashed wall and unlocked the door. Mr. Thomas came out of the loo. He was wearing a grey blanket to which flakes of pastry adhered. He gave a sobbing cry. "My house," he said. "Where's my house?"

"Search me," the driver said. His eye lit on the remains of a bath and what had once been a dresser and he began to laugh. There wasn't anything left anywhere.

"How dare you laugh," Mr. Thomas said. "It was my house. My house."

"I'm sorry," the driver said, making heroic efforts, but when he remembered the sudden check to his lorry, the crash of bricks falling, he became convulsed again. One moment the house had stood there with such dignity between the bomb-sites like a man in a top hat, and then, bang, crash, there wasn't anything left—not anything. He said, "I'm sorry. I can't help it, Mr. Thomas. There's nothing personal, but you got to admit it's funny."

MY HATE

My hate is like ripe fruit
from an orchard, which is mine.

I sink my teeth into it.
I nurse on its odd shapes.

I have grafted every new variety,
walked in my bare feet,

rotting and detached,
on the fallen ones.

Vicious circle. Unfriendly act.
I am eating the whole world.

In the caves of my ill will
I must be stopped.

—Marvin Bell

HOW TO HATE... IN ONE EASY LESSON

By Leo Rosten

When I was a sophomore at college, during the War of Jenkin's Ear, I spent many a happy afternoon shooting pool in the common room with a classmate of whom I was fond. He was a tall, pale, freckled redhead who talked a blue streak. His humor was delightful, his ebullience a tonic, and we beguiled each other with adolescent drolleries. Once, I asked him what his father did for a living. He chalked his cue, then sighed, "He's a bishop."

I brought my friend to lunch at my fraternity house one day. He was as garrulous and amusing as ever, but my exalted brothers acted rather miffed. That night, the Pooh-Bah of the lodge took me aside. "Please don't bring your friend to lunch here again. It isn't that we're prejudiced. We just don't want Negro guests."

"Negro," I gulped. "You must be out of your mind. Why, his skin is fairer than yours!"

"He's a Negro," said the Great Stone Face. "His father happens to be a well-known bishop, black as the ace of spades. We all think you ought to spend less time with your friend—and more with us."

After careful thought, I followed his advice—but reversed the equation: I spent more time with the son of the bishop and less with the sons of the bigots to whom I had pledged my troth. But don't jump to conclusions. I was *not* acting nobly or with any lump-in-the throat commitment to the brotherhood of man. I simply found the redhead too *interesting* to drop, and a far more amusing companion than anyone at the fraternity. I made my choice for entirely selfish reasons.

You see, I believe in discriminating (if not discrimination). I have practiced discriminating all my life. I discriminate against ignoramuses, phonies, bores, boors, swine, bigots and liars. I plead guilty to harboring the most violent prejudices—against people who blow their nose at the table, for instance, or yak loudly on airplanes, or call me by my first name upon being introduced.

It is because I believe in discrimi-

Reprinted by permission of Leo Rosten and *Look* magazine, December 14, 1965.

> The price of hating other human beings is loving oneself less.
> *Eldridge Cleaver*

nating that I pity those who don't. They don't gain the rewards of selectivity because they make no distinction between one Catholic or Protestant or Jew (or Mormon or doorman or foreman) and another. The prejudiced man practices the rankest form of nondiscrimination: He hates people he hasn't even met yet. This is the worst possible way of hating—especially when there are so many sound, 100-percent-American reasons for hating, as you shall see.

The bigot is the pawn of his own fears. He has to prop up a shaky ego by blind asseverations of his own superiority. He thinks he makes more of himself by making less of others.

I dislike bigots because I dislike fools who try to reason or intelligent people who rationalize. I also prefer scoundrels to sadists, musicians to Mau Mau types and psychoanalysts to psychopaths.

As for hate—well, I hate rabble-rousers, regardless of race, color, party or creed. I hate anyone who hates others enough to want to harm, harass or kill them. I believe in honest hate, based on sound evidence and reached after careful thought. The bigot, alas, proceeds on false or flimsy evidence. He is incapable of listening, much less reasoning, much less changing.

Worse than the bigot, in God's eye, is the fanatic. Bigots are often peaceful churchgoers who sing a nifty psalm; fanatics don't have that much sense of humor. Bigots are despicable, but fanatics are dangerous. A bigot's mind is shut—but so, mercifully, may be his mouth. A fanatic can't shut up. Bigotry is a disease of the soul; fanaticism is lunacy with a program. Scratch a bigot, and you uncover fear; scratch a fanatic, and you uncover rage.

I admit that I am not a top-notch, expert hater because I am a sissy about violence, even in feeling I compromise my principles by only *wishing* that certain people would drop dead. Nikita Khrushchev, for instance. I detested him as an ignorant, dangerous lout even during his gaudy hadj to Iowa's cornfields, when the American press, acting like schoolgirls, made him out to be a cute and cuddly Slavic uncle. Or Mao Tse-tung. I wish he would drop dead, too, because he is able, closed-minded and cold-blooded. I would cheer a coronary on Fidel Castro, who is a liar, a sincere demagogue and a paranoiac. I would gladly send flowers to any psychiatric ward that incarcerated George Lincoln Rockwell. I could, if pressed, extend this list to the length of Wilt Chamberlain's arm.

But hatred palls, except on the paranoid; let discrimination possess us instead. You have an absolute right to choose whom you want to associate with, or have in your home or go bowling with. But you cannot defend discrimination in public places or in tax-supported institutions. Discrimination is a matter of private privilege, not public policy.

I hold no grudge against those who don't want me in their clubs. Most private clubs are dandy places for the kind of people I don't like to spend time with. I loathe locker-room vulgarity and "socials" where camaraderie is expressed by getting drunk and making a pass at someone else's wife. My friend Groucho Marx reduced snobbery to a nutshell by resigning from a country club in these words: "I do not wish to belong to the kind of club that accepts people like me as members."

I once served on a committee that rated candidates for a certain job. We were going through a long list when the name of John B——— came up. "Not him," I groaned. "He's stupid."

After the session, a woman came up to me with blazing eyes. "You," she quivered, ". . . prejudiced! You ought to be ashamed of yourself!"

"Oh, I am," I replied. "But why now?"

"John B———!" she exploded. "How could you talk that way about a Negro?!"

"Oh, dear," I cursed. (In moments of stress I enlist steamy Victorian epithets.) "I had forgotten he's a Negro. I was judging him as a man. . . . He *is* stupid. He would be stupid if he were white—or red or yellow or as green as you look this moment."

Here is a story about race prejudice I cherish. It is true. Shortly after the war ended, Mr. Jones dropped in on his neighbor, Mr. Smith, in Beverly Hills. (Both names are fictional, to protect the guilty.) "I

know that you love living in this community," said Mr. Jones, "and that you're as proud of it as all of us are. I'm circulating this petition, I'm sure you'll be happy to sign it. It's an agreement on the part of the residents not to sell property to any except Caucasians."

Mr. Smith thought for a moment. "What about Will Rogers? He was one of the best-loved men we ever had here, our mayor. He was part Cherokee, part *Mongolian*."

Jones laughed. "I'm not talking about people like Will *Rogers!* . . . Frankly, how would you like a Negro living next door?"

"Which one?" asked Smith.

Jones blinked. "I don't get you."

"Which Negro?" Smith repeated. "It would have to be *someone*. A doctor? Lawyer? Musician? Frankly, I'd prefer any of them to the neighbors I now have. They drink—"

Mr. Smith! Once a Negro gets into a nice, all-white community, property prices go to hell!"

"No, property prices generally *rise* in a nice neighborhood that opens up to Negroes."

"But *in the long run* property values go to hell!" Jones insisted. "You would lose a lot of money!"

"How much?" asked Smith.

"I beg your pardon?"

How much would I lose?"

"If Negroes begin buying into Beverly Hills," said Jones, "you could lose between 20 and 25 thousand dollars!"

161

The white workingman is against open housing, against school busing, against hippies, yippies and draft dodgers. He's against letting blacks into unions and China into the United Nations. *Peter Binzen*

Smith considered this. "It isn't enough."

"*What?*"

"It's not enough. You see, I shave every morning. And when I shave, I look in the mirror. So I would have to look at myself every day for the rest of my life and say, 'You sold out your principles for 25 thousand dollars.'"

Jones got up angrily.

"Wait," said Smith. "I'm a reasonable man. Let's make a deal. Any man can be bought, if the sum is high enough. I'm willing to be bribed. I'll sign your petition—for, say, a million dollars. Do I alarm you? Okay, half a million. You see, I could find a way of salving my conscience. I would contribute a hundred thousand, say, to a worthy cause; that would still leave me a lot of money. Why don't you go to your friends, those who favor this petition, and buy me out? Just pay me half a million for my house. But 25 thousand? No, Mr. Jones.

Don't put so *small* a price on my conscience."

White-faced, Jones left.

The next morning, he phoned Smith. "I didn't sleep very well last night. I kept thinking about some of the things you told me. You mixed me up. I'm not sure you're right, but I don't seem able to answer the points you raised. So I've stopped circulating that petition. My name's still on it, because I'm not sure—but because I'm not sure, I'm not going to try to persuade others I'm right. Good-bye."

Voltaire said: "Prejudice is the reason of fools." Some wit called prejudice "an opinion that holds a man"; another dubbed it "the divine right of fools." But the best comment was Mark Twain's: "I'm quite sure . . . I have no race prejudices. . . . All I care to know is that a man is a human being—that is enough for me; he can't be any worse."

THE IMAGINARY JEW

By John Berryman

The second summer of the European war I spent in New York. I lived in a room just below street level on Lexington above Thirty-fourth, wrote a good deal, tried not to think about Europe, and listened to music on a small gramophone, the only thing of my own, except books, in the room. Haydn's London Symphony, his last, I heard probably fifty times in two months. One night when excited I dropped the pickup, creating a series of knocks at the beginning of the last movement where the oboe joins the strings which still, when I hear them, bring up for me my low dark long damp room and I feel the dew of heat and smell the rented upholstery. I was trying, as one says, to come back a little, uncertain and low after an exhausting year. Why I decided to do this in New York—the enemy in summer equally of soul and body, as I had known for years—I can't remember; perhaps I didn't, but we held on merely from week to week by the motive which presently appeared in the form of a young woman met the Christmas before and now the occupation of every evening not passed in solitary and restless gloom. My friends were away; I saw few other people. Now and then I went to the zoo in lower Central Park and watched with interest the extraordinary behavior of a female badger. For a certain time she quickly paced the round of her cage. Then she would approach the side wall from an angle in a determined, hardly perceptible, unhurried trot; suddenly, when an inch away, point her nose up it, follow her nose up over her back, turning a deft and easy somersault, from which she emerged on her feet moving swiftly and unconcernedly away, as if the action had been no affair of hers, indeed she had scarcely been present. There was another badger in the cage who never did this, and nothing else about her was remarkable; but this competent disinterested somersault she enacted once every five or ten minutes as long as I watched her—quitting the wall, by the way, always at an angle in fixed relation to the angle at which she arrived at it. It is no longer possible to experience the pleasure I knew each time she lifted

Reprinted by permission of John Berryman from *The Kenyon Review*, Autumn, 1945.

her nose and I understood again that she would not fail me, or feel the mystery of her absolute disclaimer—she has been taken away or died.

The story I have to tell is no further a part of that special summer than a nightmare takes its character, for memory, from the phase of the moon one noticed on going to bed. It could have happened in another year and in another place. No doubt it did, has done, will do. Still, so weak is the talent of the mind for pure relation—immaculate apprehension of *p* alone—that everything helps us, as when we come to an unknown city: architecture, history, trade practices, folklore. Even more anxious our approach to a city—like my small story—which we have known and forgotten. Yet how little we can learn! Some of the history is the lonely summer. Part of the folklore, I suppose, is which I now unwillingly rehearse, the character which experience has given to my sense of the Jewish people.

Born in a part of the South where no Jews had come, or none had stayed, and educated thereafter in states where they are not numerous, I somehow arrived at a metropolitan university without any clear idea of what in modern life a Jew was—without even a clear consciousness of having seen one. I am unable now to explain this simplicity or blindness. I had not escaped, of course, a sense that humans somewhat different from ourselves, called "Jews," existed as in the middle distance and were best kept there, but this sense was of the vaguest. From what it was derived I do not know; I do not recall feeling the least curiosity about it, or about Jews; I had, simply, from the atmosphere of an advanced heterogeneous democratic society, ingathered a gently negative attitude toward Jews. This I took with me, untested, to college, where it received neither confirmation nor stimulus for two months. I rowed and danced and cut classes and was political; by mid-November I knew most of the five hundred men in my year. Then the man who rowed Number Three, in the eight of which I was bow, took me aside in the shower one afternoon and warned me not to be so chatty with Rosenblum.

I wondered why not. Rosenblum was stroke, a large handsome amiable fellow, for whose ability in the shell I felt great respect and no doubt envy. Because the fellows in the house wouldn't like it, my friend said. "What have they against him?" "It's only because he's Jewish," explained my friend, a second-generation Middle European.

I hooted at him, making the current noises of disbelief, and went back under the shower. It did not occur to me that he could be right. But next day when I was talking with Herz, the coxswain, whom I knew very well, I remembered the label with some annoyance, and told Herz about it as a curiosity. Herz looked at me oddly, lowering his head, and said after a pause, "Why Al *is* Jewish, didn't you know that?" I was amazed. I said it was absurd, he couldn't be! "Why not?" said Herz, who must have been as astonished as I was. "Don't you know I'm Jewish?"

I did not know, of course, and ignorance has seldom cost me such humiliation. Herz did not guy me; he went off. But greater than my shame at not knowing something known, apparently, without effort to everyone else, were my emotions for what I then quickly discovered. Asking careful questions during the next week, I learned that about a third of the men I spent time with in college were Jewish, that they knew it, and the others knew it; that some of the others disliked them for it, and they knew this also; that certain houses existed *only* for Jews,

There is a natural prejudice that prompts men to despise whoever has been their inferior long after he has become their equal. *Alexis de Tocqueville*

who were excluded from the rest; and that what in short I took to be an idiotic state was deeply established, familiar, and acceptable to everyone. This discovery was the beginning of my instruction in social life proper—construing social life as that from which political life issues like a somatic dream.

My attitude toward my friends did not alter on this revelation. I merely discarded the notion that Jews were a proper object for any special attitude; my old sense vanished. This was in 1933. Later, as word of the German persecution filtered into this country, some sentimentality undoubtedly corrupted my no-attitude. I denied the presence of obvious defects in particular Jews, feeling that to admit them would be to side with the sadists and murderers. Accident allotting me close friends who were Jewish, their disadvantages enraged me. Gradually, and against my sense of impartial justice, I became the anomaly which only a partial society can produce, and for which it has no name known to the lexicons. In one area, not exclusively, "nigger-lover" is flung in a proximate way; but for a special sympathy and liking for Jews—which became my fate, so that I trembled when I heard one abused in talk—we have no term. In this condition I still was during the summer of which I speak. One further circumstance may be mentioned, as a product, I believe, of this curious training. I am spectacularly unable to identify Jews as Jews—by name, cast of feature, accent, or environment—and this has been true, not only of course before the college incident, but during my whole life since. Even names to anyone else patently Hebraic rarely suggest to me anything. And when once I learn that So-and-so is Jewish, I am likely to forget it. Now Jewishness—the religion or the race—may be a fact as striking and informative as someone's past heroism or his Christianity or his understanding of the subtlest human relations, and I feel sure that something operates to prevent my utilizing the plain signs by which such characters—in a Jewish man or woman—my be identified, and prevent my retaining the identification once it is made.

So to the city my summer and a night in August. I used to stop on Fourteenth Street for iced coffee, walking from the Village home (or to my room rather) after leaving my friend, and one night when I came out I wandered across to the island of trees and grass and concrete walks raised in the center of Union Square. Here men—a few women, old—sit in the evenings of summer, looking at papers or staring off or talking, and knots of them stay on, arguing, very late; these the unemployed or unemployable, the sleepless, the malcontent. There are no formal orators, as at Columbus Circle in the nineteen-thrities and at Hyde Park Corner. Each group is dominated by several articulate and strong-lunged persons who battle each other with prejudices and desires, swaying with intensity, and take on from time to time the interrupters: a forum at the bottom of the pot—Jefferson's fear, Whitman's hope, the dream of the younger Lenin. It was now about one o'clock, almost hot, and many men were still out. I stared for a little at the equestrian statue, obscure in the night on top of its pedestal, thinking that misty Rider would sweep away again all these men at his feet, whenever he liked—what symbol for power yet in a mechanical age rivals the mounted man?—and moved to the nearest group; or I plunged to it.

The dictator to the group was old, with dark cracked skin, fixed eyes in an excited face, leaning forward madly on his bench toward the half-dozen men in semicircle before him. "It's bread! It's bread!" he was saying. "It's bittersweet. All the bitter and all the sweetness. Of an overture. What else do you want? When you ask for steak and potatoes, do you want pastry with it? It's bread! It's bread! Help yourself! Help yourself!"

The listeners stood expressionless, except one who was smiling with contempt and interrupted now.

"Never a happy minute, never a happy minute!" the old man cried. "It's good to be dead! Some men should kill themselves."

"Don't you want to live?" said the smiling man.

"Of course I want to live. Everyone wants to live! If death comes suddenly, it's better. It's better!"

With pain I turned away. The next group were talking diffusely and angrily about the mayor, and I passed to a third, where a frantic olive-skinned young man with a fringe of silky beard was exclaiming:

"No restaurant in New York has the Last Supper! No. When people sit down to eat they should think of that!"

"Listen," said a white-shirted student on the rail, glancing around for

---

There are more things to admire in man than to despise.   *Albert Camus*

---

approbation, "Listen, if I open a restaurant and put *The Last Supper* up over the door, how much money do you think I'd lose? Ten thousand dollars?"

The fourth cluster was larger and appeared more coherent. A savage argument was in progress between a man of fifty with an oily red face, hatted, very determined in manner, and a muscular fellow half his age with heavy eyebrows, coatless, plainly Irish. Fifteen or twenty men were packed around them, and others on a bench near the rail against which the Irishman was lounging were attending also. I listened for a few minutes. The question was whether the President was trying to get us into the war—or rather, whether this was legitimate, since the Irishman claimed that Roosevelt was a goddamned warmonger whom all the real people in the country hated, and the older man claimed that we should have gone into the f—ing war when France fell a year before, as everybody in the country knew except a few immigrant rats. Redface talked ten times as much as the Irishman, but he was not able to establish any advantage that I could see. He ranted, and then Irish either repeated shortly and fiercely what he had said last, or shifted his ground. The audience were silent—favoring whom I don't know, but evidently much interested. One or two men pushed out of the group, others arrived behind me, and I was eddied forward toward the disputants. The young Irishman broke suddenly into a tirade by the man with the hat:

"You're full of s—. Roosevelt even tried to get us in with the communists in the Spanish war. If he could have done it we'd have been burning churches down like the rest of the Reds."

"No, that's not right," I heard my own voice, and pushed forward, feeling blood in my face, beginning to tremble. "No, Roosevelt, as a matter of fact, helped Franco by non-intervention, at the same time that Italians and German planes were fighting against the Government and arms couldn't get in from France."

"What's that? What are you, a Jew?" He turned to me contemptuously, and was back at the older man before I could speak. "The only reason we weren't over there four years ago is because you can only screw us so much. Then we quit. No New Deal bastard could make us go help the goddamned communists."

"That ain't the question, it's if we want to fight *now* or *later*. Them Nazis ain't gonna sit!" shouted the red-faced man. "They got Egypt practically, and then it's India if it ain't England first. It ain't a question of the communists, the communists are on Hitler's side. I tellya we can wait and wait and chew and spit and the first thing you know they'll be in England, and then who's gonna help us when they start after us? Maybe Brazil? Get wise to the world! Spain don't matter now one way or the other, they ain't gonna help and they can't hurt. It's Germany and Italy and Japan, and if it ain't too late now it's gonna be. Get wise to yourself. We shoulda gone in—"

"What with?" said the Irishman with disdain. "Pop, pop. Wooden machine guns?"

"We were as ready a year ago as we are now. Defense don't mean nothing, you gotta have to fight!"

"No, we're much better off now," I said, "than we were a year ago. When England went in, to keep its word to Poland, what good was it to Poland? The German Army—"

"Shut up, you Jew," said the Irishman.

"I'm not a Jew," I said to him. "What makes—"

"Listen, Pop," he said to the man in the hat, "it's O.K. to shoot your mouth off, but what the hell have you got to do with it? You aren't gonna do any fighting."

"Listen," I said.

"You sit on your big ass and talk about who's gonna fight who. Nobody's gonna fight anybody. If we feel hot, we ought to clean up some of the sons of bitches here before we go sticking our nuts anywhere to help England. We ought to clean up the sons of bitches in Wall Street and Washington before we take any ocean trips. You want to know something? You know why Germany's winning everything in this war? Because there ain't no Jews back home. There ain't no more Jews, first shouting war like this one here"—nodding at me— "and then skinning off to the synagogue with the profits. Wake up, Pop! You must have been around in the last war, you ought to know better."

I was too nervous to be angry or resentful. But I began to have a sense of oppression in breathing. I took the Irishman by the arm.

"Listen, I told you I'm not a Jew."

"I don't give a damn what you are." He turned his half-dark eyes to me, wrenching his arm loose. "You talk like a Jew."

"What does that mean?" Some part of me wanted to laugh. "How does a Jew talk?"

"They talk like you, buddy."

"That's a fine argument! But if I'm not a Jew, my talk only—"

"You probably are a Jew. You look like a Jew."

"I *look* like a Jew? Listen"—I swung around eagerly to a man standing next to me—"do I look like a Jew? It doesn't matter whether I do or not—a Jew is as good as anybody and better than this son of a bitch." I was not exactly excited, I was trying to adapt my language as my need for the crowd, and sudden respect for its judgment possessed me. "But in fact I'm not Jewish and I don't look Jewish. Do I?"

The man looked at me quickly and said, half to me and half to the Irishman, "Hell, I don't know. Sure he does."

A wave of disappointment and outrage swept me almost to tears. I felt like a man betrayed by his brother. The lamps seemed brighter and vaguer, the night large. Glancing 'round, I saw sitting on a bench near me a tall, heavy, serious-looking man of thirty, well dressed, whom I had noticed earlier, and appealed to him, "Tell me, do I look Jewish?"

But he only stared up and waved his head vaguely. I saw with horror that something was wrong with him.

"You look like a Jew. You talk like a Jew. You *are* a Jew," I heard the Irishman say.

I heard murmuring among the men, but I could see nothing very clearly. It seemed very hot. I faced the Irishman again helplessly, holding my voice from rising.

"I'm *not* a Jew," I told him. "I might be, but I'm not. You have no bloody reason to think so, and you can't make me a Jew by simply repeating like an idiot that I am."

"Don't deny it, son," said the red-faced man, "stand up to him."

"God damn it"—suddenly I was furious, whirling like a fool (was I afraid of the Irishman? had he conquered me?) on the red-faced man—"I'm *not* denying it! Or rather I am, but only because I'm not a Jew! I despise renegades, I hate Jews who turn on their people, if I were a Jew I would say so, I would be proud to be. What is the vicious opinion of a man like this to me if I were a Jew? But I'm not. Why the hell should I admit I am if I'm not?"

"Jesus, the Jew is excited," said the Irishman.

"I have a right to be excited, you son of a bitch. Suppose I call you a Jew. Yes, you're a Jew. Does that mean anything?"

"Not a damn thing." He spat over the rail past a man's head.

"Prove that you're not. I say you are."

"Now listen, you Jew. I'm a Catholic."

"So am I, or I was born one, I'm not one now. I was born a Catholic." I was a little calmer but goaded, obsessed with the need to straighten this out. I felt that everything for everyone there depended on my proving him wrong. If *once* this evil for which we have not even a name could be exposed to the rest of the men as empty—if I could *prove* I was not a Jew—it would fall to the ground, neither would anyone else be a Jew to be accused. Then it could be trampled on. Fascist America was at stake. I listened, intensely anxious for our fate.

"Yeah?" said the Irishman. "Say the Apostles' Creed."

Memory went swirling back. I could hear the little bell die as I hushed it and set it on the felt. Father Boniface looked at me tall from the top of the steps and smiled, greeting me in the darkness before dawn as I came to serve, the men pressed around me under the lamps, and I could remember nothing but *visibilium omnium, et invisibilium.*

"I don't remember it."

The Irishman laughed with his certainty.

The papers in my pocket; I thought them over hurriedly. In my wallet. What would they prove? Details of ritual, Church history: anyone could learn them. My piece of Irish blood. Shame, shame: shame for my ruthless people. I will not be his blood. I wish I were a Jew, I would change my blood, to be able to say *Yes* and defy him.

"I'm not a Jew." I felt a fool. "You only say so. You haven't any evidence in the world."

He leaned forward from the rail, close to me. "Are you cut?"

Shock, fear ran through me before I could make any meaning out of his words. Then they ran faster, and I felt confused.

From that point nothing is clear for me. I stayed a long time—it seemed impossible to leave, showing him victor to them—thinking of possible allies and new plans of proof, but without hope. I was tired to the marrow. The arguments rushed on, and I spoke often now but seldom was heeded except by an old fat woman, very short and dirty, who listened intently to everyone. Heavier and heavier appeared to me to press upon us in the fading night our general guilt.

In the days following, as my resentment died, I saw that I had not been a victim altogether unjustly. My persecutors were right: I was a Jew. The imaginary Jew I was was as real as the imaginary Jew hunted down, on other nights and days, in a real Jew. Every murderer strikes the mirror, the lash of the torturer falls on the mirror and cuts the real image, and the real and the imaginary blood flow down together.

MUSÉE DES BEAUX ARTS

About suffering they were never wrong,
The Old Masters: how well they understood
Its human position; how it takes place
While someone else is eating or opening a window or
    just walking dully along;
How, when the aged are reverently, passionately
    waiting
For the miraculous birth, there always must be
Children who did not specially want it to happen,
    skating
On a pond at the edge of the wood:
They never forgot
That even the dreadful martyrdom must run its
    course
Anyhow in a corner, some untidy spot
Where the dogs go on with their doggy life and the
    torturer's horse
Scratches its innocent behind on a tree.

In Brueghel's *Icarus*,* for instance: how everything
    turns away
Quite leisurely from the disaster; the plowman may
Have heard the splash, the forsaken cry,
But for him it was not an important failure; the sun
    shone
As it had to on the white legs disappearing into the
    green
Water; and the expensive delicate ship that must
    have seen
Something amazing, a boy falling out of the sky,
Had somewhere to get to and sailed calmly on.

—*W. H. Auden*

*In Greek mythology, son of Daedalus. He flew with his
father from Crete; but the sun melted the wax with which
his wings were fastened on, and he fell into the sea, hence
called the Icarian.

What a man believes may be ascertained not from his creed. But from the assumption on which he habitually acts.   *George Bernard Shaw*

The Fall of Icarus: Pieter Brueghel.

ONLY THE DEAD KNOW BROOKLYN

By Thomas Wolfe

Dere's no guy livin' dat knows Brooklyn t'roo an' t'roo, because it'd take a guy a lifetime just to find his way aroun' duh f——town.

So like I say, I'm waitin' for my train t' come when I sees dis big guy standin' deh—dis is duh foist I eveh see of him. Well, he's lookin' wild, y'know, an' I can see dat he's had plenty, but still he's holdin' it; he talks good an' is walkin' straight enough. So den, dis big guy steps up to a little guy dat's standin' deh, an' says, "How d'yuh get t' Eighteent' Avenoo an' Sixty-sevent' Street?" he says.

"Jesus! Yuh got me, chief," duh little guy says to him. "I ain't been heah long myself. Where is duh place?" he says. "Out in duh Flatbush section somewhere?"

"Nah," duh big guy says. "It's out in Bensonhoist. But I was neveh deh befoeh. How d'yuh get deh?"

"Jesus," duh little guy says, scratchin' his head, y'know—yuh could see duh little guy didn't know his way about—"yuh got me, chief. I neveh hoid of it. Do any of youse guys know where it is?" he says to me.

"Sure," I says. "It's out in Bensonhoist. Yuh take duh Fourt' Avenoo express, get off at Fifty-nint' Street, change to a Sea Beach local deh, get off at Eighteent' Avenoo an' Sixty-toid, an' den walk down foeh blocks. Dat's all yuh got to do," I says.

"G'wan!" some wise guys dat I neveh seen befoeh pipes up. "Whatcha talkin' about?" he says—oh, he was wise, y'know. "Duh guy is crazy! I tell yuh what yuh do," he says to duh big guy. "Yuh change to duh West End line at Toity-sixt'," he tells him. "Get off at Noo Utrecht an' Sixteen't Avenoo," he says. "Walk two blocks oveh, foeh blocks up," he says, "an' you'll be right deh." Oh, a *wise* guy, y'know.

"Oh, yeah?" I says. "Who told *you* so much?" He got me sore because he was so wise about it. "How long you been livin' heah?" I says.

Reprinted by permission of Charles Scribner's Sons from Thomas Wolfe, *From Death to Morning* (New York: Charles Scribner's Sons, 1963).

"All my life," he says. "I was bawn in Williamsboig," he says. "An I can tell you t'ings about dis town you neveh hoid of," he says.

"Yeah?" I says.

"Yeah," he says.

"Well, den, you can tell me t'ings about dis town dat nobody else has eveh hoid of, either. Maybe you make it all up yoehself at night," I says, "befoeh you go to sleep—like cuttin' out papeh dolls, or somp'n."

"Oh, yeah?" he says. "You're pretty wise, ain't yuh?"

"Oh, I don't know," I says. "Duh boids ain't usin' my head for Lincoln's statue yet," I says. "But I'm wise enough to know a phony when I see one."

"Yeah?" he says. "A wise guy, huh? Well, you're so wise dat someone's goin' t'bust yuh one right on duh snoot some day," he says. "Dat's how wise *you* are."

Well, my train was comin', or I'da smacked him den and dere, but when I seen duh train was comin', all I said was, "All right, mugg! I'm sorry I can't stay to take keh of you, but I'll be seein' yuh sometime, I hope, out in duh cemetery." So den I says to duh big guy, who'd been standin' deh all duh time, "You come wit me," I says. So when we gets onto duh train I says to him, "Where yuh goin' out in Bensonhoist?" I says. "What numbeh are yuh lookin' for?" I says. *You* know—I t'ought if he told me duh address I might be able to help him out.

"Oh," he says. "I'm not lookin' for no one. I don't know no one out deh."

"Then whatcha goin' out deh for?" I says.

"Oh," duh guy says, "I'm just goin' out to see duh place," he says. "I like duh sound of duh name—Bensonhoist, y'know—so I t'ought I'd go out an' have a look at it."

"Whatcha tryin t'hand me?" I says. "Whatcha tryin t'do—kid me?" *You* know, I t'ought duh guy was bein' wise wit me.

"No," he says, "I'm tellin' yuh duh troot. I like to go out an' take a look at places wit nice names like dat. I like to go out an' look at all kinds of places," he says.

"How'd yuh know deh was such a place," I says, "if yuh neveh been deh befoeh?"

"Oh," he says, "I got a map."

"A *map*?" I says.

"Sure," he says, "I got a map dat tells me about all dese places. I take it wit me every time I come out heah," he says.

And Jesus! Wit dat, he pulls it out of his pocket, an' so help me, but he's *got* it—he's tellin' duh troot—a big map of duh whole f——place with all duh different paths mahked out. You know—Canarsie an' East Noo Yawk an' Flatbush, Bensohnhoist, Sout' Brooklyn, duh Heights, Bay Ridge, Greenpernt—duh whole goddam layout, he's got it right deh on duh map.

"You been to any of dose places?" I says.

"Sure," he says, "I been to most of 'em. I was down in Red Hook just last night," he says.

"Jesus! Red Hook!" I says. "Whatcha do down deh?"

"Oh," he says, "nuttin much. I just walked aroun'. I went into a coupla places an' had a drink," he says, "but most of the time I just walked aroun'."

Just walked aroun'?" I says.

"Sure," he says, "just lookin' at t'ings, y'know."

"Where'd yuh go?" I asts him.

"Oh," he says, "I don't know duh name of duh place, but I could find it on my map," he says. "One time I was walkin' across some big fields where deh ain't no houses," he says, "but I could see ships oveh deh all lighted up. Dey was loadin'. So I walks across duh fields," he says, "to where duh ships are."

"Sure," I says, "I know where you was. You was down to duh Erie Basin."

"Yeah," he says, "I gues dat was it. Dey had some of dose big elevators an' cranes an' dey was loadin' ships, an' I could see some ships in drydock all lighted up, so I walks across duh fields to where dey are," he says.

"Den what did yuh do?" I says.

"Oh," he says, "nuttin much. I came on back across duh fields after a while an' went into a coupla places an' had a drink."

"Didn't nuttin' happen while yuh was in dere?" I says.

"No," he says. "Nuttin' much. A coupla guys was drunk in one of duh places an' started a fight, but dey bounced 'em out," he says, "an' den one of duh guys stahted to come back again, but duh bartender gets his baseball bat out from under duh counteh, so duh guy goes on."

174

"Jesus!" I said. "Red Hook!"

"Sure," he says. "Dat's where it was, all right."

"Well, you keep outa deh," I says. "You stay away from deh."

"Why?" he says. "What's wrong wit it?"

"Oh," I says, "It's a good place to stay away from, dat's all. It's a good place to keep out of."

"Why?" he says. "Why is it?"

Jesus! Whatcha gonna do wit a guy as dumb as dat? I saw it wasn't no use to try to tell him nuttin', he wouldn't know what I was talking' about, so I just says to him, "Oh, nuttin'. Yuh might get lost down deh, dat's all."

"Lost?" he says. "No, I wouldn't get lost. I got a map," he says.

A map! Red Hook! Jesus.

So den duh guy begins to ast me all kinds of nutty questions: how big was Brooklyn an' could I find my way aroun' in it, an' how long would it take a guy to know duh place.

"Listen!" I says. "You get dat idea outa yoeh head right now," I says. "You ain't neveh gonna get to know Brooklyn," I says. "Not in a hunderd yeahs. I been livin' heah all my life," I says, "an' I don't even know all deh is to know about it, so how do you expect to know duh town," I says, "when you don't even live heah?"

"Yes," he says, "but I got a map to help me find my way about."

"Map or no map," I says, "yuh ain't gonna get to know Brooklyn wit no map," I says.

"Can you swim?" he says, just like dat. Jesus! By dat time, y'know, I begun to see dat duh guy was some kind of nut. He'd had plenty to drink, of course, but he had dat crazy look in his eye I didn't like. "Can you swim?" he says.

"Sure," I says. "Can't you?"

"No," he says. "Not more'n a stroke or two. I neveh loined good."

"Well, it's easy," I says. "All yuh need is a little confidence. Duh way I loined, me older bruddeh pitched me off duh dock one day when I was eight yeahs old, cloes an' all. 'You'll swim,' he says. 'You'll swim all right—or drown.'

An' believe me, I *swam!* When yuh know yuh got to, you'll do it. Duh only t'ing yuh need is confidence. An' once you've loined," I says, "you've got nuttin' else to worry about. You'll neveh forget it. It's somp'n dat stays wit yuh as long as yuh live."

"Can yuh swim good?" he says.

"Like a fish," I tells him. "I'm a regulah fish in duh wateh," I says. "I loined to swim right off duh docks wit all duh oddeh kids," I says.

"What would you do if yuh saw a man drownin'?" duh guy says.

"Do? Why, I'd jump in an' pull him out," I says. "Dat's what I'd do."

"Did yuh eveh see a man drown?" he says.

"Sure," I says. "I see two guys—bot' times at Coney Island. Dey got out too far, an' neider one could swim. Dey drowned befoeh anyone could get to 'em."

"What becomes of people after dey've drowned out heah?" he says.

"Drowned out where?" I says.

"Out heah in Brooklyn."

"I don't know whatcha mean," I says. "Neveh hoid of no one drownin' heah in Brooklyn, unless you mean a swimmin' pool. Yuh can't drown in Brooklyn," I says. "Yuh gotta drown somewhere else—in duh ocean, where dere's wateh."

"Drownin'," duh guy says, lookin' at his map. "Drownin'," Jesus! I could see by den he was some kind of nut, he had dat crazy expression in his eyes when he looked at you, an' I didn't know what he might do. So we was comin' to a station, an' it wasn't my stop, but I got off anyway, an' waited for duh next train.

"Well, so long, chief," I says. "Take it easy, now."

"Drownin'," duh guy says, lookin' at his map. "Drownin'."

Jesus! I've t'ought about day guy a t'ousand times since den an' wondered what eveh happened to 'm goin' out to look at Bensonhoist because he liked duh name! Walkin' aroun' t'roo Red Hook by himself at night an' lookin' at his map! How many people did I see get drowned out heah in Brooklyn! How long would it take a guy wit a good map to know all deh was to know about Brooklyn!

Jesus! What a nut *he* was! I wondeh what eveh happened to 'im, anyway! I wondeh if someone knocked him on duh head, or if he's still wanderin' aroun' in duh subway in duh middle of duh night wit his little map! Duh poor guy! Say, I've got to laugh, at dat, when I t'ink about him! Maybe he's found out by now dat he'll neveh live long enough to know duh whole of Brooklyn. It'd take a guy a lifetime to know Brooklyn t'roo an' t'roo. An' even den, yuh wouldn't know it all.

Among the oddest of men is that man who has deep feeling, and a deep desire to communicate it and cannot do so, either because he will not try to, or he cannot. These are the strange people of the world. They vary from the slightly odd to the assassin. They are all urked, emotionally.

Charles McCabe

THE HOLLOW MEN

A penny for the Old Guy

I

We are the hollow men
We are the stuffed men
Leaning together
Headpiece filled with straw. Alas!
Our dried voices, when
We whisper together
Are quiet and meaningless
As wind in dry grass
Or rat's feet over broken glass
In our dry cellar

Shape without form, shade without color,
Paralyzed force, gesture without motion;

Those who have crossed
With direct eyes, to death's other Kingdom
Remember us—if at all—not as lost
Violent souls, but only
As the hollow men
The stuffed men.

II

Eyes I dare not meet in dreams
In death's dream kingdom
These do not appear:
There, the eyes are

Reprinted by permission of Faber and Faber from T. S. Eliot, *Collected Poems 1909–1962* (London: Faber and Faber). Also by permission of Harcourt, Brace and World, New York.

Sunlight on a broken column
There, is a tree swinging
And voices are
In the wind's singing
More distant and more solemn
Than a fading star.

Let me be no nearer
In death's dream kingdom
Let me also wear
Such deliberate disguises
Rat's skin, crowskin, crossed staves
In a field
Behaving as the wind behaves
No nearer—
Not that final meeting
In the twilight kingdom

III

This is the dead land
This is cactus land
Here the stone images
Are raised, here they receive
The supplication of a dead man's hand
Under the twinkle of a fading star.
Is it like this
In death's other kingdom

Waking alone
At the hour when we are
Trembling with tenderness
Lips that would kiss
Form prayers to broken stone.

IV

The eyes are not here
There are no eyes here
In this valley of dying stars
In this hollow valley
This broken jaw of our lost kingdoms
In this last of meeting places
We grope together
And avoid speech
Gathered on this beach of the tumid river
Sightless, unless
The eyes reappear
As the perpetual star
Multifoliate rose
Of death's twilight kingdom
The hope only
Of empty men.

V

Here we go round the prickly pear
Prickly pear prickly pear
Here we go round the prickly pear
At five o'clock in the morning.
Between the idea
And the reality

Between the motion
And the act
Falls the Shadow

For Thine is the Kingdom

Between the conception
And the creation
Between the emotion
And the response
Falls the Shadow

Life is very long

Between the desire
And the spasm
Between the potency
And the existence
Between the essence
And the descent
Falls the Shadow

For Thine is the Kingdom

For Thine is
Life is
For Thine is the

This is the way the world ends
This is the way the world ends
This is the way the world ends
Not with a bang but a whimper.

—T. S. Eliot

LONELINESS

POVERTY

INJUSTICE

LINES TO CROSS

Now the trumpet summons us again—
not as a call to bear arms, though arms
we need; not as a call to battle, though
embattled we are; but a call to bear the
burden of a long twilight struggle, year in
and year out, "rejoicing in hope, patient
in tribulation," a struggle against the
common enemies of man: tyranny,
poverty, disease and war itself.
John Fitzgerald Kennedy

Not to care—for the old, the poor, for your
fellow man whose skin may not be the
same color as yours—is ultimately to be
alone, to walk in loneliness.

All man's history is an endeavor to shatter
his loneliness.
Norman Cousins

The Cry (1895): Edvard Munch.

Sometimes it is necessary for men to scream against a world they never made, and cannot control.
T. R. Fenrenbach

THE MEMBER OF THE WEDDING

By Carson McCullers

PART ONE

It happened that green and crazy summer when Frankie was twelve years old. This was the summer when for a long time she had not been a member. She belonged to no club and was a member of nothing in the world. Frankie had become an unjoined person who hung around in doorways, and she was afraid. In June the trees were bright dizzy green, but later the leaves darkened, and the town turned black and shrunken under the glare of the sun. At first Frankie walked around doing one thing and another. The sidewalks of the town were gray in the early morning and at night, but the noon sun put a glaze on them, so that the cement burned and glittered like glass. The sidewalks finally became too hot for Frankie's feet, and also she got herself in trouble. She was in so much secret trouble that she thought it was better to stay at home—and at home there was only Berenice Sadie Brown and John Henry West. The three of them sat at the kitchen table, saying the same things over and over, so that by August the words began to rhyme with each other and sound strange. The world seemed to die each afternoon and nothing moved any longer. At last the summer was like a green sick dream, or like a silent crazy jungle under glass. And then, on the last Friday of August, all this was changed: it was so sudden that Frankie puzzled the whole blank afternoon, and still she did not understand.

"It is so very queer," she said. "The way it all just happened."

"Happened? Happened?" said Berenice.

John Henry listened and watched them quietly.

"I have never been so puzzled."

"But puzzled about what?"

"The whole thing," Frankie said.

And Berenice remarked: "I believe the sun has fried your brains."

"Me too," John Henry whispered.

Reprinted by permission of Houghton Mifflin Company from Carson McCullers, *The Member of the Wedding* (Boston: Houghton Mifflin).

Frankie herself almost admitted maybe so. It was four o'clock in the afternoon and the kitchen was square and gray and quiet. Frankie sat at the table with her eyes half closed, and she thought about a wedding. She saw a silent church, a strange snow slanting down against the colored windows. The groom in this wedding was her brother, and there was a brightness where his face should be. The bride was there in a long white train, and the bride also was faceless. There was something about this wedding that gave Frankie a feeling she could not name.

"Look here at me," said Berenice. "You jealous?"

"Jealous?"

"Jealous because your brother going to be married?"

"No," said Frankie. "I just never saw any two people like them. When they walked in the house today it was so queer."

"You jealous," said Berenice. "Go and behold yourself in the mirror. I can see from the color in your eye."

There was a watery kitchen mirror hanging above the sink. Frankie looked, but her eyes were gray as they always were. This summer she was grown so tall that she was almost a big freak, and her shoulders were narrow, her legs too long. She wore a pair of blue black shorts, a B.V.D. undervest, and she was barefooted. Her hair had been cut like a boy's, but it had not been cut for a long time and was now not even parted. The reflection in the glass was warped and crooked, but Frankie knew well what she looked like; she drew up her left shoulder and turned her head aside.

"Oh," she said. "They were the two prettiest people I ever saw. I just can't understand how it happened."

"But what, Foolish?" said Berenice. "Your brother come home with the girl he means to marry and took dinner today with you and your Daddy. They intend to marry at her home in Winter Hill this coming Sunday. You and your Daddy are going to the wedding. And that is the A and the Z of the matter. So whatever ails you?"

"I don't know," said Frankie. "I bet they have a good time every minute of the day."

"Less us have a good time," John Henry said.

"Us have a good time?" Frankie asked. "Us?"

The three of them sat at the table again and Berenice dealt the cards for three-handed bridge. Berenice had been the cook since Frankie could remember. She was very black and broad-shouldered and short. She always said that she was thirty-five years old, but she had been saying that at least three years. Her hair was parted, plaited, and greased close to the skull, and she had a flat and quiet face. There was only one thing wrong about Berenice—her left eye was bright blue glass. It stared out fixed and wild from her quiet, colored face, and why she had wanted a blue eye nobody human would ever know. Her right eye was dark and sad. Berenice dealt slowly, licking her thumb when the sweaty cards stuck together. John Henry watched each card as it was being dealt. His chest was white and wet and naked, and he wore around his neck a tiny lead donkey tied by a string. He was blood kin to Frankie, first cousin, and all summer he would eat dinner and spend the day with her, or eat supper and spend the night; and she could not make him go home. He was small to be six years old, but he had the largest knees that Frankie had ever seen, and on one of them there was always a scab or a bandage where he had fallen down and skinned himself. John Henry had a little screwed white face and he wore tiny gold-rimmed glasses. He watched all of the cards very carefully, because he was in debt; he owed Berenice more than five million dollars.

"I bid one heart," said Berenice.

"A spade," said Frankie.

"I want to bid spades," said John Henry. "That's what I was going to bid."

"Well, that's your tough luck. I bid them first."

"Oh, you fool jackass!" he said. "It's not fair!"

"Hush quarreling," said Berenice. "To tell the truth, I don't think either one of you got such a grand hand to fight over the bid about. I bid two hearts."

"I don't give a durn about it," Frankie said. "It is immaterial with me."

As a matter of fact this was so: she played bridge that afternoon like John Henry, just putting down any card that suddenly occurred to her. They sat together in the kitchen, and the kitchen was a sad and ugly room. John Henry had covered the walls with queer, child drawings, as far up as his arm would reach. This gave the kitchen a crazy look, like that of a room in the crazy-house. And now the old kitchen made Frankie sick. The name for what had happened to her Frankie did not know, but she could feel her squeezed heart beating against the table edge.

"The world is certainly a small place," she said.

"What makes you say that?"

"I mean sudden," said Frankie. "The world is certainly a sudden place."

"Well, I don't know," said Bernice. "Sometimes sudden and sometimes slow."

Frankie's eyes were half closed, and to her own ears her voice sounded ragged, far away:

"To me it is sudden."

For only yesterday Frankie had never thought seriously about a wedding. She knew that her only brother, Jarvis, was to be married. He had become engaged to a girl in Winter Hill just before he went to Alaska. Jarvis was a corporal in the army and he had spent almost two years in Alaska. Frankie had not seen her brother for a long, long time, and his face had become masked and changing, like a face seen under water. But Alaska! Frankie had dreamed of it constantly, and especially this summer it was very real. She saw the snow and frozen sea and ice glaciers, Esquimau igloos and polar bears and the beautiful Northern lights. When Jarvis had first gone to Alaska, she had sent him a box of home-made fudge, packing it carefully and wrapping each piece separately in waxed paper. It had thrilled her to think that her fudge would be eaten in Alaska, and she had a vision of her brother passing it around to furry Esquimaux. Three months later, a thank-you letter had come from Jarvis with a five-dollar bill enclosed. For a while she mailed candy almost every week, sometimes divinity instead of fudge, but Jarvis did not send her another bill, except at Christmas time. Sometimes his short letters to her father disturbed her a little. For instance, this summer he mentioned once that he had been in swimming and that the mosquitoes were something fierce. This letter jarred upon her dream, but after a few days of bewilderment, she returned to her frozen seas and snow. When Jarvis had come back from Alaska, he had gone straight to Winter Hill. The bride was named Janice Evans and the plans for the wedding were like this: her brother had wired that he and the bride were coming this Friday to spend the day, then on the following Sunday there was to be the wedding at Winter Hill. Frankie and her father were going to the wedding, traveling nearly a hundred miles to Winter Hill, and Frankie had already packed a suitcase. She looked forward to the time her brother and the bride should come, but she did not picture them to herself, and did not think about the wedding. So on the day before the visit she only commented to Berenice:

"I think it's a curious coincidence that Jarvis would get to go to Alaska and that the very bride he picked to marry would come from a place called Winter Hill. Winter Hill," she repeated slowly, her eyes closed, and the name blended with dreams of Alaska and cold snow. "I wish tomorrow was Sunday instead of Friday. I wish I had already left town."

"Sunday will come," said Berenice.

"I doubt it," said Frankie. "I've been ready to leave this town so long. I wish I didn't have to come back here after the wedding. I wish I was going somewhere for good. I wish I had a hundred dollars and could just light out and never see this town again."

"It seems to me you wish for a lot of things," said Berenice.

"I wish I was somebody else except me."

So the afternoon before it happened was like the other August afternoons. Frankie had hung around the kitchen, then toward dark she had gone out into the yard. The scuppernong arbor behind the house was purple and dark in the twilight. She walked slowly. John Henry West was sitting beneath the August arbor in a wicker chair, his legs crossed and his hands in his pockets.

"What are you doing?" she asked.

"I'm thinking."

Christina's World: Andrew Wyeth.

"About what?"

He did not answer.

Frankie was too tall this summer to walk beneath the arbor as she had always done before. Other twelve-year-old people could still walk around inside, give shows, and have a good time. Even small grown ladies could walk underneath the arbor. And already Frankie was too big; this year she had to hang around and pick from the edges like the grown people. She stared into the tangle of dark vines, and there was the smell of crushed scuppernongs and dust. Standing beside the arbor, with dark coming on, Frankie was afraid. She did not know what caused this fear, but she was afraid.

"I tell you what," she said. "Suppose you eat supper and spend the night with me."

John Henry took his dollar watch from his pocket and looked at it as though the time would decide whether or not he would come, but it was too dark under the arbor for him to read the numbers.

"Go on home and tell Aunt Pet. I'll meet you in the kitchen."

"All right."

She was afraid. The evening sky was pale and empty and the light from the kitchen window made a yellow square reflection in the darkening yard. She remembered that when she was a little girl she believed that three ghosts were living in the coal house, and one of the ghosts wore a silver ring.

She ran up the back steps and said: "I just now invited John Henry to eat supper and spend the night with me."

Berenice was kneading a lump of biscuit dough, and she dropped it on the flour-dusted table. "I thought you were sick and tired of him."

"I am sick and tired of him," said Frankie. "But it seemed to me he looked scared."

"Scared of what?"

Frankie shook her head. "Maybe I mean lonesome," she said finally.

"Well, I'll save him a scrap of dough."

After the darkening yard the kitchen was hot and bright and queer. The walls of the kitchen bothered Frankie—the queer drawings of Christmas trees, airplanes, freak soldiers, flowers. John Henry had started the first pictures one long afternoon in June, and having already ruined the wall, he went on and drew whenever he wished. Sometimes Frankie had drawn also. At first her father had been furious about the walls, but later he said for them to draw all the pictures out of their systems, and he would have the kitchen painted in the fall. But as the summer lasted, and would not end, the walls had begun to bother Frankie. That evening the kitchen looked strange to her, and she was afraid.

She stood in the doorway and said: "I just thought I might as well invite him."

So at dark John Henry came to the back door with a little week-end bag. He was dressed in his white recital suit and had put on shoes and socks. There was a dagger buckled to his belt. John Henry had seen snow. Although he was only six years old, he had gone to Birmingham last winter and there he had seen snow. Frankie had never seen snow.

"I'll take the week-end bag," said Frankie. "You can start right in making a biscuit man."

"O.K."

John Henry did not play with the dough; he worked on the biscuit man as though it were a very serious business. Now and then he stopped off, settled his glasses with his little hand, and studied what he had done. He was like a tiny watchmaker, and he drew up a chair and knelt on it so that he could get directly over the work. When Berenice gave him some raisins, he did not stick them all around as any other human child would do; he used only two for the eyes; but immediately he realized they were too large—so he divided one raisin carefully and put in eyes, two specks for the nose, and a little grinning raisin mouth. When he had finished, he wiped his hands on the seat of his shorts, and there was a little biscuit man with separate fingers, a hat on, and even walking stick. John Henry had worked so hard that the dough was now gray and wet. But it was a perfect little biscuit man, and, as a matter of fact, it reminded Frankie of John Henry himself.

"I better entertain you now," she said.

They ate supper at the kitchen table with Berenice, since her father had telephoned that he was working late at his jewelry store. When Berenice brought the biscuit man from the oven, they saw that it looked exactly like any biscuit man ever made by a child—it had swelled so that all the work of John Henry had been cooked out, the fingers were run together, and the walking stick resembled a sort of tail. But John Henry just looked at it through his glasses, wiped it with his napkin, and buttered the left foot.

It was a dark, hot August night. The radio in the dining room was playing a mixture of many stations: a war voice crossed with the gabble of an advertiser, and underneath there was the sleazy music of a sweet band. The radio had stayed on all the summer long, so finally it was a sound that as a rule they did not notice. Sometimes, when the noise became so loud that they could not hear their own ears, Frankie would turn it down a little. Otherwise, music and voices came and went and crossed and twisted with each other, and by August they did not listen any more.

"What do you want to do?" asked Frankie. "Would you like for me to read to you out of Hans Brinker or would you rather do something else?"

"I rather do something else," he said.

"What?"

"Less play out."

"I don't want to," Frankie said.

"There's a big crowd going to play out tonight."

"You got ears," Frankie said. "You heard me."

John Henry stood with his big knees locked, then finally he said: "I think I better go home."

"Why, you haven't spent the night! You can't eat supper and just go on off like that."

"I know it," he said quietly. Along with the radio they could hear the voices of the children playing in the night. "But less go out, Frankie. They sound like they having a mighty good time."

"No they're not," she said. "Just a lot of ugly silly children. Running and hollering and running and hollering. Nothing to it. We'll go upstairs and unpack your week-end bag."

Frankie's room was an elevated sleeping porch which had been built onto the house, with a stairway leading up from the kitchen. The room was furnished with an iron bed, a bureau, and a desk. Also Frankie had a motor which could be turned on and off; the motor could sharpen knives, and, if they were long enough, it could be used for filing down your fingernails. Against the wall was the suitcase packed and ready for the trip to Winter Hill. On the desk there was a very old typewriter, and Frankie sat down before it, trying to think of any letters she could write: but there was nobody for her to write to, as every possible letter had already been answered, and answered even several times. So she covered the typewriter with a raincoat and pushed it aside.

"Honestly," John Henry said, "don't you think I better go home?"

"No," she answered, without looking around at him. "You sit there in the corner and play with the motor."

Before Frankie there were now two objects—a lavender seashell and a glass globe with snow inside that could be shaken into a snowstorm. When she held the seashell to her ear, she could hear the warm wash of the Gulf of Mexico, and think of a green palm island far away. And she could hold the snow globe to her narrowed eyes and watch the whirling white flakes fall until they blinded her. She dreamed of Alaska. She walked up a cold white hill and looked on a snowy wasteland far below. She watched the sun make colors in the ice, and heard dream voices, saw dream things. And everywhere there was the cold white gentle snow.

"Look," John Henry said, and he was staring out of the window. "I think those big girls are having a party in their clubhouse."

"Hush!" Frankie screamed suddenly. "Don't mention those crooks to me."

There was in the neighborhood a clubhouse, and Frankie was not a member. The members of the club were girls who were thirteen and fourteen and even fifteen years old. They had parties with boys on Saturday night. Frankie knew all of the club members, and until this summer she had been like a younger member of their crowd, but now they had this club and she was not a member. They had said she was too young and mean. On Saturday night she could hear the terrible music and see from far away their light. Sometimes she went around to the alley behind the clubhouse and stood near a honeysuckle fence. She stood in the alley and watched and listened. They were very long, those parties.

"Maybe they will change their mind and invite you," John Henry said.

"The son-of-a-bitches."

Frankie sniffled and wiped her nose in the crook of her arm. She sat down on the edge of the bed, her shoulders slumped and her elbows resting on her knees. "I think they have been spreading it all over town that I smell bad," she said. "When I had those boils and that black bitter smelling ointment, old Helen Fletcher asked what was that funny smell I had. Oh, I could shoot every one of them with a pistol."

She heard John Henry walking up to the bed, and then she felt his hand patting her neck with tiny little pats. "I don't think you smell so bad," he said. "You smell sweet."

"The son-of-a-bitches," she said again. "And there was something else. They were talking nasty lies about married people. When I think of Aunt Pet and Uncle Ustace. And my own father! The nasty lies! I don't know what kind of fool they take me for."

"I can smell you the minute you walk in the house without even looking to see if it is you. Like a hundred flowers."

"I don't care," she said. "I just don't care."

"Like a thousand flowers," said John Henry, and still he was patting his sticky hand on the back of her bent neck.

Frankie sat up, licked the tears from around her mouth, and wiped off her face with her shirttail. She sat still, her nose widened, smelling herself. Then she went to her suitcase and took out a bottle of Sweet Serenade. She rubbed some on the top of her head and poured some more down inside the neck of her shirt.

"Want some on you?"

John Henry was squatting beside her open suitcase and he gave a little shiver when she poured the perfume over him. He wanted to meddle in her traveling suitcase and look carefully at every thing she owned. But Frankie only wanted him to get a general impression, and not count and know just what she had and what she did not have. So she strapped the suitcase and pushed it back against the wall. "Boy!" she said. "I bet I use more perfume than anybody in this town."

The house was quiet except for the low rumble of the radio in the dining room downstairs. Long ago her father had come home and Berenice had closed the back door and gone away. There was no longer the sound of children's voices in the summer night.

"I guess we ought to have a good time," said Frankie.

But there was nothing to do. John Henry stood, his knees locked and his hands clasped behind his back, in the middle of the room. There were moths at the window—pale green moths and yellow moths that fluttered and spread their wings against the screen.

"Those beautiful butterflies," he said. "They are trying to get in."

Frankie watched the soft moths tremble and press against the window screen. The moths came every evening when the lamp on her desk was lighted. They came from out of the August night and fluttered and clung against the screen.

"To me it is the irony of fate," she said. "The way they come here. Those moths could fly anywhere. Yet they keep hanging around the windows of this house."

John Henry touched the gold rim of his glasses to settle them on his nose and Frankie studied his flat little freckled face.

"Take off those glasses," she said suddenly.

John Henry took them off and blew on them. She looked through the glasses and the room was loose and crooked. Then she pushed back her chair and stared at John Henry. There were two damp white circles around his eyes.

"I bet you don't need those glasses," she said. She put her hand down on the typewriter, "What is this?"

"The typewriter," he said.

Frankie picked up the shell. "And this?"

"The shell from the Bay."

"What is that little thing crawling there on the floor?"

"Where?" he asked, looking around him.

"That little thing crawling along near your feet."

"Oh," he said. He squatted down. "Why, it's an ant. I wonder how it got up here."

Frankie tilted back in her chair and crossed her bare feet on her desk. "If I were you I'd just throw those glasses away," she said. "You can see good as anybody."

John Henry did not answer.

"They don't look becoming."

She handed the folded glasses to John Henry and he wiped them with his pink flannel glasses rag. He put them back on and did not answer.

"O.K." she said. "Suit yourself. I was only telling you for your own good."

They went to bed. They undressed with their backs turned to each other and then Frankie switched off the motor and the light. John Henry knelt down to say his prayers and he prayed for a long time, not saying the words aloud. Then he lay down beside her.

"Good night," she said.

"Good night."

Frankie stared up into the dark. "You know it is still hard for me to realize that the world turns around at the rate of about a thousand miles an hour."

"I know it," he said.

"And to understand why it is that when you jump up in the air you don't come down in Fairview or Selma or somewhere fifty miles away."

John Henry turned over and made a sleepy sound.

"Or Winter Hill," she said. "I wish I was starting for Winter Hill right now."

Already John Henry was asleep. She heard him breathe in the darkness, and now she had what she had wanted so many nights that summer; there was somebody sleeping in the bed with her. She lay in the dark and listened to him breathe, then after a while she raised herself on her elbow. He lay freckled and small in the moonlight, his chest white and naked, and one foot hanging from the edge of the bed. Carefully she put her hand on his stomach and moved closer; it felt as though a little clock was ticking inside him and he smelled of sweat and Sweet Serenade. He smelled like a sour little rose. Frankie leaned down and licked him behind the ear. Then she breathed deeply, settled herself with her chin on his sharp damp shoulder, and closed her eyes: for now, with somebody sleeping in the dark with her, she was not so much afraid.

The only thing I desire is to remain young enough to be able to tell myself that I still have time to do all the things I know I never will.   *Faith E. Beebe*

I WONDER HOW MANY PEOPLE IN THIS CITY

I wonder how many people in this city
live in furnished rooms.
Late at night when I look out at the buildings
I swear I see a face in every window
looking back at me,
and when I turn away
I wonder how many go back to their desks
and write this down.

—*Leonard Cohen*

Reprinted by permission of The Viking Press from Leonard
Cohen, *The Spice-Box of Earth* (New York: The Viking
Press). Also by permission of McClelland and Stewart,
Canada.

191

THE LONELY MAN

A cat sits on the pavement by the house.
It lets itself be touched, then slides away.
A girl goes by in a hood; the winter noon's
Long shadows lengthen. The cat is gray,
It sits there. It sits there all day, every day.

A collie bounds into my arms: he is a dog
And, therefore, finds nothing human alien.
He lives at the preacher's with a pair of cats.
The soft half-Persian sidles to me;
Indoors, the old white one watches blindly.

How cold it is! Some snow slides from a roof
When a squirrel jumps off it to a squirrel-proof
Feeding-station; and, a lot and two yards down,
A fat spaniel snuffles out to me
And sobers me with his untrusting frown.

He worries about his yard: past it, it's my affair
If I halt Earth in her track—his duty's done.
And the cat and the collie worry about the old one:
They come, when she's out too, so uncertainly. . . .
It's my block; I know them, just as they know me.

As for the others, those who wake up every day
And feed these, keep the houses, ride away
To work—I don't know them, they don't know me.
Are we friends or enemies? Why, who can say?
We nod to each other sometimes, in humanity,

Or search one another's faces with a yearning
Remnant of faith that's almost animal. . . .
The gray cat that just sits there: surely it is learning
To be a man; will find, soon, *some especial
Opening in a good firm for a former cat.*

—*Randall Jarrell*

Reprinted by permission of Atheneum Publishers from *The
Woman at the Washington Zoo* by Randall Jarrell. Copyright ©
1954, 1960 by Randall Jarrell.

A MOTHER IN MANNVILLE

By Marjorie Kinnan Rawlings

The orphanage is high in the Carolina mountains. Sometimes in winter the snowdrifts are so deep that the institution is cut off from the village below, from all the world. Fog hides the mountain peaks, the snow swirls down the valleys, and a wind blows so bitterly that the orphanage boys who take the milk twice daily to the baby cottage reach the door with fingers stiff in an agony of numbness.

"Or when we carry trays from the cookhouse for the ones that are sick," Jerry said, "we get our faces frostbit, because we can't put our hands over them. I have gloves," he added. "Some of the boys don't have any."

He liked the late spring, he said. The rhododendron was in bloom, a carpet of color, across the mountainsides, soft as the May winds that stirred the hemlocks. He called it laurel.

"It's pretty when the laurel blooms," he said. "Some of it's pink and some of it's white."

I was there in the autumn. I wanted quiet, isolation, to do some troublesome writing. I wanted mountain air to blow out the malaria from too long a time in the subtropics. I was homesick, too, for the flaming of maples in October, and for corn shocks and pumpkins and black-walnut trees and the lift of hills. I found them all, living in a cabin that belonged to the orphanage, half a mile beyond the orphanage farm. When I took the cabin, I asked for a boy or man to come and chop wood for the fireplace. The first few days were warm, I found what wood I needed about the cabin, no one came, and I forgot the order.

I looked up from my typewriter one late afternoon, a little startled. A boy stood at the door, and my pointer dog, my companion, was at his side and had not barked to warn me. The boy was probably twelve years old, but undersized. He wore overalls and a torn shirt, and was barefooted.

He said, "I can chop some wood today."

I said, "But I have a boy coming from the orphanage."

"I'm the boy."

"You? But you're small."

Reprinted by permission of Charles Scribner's Sons from Marjorie Kinnan Rawlings, *When the Whippoorwill* (New York: Charles Scribner's Sons, 1964).

"Size don't matter, chopping wood," he said. "Some of the big boys don't chop good. I've been chopping wood at the orphanage a long time."

I visualized mangled and inadequate branches for my fires. I was well into my work and not inclined to conversation. I was a little blunt.

"Very well. There's the ax. Go ahead and see what you can do."

I went back to work, closing the door. At first the sound of the boy dragging brush annoyed me. Then he began to chop. The blows were rhythmic and steady, and shortly I had forgotten him, the sound no more of an interruption than a constant rain. I suppose an hour and a half passed, for when I stopped and stretched, and heard the boy's steps on the cabin stoop, the sun was dropping behind the farthest mountain, and the valleys were purple with something deeper than the asters.

The boy said, "I have to go to supper now. I can come again tomorrow evening."

I said, "I'll pay you now for what you've done," thinking I should probably have to insist on an older boy. "Ten cents an hour?"

Anything is all right."

We went back to the cabin. An astonishing amount of solid wood had been cut. There were cherry logs and heavy roots of rhododendron, and blocks from the waste pine and oak left from the building of the cabin.

"But you've done as much as a man," I said. "This is a splendid pile."

I looked at him, actually, for the first time. His hair was the color of the corn shocks and his eyes, very direct, were like the mountain sky when rain is pending—gray, with a shadowing of that miraculous blue. As I spoke, a light came over him, as though the setting sun had touched him with the same suffused glory with which it touched the mountains. I gave him a quarter.

"You may come tomorrow," I said, "and thank you very much."

He looked at me, and at the coin, and seemed to want to speak, but could not, and turned away.

"I'll split kindling tomorrow," he said over his thin ragged shoulder. "You'll need kindling and medium wood and logs and backlogs."

At daylight I was half awakened by the sound of chopping. Again it was so even in texture that I went back to sleep. When I left my bed in the cool morning, the boy had come and gone, and a stack of kindling was neat against the cabin wall. He came again after school in the afternoon and worked until time to return to the orphanage. His name was Jerry; he was twelve years old, and he had been at the orphanage since he was four. I could picture him at four, with the same grave gray-blue eyes and the same—independence? No, the word that comes to me is "integrity."

The word means something very special to me, and the quality for which I use it is a rare one. My father had it—there is another of whom I am almost sure —but almost no man of my acquaintance possesses it with the clarity, the purity, the simplicity of a mountain stream. But the boy Jerry had it. It is bedded on courage, but it is more than brave. It is honest, but it is more than honesty. The ax handle broke one day. Jerry said the woodshop at the orphanage would repair it. I brought money to pay for the job and he refused it.

"I'll pay for it," he said. "I broke it. I brought the ax down careless."

"But no one hits accurately every time," I told him. "The fault was in the wood of the handle. I'll see the man from whom I bought it."

> It is a little lonely in the desert . . . It is also lonely among men.
>
> *Antoine de Saint-Exupéry*

It was only then that he would take the money. He was standing back of his own carelessness. He was a free-will agent and he chose to do careful work, and if he failed, he took the responsibility without subterfuge.*

And he did for me the unnecessary thing, the gracious thing, that we find done only by the great of heart. Things no training can teach, for they are done on the instant, with no predicted experience. He found a cubbyhole beside the fireplace that I had not noticed. There, of his own accord, he put kindling and "medium" wood, so that I might always have dry fire material ready in case of sudden wet weather. A stone was loose in the rough walk to the cabin. He dug a deeper hole and steadied it, although he came, himself, by a short cut over the bank. I found that when I tried to return his thoughtfulness with such things as candy and apples, he was wordless. "Thank you" was, perhaps, an expression for which he had no use, for his courtesy was instinctive. He only looked at the gift and at me, and a curtain lifted, so that I saw deep into the clear well of his eyes, and gratitude was there, and affection, soft over the firm granite of his character.

He made simple excuses to come and sit with me. I could no more have turned him away than if he had been physically hungry. I suggested once that the best time for us to visit was just before supper, when I left off my writing. After that, he waited always until my typewriter had been some time quiet. One day I worked until nearly dark. I went outside the cabin, having forgotten him. I saw him going up over the hill in the twilight toward the orphanage. When I sat down on my stoop, a place was warm from his body where he had been sitting.

He became intimate, of course, with my pointer, Pat. There is a strange communion between a boy and a dog. Perhaps they possess the same singleness of spirit, the same kind of wisdom. It is difficult to explain, but it exists. When I went across the state for a week end, I left the dog in Jerry's charge. I gave him the dog whistle and the key to the cabin, and left sufficient food. He was to come two or three times a day and let out the dog, and feed and exercise him. I should return Sunday night, and Jerry would take out the dog for the last time Sunday afternoon and then leave the key under an agreed hiding place.

My return was belated and fog filled the mountain passes so treacherously that I dared not drive at night. The fog held the next morning, and it was Monday noon before I reached the cabin. The dog had been fed and cared for that morning. Jerry came early in the afternoon, anxious.

"The superintendent said nobody would drive in the fog," he said. "I came just before bedtime last night and you hadn't come. So I brought Pat some of my breakfast this morning. I wouldn't have let anything happen to him."

"When I heard about the fog, I thought you'd know."

He was needed for work at the orphanage and he had to return at once. I gave him a dollar in payment, and he looked at it and went away. But that night he came in the darkness and knocked at the door.

*Free-will agent, one who himself has determined the details of this work.

"Come in, Jerry," I said, "If you're allowed to be away this late."

"I told maybe a story," he said. "I told them I thought you would want to see me."

"That's true," I assured him, and I saw his relief. "I want to hear about how you managed with the dog."

He sat by the fire with me, with no other light, and told me of their two days together. The dog lay close to him, and found a comfort there that I did not have for him. And it seemed to me that being with my dog, and caring for him, had brought the boy and me, too, together, so that he felt that he belonged to me as well as to the animal.

"He stayed right with me," he told me, "except when he ran in the laurel. He likes the laurel. I took him up over the hill and we both ran fast. There was a place where the grass was high and I lay down in it and hid. I could hear Pat hunting for me. He found my trail and he barked. When he found me, he acted crazy, and he ran around and around me, in circles."

We watched the flames.

"That's an apple log," he said. "It burns the prettiest of any wood."

We were very close.

He was suddenly impelled to speak of things he had not spoken of before, nor had I cared to ask him.

"You look a little bit like my mother," he said. "Especially in the dark, by the fire."

"But you were only four, Jerry, when you came here. You have remembered how she looked, all these years?"

"My mother lives in Mannville," he said.

For a moment, finding that he had a mother shocked me as greatly as anything in my life has ever done, and I did not know why it disturbed me. Then I understood my distress. I was filled with a passionate resentment that any woman should go away and leave her son. A fresh anger added itself. A son like this one—. The orphanage was a wholesome place, the executives were kind, good people, the food was more than adequate, the boys were healthy, a ragged shirt was no hardship, nor the doing of clean labor. Granted, perhaps, that the boy felt no lack, what blood fed the veins of a woman who did not yearn over her own child's lean body? At four he would have looked the same as now. Nothing, I thought, nothing in life could change those eyes. His quality must be apparent to an idiot, a fool. I burned with questions I could not ask. In any case, I was afraid, there would be pain.

"Have you seen her, Jerry—lately?"

"I see her every summer. She sends for me."

I wanted to cry out, "Why are you not with her? How can she let you go away again?"

He said, "She comes up here from Mannville whenever she can. She doesn't have a job now."

His face shone in the firelight.

She wanted to give me a puppy, but they can't let any one boy keep a puppy. You memember the suit I had on last Sunday?" He was plainly proud. "She sent me that for Christmas. The Christmas before that"—he drew a long breath, savoring the memory—"she sent me a pair of skates."

"Roller skates?"

My mind was busy, making pictures of her, trying to understand her. She had not, then, entirely deserted or forgotten him. But why, then—I thought, "I must not condemn her without knowing."

"Roller skates. I let the other boys use them. They're always borrowing them. But they're careful of them."

What circumstances other than poverty—

"I'm going to take the dollar you gave me for taking care of Pat," he said, "and buy her a pair of gloves."

I could only say, "That will be nice. Do you know her size?"

"I think it's 8½," he said.

He looked at my hands.

"Do you wear 8½" he asked.

"No. I wear a smaller size, a 6."

"Oh! Then I guess her hands are bigger than yours."

I hated her. Poverty or no, there was other food than bread, and the soul could starve as quickly as the body. He was taking his dollar to buy gloves for her big stupid hands, and she lived away from him, in Mannville, and contented herself with sending him skates.

"She likes white gloves," he said. "Do you think I can get them for a dollar?"

"I think so," I said.

I decided that I should not leave the mountains without seeing her and knowing for myself why she had done this thing.

The human mind scatters its interests as though made of thistledown, and every wind stirs and moves it. I finished my work. It did not please me, and I gave my thoughts to another field. I should need some Mexican material.

I made arrangements to close my Florida place. Mexico immediately, and doing the writing there, if conditions were favorable. Then, Alaska with my brother. After that, heaven knew what or where.

I did not take time to go to Mannville to see Jerry's mother, nor even to talk with the orphanage officials about her. I was a trifle abstracted about the boy, because of my work and plans. And after my first fury at her—we did not speak of her again—his having a mother, any sort at all, not far away, in Mannville, relieved me of the ache I had had about him. He did not question the anomalous relation. He was not lonely. It was none of my concern.

He came every day and cut my wood and did small helpful favors and stayed to talk. The days had become cold, and often I let him come inside the cabin. He would lie on the floor in front of the fire, with one arm across the pointer, and they would both doze and wait quietly for me. Other days they ran with a common ecstasy through the laurel, and since the asters were now gone, he brought me back vermilion maple leaves, and chestnut boughs dripping with imperial yellow. I was ready to go.

I said to him, "You have been my good friend, Jerry. I shall often think of you and miss you. Pat will miss you too. I am leaving tomorrow."

He did not answer. When he went away, I remember that a new moon hung over the mountains, and I watched him go in silence up the hill. I expected him the next day, but he did not come. The details of packing my personal belongings, loading my car, arranging the bed over the seat, where the dog would ride, occupied me until late in the day. I closed the cabin and started the car, noticing that the sun was in the west and I should do well to be out of the mountains by nightfall. I stopped by the orphanage and left the cabin key and money for my light bill with Miss Clark.

"And will you call Jerry for me to say good-by to him?"

"I don't know where he is," she said. "I'm afraid he's not well. He didn't eat his dinner this noon. One of the other boys saw him going over the hill into the laurel. He was supposed to fire the boiler this afternoon. It's not like him; he's unusually reliable."

I was almost relieved, for I knew I should never see him again, and it would be easier not to say good-by to him.

I said, "I wanted to talk with you about his mother—why he's here—but I'm in more of a hurry than I expected to be. It's out of the question for me to see her now too. But here's some money I'd like to leave with you to buy things for him at Christmas and on his birthday. It will be better than for me to try to send him things. I could so easily duplicate—skates, for instance."

She blinked her honest spinster's eyes.

"There's not much use for skates here," she said.

Her stupidity annoyed me.

"What I mean," I said, "is that I don't want to duplicate things his mother sends him. I might have chosen skates if I didn't know she had already given them to him."

She stared at me.

"I don't understand," she said. "He has no mother. He has no skates."

LONELINESS

By Rollo May

Another characteristic of modern people is loneliness. They describe this feeling as one of being "on the outside," isolated, or, if they are sophisticated, they say that they feel alienated. They emphasize how crucial it is for them to be invited to this party or that dinner, not because they especially want to go (though they generally do go) nor because they will get enjoyment, companionship, sharing of experience and human warmth in the gathering (very often they do not, but are simply bored). Rather, being invited is crucial because it is a proof that they are not alone. Loneliness is such an omnipotent and painful threat to many persons that they have little conception of the positive values of solitude, and even at times are very frightened at the prospect of being alone. Many people suffer from "the fear of finding oneself alone," remarks André Gide, "and so they don't find themselves at all."

The feeling of emptiness and loneliness go together. When persons, for example, are telling of a break-up in a love relationship, they will often not say they feel sorrow or humiliation over a lost conquest; but rather that they feel "emptied." The loss of the other leaves an inner "yawning void," as one person put it.

The reasons for the close relation between loneliness and emptiness are not difficult to discover. For when a person does not know with any inner conviction what he wants or what he feels; when, in a period of traumatic change, he becomes aware of the fact that the conventional desires and goals he has been taught to follow no longer bring him any security or give him any sense of direction, when, that is, he

feels an inner void while he stands amid the outer confusion of upheaval in his society, he senses danger; and his natural reaction is to look around for other people. They, he hopes, will give him some sense of direction, or at least some comfort in the knowledge that he is not alone in his fright. Emptiness and loneliness are thus two phases of the same basic experience of anxiety.

Perhaps the reader can recall the anxiety which swept over us like a tidal wave when the first atom bomb exploded over Hiroshima, when we sensed our grave danger—sensed, that is, that we might be the last generation—but did not know in which direction to turn. At that moment the reaction of great numbers of people was, strangely enough, a sudden, deep loneliness. Norman Cousins, endeavoring in his essay *Modern Man Is Obsolete* to express the deepest feelings of intelligent people at that staggering historical moment, wrote not about how to protect one's self from atomic radiation, or how to meet political problems, or the tragedy of man's self-destruction. Instead his editorial was a mediation on loneliness. "All man's history," he proclaimed, "is an endeavor to shatter his loneliness."

Feelings of loneliness occur when one feels empty and afraid not simply because one wants to be protected by the crowd, as a wild animal is protected by being in a pack. Nor is the longing for others simply an endeavor to fill the void within one's self— though this certainly is one side of the need for human companionship when one feels empty or anxious. The more basic reason is that the human being gets his original experiences of being

Reprinted by permission of W. W. Norton & Company from Rollo May, *Man's Search for Himself* (New York: W. W. Norton & Company, 1953).

198

a self out of his relatedness to other persons, and when he is alone, without other persons, he is afraid he will lose this experience of being a self. Man, the biosocial mammal, not only is dependent on other human beings such as his father and mother for his security during a long childhood; he likewise receives his consciousness of himself, which is the basis of his capacity to orient himself in life, from these early relationships. These important points we will discuss more thoroughly in a later chapter—here we wish only to point out that part of the feeling of loneliness is that man needs relations with other people in order to orient himself.

But another important reason for the feeling of loneliness arises from the fact that our society lays such a great emphasis on being socially accepted. It is our chief way of allaying anxiety, and our chief mark of prestige. Thus we always have to prove we are a "social success" by being forever sought after and by never being alone. If one is well-liked, that is, socially successful—so the idea goes—one will rarely be alone; not to be liked is to have lost out in the race. In the days of the gyroscopeman and earlier, the chief criterion of prestige was financial success: now the belief is that if one is well-liked, financial success and prestige will follow. "Be well-liked," Willie Loman in *Death of a Salesman* advises his sons, "and you will never want."

The reverse side of modern man's loneliness is his great fear of being alone. In our culture it is permissible to say you are lonely, for that is a way of admitting that it is not good to be alone. The melancholy romantic songs present this sentiment, with the appropriate nostalgia:

Me and my shadow,
Not a soul to tell our troubles to . . .

Just me and my shadow,
All alone and feeling blue.*

And it is permissible to want to be alone temporarily to "get away from it all." But if one mentioned at a party that he liked to be alone, not for a rest or an escape, but for its own joys, people would think that something was vaguely wrong with him— that some pariah aura of untouchability or sickness hovered round him. And if a person is alone very much of the time, people tend to think of him as a failure, for it is inconceivable to them that he would choose to be alone.

This fear of being alone lies behind the great need of people in our society to get invited places, or if they invite someone else, to have the other accept. The pressure to keep "dated up" goes way beyond such realistic motives as the pleasure and warmth people get in each other's company, the enrichment of feelings, ideas and experiences, or the sheer pleasure of relaxation. Actually, such motives have very little to do with the compulsion to get invited. Many of the more sophisticated persons are well aware of these points, and would like to be able to say "No"; but they very much want the *chance* to go, and to turn down invitations in the usual round of social life means sooner or later one won't get invited. The cold fear that protrudes its icy head from subterranean levels is that one would then be shut out entirely, left on the outside.

To be sure, in all ages people have been afraid of loneliness and have tried to escape it. Pascal in the seventeenth century observed the great efforts people make to divert themselves, and he opined that the purpose of the bulk of these diversions was to enable people to avoid thoughts of themselves. Kierkegaard a hundred years ago wrote that in his age "one does everything possible by way of diversions and the Janizary music of loud-voiced enterprises to keep lonely thoughts away, just as in the forests of America they keep away wild beasts by torches, by yells, by the sound of cymbals." But the difference in our day is that the fear of loneliness is much more extensive, and the defenses against it—diversions, social rounds, and "being liked"—are more rigid and compulsive.

Let us paint an impressionistic picture of a somewhat extreme though not otherwise unusual example of the fear of loneliness in our society as seen in the social activities at summer resorts. Let us take a typical, averagely well-to-do summer colony on the seashore, where people are vacationing and therefore do not have their work available for the time being as escape and support. It is of crucial importance for these people to keep up the continual merry-go-round of cocktail parties, despite the fact that they meet the same people every day at the parties, drink the same cocktails, and talk of the same subjects or lack of subjects. What is important is not what is said, but that some talk be continually going on. Silence is the great crime, for silence is lonely and frightening. One shouldn't feel much, nor put much meaning into what one says: what you say seems to have more effect if you don't try to understand. One has the strange impression that these people are all afraid of something—what is it? It is as if the "yatata" were a primitive tribal ceremony, a witch dance calculated to appease some god. There is a god, or rather a demon, they are trying to appease: it is the specter of loneliness which hovers outside like the fog drifting in from the sea. One will have to meet this specter's leering terror

for the first half-hour one is awake in the morning anyway, so let one do everything possible to keep it away now. Figuratively speaking, it is the specter of death they are trying to appease—death as the symbol of ultimate separation, aloneness, isolation from other human beings.

Admittedly, the above illustration is extreme. In the day-to-day experience of most of us, the fear of being alone may not crop up in intense form very often. We generally have methods of "keeping lonely thoughts away," and our anxiety may appear only in occasional dreams of fright which we try to forget as soon as possible in the morning. But these differences in intensity of the fear of loneliness, and the relative success of our defenses against it, do not change the central issue. Our fear of loneliness may not be shown by anxiety as such, but by subtle thoughts which pop up to remind us, when we discover we were not invited to so-and-so's party, that someone else likes us even if the person in question doesn't, or to tell us that we were successful or popular in such-and-such other time in the past. Often this reassuring process is so automatic that we are not aware of it in itself, but only of the ensuing comfort to our self-esteem. If we as citizens of the middle twentieth century look honestly into ourselves, that is, look below our customary pretenses, do we not find this fear of isolation as an almost constant companion, despite its many masquerades?

The fear of being alone derives much of its terror from our anxiety lest we *lose our awareness of ourselves*. If people contemplate being alone for longish periods of time, without anyone to talk to or any radio to eject noise into the air, they generally are afraid that they would be at "loose ends," would lose the boundaries for themselves, would have nothing to bump up against, nothing by which to orient themselves. It is interesting that they sometimes say that if they were alone for long they wouldn't be able to work or play in order to get tired; and so they wouldn't be able to sleep. And then, though they generally cannot explain this, they would lose the distinction between wakefulness and sleep, just as they lose the distinction between the subjective self and the objective world around them.

Every human being gets much of his sense of his own reality out of what others say to him and think about him. But many modern people have gone so far in their dependence on others for their feeling of reality that they are afraid that without it they would lose the sense of their own existence. They feel they would be "dispersed," like water flowing every which way on the sand. Many people are like blind men feeling their way along in life only by means of touching a succession of other people.

In its extreme form, this fear of losing one's orientation is the fear of psychosis. When persons actually are on the brink of psychosis, they often have an urgent need to seek out some contact with other human beings. This is sound, for such relating gives them a bridge to reality.

But the point we are discussing here has a different origin. Modern Western man, trained through four centuries of emphasis on rationality, uniformity, and mechanics, has consistently endeavored, with unfortunate success, to repress the aspects of himself which do not fit these uniform and mechanical standards. Is it not too much to say that modern man, sensing his own inner hollowness, is afraid that if he should not have his regular associates around him, should not have the talisman of his daily program and his routine of work, if he should forget what time it is, that he would feel, though in an inarticulate way, some threat like that which one experiences on the brink of psychosis? When one's customary ways of orienting oneself are threatened, and one is without other selves around one, one is thrown back on inner resources and inner strength, and this is what modern people have neglected to develop. Hence loneliness is a real, not imaginary, threat to so many of them.

Social acceptance, "being liked," has so much power because it holds the feelings of loneliness at bay. A person is surrounded with comfortable warmth; he is merged in the group. He is reabsorbed—as though, in the extreme psychoanalytic symbol, he were to go back into the womb. He temporarily loses his loneliness; but it is at the price of giving up his existence as an identity in his own right. And he renounces the one thing which would get him constructively over the loneliness in the long run, namely the developing of his own inner resources, strength and sense of direction, and using this as a basis for meaningful relations with others. The "stuffed men" are bound to become more lonely no matter how much they "lean together"; for hollow people do not have a base from which to learn to love.

MR. FLOOD'S PARTY

Old Eben Flood, climbing alone one night
Over the hill between the town below
And the forsaken upland hermitage
That held as much as he should ever know
On earth again of home, paused warily.
The road was his with not a native near;
And Eben, having leisure, said aloud,
For no man else in Tilbury Town to hear:

"Well, Mr. Flood, we have the harvest moon
Again, and we may not have many more;
The bird is on the wing, the poet says,
And you and I have said it here before.
Drink to the bird." He raised up to the light
The jug that he had gone so far to fill,
And answered huskily: "Well, Mr. Flood,
Since you propose it, I believe I will."

Alone, as if enduring to the end
A valiant armor of scarred hopes outworn,
He stood there in the middle of the road
Like Roland's ghost winding a silent horn.
Below him, in the town among the trees,
Where friends of other days had honored him,
A phantom salutation of the dead
Rang thinly till old Eben's eyes were dim.

Then, as a mother lays her sleeping child
Down tenderly, fearing it may awake,
He set the jug down slowly at his feet
With trembling care, knowing that most things break;

Reprinted by permission of The Macmillan Company from
Edwin Arlington Robinson, *Collected Poems* (New York:
Macmillan, 1949).

And only when assured that on firm earth
It stood, as the uncertain lives of men
Assuredly did not, he paced away,
And with his hand extended paused again:

"Well, Mr. Flood, we have not met like this
In a long time; and many a change has come
To both of us, I fear, since last it was
We had a drop together. Welcome home!"
Convivially returning with himself,
Again he raised the jug up to the light;
And with an acquiescent quaver said:
"Well, Mr. Flood, if you insist, I might.

"Only a very little, Mr. Flood—
For auld lang syne. No more, sir; that will do."
So, for the time, apparently it did,
And Eben evidently thought so too;
For soon amid the silver loneliness
Of night he lifted up his voice and sang,
Secure, with only two moons listening,
Until the whole harmonious landscape rang—

"For auld lang syne." The weary throat gave out,
The last word wavered, and the song was done.
He raised again the jug regretfully
And shook his head, and was again alone.
There was not much that was ahead of him,
And there was nothing in the town below—
Where strangers would have shut the many doors
That many friends had opened long ago.

—*Edwin Arlington Robinson*

BIG BLONDE

By Dorothy Parker

I

Hazel Morse was a large, fair woman of the type that incites some men when they use the word "blonde" to click their tongues and wag their heads roguishly. She prided herself upon her small feet and suffered for her vanity, boxing them in snub-toed, high-heeled slippers of the shortest bearable size. The curious things about her were her hands, strange terminations to the flabby white arms splattered with pale tan spots—long, quivering hands with deep and convex nails. She should not have disfigured them with little jewels.

She was not a woman given to recollections. At her middle thirties, her old days were a blurred and flickering sequence, an imperfect film, dealing with the actions of strangers.

In her twenties, after the deferred death of a hazy widowed mother, she had been employed as a model in a wholesale dress establishment—it was still the day of the big woman, and she was then prettily colored and erect and high-breasted. Her job was not onerous, and she met numbers of men and spent numbers of evenings with them, laughing at their jokes and telling them she loved their neckties. Men liked her, and she took it for granted that the liking of many men was a desirable thing. Popularity seemed to her to be worth all the work that had to be put into its achievement. Men liked you because you were fun, and when they liked you they took you out, and there you were. So, and successfully, she was fun. She was a good sport. Men like a good sport.

No other form of diversion, simpler or more complicated, drew her attention. She never pondered if she might not be better occupied doing something else. Her ideas, or, better, her acceptances, ran right along with those of the other substantially built blondes in whom she found her friends.

When she had been working in the dress establishment some years she met Herbie Morse. He was thin, quick, attractive, with shifting lines about his shiny,

Reprinted by permission of The Viking Press from Dorothy Parker, *The Portable Dorothy Parker* (New York: The Viking Press, 1957). Copyright © 1957 by Dorothy Parker.

brown eyes and a habit of fiercely biting at the skin around his finger nails. He drank largely; she found that entertaining. Her habitual greeting to him was an allusion to his state of the previous night.

"Oh, what a peach you had," she used to say, through her easy laugh.."I thought I'd die, the way you kept asking the waiter to dance with you."

She liked him immediately upon their meeting. She was enormously amused at his fast, slurred sentences, his interpolations of apt phrases from vaudeville acts and comic strips; she thrilled at the feel of his lean arm tucked firm beneath the sleeve of her coat; she wanted to touch the wet, flat surface of his hair. He was as promptly drawn to her. They were married six weeks after they had met.

She was delighted at the idea of being a bride; coquetted with it, played upon it. Other offers of marriage she had had, and not a few of them, but it happened that they were all from stout, serious men who had visited the dress establishment as buyers; men from Des Moines and Houston and Chicago and, in her phrase, even funnier places. There was always something immensely comic to her in the thought of living elsewhere than New York. She could not regard as serious proposals that she share a western residence.

She wanted to be married. She was nearing thirty now, and she did not take the years well. She spread and softened, and her darkening hair turned her to inexpert dabblings with peroxide. There were times when she had little flashes of fear about her job. And she had had a couple of thousand evenings of being a good sport among her male acquaintances. She had come to be more conscientious than spontaneous about it.

Herbie earned enough, and they took a little apartment far uptown. There was a Mission-furnished dining-room with a hanging central light globed in liver-colored glass; in the living-room were an "over-stuffed suite," a Bostern fern, and a reproduction of the Henner "Magdalene" with the red hair and the blue draperies; the bedroom was in gray enamel and old rose, with Herbie's photograph on Hazel's dressing-table and Hazel's likeness on Herbie's chest of drawers.

She cooked—and she was a good cook—and marketed and chatted with the delivery boys and the colored laundress. She loved the flat, she loved her life, she loved Herbie. In the first months of their marriage, she gave him all the passion she was ever to know.

She had not realized how tired she was. It was a delight, a new game, a holiday, to give up being a good sport. If her head ached or her arches throbbed, she complained piteously, babyishly. If her mood was quiet, she did not talk. If tears came to her eyes, she let them fall.

She fell readily into the habit of tears during the first year of her marriage. Even in her good sport days, she had been known to weep lavishly and disinterestedly on occasion. Her behavior at the theater was a standing joke. She could weep at anything in a play—tiny garments, love both unrequited and mutual, seduction, purity, faithful servitors, wedlock, the triangle.

"There goes Haze," her friends would say, watching her. "She's off again."

Wedded and relaxed, she poured her tears freely. To her who had laughed so much, crying was delicious. All sorrows became her sorrows; she was Tenderness. She would cry long and softly over newspaper accounts of kidnaped babies, deserted wives, unemployed men, strayed cats, heroic dogs. Even when the paper was no longer before her, her mind revolved upon these things and the drops slipped rhythmically over her plump cheeks.

"Honestly," she would say to Herbie, "all the sadness there is in the world when you stop to think about it!"

"Yeah," Herbie would say.

She missed nobody. The old crowd, the people who had brought her and Herbie together, dropped from their lives, lingeringly at first. When she thought of this at all, it was only to consider it fitting. This was marriage. This was peace.

But the thing was that Herbie was not amused.

For a time, he had enjoyed being alone with her. He found the voluntary isolation novel and sweet. Then it palled with a ferocious suddenness. It was as if one night, sitting with her in the steam-heated living-room, he would ask no more; and the next night he was through and done with the whole thing.

He became annoyed by her misty melancholics. At first, when he came home to find her softly tired and moody, he kissed her neck and patted her shoulder and begged her to tell her Herbie what was wrong. She loved that. But time slid by, and he found that there was never anything really, personally, the matter.

"Ah, for God's sake," he would say. "Crabbing again. All right, sit here and crab your head off. I'm going out."

And he would slam out of the flat and come back late and drunk.

She was completely bewildered by what happened to their marriage. First they were lovers; and then, it seemed without transition, they were enemies. She never understood it.

There were longer and longer intervals between his leaving his office and his arrival at the apartment. She went through agonies of picturing him run over and bleeding, dead and covered with a sheet. Then she lost her fears for his safety and grew sullen and wounded. When a person wanted to be with a person, he came as soon as possible. She desperately wanted him to want to be with her; her own hours only marked the time till he would come. It was often nearly nine o'clock before he came home to dinner. Always he had had many drinks, and their effect would die in him, leaving him loud and querulous and bristling for affronts.

He was too nervous, he said, to sit and do nothing for an evening. He boasted, probably not in all truth, that he had never read a book in his life.

"What am I expected to do—sit around this dump on my tail all night?" he would ask, rhetorically. And again he would slam out.

She did not know what to do. She could not manage him. She could not meet him.

She fought him furiously. A terrific domesticity had come upon her, and she would bite and scratch to guard it. She wanted what she called "a nice home." She wanted a sober, tender husband, prompt at dinner, punctual at work. She wanted sweet, comforting evenings. The idea of intimacy with other men was terrible to her; the thought that Herbie might be seeking entertainment in other women set her frantic.

It seemed to her that almost everything she read—novels from the drugstore lending library, magazine stories, women's pages in the papers—dealt with wives who lost their husbands' love. She could bear those, at that, better than accounts of neat, companionable marriage and living happily ever after.

She was frightened. Several times when Herbie came home in the evening, he found her determinedly dressed—she had had to alter those of her clothes that were not new, to make them fasten—and rouged.

"Let's go wild tonight, what do you say? she would hail him. "A person's got lots of time to hang around and do nothing when they're dead."

So they would go out, to chop houses and the less expensive cabarets. But it turned out badly. She could no longer find amusement in watching Herbie drink. She could not laugh at his whimsicalities, she was so tensely counting his indulgences. And she was unable to keep back her remonstrances—"Ah, come on, Herb, you've had enough, haven't you? You'll feel something terrible in the morning."

He would be immediately enraged. All right, crab; crab, crab, crab, crab, that was all she ever did. What a lousy sport *she* was! There would be scenes, and one or the other of them would rise and stalk out in fury.

She could not recall the definite day that she started drinking, herself. There was nothing separate about her days. Like drops upon a windowpane, they ran together and trickled away. She had been married six months; then a year; then three years.

She had never needed to drink, formerly. She could sit for most of a night at a table where the others were imbibing earnestly and never droop in looks or spirits, nor be bored by the doings of those about her. If she took a cocktail, it was so unusual as to cause twenty minutes or so of jocular comment. But now anguish was in her. Frequently, after a quarrel, Herbie would stay out for the night, and she could not learn from him where the time had been spent. Her heart felt tight and sore in her breast, and her mind turned like an electric fan.

She hated the taste of liquor. Gin, plain or in mixtures, made her promptly sick. After experiment, she found that Scotch whisky was best for her. She took it without water, because that was the quickest way to its effect.

Herbie pressed it on her. He was glad to see her drink. They both felt it might restore her high spirits, and their good times together might again be possible.

" 'Atta girl," he would approve her. "Let's see you get boiled, baby."

But it brought them no nearer. When she drank with him, there would be a little while of gaiety and then, strangely without beginning, they would be in a wild quarrel. They would wake in the morning not sure what it had all been about, foggy as to what had been said and done, but each deeply injured and bitterly resentful. There would be days of vengeful silence.

There had been a time when they had made up their quarrels, usually in bed. There would be kisses and little names and assurances of fresh starts. . . . "Oh, it's going to be great now, Herb. We'll have swell times. I was a crab. I guess I must have been tired. But everything's going to be swell. You'll see."

Now there were no gentle reconciliations. They resumed friendly relations only in the brief magnanimity caused by liquor, before more liquor drew them into new battles. The scenes became more violent. There were shouted invectives and pushes, and sometimes sharp slaps. Once she had a black eye. Herbie was horrified next day at sight of it. He did not go to work; he followed her about, suggesting remedies and heaping dark blame on himself. But after they had had a few drinks—"to pull themselves together"—she made so many wistful references to her bruise that he shouted at her and rushed out and was gone for two days.

Each time he left the place in a rage, he threatened never to come back. She did not believe him, nor did she consider separation. Somewhere in her head or her heart was the lazy, nebulous hope that things would change and she and Herbie settle suddenly into soothing married life. Here were her home, her furniture, her husband, her station. She summoned no alternatives.

She could no longer bustle and potter. She had no more vicarious tears; the hot drops she shed were for herself. She walked ceaselessly about the rooms, her thoughts running mechanically round and round Herbie. In those days began the hatred of being alone that she was never to overcome. You could be by yourself when things were all right, but when you were blue you got the howling horrors.

She commenced drinking alone, little, short drinks all through the day. It was only with Herbie that alcohol made her nervous and quick in offense. Alone, it blurred sharp things for her. She lived in a haze of it. Her life took on a dream-like quality. Nothing was astonishing.

A Mrs. Martin moved into the flat across the hall. She was a great blonde woman of forty, a promise in looks of what Mrs. Morse was to be. They made acquaintance, quickly became inseparable. Mrs. Morse spent her days in the opposite apartment. They drank together, to brace themselves after the drinks of the nights before.

She never confided her troubles about Herbie to Mrs. Martin. The subject was too bewildering to her to find comfort in talk. She let it be assumed that her husband's business kept him much away. It was not regarded as important; husbands, as such, played but shadowy parts in Mrs. Martin's circle.

Mrs. Martin had no visible spouse; you were left to decide for yourself whether he was or was not dead. She had an admirer, Joe, who came to see her almost nightly. Often he brought several friends with him—"The Boys," they were called. The Boys were big, red, good-humored men, perhaps forty-five, perhaps fifty. Mrs. Morse was glad of invitations to join the parties—Herbie was scarcely ever at home at night now. If he did come home, she did not visit Mrs. Martin. An evening alone with Herbie meant inevitably a quarrel, yet she would stay with him. There was always her thin and worldless idea that, maybe, this night, things would begin to be all right.

The Boys brought plenty of liquor along with them whenever they came to Mrs. Martin's. Drinking with them, Mrs. Morse became lively and good-natured and audacious. She was quickly popular. When she had drunk enough to cloud her most recent battle with Herbie, she was excited by their approbation. Crab, was she? Rotten sport, was she? Well, there were some that thought different.

Ed was one of The Boys. He lived in Utica—had "his own business" there, was the awed report—but he came to New York almost every week. He was married. He showed Mrs. Morse the then current photographs of Junior and Sister, and she praised them abundantly and sincerely. Soon it was accepted by the others that Ed was her particular friend.

He staked her when they all played poker; sat next her and occasionally rubbed his knee against hers during the game. She was rather lucky. Frequently she went home with a twenty-dollar bill or a ten-dollar bill or a handful of crumpled dollars. She was glad of them. Herbie was getting, in her words, something awful about money. To ask him for it brought an instant row.

"What the hell do you do with it?" he would say. "Shoot it all on Scotch?"

"I try to run this house half-way decent," she would retort. "Never thought of that, did you? Oh, no, his lordship couldn't be bothered with that."

Again, she could not find a definite day, to fix the beginning of Ed's proprietorship. It became his custom to kiss her on the mouth when he came in, as well as for farewell, and he gave her little quick kisses of approval all through the evening. She liked this rather more than she disliked it. She never thought of his kisses when she was not with him.

He would run his hand lingeringly over her back and shoulders.

"Some dizzy blonde, eh?" he would say. "Some doll."

One afternoon she came home from Mrs. Martin's to find Herbie in the bedroom. He had been away for several nights, evidently on a prolonged drinking bout. His face was gray, his hands jerked as if they were on wires. On the bed were two old suitcases, packed high. Only her photograph remained on his bureau, and the wide doors of his closet disclosed nothing but coat-hangers.

"I'm blowing," he said. "I'm through with the whole works. I got a job in Detroit."

She sat down on the edge of the bed. She had drunk much the night before, and the four Scotches she had had with Mrs. Martin had only increased her fogginess.

"Good job?" she said.

"Oh, yeah," he said. "Looks all right."

He closed a suitcase with difficulty, swearing at it in whispers.

"There's some dough in the bank," he said. "The bank book's in your top drawer. You can have the furniture and stuff."

He looked at her, and his forehead twitched.

"God damn it, I'm through, I'm telling you," he cried. "I'm through."

"All right, all right," she said. "I heard you, didn't I?"

She saw him as if he were at one end of a cannon and she at the other. Her head was beginning to ache bumpingly, and her voice had a dreary, tiresome tone. She could not have raised it.

"Like a drink before you go?" she asked.

Again he looked at her, and a corner of his mouth jerked up.

"Cockeyed again for a change, aren't you?" he said. "That's nice. Sure, get a couple of shots, will you?"

She went to the pantry, mixed him a stiff highball, poured herself a couple of inches of whisky and drank it. Then she gave herself another portion and brought the glasses into the bedroom. He had strapped both suitcases and had put on his hat and overcoat.

He took his highball.

"Well," he said, and he gave a sudden, uncertain laugh. "Here's mud in your eye."

"Mud in your eye," she said.

They drank. He put down his glass and took up the heavy suitcases.

"Got to get a train around six," he said.

She followed him down the hall. There was a song, a song that Mrs. Martin played doggedly on the phonograph, running loudly through her mind. She had never liked the thing.

> *Night and daytime,*
> *Always playtime.*
> *Ain't we got fun?*

At the door he put down the bags and faced her.

"Well," he said. "Well, take care of yourself. You'll be all right, will you?"

"Oh, sure," she said.

He opened the door, then came back to her, holding out his hand.

" 'By, Haze," he said. "Good luck to you."

She took his hand and shook it.

"Pardon my wet glove," she said.

When the door had closed behind him, she went back to the pantry.

She was flushed and lively when she went in to Mrs. Martin's that evening. The Boys were there, Ed among them. He was glad to be in town, frisky and loud and full of jokes. But she spoke quietly to him for a minute.

"Herbie blew today," she said. "Going to live out west."

"That so?" he said. He looked at her and played with the fountain pen clipped to his waistcoat pocket.

"Think he's gone for good, do you?" he asked.

"Yeah," she said. "I know he is. I know. Yeah."

"You going to live on across the hall just the same?" he said. "Know what you're going to do?"

"Gee, I don't know," she said. "I don't give much of a damn."

"Oh, come on, that's no way to talk," he told her. "What you need—you need a little snifter. How about it?"

"Yeah," she said. "Just straight."

She won forty-three dollars at poker. When the game broke up, Ed took her back to her apartment.

"Got a little kiss for me?" he asked.

He wrapped her in his big arms and kissed her violently. She was entirely passive. He held her away and looked at her.

"Little tight, honey?" he asked, anxiously. "Not going to be sick, are you?"

"Me?" she said. "I'm swell."

II

When Ed left in the morning, he took her photograph with him. He said he wanted her picture to look at, up in Utica. "You can have that one on the bureau," she said.

She put Herbie's picture in a drawer, out of her sight. When she could look at it, she meant to tear it up. She was fairly successful in keeping her mind from racing around him. Whisky slowed it for her. She was almost peaceful, in her mist.

She accepted her relationship with Ed without question or enthusiasm. When he was away, she seldom thought definitely of him. He was good to her; he gave her frequent presents and a regular allowance. She was even able to save.

She did not plan ahead of any day, but her wants were few, and you might as well put money in the bank as have it lying around.

When the lease of her apartment neared its end, it was Ed who suggested moving. His friendship with Mrs. Martin and Joe had become strained over a dispute at poker; a feud was impending.

"Let's get the hell out of here," Ed said. "What I want you to have is a place near the Grand Central. Make it easier for me."

So she took a little flat in the Forties. A colored maid came in every day to clean and to make coffee for her—she was "through with that housekeeping stuff," she said, and Ed, twenty years married to a passionately domestic woman, admired this romantic uselessness and felt doubly a man of the world in abetting it.

The coffee was all she had until she went out to dinner, but alcohol kept her fat. Prohibition she regarded only as a basis for jokes. You could always get all you wanted. She was never noticeably drunk and seldom nearly sober. It required a larger daily allowance to keep her misty-minded. Too little, and she was achingly melancholy.

Ed brought her to Jimmy's. He was proud, with the pride of the transient who would be mistaken for a native, in his knowledge of small, recent restaurants occupying the lower floors of shabby brownstone houses; places where, upon mentioning the name of an habitué friend, might be obtained strange whisky and fresh gin in many of their ramifications. Jimmy's place was the favorite of his acquaintances.

There, through Ed, Mrs. Morse met many men and women, formed quick friendships. The men often took her out when Ed was in Utica. He was proud of her popularity.

She fell into the habit of going to Jimmy's alone when she had no engagement. She was certain to meet some people she knew, and join them. It was a club for her friends, both men and women.

The women at Jimmy's looked remarkably alike, and this was curious, for, through feuds, removals, and opportunities of more profitable contacts, the personnel of the group changed constantly. Yet always the newcomers resembled those whom they replaced. They were all big women and stout, broad of shoulder and abundantly breasted, with faces thickly clothed in soft, high-colored flesh. They laughed loud and often, showing opaque and lusterless teeth like squares of crockery. There was about them the health of the big, yet a slight, unwholesome suggestion of stubborn preservation. They might have been thirty-six or forty-five or anywhere between.

They composed their titles of their own first names with their husbands' surnames—Mrs. Florence Miller, Mrs. Vera Riley, Mrs. Lilian Block. This gave at the same time the solidity of marriage and the glamour of freedom. Yet only one or two were actually divorced. Most of them never referred to their dimmed spouses; some, a shorter time separated, described them in terms of great biological interest. Several were mothers, each of an only child—a boy at school somewhere, or a girl being cared for by a grandmother. Often, well on towards morning, there would be displays of Kodak portraits and of tears.

They were comfortable women, cordial and friendly and irrepressibly matronly. Theirs was the quality of ease. Become fatalistic, especially about money matters, they were unworried. Whenever their funds dropped alarmingly, a new donor appeared; this had always happened. The aim of each was to have one man, permanently, to pay all her bills, in return for which she would have immediately given up other admirers and probably would have become exceedingly fond of him; for the affections of all of them were, by now, unexacting, tranquil, and easily arranged. This end, however, grew increasingly difficult yearly. Mrs. Morse was regarded as fortunate.

Ed had a good year, increased her allowance and gave her a sealskin coat. But she had to be careful of her moods with him. He insisted upon gaiety. He would not listen to admissions of aches or weariness.

"Hey, listen," he would say, "I got worries of my own, and plenty. Nobody wants to hear other people's troubles, sweetie. What you got to do, you got to be a sport and forget it. See? Well, slip us a little smile, then. That's my girl."

She never had enough interest to quarrel with him as she had with Herbie, but she wanted the privilege of occasional admitted sadness. It was strange. The other women she saw did not have to fight their moods. There was Mrs. Florence Miller who got regular crying jags, and the men sought only to cheer and comfort her. The others spent whole evenings in grieved recitals of worries and ills; their escorts paid them deep sympathy. But she was instantly undesirable when she was low in spirits. Once, at Jimmy's, when she could not make herself lively, Ed had walked out and left her.

"Why the hell don't you stay home and not go spoiling everybody's evening?" he had roared.

Even her slightest acquaintances seemed irritated if she were not conspicuously light-hearted.

"What's the matter with you, anyway? they would say. "Be your age, why don't you? Have a little drink and snap out of it."

When her relationship with Ed had continued nearly three years, he moved to Florida to live. He hated leaving her; he gave her a large check and some shares of a sound stock, and his pale eyes were wet when he said good-by. She did not miss him. He came to New York infrequently, perhaps two or three times a year, and hurried directly from the train to see her. She was always pleased to have him come and never sorry to see him go.

Charley, an acquaintance of Ed's that she had met at Jimmy's, had long admired her. He had always made opportunities of touching her and leaning close to talk to her. He asked repeatedly of all their friends if they had ever heard such a fine laugh as she had. After Ed left, Charley became the main figure in her life. She classified him and spoke of him as "not so bad." There was nearly a year of Charley; then she divided her time between him and Sydney, another frequenter of Jimmy's; then Charley slipped away altogether.

Sydney was a little brightly dressed, clever Jew. She was perhaps nearest contentment with him. He amused her always; her laughter was not forced.

He admired her completely. Her softness and size delighted him. And he thought she was great, he often told her, because she kept gay and lively when she was drunk.

"Once I had a gal," he said, "used to try and throw herself out of the window every time she got a can on. Jee-*zuss*," he added, feelingly.

Then Sydney married a rich and watchful bride, and then there was Billy. No—after Sydney came Fred, then Billy. In her haze, she never recalled how men entered her life and left it. There were no surprises. She had no thrill at their advent, nor woe at their departure. She seemed to be always able to attract men. There was never another as rich as Ed, but they were all generous to her, in their means.

Once she had news of Herbie. She met Mrs. Martin dining at Jimmy's, and the old friendship was vigorously renewed. The still admiring Joe, while on a business trip, had seen Herbie. He had settled in Chicago, he looked fine, he was living with some woman—seemed to be crazy about her. Mrs. Morse had been drinking vastly that day. She took the news with mild interest, as one hearing of the sex peccadilloes of somebody whose name is, after a moment's groping, familiar.

"Must be damn near seven years since I saw him," she commented. "Gee. Seven years."

More and more, her days lost their individuality. She never knew dates, nor was sure of the day of the week.

"My God, was that a year ago!" she would exclaim, when an event was recalled in conversation.

She was tired so much of the time. Tired and blue. Almost everything could give her the blues. Those old horses she saw on Sixth Avenue—struggling and slipping along the car-tracks, or standing at the curb, their heads dropped level with their worn knees. The tightly stored tears would squeeze from her eyes as she teetered past on her aching feet in the stubby, champagne-colored slippers.

The thought of death came and stayed with her and lent her a sort of drowsy cheer. It would be nice, nice and restful, to be dead.

There was no settled, shocked moment when she first thought of killing herself; it seemed to her as if the idea had always been with her. She pounced upon all the accounts of suicides in the newspapers. There was an epidemic of self-killings—or maybe it was just that she searched for the stories of them so eagerly that she found many. To read of them roused reassurance in her; she felt a cozy solidarity with the big company of the voluntary dead.

She slept, aided by whisky, till deep into the afternoons, then lay abed, a bottle and glass at her hand, until it was time to dress to go out for dinner. She was beginning to feel towards alcohol a little puzzled distrust, as toward an old friend who has refused a simple favor. Whisky could still soothe her for most of the time, but there were sudden, inexplicable moments when the cloud fell treacherously away from her, and she was sawed by the sorrow and bewilderment and nuisance of all living. She played voluptuously with the thought of cool, sleepy retreat. She had never been troubled by religious belief and no vision of an after-life intimidated her. She dreamed by day of never again putting on tight shoes, of never having to laugh and listen and admire, of never more being a good sport. Never.

But how would you do it? It made her sick to think of jumping from heights. She could not stand a gun. At the theater, if one of the actors drew a revolver, she crammed her fingers into her ears and could not even look at the stage until after the shot had been fired. There was no gas in her flat. She looked long at the bright blue veins in her slim wrists—a cut with a razor blade, and there you'd be. But it would hurt, hurt like hell, and there would be blood to see. Poison— something tasteless and quick and painless—was the thing. But they wouldn't sell it to you in drugstores, because of the law.

She had few other thoughts.

There was a new man now—Art. He was short and fat and exacting and hard on her patience when he was drunk. But there had been only occasionals for some time before him, and she was glad of a little stability. Too, Art must be away for weeks at a stretch, selling silks, and that was restful. She was convincingly gay with him, though the effort shook her.

"The best sport in the world," he would murmur, deep in her neck. "The best sport in the world."

One night, when he had taken her to Jimmy's, she went into the dressing-room with Mrs. Florence Miller. There, while designing curly mouths on their faces with lip-rouge, they compared experiences of insomnia.

"Honestly," Mrs. Morse said, "I wouldn't close an eye if I didn't go to bed full of Scotch. I lie there and toss and turn and toss and turn. Blue! Does a person get blue lying awake that way!"

"Say, listen, Hazel," Mrs. Miller said, impressively, "I'm telling you I'd be awake for a year if I didn't take veronal. That stuff makes you sleep like a fool."

"Isn't it poison, or something?" Mrs. Morse asked.

"Oh, you take too much and you're out for the count," said Mrs. Miller. "I just take five grains—they come in tablets. I'd be scared to fool around with it. But five grains, and you cork off pretty."

"Can you get it anywhere?" Mrs. Morse felt superbly Machiavellian.

"Get all you want in Jersey," said Mrs. Miller. "They won't give it to you here without you have a doctor's prescription. Finished? We'd better go back and see what the boys are doing."

That night, Art left Mrs. Morse at the door of her apartment; his mother was in town. Mrs. Morse was still sober, and it happened that there was no whisky left in her cupboard. She lay in bed, looking up at the black ceiling.

She rose early, for her, and went to New Jersey. She had never taken the tube, and did not understand it. So she went to the Pennsylvania Station and bought a railroad ticket to Newark. She thought of nothing in particular on the trip out. She looked at the uninspired hats of the women about her and gazed through the smeared window at the flat, gritty scene.

In Newark, in the first drug-store she came to, she asked for a tin of talcum powder, a nailbrush, and a box of veronal tablets. The powder and brush were to make the hypnotic seem also a casual need. The clerk was entirely unconcerned. "We only keep them in bottles," he said, and wrapped up for her a little glass vial containing ten white tablets, stacked one on another.

She went to another drug-store and bought a face-cloth, an orange-wood stick, and a bottle of veronal tablets. The clerk was also uninterested.

"Well, I guess I got enough to kill an ox," she thought, and went back to the station.

At home, she put the little vials in the drawer of her dressing-table and stood looking at them with a dreamy tenderness.

"There they are, God bless them," she said, and she kissed her finger-tip and touched each bottle.

The colored maid was busy in the living-room.

"Hey, Nettie," Mrs. Morse called. "Be an angel, will you? Run around to Jimmy's and get me a quart of Scotch."

She hummed while she awaited the girl's return.

During the next few days, whisky ministered to her as tenderly as it had done when she first turned to its aid. Alone, she was soothed and vague, at Jimmy's she was the gayest of the groups. Art was delighted with her.

Then, one night, she had an appointment to meet Art at Jimmy's for an early dinner. He was to leave afterward on a business excursion, to be away for a week. Mrs. Morse had been drinking all the afternoon; while she dressed to go out, she felt herself rising pleasurably from drowsiness to high spirits. But as she came out into the street the effects of the whisky deserted her completely, and she was filled with a slow, grinding wretchedness so horrible that she stood swaying on the pavement, unable for a moment to move forward. It was a gray night with spurts of mean, thin snow, and the streets shone with dark ice. As she slowly crossed Sixth Avenue, consciously dragging one foot past the other, a big, scarred horse pulling a rickety express-wagon crashed to his knees before her. The driver swore and screamed and lashed the beast insanely, bringing the whip back over his shoulder for every blow, while the horse struggled to get a footing on the slippery asphalt. A group gathered and watched with interest.

Art was waiting, when Mrs. Morse reached Jimmy's.

"What's the matter with you, for God's sake?" was his greeting to her.

"I saw a horse," she said. "Gee, I—a person feels sorry for horses. I—it isn't just horses. Everything's kind of terrible, isn't it? I can't help getting sunk."

"Ah, sunk, me eye," he said. "What's the idea of all the bellyaching? What have you got to be sunk about?"

"I can't help it," she said.

"Ah, help it, me eye," he said. "Pull yourself together, will you? Come on and sit down, and take that face off you."

She drank industriously and she tried hard, but she could not overcome her melancholy. Others joined them and commented on her gloom, and she could do no more for them than smile weakly. She made little dabs at her eyes with her handkerchief, trying to time her movements so they would be unnoticed, but several times Art caught her and scowled and shifted impatiently in his chair.

When it was time for him to go to his train, she said she would leave, too, and go home.

"And not a bad idea, either," he said. "See if you can't sleep yourself out of it. I'll see you Thursday. For God's sake, try and cheer up by then, will you?"

"Yeah," she said. "I will."

In her bedroom, she undressed with a tense speed wholly unlike her usual slow uncertainty. She put on her nightgown, took off her hair-net and passed the comb quickly through her dry, vari-colored hair. Then she took the two little vials from the drawer and carried them into the bathroom. The splintering misery had gone from her, and she felt the quick excitement of one who is about to receive an anticipated gift.

She uncorked the vials, filled a glass with water and stood before the mirror, a tablet between her fingers. Suddenly she bowed graciously to her reflection, and raised the glass to it.

"Well, here's mud in your eye," she said.

The tablets were unpleasant to take, dry and powdery and sticking obstinately half-way down her throat. It took her a long time to swallow all twenty of them. She stood watching her reflection with deep, impersonal interest, studying the movements of the gulping throat. Once more she spoke aloud.

"For Gȯd's sake, try and cheer up by Thursday, will you?" she said. "Well, you know what he can do. He and the whole lot of them."

She had no idea how quickly to expect effect from the veronal. When she had taken the last tablet, she stood uncertainly, wondering, still with a courteous, vicarious interest, if death would strike her down then and there. She felt in no way strange, save for a slight stirring of sickness from the effort of swallowing the tablets, nor did her reflected face look at all different. It would not be immediate, then; it might even take an hour or so.

She stretched her arms high and gave a vast yawn.

"Guess I'll go to bed," she said. "Gee, I'm nearly dead."

That struck her as comic, and she turned out the bathroom light and went in and laid herself down in her bed, chuckling softly all the time.

"Gee, I'm nearly dead," she quoted. "That's a hot one!"

III

Nettie, the colored maid, came in late the next afternoon to clean the apartment, and found Mrs. Morse in her bed. But then, that was not unusual. Usually, though, the sounds of cleaning waked her, and she did not like to wake up. Nettie, an agreeable girl, had learned to move softly about her work.

But when she had done the living-room and stolen in to tidy the little square bedroom, she could not avoid a tiny clatter as she arranged the objects on the dressing-table. Instinctively, she glanced over her shoulder at the sleeper, and without warning a sickly uneasiness crept over her. She came to the bed and stared down at the woman lying there.

Mrs. Morse lay on her back, one flabby, white arm flung up, the wrist against her forehead. Her stiff hair hung untenderly along her face. The bed covers were pushed down, exposing a deep square of soft neck and a pink nightgown, its fabric worn uneven by many launderings; her great breasts, freed from their tight confiner, sagged beneath her arm-pits. Now and then she made knotted, snoring sounds, and from the corner of her opened mouth to the blurred turn of her jaw ran a lane of crusted spittle.

"Mis' Morse," Nettie called. "Oh, Mis' Morse! It's terrible late."

Mrs. Morse made no move.

"Mis' Morse," said Nettie. "Look, Mis' Morse. How'm I goin' get this bed made?"

Panic sprang upon the girl. She shook the woman's hot shoulder.

"Ah, wake up, will yuh?" she whined. "Ah, please wake up."

Suddenly the girl turned and ran out in the hall to the elevator door, keeping her thumb firm on the black, shiny button until the elderly car and its Negro attendant stood before her. She poured a jumble of words over the boy, and led him back to the apartment. He tiptoed creakingly in to the bedside; first gingerly, then so lustily that he left marks in the soft flesh, he prodded the unconscious woman.

"Hey, there!" he cried, and listened intently, as for an echo.

"Jeez. Out like a light," he commented.

At his interest in the spectacle, Nettie's panic left her. Importance was big in both of them. They talked in quick, unfinished whispers, and it was the boy's suggestion that he fetch the young doctor who lived on the ground floor. Nettie hurried along with him. They looked forward to the limelit moment of breaking their news of something untoward, something pleasurably unpleasant. Mrs. Morse had become the medium of drama. With no ill wish to her, they hoped that her state was serious, that she would not let them down by being awake and normal on their return. A little fear of this determined them to make the most, to the doctor, of her present condition. "Matter of life and death," returned to Nettie from her thin store of reading. She considered startling the doctor with the phrase.

The doctor was in and none too pleased at interruption. He wore a yellow and blue striped dressing-gown, and he was lying on his sofa, laughing with a dark girl, her face scaly with inexpensive powder, who perched on the arm. Half-emptied highball glasses stood beside them, and her coat and hat were neatly hung up with the comfortable implication of a long stay.

Always something, the doctor grumbled. Couldn't let anybody alone after a hard day. But he put some bottles and instruments into a case, changed his dressing-gown for his coat and started out with the Negroes.

"Snap it up there, big boy," the girl called after him. "Don't be all night."

The doctor strode loudly into Mrs. Morse's flat and on to the bedroom, Nettie and the boy right behind him. Mrs. Morse had not moved; her sleep was as deep, but soundless, now. The doctor looked sharply at her, then plunged his thumbs into the lidded pits above her eyeballs and threw his weight upon them. A high, sickened cry broke from Nettie.

"Look like he tryin' to push her right on th'ough the bed," said the boy. He chuckled.

Mrs. Morse gave no sign under the pressure. Abruptly the doctor abandoned it, and with one quick movement swept the covers down to the foot of the bed. With another he flung her nightgown back and lifted the thick, white legs, cross-hatched with blocks of tiny, iris-colored veins. He pinched them repeatedly, with long, cruel nips, back of the knees. She did not awaken.

"What's she been drinking?" he asked Nettie, over his shoulder.

With the certain celerity of one who knows just where to lay hands on a thing, Nettie went into the bathroom, bound for the cupboard where Mrs. Morse kept her whisky. But she stopped at the sight of the two vials, with their red and white labels, lying before the mirror. She brought them to the doctor.

"Oh, for the Lord Almighty's sweet sake!" he said. He dropped Mrs. Morse's legs, and pushed them impatiently across the bed. "What did she want to go taking that tripe for? Rotten yellow trick, that's what a thing like that is. Now we'll have to pump her out, and all that stuff. Nuisance, a thing like that is; that's what it amounts to. Here, George, take me down in the elevator. You wait here, maid. She won't do anything."

"She won't die on me, will she?" cried Nettie.

"No," said the doctor. "God, no. You couldn't kill her with an ax."

IV

After two days, Mrs. Morse came back to consciousness, dazed at first, then with a comprehension that brought with it the slow, saturating wretchedness.

"Oh, Lord, oh, Lord," she moaned, and tears for herself and for life striped her cheeks.

Nettie came in at the sound. For two days she had done the ugly, incessant tasks in the nursing of the unconscious, for two nights she had caught broken bits of sleep on the living-room couch. She looked coldly at the big, blown woman in the bed.

"What you been tryin' to do, Mis' Morse?" she said. "What kine o' work is that, takin' all that stuff?"

"Oh, Lord," moaned Mrs. Morse, again, and she tried to cover her eyes with her arms. But the joints felt stiff and brittle, and she cried out at their ache.

"Tha's no way to ack, takin' them pills," said Nettie. "You can thank you' stars you heah at all. How you feel now?"

"Oh, I feel great," said Mrs. Morse. "Swell, I feel."

Her hot, painful tears fell as if they would never stop.

"Tha's no way to take on, cryin' like that," Nettie said. "After what you done. The doctor, he says he could have you arrested, doin' a thing like that. He was fit to be tied, here."

"Why couldn't he let me alone?" wailed Mrs. Morse. "Why the hell couldn't he have?"

"Tha's terr'ble, Mis' Morse, swearin' an' talkin' like that," said Nettie, "after what people done for you. Here I ain' had no sleep at all for two nights, an' had to give up goin' out to my other ladies!"

"Oh, I'm sorry, Nettie," she said. "You're a peach. I'm sorry I've given you so much trouble. I couldn't help it. I just got sunk. Didn't you ever feel like doing it? When everything looks just lousy to you?"

"I wouldn' think o' no such thing," declared Nettie. "You got to cheer up. Tha's what you got to do. Everybody's got their troubles."

"Yeah," said Mrs. Morse. "I know."

"Come a pretty picture card for you," Nettie said. "Maybe that will cheer you up."

She handed Mrs. Morse a post-card. Mrs. Morse had to cover one eye with her hand, in order to read the message; her eyes were not yet focusing correctly.

It was from Art. On the back of a view of the Detroit Athletic Club he had written: "Greeting and salutations. Hope you have lost that gloom. Cheer up and don't take any rubber nickles. See you on Thursday."

She dropped the card to the floor. Misery crushed her as if she were between great smooth stones. There passed before her a slow, slow pageant of days spent lying in her flat, of evenings at Jimmy's being a good sport, making herself laugh and coo at Art and other Arts; she saw a long parade of weary horses and shivering beggars and all beaten, driven, stumbling things. Her feet throbbed as if she had crammed them into the stubby champagne-colored slippers. Her heart seemed to swell and harden.

"Nettie," she cried, "for heaven's sake pour me a drink, will you?"

The maid looked doubtful.

"Now you know, Mis' Morse," she said, "you been near daid. I don' know if the doctor he let you drink nothin' yet."

"Oh, never mind him," she said. "You get me one, and bring in the bottle. Take one yourself."

"Well," said Nettie.

She poured them each a drink, deferentially leaving hers in the bathroom to be taken in solitude, and brought Mrs. Morse's glass in to her.

Mrs. Morse looked into the liquor and shuddered back from its odor. Maybe it would help. Maybe, when you have been knocked cold for a few days, your very first drink would give you a lift. Maybe whisky would be her friend again. She prayed without addressing a God, without knowing a God. Oh, please, please let her be able to get drunk, please keep her always drunk.

She lifted the glass.

"Thanks, Nettie," she said. "Here's mud in your eye."

The maid giggled. "Tha's the way, Mis' Morse," she said. "You cheer up, now."

"Yeah," said Mrs. Morse. "Sure."

THE OLD AGE HOME

Voluntarily walled themselves up inside the stone,
Because life no longer held for them a way of getting
      along—
On the shores of the reservoir as if it was some
      wisdom of the town's
They have stored up in them by having lived in it;
Each day cared for by a world that no longer has
      meaning:
Food prepared on trays sent up from below,
Beds from which they need only arise to return to
      them made;
Entertainment, what pastimes they can devise for
      themselves
Or the moving figures on the screen in the solarium.
Aged men and aged women passing their days
Stirring a little dust in the corridors—combing their
      hair
In bathrobes as they once did for their dinner dates,
Putting on a touch of lipstick to add color to their face;
Gestures made in expiation of wounds that have
      healed:
Sly smiles, overtures of commiseration, minor
      gallantries;
An intercourse arisen out of the knowledge of the
      old failures—
Being able to get along now because they no longer are
An expression of the reason why; making of infirmity
      a life.

What society has raised to the colloquies of the past,
Looking out over a body of water toward a graveyard
      on a hill;
Surrounded by the unintelligible order of nature
      renewing itself,
They have raised this institution of brick to preserve
      them:
The old rocking on balconies or strolling along
      flowered paths,
At the edge of that lake looking out toward that
      further hill.
The gulf of their existence between them and their
      final end—
All that they once took for their image reflected in
      life,
Now only become the dimensions of space through
      which they see:

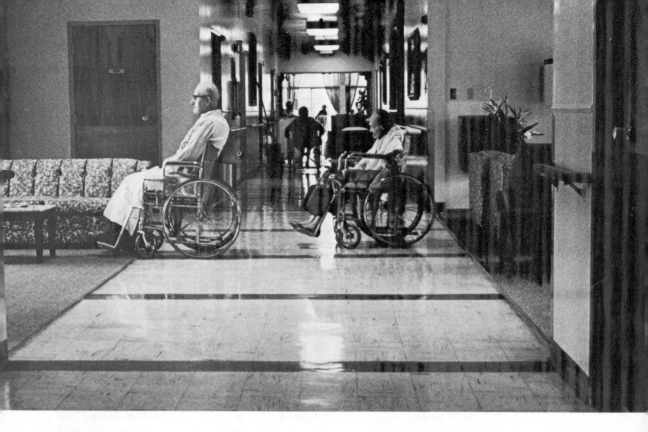

The nursing home today holds a terror for the aged that Bedlam once held for the insane, the chain gangs once held for convicts, and that sweat shops once held for children.

Richard Garvin and Robert E. Burger, Where They Go To Die

The hole of their dreams, broken off bits of desire,
    the emptiness
That always lay just beyond their fulfillment;
    wisdom
Written out in the soul in words: the forms of life
    without its needs.
The sun setting in the west over the graveyard
Casts up in the heavens the promise of an existence
    beyond it;
The stones, a monument to the last point of their
    identity
As they go on in the world as others—in the lake
The colors reflected like the story of a life going on
    above it:
It is the water that bubbles up in the fountains in
    our studies.

    —Theodore Holmes

A VISIT OF CHARITY

By Eudora Welty

It was mid-morning—a very cold, bright day. Holding a potted plant before her, a girl of fourteen jumped off the bus in front of the Old Ladies' Home, on the outskirts of town. She wore a red coat, and her straight yellow hair was hanging down loose from the pointed white cap all the little girls were wearing that year. She stopped for a moment beside one of the prickly dark shrubs with which the city had beautified the Home, and then proceeded slowly toward the building, which was of whitewashed brick and reflected the winter sunlight like a block of ice. As she walked vaguely up the steps she shifted the small pot from hand to hand; then she had to set it down and remove her mittens before she could open the heavy door.

"I'm a Campfire Girl. . . . I have to pay a visit to some old lady," she told the nurse at the desk. This was a woman in a white uniform who looked as if she were cold; she had close-cut hair which stood up on the very top of her head exactly like a sea wave. Marian, the little girl, did not tell her that this visit would give her a minimum of only three points in her score.

"Acquainted with any of our residents?" asked the nurse. She lifted one eyebrow and spoke like a man.

"With any old ladies? No—but—that is, any of them will do," Marian stammered. With her free hand she pushed her hair behind her ears, as she did when it was time to study Science.

The nurse shrugged and rose. "You have a nice *multiflora cineraria* there," she remarked as she walked ahead down the hall of closed doors to pick out an old lady.

There was loose, bulging linoleum on the floor. Marian felt as if she were walking on the waves, but the nurse paid no attention to it. There was a smell in the hall like the interior of a clock. Everything was silent until, behind one of the doors, an old lady of some kind cleared her throat like a sheep bleating. This decided the nurse. Stopping in her tracks, she first extended her arm, bent her

Reprinted by permission of Harcourt, Brace & World from Eudora Welty, *A Curtain of Green and Other Stories* (New York: Harcourt, Brace & World, 1941).

elbow, and leaned forward from the hips—all to examine the watch strapped to her wrist; then she gave a loud double-rap on the door.

"There are two in each room," the nurse remarked over her shoulder.

"Two what?" asked Marian without thinking. The sound like a sheep's bleating almost made her turn around and run back.

One old woman was pulling the door open in short, gradual jerks, and when she saw the nurse a strange smile forced her old face dangerously awry. Marian, suddenly propelled by the strong, impatient arm of the nurse, saw next the side-face of another old woman, even older, who was laying flat in bed with a cap on and a counterpane drawn up to her chin.

"Visitor," said the nurse, and after one more shove she was off up the hall.

Marian stood tongue-tied; both hands held the potted plant. The old woman, still with that terrible, square smile (which was a smile of welcome) stamped on her bony face, was waiting. . . . Perhaps she said something. The old woman in bed said nothing at all, and she did not look around.

Suddenly Marian saw a hand, quick as a bird claw, reach up in the air and pluck the white cap off her head. At the same time, another claw to match drew her all the way into the room, and the next moment the door closed behind her.

"My, my, my," said the old lady at her side.

Marian stood enclosed by a bed, a washstand and a chair; the tiny room had altogether too much furniture. Everything smelled wet—even the bare floor. She held onto the back of the chair, which was wicker and felt soft and damp. Her heart beat more and more slowly, her hands got colder and colder, and she could not hear whether the old women were saying anything or not. She could not see them very clearly. How dark it was! The window shade was down, and the only door was shut. Marian looked at the ceiling. . . . It was like being caught in a robbers' cave, just before one was murdered.

"Did you come to be our little girl for a while?" the first robber asked.

Then something was snatched from Marian's hand—the little potted plant.

"Flowers!" screamed the old woman. She stood holding the pot in an undecided way. "Pretty flowers," she added.

Then the old woman in bed cleared her throat and spoke. "They are not pretty," she said, still without looking around, but very distinctly.

Marian suddenly pitched against the chair and sat down in it.

"Pretty flowers," the first old woman insisted. "Pretty—pretty . . ."

Marian wished she had the little pot back for just a moment—she had forgotten to look at the plant herself before giving it away. What did it look like?

"Stinkweeds," said the other old woman sharply. She had a bunchy white forehead and red eyes like a sheep. Now she turned them toward Marian. The fogginess seemed to rise in her throat again, and she bleated, "Who—are—you?"

To her surprise, Marian could not remember her name. "I'm a Campfire Girl," she said finally.

"Watch out for the germs," said the old woman like a sheep, not addressing anyone.

"One came out last month to see us," said the first old woman.

A sheep or a germ? wondered Marian dreamily, holding onto the chair.

"Did not!" cried the other old woman.

"Did so! Read to us out of the Bible, and we enjoyed it!" screamed the first.

"Who enjoyed it!" said the woman in bed. Her mouth was unexpectedly small and sorrowful, like a pet's.

"We enjoyed it," insisted the other. "You enjoyed it—I enjoyed it."

"We all enjoyed it," said Marian, without realizing that she had said a word.

The first old woman had just finished putting the potted plant high, high on the top of the wardrobe, where it could hardly be seen from below. Marian wondered how she had ever succeeded in placing it there, how she could ever have reached so high.

"You mustn't pay any attention to old Addie," she now said to the little girl. "She's ailing today."

"Will you shut your mouth?" said the woman in bed. "I am not."

"You're a story."

"I can't stay but a minute—really, I can't," said Marian suddenly. She looked down at the wet floor and thought that if she were sick in here they would have to let her go.

With much to-do the first old woman sat down in a rocking chair—still another piece of furniture!—and began to rock. With the fingers of one hand she touched a very dirty cameo pin on her chest. "What do you do at school?" she asked.

"I don't know . . ." said Marian. She tried to think but she could not.

"Oh, but the flowers are beautiful," the old woman whispered. She seemed to rock faster and faster; Marian did not see how anyone could rock so fast.

"Ugly," said the woman in bed.

"If we bring flowers—" Marian began, and then fell silent. She had almost said that if Campfire Girls brought flowers to the Old Ladies' Home, the visit would count one extra point, and if they took a Bible with them on the bus and read to the old ladies, it counted double. But the old woman had not listened, anyway; she was rocking and watching the other one, who watched back from the bed.

"Poor Addie is ailing. She has to take medicine—see?" she said, pointing a horny finger at a row of bottles on the table, and rocking so high that her black comfort shoes lifted off the floor like a little child's.

"I am no more sick than you are," said the woman in bed.

"Oh, yes you are!"

"I just got more sense than you have, that's all," said the other old woman, nodding her head.

"That's only the contrary way she talks when *you all* come," said the first old lady with sudden intimacy. She stopped the rocker with a neat pat of her feet and leaned toward Marian. Her hand reached over—it felt like a petunia leaf, clinging and just a little sticky.

"Will you hush! Will you hush!" cried the other one.

Marian leaned back rigidly in her chair.

"When I was a little girl like you, I went to school and all," said the old woman in the same intimate, menacing voice. "Not here—another town. . . ."

"Hush!" said the sick woman. "You never went to school. You never came and you never went. You never were anything—only here. You never were born! You don't know anything. Your head is empty, your heart and hands and your old black purse are all empty, even that little old box that you brought with you you brought empty—you showed it to me. And yet you talk, talk, talk, talk, talk

OLD MEN

People expect old men to die,
They do not really mourn old men.
Old men are different. People look
At them with eyes that wonder when . . .
People watch with unshocked eyes;
But the old men know when an old man dies.

— *Ogden Nash*

Reprinted by permission of Little, Brown and Company from Ogden Nash. *Verses from 1929 On* (Boston: Little, Brown and Company, 1933).

WHO CARES FOR THE AGED?

By Robert E. Burger

Approximately one of every ten Americans is over sixty-five, and the proportion is increasing every year. Two-thirds of these Americans suffer from some chronic condition—high blood pressure, arthritis, diabetes, or other afflictions. Yet there are only about 30,000 institutions of all kinds designed to take care of them—with enough beds to handle only one out of fifty. The majority of the aged, in addition, do not qualify for either Medicare or Medicaid. The *median* annual income for the single person over sixty-five is $1,055, and 30 percent—single or married—live in poverty. Their families, therefore, must be able to pay what amounts to half of a normal take-home wage per month for even the most limited care.

The financial dilemma posed by nursing homes reflects a more fundamental question. What is the place of the aged in America? Most Americans have accepted the assumption that the aged are better off by themselves. We seem to believe that their medical needs are different, and that

they can be treated more efficiently as a group; that their interests and their sensibilities are protected when they are among others of their own age; and that they live longer, happier lives away from the pressures of the competitive, youthful world. All of these assumptions are fundamentally incorrect, but the pressures leading to them are easy to understand. We have not been able to face the basic medical need of the aged—rehabilitation. A definitive study in 1966 of 2,000 public-welfare patients of New York nursing homes concluded that, "extensive rehabilitation of aged residents in nursing homes is neither practical nor socially productive. . . . Maximum rehabilitation efforts should be applied earlier, and in other sites than nursing homes. We have habitually viewed the nursing home not as a place for rehabilitation at all, but as "the last resort" for a "difficult" older person. Thus, the basic technique of rehabilitation—keeping the patient active—has been systematically precluded by the way such homes are

Reprinted by permission of Robert E. Burger.

filled and financed. Bedridden patients receive a higher welfare payment, require less attention, and seldom leave.

The rapid industrialization of America has also stripped our aged of the responsibilities and functions they

---

The generation gap is not a matter of chronological age—it is a matter of being turned on or turned off to what's happening today.

Helen Berryhill

possessed in an agrarian society. Unproductive, they soon feel unwanted. And so the pressures for separation from society grow on both sides, a tendency that seems to have psychological validity among younger and younger age groups. The executive "retires early" because his fifty-ish age level has put him out of contention for a promotion. The blue collar worker buys a condominium in a "retirement village" (minimum age, once fifty-three, is now down to forty-five), because his grown children have no real contact with him.

These psychological pressures, working to widen the gap between the old and young, have received unexpected impetus from another source. The miracle that has made old age possible for many more Americans has also made it more frustrating. Modern medicine has increased the life expectancy for American men from forty-nine years in 1900 to almost seventy years today. Yet the life expectancy for men at the age of sixty-five is fourteen additional years, compared to thirteen in 1900. We have prolonged life in general, thereby creating a larger group of the aged; but we have not prolonged the life of the aged. Worse, we have not made the life of the aged meaningful or in any sense self-sufficient. Instead, we have placed most of the burdens of health care on the shoulders of the aged and their families.

The American "solution"—nursing homes, homes for the aged, rest homes, retirement villages—begs the question of whether the aged are better off away from society. We have been able to hide the problem of the impossible demands of medical attention for the aged only by putting the aged who are ill out of public sight.

The latest fad in the stock market, according to financial columnist Sylvia Porter, is the nursing home business. Even before Medicare was

voted in, such firms as Holiday Inn and Sheraton Hotels were planning nursing home chains. At least seven chains are now publicly owned and, according to *Business Week*, "most have become high fliers." Federally financed programs are obviously behind this boomlet, as they are responsible for the construction of housing for the aged in low-income redevelopment projects. Tax laws have also made church-sponsored old-age apartment complexes financially feasible. It would seem that, although the cost to the individual family may still be high, care for the aged is catching up with the medical and environmental problem.

A basic misconception, however, clouds the issue. Medicare covers only a small minority of the aged—those who require post-hospital care for a maximum of 100 days. In the language of the bill, Title XVIII of the Social Security Act of 1967, a Medicare patient is one who needs "extended care" in a "medically oriented" facility. "Extended" means extended from a hospital, not extended in time or extensive in nature. The idea of Medicare was to take old people out of hospitals when they could be treated adequately in a nursing home near a hospital before going home. Medicare pays $16 a day for room, board, and medical care to the nursing home, for each qualified patient. It is not intended to provide a solution for old people who wish to retire from society.

The nursing home chains touted in financial circles have been developed merely for the specialized need of providing hospital-related, short-term care. It is a sad commentary on the standards of nursing homes prior to Medicare that such a wide-open market exists for facilities that meet even the nominal requirements

Loneliness, isolation, and sickness are the affliction of the aged in every economic class. But for those who are poor, there is an intensification of these tragedies. They are more lonely, more isolated, sicker.

Michael Harrington,
The Other America

of Title XVIII. To qualify under Medicare, a home must have a physician and a registered nurse "on call" around the clock—and, since the home must be affiliated with a hospital in the first place, this presents no problem. The physical-therapy specialists required by Medicare would also be only a matter of cost, not availability.

In the strictest sense of the phrase, these Medicare facilities are nursing homes. Yet the expression has been used so loosely in the past that a new nomenclature has been felt necessary. Such homes are officially referred to as "medically oriented nursing homes."

Non-medically oriented nursing homes, a contradiction in terms, make up the market for long-term or terminal care of the aged. Such facilities, as well as the more aptly described rest homes and homes for the aged, benefit from another provision of the 1967 Social Security Act, Title XIX. Dubbed "Medicaid" but usually confused with Medicare, this legislation is far broader in application and depends on matching programs established state by state. The Medicaid program is really nothing new as far as the aged are concerned, nor, in many cases, does it increase the level of care for the aged offered in state welfare programs. Institutions are paid about the same amounts under Medicaid as they were under previous programs (a basic rate of about $300 a month per patient), but more of the money now comes from Washington. Medicaid simply provides a financial base for medical assistance to citizens of all ages who fall in certain income categories. Residents of New York State are familiar with the comprehensive program initiated by Governor Rockefeller under the Medicaid program, which directly affects about one out of ten people in New York City. Besides dramatizing the skyrocketing costs of providing adequate medical care for the general public, Medicaid initially gave promise of establishing some kind of uniformity and enforceable standards among participating doctors and institutions.

Yet Medicaid has proved to be toothless in regulating the institutions that are subsidized by this law to care for the aged. "Welfare" or "MAA" (Medical Assistance to the Aged) patients and the homes that will take them are still the responsibility of *state* licensing agencies. This was assured by powerful lobbying by nursing home associations in writing key provisions of Medicaid. For years, state authorities have grappled with the problem of how to regulate substandard homes for the aged when strict enforcement would bring only further hardship on their patients. When threatened with being closed up for persistent violations, operators of ragtag homes shrug, "What do you want us to do—throw them out in the street?"

Of the roughly 30,000 institutions offering long-term care for the aged, more than half make no pretense of offering adequate nursing care. The law in most states requires a registered nurse or a licensed practical nurse to be in attendance eight hours a day at homes that care for MAA patients. But the standards for a "practical nurse" hardly measure up to the demands of aged patients with both psychological and medical problems. The shortage of registered nurses for good paying jobs in hospitals suggests the quality of care offered by registered nurses in nursing homes—whose average salary breaks down to $2.40 an hour. Practical nurses average $1.65, and the national average for all employees in nursing homes is less than $1.25. "Nurse's Aide" has become almost a meaningless designation in the trade, yet it is constantly used by nursing home operators to rationalize their fees. If a licensing agency finds that a home is ignoring the requirement of having a professional nurse on duty, a "grace period" is extended until the situation can be remedied. Some homes have been in "grace periods" for a year at a time. The Oregon Board of Health only expressed the common dilemma when it stated, "It is a hoax on the public to call these institutions for old people 'nursing homes' when there is no nursing service."

The hoax is perpetuated by individual states, however, in refusing to reorganize their agencies which regulate the field. And the $300 or more per month paid by the state for each welfare patient subsidizes substandard homes and spawns new ones.

At the other end of the medical profession, an equally destructive masquerade goes on. This is the practice of doctors setting up or sponsoring a nursing home to which they refer patients without disclosing their interest. Several years ago, Consumers Union termed this a "festering scandal that warrants prompt attention by the American Medical Association." The AMA, however, lobbies side by side with the American Nursing Home Association. Far from being attended to, this problem of conflict of interest has been openly dismissed by the new nursing home promoters. (Four Seasons Nursing Centers of America, Inc., is one of many developers who finance their homes by selling interests to physicians. Four Seasons reports that 50 per cent of its beds are often filled by referrals from their doctor-owners.)

Potentially more dangerous than conflict of interest is the moral and financial weight that the medical profession is throwing behind nursing homes as *the* solution to the problems of the aged. Rehabilitation is simply not a profitable field for investment.

It can be argued that at least these new physician-sponsored homes are correcting the abuses that have plagued the industry for the last thirty years. Yet, for every new home with private rooms, a beauty parlor, a cocktail hour, and physical therapists (at $600–$900 a month), there are a dozen that exist by cutting all possible corners to make a $300 a month subsidy from the state profitable.

According to the National Fire Prevention Association, the most dangerous place to be in America, with respect to fire, is in a nursing home. Nursing home fires are especially terrifying because of the helplessness of their victims. The NFPA has stated that deaths resulting from these fires could be greatly reduced or eliminated if sprinkler systems were universally required. But in many states, such a regulation has been systematically opposed by nursing-home or homes-for-the-aged groups on the grounds that it would put many homes out of business. In the most disastrous fire in Ohio's history, a modern, concrete-block structure became a funeral pyre for sixty-three aged patients in 1963— yet the state association successfully blocked a sprinkler ordinance that might have made such a fire impossible.

A second abuse is the threat to health in general. Gerontologists tell us that one of the most dangerous treatments for non-psychotic seniles is enforced inactivity. Under the pressure of Medicaid payments (and other "welfare" payments before Medicaid), patients are confined to bed more often than necessary, to earn a $3 to $5 additional subsidy. They are also easier to deal with, pose less of an insurance hazard from falls, and are more permanent guests.

Mere confinement to a bed, moreover, is only the beginning of the health hazard to the patient. In the typically understaffed home, the patient is not turned in his bed often enough to prevent the dreaded decubitus ulcer (euphemistically, a bedsore), an open wound which is as painful as it is difficult to arrest. The misuse of drugs, either to control patients or to cut expenses, is widespread and leads to irreversible medical problems that untrained help cannot be expected to handle. A less publicized abuse is the deprivation of those small conveniences and human activities that make up the stuff of life and, in many cases, are all that make life worth living. Food, for example, is a constant problem in the substandard home. In the states with admittedly the best nursing homes, the average spent per patient per day for food is 94 cents—and this is according to the homes' own figures supplied to justify the highest possible welfare rate. The patient's sense of purpose, or even the mere feeling of accomplishing something is absent— and this void is exploited by unscrupulous nursing home operators to cow the patients, to prevent exposure of other abuses, or to magnify their own importance. One of the most common complaints from visitors to nursing homes is the disregard for the privacy of patients. Operators often conduct an inspection tour for the benefit of prospective customers without the faintest apology to the dumbfounded patients on exhibition.

Perhaps the basic abuse is the insult to the patient as a person. Sometimes this occurs by intention. The notorious "life-care contract," for instance, amounts to an insurance policy, paid in advance by the patient or his family in a lump sum, and guarantees a bed as long as the patient lives. Whether he lives or dies, however, the money is in the hands of the person who stands to benefit from the patient's early demise. By stripping the patient of his will to live—through daily sniping, snubs, and slurs—a nursing home can kill a man. Even where life-care contracts are simply a reasonable bet by both parties, the unconscious resentment of a guest who is "overdue" cannot fail to have its effect.

In spite of numerous newspaper exposés, voluminous testimony at Congressional hearings, and an endless recitation of personal experiences by nurses, patients, and their relatives, the official stance of the industry is first to deny the existence of a problem, and second to blame any documented abuses on government red tape. When the Attorney General of California recently issued a report charging an $8-million "bilking" of MediCal by doctors, pharmacies, hospitals, and nursing homes, spokesmen for these groups called the accusation "unfounded." "Only a small minority" always seems to be the culprit. Yet the state, which pays an average of $140,000 a year to each home under MediCal, claims that *most* of these homes are guilty of double billing, over-servicing, padding, or all three.

The Department of Health, Education and Welfare has promised a nationwide review of Medicare and Medicaid as a result of the California scandal. This review could well be the opportunity for a look into the social and medical aspects of our old-age institutions as well as their financial meanderings.

Hopefully legislators and government agencies will examine the obvious alternatives to institutional care of the aged. In the parallel field of the mentally handicapped, "de-institutionalization" has already begun. Three-fourths of the population of the village of Botton, England, consist of mentally handicapped adults who have achieved a degree of isolation consistent with their malady but have, at the same time, avoided the hospital atmosphere and psychological imprisonment of an institution. At recent conferences in the United States, specialists in this field have called for an end to the "bounty" that government agencies confer on institutions for each handicapped inmate, thereby frustrating any other form of care.

Among the alternatives to institutional care of the aged are two general courses of action: greater stress on rehabilitation, and assistance to the aged as persons rather than as patients. Rehabilitation, socially and psychologically as well as physically, will have to be made as profitable as "terminal care" for any chance of success on a large scale. Medicare, with its higher medical standards and limitation to short-term care, is a step in this direction. Unfortunately, its impetus has been all but smothered in the far broader and less selective provisions of Medicaid.

Perhaps the most direct method of encouraging rehabilitation is simply to offer Medicare and Medicaid benefits to the person rather than to the institution that claims him as a patient. Payments could be made to the family for medical treatments under the supervision of their doctor and for nursing care when no adult relatives are at home. If this seems a less efficient method than mass-care in an institution, consider the success of Homemakers, Inc. This profit-minded operation now has franchises in some fifteen major cities, offering in-home

nursing or attendant care at well under the cost of a nursing or rest home. Similar services are offered in some metropolitan areas by non-profit groups.

The point is that Medicare provides only for emergency in-home care, and Medicaid offers a maximum of four hours a day. Far too many old people who desperately require some sort of personal care therefore find themselves caught in a trap between the regulations of federal and state programs—simply because these programs are built on institutional requirements other than the variety of personal needs. HEW officials are now exploring an "intermediate" form of Medicare that would recognize more general medical needs of old people other than post-hospital recuperation. Given our commitment to institutions, this at least offers a measure of relief for the present.

Amendments to Medicaid, to become effective in 1969, indicate that Congress is not unaware of the drawbacks of the present system. Although state agencies must still police the program, benefits are to be broadened beyond institutional care, and higher standards will be required—such as disclosure of ownership of nursing homes, accounting for drugs, and a level of health services similar to that of Medicare. By December 31, 1969, national fire safety regulations will go into effect for Medicaid facilities.

Strict enforcement of Medicaid provisions at the state level will have to come before the stranglehold of substandard institutions can be broken. Nursing home associations must realize that such enforcement and such exposés as the Attorney General's report in California can only help them, not hurt them. The need for good nursing homes will remain for a long time to come in a competitive, profit-motivated society. At the same time, the more basic need for a just, human, and respectful treatment of 20,000,000 aged Americans cannot remain unfulfilled.

Charles Boucher, senior medical officer in the British Ministry of Health, says: "our philosophy is that old people want to remain at home, in their own houses, surrounded by their own possessions, their own memories. We don't mind whether it is a good home, a bad home, a tiny home. That's where we believe they should be . . . where they feel secure, where they've got confidence. It's tempting to think that it's a matter of institutions and that sort of thing. I think it is rather like condemning old cars to the scrap heap."

THE MOTHER

By Paddy Chayefsky

Philco Television Playhouse
April 4, 1954

Director: DELBERT MANN
Producer: FRED COE
Associate Producer: GORDON DUFF

Cast

Old Lady: CATHLEEN NESBITT
Daughter: MAUREEN STAPLETON
Boss: DAVID OPATOSHU
Son-in-law: GEORGE L. SMITH
Negro Woman: ESTELLE HEMSLEY
Sister: PERRY WILSON
Mrs. Geegan: KATHERINE HYNES
Mrs. Kline: DORA WEISSMAN
Bookkeeper: ANNA BERGER
Puerto Rican Girl: VIOLETA DIAZ

Reprinted by permission of Simon & Schuster from *Best Television Plays* (New York: Simon & Schuster, 1955).

SON-IN-LAW (*From under the blankets*): What time is it?

DAUGHTER (*Still seated heavily on the edge of the bed*): It's half past six.

SON-IN-LAW (*From under the blankets*): What did you set it so early for?

DAUGHTER: I wanna call my mother (*She looks out at the window, the rain driving fiercely against it*) For heaven's sake, listen to that rain! She's not going down today, I'll tell you that, if I have to go over there and chain her in her bed. . . . (*She stands, crosses to the window, studies the rain*) Boy, look at it rain.

SON-IN-LAW (*Still under the covers*): What?

DAUGHTER: I said, it's raining.

She makes her way, still heavy with sleep, out of the bedroom into the foyer of the apartment. She pads in her bare feet and pajamas down the foyer to the telephone table, sits on the little chair, trying to clear her head of sleep. A baby's cry is suddenly heard in an off room. The young woman absently goes "Sshh." The baby's cry stops. The young woman picks up the receiver of the phone and dials. She waits. Then . . .

DAUGHTER: Ma? This is Annie. Did I wake you up? . . . I figured you'd be up by now. . . . Ma, you're not going downtown today, and I don't wanna hear no arguments . . . Ma, have you looked out the window? It's raining like . . . Ma, I'm not gonna let you go downtown today, do you hear me? . . . I don't care, Ma . . . Ma, I don't care . . . Ma, I'm coming over. You stay there till . . . Ma, stay there till I come over. I'm getting dressed right now. I'll drive over in the car. It won't take me ten minutes . . . Ma, you're not going out in this rain. It's not enough that you almost fainted in the subway yesterday . . . Ma, I'm hanging up, and I'm coming over right now. Stay there . . . all right, I'm hanging up . . .

She hangs up, sits for a minute, then rises and shuffles quickly back up the foyer and back into her bedroom. She disappears into the bathroom, unbuttoning the blouse of her pajamas. She leaves the bathroom door open, and a shaft of light suddenly shoots out into the dark bedroom.

SON-IN-LAW (*Awake now, his head visible over the covers*): Did you talk to her?

DAUGHTER (*Off in bathroom*): Yeah, she was all practically ready to leave.

SON-IN-LAW: Look, Annie, I don't wanna tell you how to treat your own mother, but why don't you leave her alone? It's obviously very important to her to get a job for herself. She wants to support herself. She doesn't want to be a burden on her children. I respect her for that. An old lady, sixty-six years old, going out and looking for work. I think that shows a lot of guts.

The daughter comes out of the bathroom. She has a blouse on now and a half-slip.

DAUGHTER (*Crossing to the closet*): George, please, you don't know what you're talking about, so do me a favor, and don't argue with me. I'm not in a good mood. (*She opens the closet, studies the crowded rack of clothes*) I'm turning on the light, so get your eyes ready. (*She turns on the light. The room is suddenly bright. She blinks and pokes in the closet for a skirt, which she finally extracts*) My mother worked like a dog all her life, and she's not gonna spend the rest of her life bent over a sewing machine. (*She slips into her skirt*) She had one of her attacks in the subway yesterday. I was never so scared in my life when that cop called yesterday. (*She's standing in front of her mirror now, hastily arranging her hair*) My mother worked like a dog to raise me and my brother and

my sister. She worked in my old man's grocery store till twelve o'clock at night. We owe her a little peace of mind, my brother and my sister and me. She sacrificed plenty for us in her time. (*She's back at the closet, fishing for her topcoat*) And I want her to move out of that apartment. I don't want her living alone. I want her to come live here with us, George, and I don't want any more arguments about that either. We can move Tommy in with the baby, and she can have Tommy's room. And that reminds me —the baby cried for a minute there. If she cries again, give her her milk because she went to sleep without her milk last night. (*She has her topcoat on now and is already at the door to the foyer*) All right, I'll probably be back in time to make you breakfast. Have you got the keys to the car? . . . (*She nervously pats the pocket of her coat*) No, I got them. All right, I'll see you. Good-by, George . . .

She goes out into the foyer.

SON-IN-LAW: Good-by, Annie . . .

Off in some other room, the baby begins to cry again, a little more insistently. The husband raises his eyebrows and listens for a moment. When it becomes apparent that the baby isn't going to stop, he sighs and begins to get out of bed.

Dissolve to: The old lady standing by the window again. She is fully dressed now, however, even to the black coat and hat. The coat is unbuttoned. For the first time, we may be aware of a black silk mourning band that the old lady has about the sleeve of her coat. Outside, the rain has abated considerably. It is drizzling lightly now. The old lady turns to her daughter, standing at the other end of the bedroom, brushing the rain from her coat. When the old lady speaks, it is with a mild, but distinct, Irish flavor.

OLD LADY: It's letting up a bit.

DAUGHTER (*Brushing off her coat*): It isn't letting up at all. It's gonna stop and start all day long.

The old lady starts out of her bedroom, past her daughter, into her living room.

OLD LADY: I'm going to make a bit of coffee for myself and some Rice Krispies. Would you like a cup?

The daughter turns and starts into the living room ahead of her mother.

DAUGHTER: I'll make it for you.

OLD LADY: You won't make it for me. I'll make it myself.

She crowds past the daughter and goes to the kitchen. At the kitchen doorway, she turns and surveys her daughter.

OLD LADY: Annie, you know, you can drive somebody crazy, do you know that?

DAUGHTER: I can drive somebody crazy! *You're* the one who can drive somebody crazy.

OLD LADY: Will you stop hovering over me like I was a cripple in a wheel chair. I can make my own coffee, believe me. Why did you come over here? You've got a husband and two kids to take care of. Go make coffee for them, for heaven's sakes.

She turns and goes into the kitchen, muttering away. She opens a cupboard and extracts a jar of instant coffee.

OLD LADY: I've taken to making instant coffee, would you like a cup?

The daughter is standing on the threshold of the kitchen now, leaning against the doorjamb.

DAUGHTER: All right, make me a cup, Ma.

The old lady takes two cups and saucers out and begins carefully to level out a teaspoonful of the instant coffee into each. The daughter moves into the kitchen, reaches up for something in the cupboard.

DAUGHTER: Where do you keep the saccharin, Ma?

The old lady wheels and slaps the daughter's outstretched arms down.

OLD LADY: Annie, I'll get it myself! (*She points a finger into the living room*) Go in there and sit down, will you? I'll bring the cup in to you!

The daughter leans back against the doorjamb, a little exasperated with the old lady's petulant independence. The old lady now takes an old teapot and sets it on the stove and lights a flame under it.

OLD LADY: You can drive me to the subway if you want to do something for me.

DAUGHTER: Ma, you're not going downtown today.

OLD LADY: I want to get down there extra early today on the off-chance that they haven't given the job to someone else. What did I do with that card from the New York State Employment Service? . . .

She shuffles out of the kitchen, the daughter moving out of the doorway to give her passage. The old lady goes to the table in the living room on which sits her battered black purse. She opens it and takes out a card.

OLD LADY: I don't want to lose that. (*She puts the white card back into her purse*) I'm pretty sure I could have held onto this job, because the chap at the Employment Service called up the boss, you see, over the phone, and he explained to the man that I hadn't worked in quite a number of years . . .

DAUGHTER (*Muttering*): Quite a number of years . . .

OLD LADY: . . . and that I'd need a day or so to get used to the machines again.

DAUGHTER: Did the chap at the Employment Service explain to the boss that it's forty years that you haven't worked?

OLD LADY (*Crossing back to the kitchen*): . . . and the boss understood this, you see, so he would have been a

239

little lenient with me. But then, of course, I had to go and faint in the subway, because I was in such a hurry to get down there, you know, I didn't even stop to eat my lunch. I had brought along some sandwiches, you see, cheese and tomatoes. Oh, I hope he hasn't given the job to anyone else . . .

The old lady reaches into the cupboard again for a bowl of sugar, an opened box of Rice Krispies, and a bowl. The daughter watches her as she turns to the refrigerator to get out a container of milk.

DAUGHTER: Ma, when are you gonna give up?

The old lady frowns.

OLD LADY: Annie, please . . .

She pours some Rice Krispies into the bowl.

DAUGHTER: Ma, you been trying for three weeks now. If you get a job, you get fired before the day is over. You're too old, Ma, and they don't want to hire old people : . . .

OLD LADY: It's not the age . . .

DAUGHTER: They don't want to hire white-haired old ladies.

OLD LADY: It's not the age at all! I've seen plenty old people with white hair and all, sitting at those machines.

The shop where I almost had that job and he fired me the other day, there was a woman there, eighty years old if she was a day, an old crone of a woman, sitting there all bent over, her machine humming away. The chap at the Employment Service said there's a lot of elderly people working in the needle trades. The young people nowadays don't want to work for thirty-five, forty dollars a week, and there's a lot of old people working in the needle trades.

DAUGHTER: Well, whatever it is, Ma . . .

OLD LADY (*Leaning to her daughter*): It's my fingers. I'm not sure of them any more. When you get old, y'know, you lose the sureness in your fingers. My eyes are all right, but my fingers tremble a lot. I get very excited, y'know, when I go in for a tryout, y'know. And I'll go in, y'know, and the boss'll say: "Sit down, let's see what you can do." And I get so excited. And my heart begins thumping so that I can hardly see to thread the needle. And they stand right over you, y'know, while you're working. They give you a packet of sleeves or a shirt or something to put a hem on. Or a seam or something, y'know. It's simple work, really. Single-needle machine. Nothing fancy. And it seems to me I do it all right, but they fire me all the time. They say: "You're too slow." And I'm working as fast as I can. I think, perhaps, I've lost the ability in my fingers. And that's what scares me the most. It's not the age. I've seen plenty of old women working in the shops.

She has begun to pour some milk into her bowl of cereal; but she stops now and just stands, staring bleakly down at the worn oilcloth on her cupboard.

DAUGHTER: (*Gently*): Ma, you worked all your life. Why don't you take it easy?

OLD LADY: I don't want to take it easy. Now that your father's dead and in the grave I don't know what to do with myself.

DAUGHTER: Why don't you go out, sit in the park, get a little sun like the other old women?

OLD LADY: I sit around here sometimes, going crazy. We had a lot of fights in our time, your father and I, but I must admit I miss him badly. You can't live with someone forty-one years and not miss him when he's dead. I'm glad that he died for his own sake—it may sound hard of me to say that—but I am glad. He was in nothing but pain the last few months, and he was a man who could never stand pain. But I do miss him.

DAUGHTER (*Gently*): Ma, why don't you come live with George and me?

OLD LADY: No, no, Annie, you're a good daughter. . . .

DAUGHTER: We'll move Tommy into the baby's room, and you can have Tommy's room. It's the nicest room in the apartment. It gets all the sun . . .

OLD LADY: I have wonderful children. I thank God every night for that. I . . .

DAUGHTER: Ma, I don't like you living here alone . . .

OLD LADY: Annie, I been living in this house for eight years, and I know all the neighbors and the store people, and if I lived with you, I'd be a stranger.

DAUGHTER: There's plenty of old people in my neighborhood. You'll make friends.

OLD LADY: Annie, you're a good daughter, but I want to keep my own home. I want to pay my own rent. I don't want to be some old lady living with her children. If I can't take care of myself, I just as soon be in the grave with your father. I don't want to be a burden on my children . . .

DAUGHTER: Ma, for heaven's sakes . . .

OLD LADY: More than anything else, I don't want to be a burden on my children. I pray to God every night to let me keep my health and my strength so that I won't have to be a burden on my children . . . (*The teapot suddenly hisses. The old lady looks up*) Annie, the pot is boiling. Would you pour the water in the cups?

The daughter moves to the stove.

The old lady, much of her ginger seemingly sapped out of her, shuffles into the living room. She perches on the edge of one of the wooden chairs.

OLD LADY: I been getting some pains in my shoulder the last week or so. I had the electric heating pad on practically the whole night. . . . (*She looks up toward the windows again*) It's starting to rain a little harder again. Maybe, I won't go downtown today after all. Maybe, if it clears up a bit, I'll go out and sit in the park and get some sun.

In the kitchen, the daughter pours the boiling water into each cup, stirs.

DAUGHTER (*To her mother, off in the living room*): Is this all you're eating for breakfast, Ma? Let me make you something else . . .

Dissolve to: A park bench. The old lady and two other old ladies are seated, all bundled up in their cheap cloth coats with the worn fur collars. The second old lady is also Irish. Her name is Mrs. Geegan. The third old lady is possibly Jewish, certainly a New Yorker by intonation. Her name is Mrs. Kline. The rain has stopped; it is a clear, bright, sunny March morning.

OLD LADY: . . . Well, it's nice and clear now, isn't it? It was raining something fierce around seven o'clock this morning.

MRS. GEEGAN (*Grimacing*): It's too ruddy cold for me. I'd go home except my daughter-in-law's cleaning the house, and I don't want to get in her way.

MRS. KLINE: My daughter-in-law should drop dead tomorrow.

MRS. GEEGAN: My daughter-in-law gets into an awful black temper when she's cleaning.

MRS. KLINE: My daughter-in-law should grow rice and own a hotel with a thousand rooms and be found dead in every one of them.

MRS. GEEGAN (*To the old lady*): I think I'll go over and visit Missus Halley in a little while, would you like to go? She fell down the stairs and broke her hip, and they're suing the owners of the building. I saw her son yesterday, and he says she's awful weak. When you break a hip at that age, you're as good as in the coffin. I don't like to visit Missus Halley. She's always so gloomy about things. But it's a way of killing off an hour or so to lunch. A little later this afternoon, I thought I'd go to confession. It's so warm and solemn in the church. Do you go to Saint John's? I think it's ever so much prettier than Our Lady of Visitation. Why don't you come to Missus Halley's with me Missus Fanning? Her son's a sweet man, and there's always a bit of fruit they offer·you.

OLD LADY: I don't believe I know a Missus Halley.

MRS. GEEGAN: Missus Halley, the one that fell down the stairs last week and dislocated her hip. They're suing the owners of the building for forty thousand dollars.

MRS. KLINE: They'll settle for a hundred, believe me.

MRS. GEEGAN: Oh, it's chilly this morning. I'd go home, but my daughter-in-law is cleaning the house, and she doesn't like me to be about when she's cleaning. I'd like a bottle of beer, that's what I'd like. Oh, my mouth is fairly watering for it. I'm not allowed to have beer, you know. I'm a diabetic. You don't happen to have a quarter on you, Missus Fanning? We could buy a bottle and split it between us. I'd ask my son for it, but they always want to know what I want the money for.

OLD LADY (*Looking sharply at Mrs. Geegan*): Do you have to ask your children for money?

MRS. GEEGAN: Oh, they're generous. They always give me money whenever I ask. But I'm not allowed to have beer, you see, and they wouldn't give me the twenty-five cents for that. What do I need money for anyway? Go to the movies? I haven't been to the movies in more than a year, I think. I just like a dollar every now and then for an offering at mass. Do you go to seven o'clock novena, Missus Fanning? It's a good way to spend an hour, I think.

OLD LADY: Is that what you do with your day, Missus Geegan? Visit dying old ladies and go to confession?

MRS. GEEGAN: Well, I like to stay in the house a lot, watching television in the afternoons, with the kiddie shows and a lot of dancing and Kate Smith and shows like that. But my daughter-in-law's cleaning up today, and she doesn't like me around the house when she's cleaning, so I came out a bit early to sit in the park.

The old lady regards Mrs. Geegan for a long moment.

MRS. KLINE: My daughter-in-law, she should invest all her money in General Motors stock, and they should go bankrupt.

A pause settles over the three old ladies. They just sit, huddled, their cheeks pressed into the fur of their collars. After a moment, the old lady shivers noticeably.

OLD LADY: It's a bit chilly. I think I'll go home. (*She rises*) Good-by, Missus Geegan . . . Good-by, Missus . . .

The other two old ladies nod their good-bys. The old lady moves off screen. We hold for a moment on the remaining two old ladies, sitting, shoulders hunched against the morning chill, faces pressed under their collars, staring bleakly ahead.

Dissolve to: Door of the old lady's

apartment. It opens, and the old lady comes in. She closes the door behind her, goes up the small foyer to the living room. she unbuttons her coat and walks aimlessly around the room, into the bedroom and out again, across the living room and into the kitchen, and then out of the kitchen. She is frowning as she walks and rubs her hands continually as if she is quite cold. Suddenly she goes to the telephone, picks it up, dials a number, waits.

OLD LADY (*Snappishly*): Is this Mister McCleod? This is Missus Fanning in Apartment 3F! The place is a refrigerator up here! It's freezing! I want some steam! I want it right now! That's all there is to it! I want some steam right now!

She hangs up sharply, turns—scowling—and sits heavily down on the edge of a soft chair, scowling, nervous, rocking a little back and forth. Then abruptly she rises, crosses the living room to the television set, clicks it on. She stands in front of it, waiting for a picture to show. At last the picture comes on. It is the WPIX station signal, accompanied by the steady high-pitched drone that indicates there are no programs on yet. She turns the set off almost angrily.

She is beginning to breathe heavily now. She turns nervously and looks at the large ornamental clock on the sideboard. It reads ten minutes after eleven. She goes to the small dining table and sits down on one of the hard-back chairs. Her black purse is still on the table, as it was during the scene with her daughter. Her eyes rest on it for a moment; then she reaches over, opens the purse, and takes out the white employment card. She looks at it briefly, expressionlessly. Then she returns it to the purse and reclasps the purse. Again she sits for a moment, rigid, expressionless. Then suddenly she stands, grabs the purse, and

starts out the living room, down the foyer, to the front door of her apartment —buttoning her coat as she goes. She opens the door, goes out.

Camera stays on door as it is closed. There is the noise of a key being inserted into the lock. A moment later the bolts on the lock shift into locked position. Hold.

Fade out.

ACT II

Fade in: Film. Lunchtime in the needletrade district of New York—a quick montage of shots of the streets, jammed with traffic, trucks, and working people hurrying to the dense little luncheonettes for their lunch.

Dissolve to: Interior of the Tiny Tots Sportswear Co., Inc., 137 West Twenty-seventh Street, on the eighth floor. It is lunchtime. We dissolve in on some of the women operators at their lunch. They are seated at their machines, of which there are twenty—in two rows of ten, facing each other. Not all of the operators eat their lunch in: about half go downstairs to join the teeming noontime crowds in the oily little restaurants of the vicinity. The ten-or-so women whom we see—munching their sandwiches and sipping their containers of coffee and chattering shrilly to one another—all wear worn house dresses. A good proportion of the operators are Negro and Puerto Rican. Not a few of them are gray-haired, or at least unmistakably middle-aged.

The rest of the shop seems to consist of endless rows of pipe racks on which hang finished children's dresses, waiting to be shipped. In the middle of these racks is a pressing machine and sorting table at which two of the three men who work in the shop eat their lunch. At the far end of the loft—in a corner so dark

*that a light must always be on over it—
it is an old, battered roll-top desk at
which sits the bookkeeper, an angular
woman of thirty-five, differentiated from
the hand workers in that she wears a
clean dress.*

*Nearby is the boss, a man in his
thirties. He is bent over a machine, working on it with a screw driver. The boss is
really a pleasant man; he works under
the illusion, however, that gruffness is a
requisite quality of an executive.*

*Somehow, a tortured passageway
has been worked out between the racks
leading to the elevator doors; it is the
only visible exit and entrance to the loft.*

*As we look at these doors, there is a
growing whirring and clanging announc-
ing the arrival of the elevator. The doors
slide reluctantly open, and the old lady
enters the shop. The elevator doors slide
closed behind her. She stands surrounded
by pipe racks, a little apprehensive. The
arrival of the elevator has caused some
of the people to look up briefly. The old
lady goes to the presser, a Puerto Rican.*

OLD LADY: Excuse me, I'm looking
for the boss.

*The presser indicates with his hand
the spot where the boss is standing,
working on the machine. The old lady
picks her way through the cluttered pipe
racks to the bookkeeper, who looks up
at her approach. The boss also looks up
briefly at her approach, but goes back to
his work. The old lady opens her purse,
takes out the white card, and proffers it to
the bookkeeper. She mutters something.*

BOOKKEEPER: Excuse me, I can't
hear what you said.

OLD LADY: I said, I was supposed
to be here yesterday, but I was sick in
the subway—I fainted, you see and . . .

The boss now turns to the old lady.

BOSS: What? . . . What? . . .

OLD LADY: I was sent down from
the . . .

BOSS: What?

OLD LADY: (*Louder*): I was sent

down from the New York State Employment Service. I was supposed to
be here yesterday.

BOSS: Yes, so what happened?

OLD LADY: I was sick. I fainted in
the subway.

BOSS: What?

OLD LADY: (*Louder*): I was sick.
The subway was so hot there, you see
—there was a big crush at a Hundred
and Forty-ninth Street . . .

BOSS: You was supposed to be
here yesterday.

OLD LADY: I had a little trouble.
They had my daughter down there
and everything. By the time I got down
here, it was half past five, and the fellow on the elevator—not the one that
was here this morning—another fellow
entirely. An old man it was. He said
there was nobody up here. So I was
going to come down early this morning, but I figured you probably had
the job filled anyway. That's why I
didn't come down till now.

BOSS: What kind of work do you
do?

OLD LADY: Well, I used to do all
sections except joining and zippers,
but I think the fellow at the Employment Service explained to you that
it's been a number of years since I
actually worked in a shop.

BOSS: What do you mean, a number of years?

OLD LADY: (*Mumbling*): Well, I
did a lot of sewing for the Red Cross
during the war, y'know, but I haven't
actually worked in a shop since 1916.

BOSS (*Who didn't quite hear her
mumbled words*): What?

OLD LADY (*Louder*): Nineteen sixteen. October.

BOSS: Nineteen sixteen.

OLD LADY: I'm sure if I could work
a little bit, I would be fine. I used to
be a very fast worker.

BOSS: Can you thread a machine?
The old lady nods.

He starts off through the maze of pipe racks to the two rows of machines. The old lady follows after him, clutching her purse and the white card, her hat still sitting on her head, her coat still buttoned. As they go up the rows of sewing machines, the other operators look up to catch covert glimpses of the new applicant. The boss indicates one of the open machines.

BOSS: All right. Siddown. Show me how you thread a machine.

The old lady sets her purse down nervously and takes the seat behind the machine. The other operators have all paused in their eating to watch the test. The old lady reaches to her side, where there are several spools of thread.

OLD LADY: What kind of thread, white or black? . . .

BOSS: White! White!

She fumblingly fetches a spool of white thread and, despite the fact she is obviously trembling, she contrives to thread the machine—a process which takes about half a minute. The boss stands towering over her.

BOSS: Can you sleeve?

The old lady nods, desperately trying to get the thread through the eye of the needle and over the proper holes.

BOSS: It's a simple business. One seam.

He reaches into the bin belonging to the machine next to the one the old lady is working on and extracts a neatly tied bundle of sleeve material. He drops it on the table beside the old lady.

BOSS: All right, make a sleeve. Let's see how you make a sleeve.

He breaks the string and gives her a piece of sleeve material. She takes it, but is so nervous it falls to the floor. She hurriedly bends to pick it up, inserts the sleeve into the machine, and hunches into her work—her face screwed tight with intense concentration. She has still not unbuttoned her coat, and beads of sweat begin to appear on her brow. With pains-taking laboriousness, she slowly moves the sleeve material into the machine. The boss stands, impatient and scowling.

BOSS: Mama, what are you weaving there, a carpet? It's a lousy sleeve, for Pete's sake.

OLD LADY: I'm a little unsure. My fingers are a little unsure . . .

BOSS: You gotta be fast, Mama. This is week work. It's not piecework. I'm paying you by the hour. I got twenny dozen cottons here, gotta be out by six o'clock. The truckman isn't gonna wait, you know . . . Mama, Mama, watch what you're doing there . . . (*He leans quickly forward and reguides the material*) A straight seam, for heaven's sake! You're making it crooked . . . Watch it! Watch it! Watch what you're doing there, Mama . . . All right, sew. Don't let me make you nervous. Sew . . . Mama, wadda you sewing there, an appendicitis operation? It's a lousy sleeve. How long you gonna take? I want operators here, not surgeons . . .

Through all this, the terrified old lady tremblingly pushes the material through the machine. Finally she's finished. She looks up at the boss, her eyes wide with apprehension, ready to pick up her purse and dash out to the street. The boss picks up the sleeve, studies it, then drops it on the table, mutters.

BOSS: All right, we'll try you out for awhile . . .

He turns abruptly and goes back through the pipe racks to the desk. The old lady sits, trembling, a little slumped, her coat still buttoned to the collar. A middle-aged Negro woman, sitting at the next machine over her lunch, leans over to the old lady.

NEGRO WOMAN (*Gently*): Mama, what are you sitting there in your hat and coat for? Hang them up, honey. You go through that door over there.

She points to a door leading into a

built-in room. The old lady looks up slowly at this genuine sympathy.

NEGRO WOMAN: Don't let him get you nervous, Mama. He likes to yell a lot, but he's okay.

The tension within the old lady suddenly bursts out in the form of a soft, staccato series of sighs. She quickly masters herself.

OLD LADY (*Smiling at the Negro woman*): I'm a little unsure of myself. My fingers are a little unsure.

Cut to: The boss, standing by the desk. He leans down to mutter to the bookkeeper.

BOSS (*Muttering*): How could I say no, will you tell me? How could I say no? . . .

BOOKKEEPER: Nobody says you should say no.

BOSS: She was so nervous, did you see how nervous she was? I bet you she's seventy years old. How could I say no?

(*The telephone suddenly rings*) Answer . . .

The bookkeeper picks up the receiver.

BOOKKEEPER (*On the phone*): Tiny Tots Sportswear . . .

BOSS (*In a low voice*): Who is it?

BOOKKEEPER (*On phone*): He's somewhere on the floor. Mister Raymond. I'll see if I can find him . . .

BOSS (*Frowning*): Which Raymond is it, the younger one or the older one?

BOOKKEEPER: The younger one.

BOSS: You can't find me.

The bookkeeper starts to relay this message, but the boss changes his mind. He takes the receiver.

BOSS: Hello Jerry? This is Sam . . . Jerry, for heaven's sake, the twenty dozen just came at half past nine this morning . . . Jerry, I told you six o'clock; it'll be ready six o'clock . . . (*Suddenly lowers his voice, turns away from the bookkeeper, embarrassed at the pleading he's going to have to go through now*) Jerry, about that fifty dozen faille sports suits . . . Have a heart, Jerry, I need the work. I haven't got enough work to keep my girls. Two of them left yesterday . . . Jerry, please, what kind of living can I make on these cheap cottons? Give me a fancier garment . . . It's such small lots, Jerry. At least give me big lots . . . (*Lowering his voice even more*) Jerry, I hate to appeal to you on this level, but I'm your brother-in-law, you know. . . . Things are pretty rough with me right now, Jerry. Have a heart. Send me over the fifty dozen failles you got in yesterday. I'll make a rush job for you . . . please, Jerry, why do you have to make me crawl? All right, I'll have this one for you five o'clock . . . I'll call up the freight man now. How about the failles? . . . Okay, Jerry, thank you, you're a good fellow. . . . All right, five o'clock. I'll call the freight man right now . . . Okay . . . *He hangs up, stands a moment, sick at his own loss of dignity. He turns to the bookkeeper, head bowed.*

BOSS: My own brother-in-law . . .

He shuffles away, looks up. The old lady, who had gone into the dressing room to hang up her coat and hat, comes out of the dressing room now. The boss wheels on her.

BOSS: Watsa matter with you? I left you a bundle of sleeves there! You're not even in the shop five minutes, and you walk around like you own the place! (*He wheels to the other operators*) All right! Come on! Come on! What are you sitting there? Rush job! Rush job! Let's go! Five o'clock the freight man's coming! Let's go! Let's go!

Cut to: The bedroom of the daughter's and son-in-law's apartment. The bed has been made, the room cleaned up. The blinds have been drawn open, and the room is nice and bright. The son-in-law sits on one of the straight-back chairs, slumped a little, surly, scowling. The daughter sits erectly on the bed, her back to her husband, likewise scowling. Apparently, angry words have passed between them. The doorbell buzzes off. Neither of them moves for a moment. Then the daughter rises. At her move, the son-in-law begins to gather himself together.

SON-IN-LAW: I'll get it.

The daughter moves—in sullen, quick silence—past him and out into the foyer. The son-in-law, who has started to rise, sits down again.

In the hallway, the daughter pads down to the front door of the apartment. She is wearing a house dress now and house slippers. She opens the door. Waiting at the door is an attractive young woman in her early thirties, in coat and hat.

DAUGHTER: Hello, Marie, what are you doing here?

SISTER: Nothing. I just came by a couple of minutes, that's all. I just brought the kids back to school, I thought I'd drop in for a minute, that's all. How's George?

She comes into the apartment. The daughter closes the door after her. The sister starts down the hallway.

DAUGHTER: You came in right in the middle of an argument.

The son-in-law is now standing in the bedroom doorway.

SON-IN-LAW (*To the sister*): Your sister drives me crazy.

SISTER: Watsa matter now?

DAUGHTER (*Following her sister up the foyer*): Nothing's the matter. How's Jack? The kids?

The two women go into the bedroom, the son-in-law stepping back to let them in.

SISTER: They're fine. Jack's got a little cold, nothing important. I just took the kids back to school, and I thought I'd drop in, see if you feel like going up to Fordham Road do a

little shopping for a couple of hours. (*To the son-in-law*) What are you doing home?

SON-IN-LAW: It's my vacation. We were gonna leave the kids with my sister, drive downna Virginia, North Carolina, get some warm climate. But your crazy sister don't wanna go. She don't wanna leave your mother . . . (*Turning to his wife*) Your mother can take care of herself better than we can. She's a tough old woman. . . . How many vacations you think I get a year? I don't wanna sit in New York for two weeks, watching it rain.

SISTER: Go ahead, Annie. Me and Frank will see that Mom's all right.

DAUGHTER: Sure, you and Frank. Look, Marie, I was over to see Mom this morning . . .

SON-IN-LAW: Half past six she got up this morning, to go over to see your mother . . .

DAUGHTER: After what happened yesterday, I decided to put my foot down. Because Mom got no business at her age riding up and down in the subways. You know how packed they are. Anyway, I called Mom on the phone, and she gave me the usual arguments. You know Mom. So anyway, I went over to see her, and she was very depressed. We talked for about an hour, and she told me she's been feeling very depressed lately. It's no good Mom living there alone, and you know it, Marie. Anyway, I think I finally convinced her to move out of there and come and live over here.

SON-IN-LAW: You didn't convince me.

DAUGHTER: George, please . . .

SON-IN-LAW: Look, Annie, I like your mother. We get along fine. We go over visit her once, twice a week, fine. What I like about her is that she doesn't hang all over you like my mother does.

DAUGHTER: This is the only thing

I ever asked you in our whole marriage . . .

SON-IN-LAW: This is just begging for trouble. You know that in the bottom of your heart . . .

DAUGHTER: I don't wanna argue any more about it . . .

SISTER: Look, Annie, I think George is right, I think . . .

The daughter suddenly wheels on her sister, a long-repressed fury trembling out of her.

DAUGHTER: (*Literally screaming*): You keep outta this! You hear me? You never cared about Mom in your whole life! How many times you been over there this week? How many times? I go over every day! Every day! And I go over in the evenings too sometimes!

The sister turns away, not a little shaken by this fierce onslaught. The daughter sits down on the bed again, her back to both her husband and sister, herself confused by the ferocity of her outburst. The son-in-law looks down, embarrassed, at the floor. A moment of sick silence fills the room. Then without turning, but in a much lower voice, the daughter goes on.

DAUGHTER: George, I been a good wife to you. Did I ever ask you for mink coats or anything? Anything you want has always been good with me. This is the only thing I ever ask of you. I want my mother to live here with me where I can take care of her.

The son-in-law looks up briefly at his wife's unrelenting back and then back to the floor again.

SON-IN-LAW: All right, Annie. I won't argue any more with you about it.

SISTER: I guess I better go because I want to get back in the house before three o'clock when the kids come home from school.

Nobody says anything, so she starts for the door. The son-in-law, from his sitting position, looks up briefly at her as she passes, but she avoids his eyes. He stands, follows her out into the foyer. They proceed silently down the foyer to the doorway. Here they pause a minute. The scene is conducted in low, intense whispers.

SON-IN-LAW: She don't mean nothing, Marie. You know that.

SISTER: I know, I know . . .

SON-IN-LAW: She's a wonderful person. She'd get up at three o'clock in the morning for you. There's nothing she wouldn't do for her family.

SISTER: I know, George. I know Annie better than you know her. When she's sweet, she can be the sweetest person in the world. She's my kid sister but many's the time I came to her to do a little crying. But she's gonna kill my mother with all her sacrifices. She's trying to take away my mother's independence. My mother's been on her own all her life. That's the only way she knows how to live. I went over to see my mother yesterday. She was depressed. It broke my heart because I told Jack; I said: "I think my mother's beginning to give up." My mother used to be so sure of herself all the time, and yesterday she was talking there about how maybe she thinks she is getting a little old to work. It depressed me for the rest of the day . . .

SON-IN-LAW: Marie, you know that I really like your mother. If I thought it would work out at all, I would have no objection to her coming to live here. But the walls in this place are made of paper. You can hear everything that goes on in the next room, and . . .

SISTER: It's a big mistake if she comes here. She'll just dry up into bones inside a year.

SON-IN-LAW: Tell that to Annie. Would you do that for me, please?

SISTER: You can't tell Annie nothing. Annie was born at a wrong time. The doctor told my mother she was gonna die if she had Annie, and my mother has been scared of Annie ever since. And if Annie thinks she's gonna get my mother to love her with all these sacrifices, she's crazy. My mother's favorite was always our big brother Frank, and Annie's been jealous of him as long as I know. I remember one time when we were in Saint John's school on Daly Avenue— I think Annie was about ten years old, and . . . oh, well, look, I better go. I'm not mad at Annie. She's been like this as long as I know her. (*She opens the door*) She's doing the worst thing for my mother, absolutely the worst thing. I'll see you, George.

SON-IN-LAW: I'll see you.

The sister goes out, closing the door after her. The son-in-law stands a moment. Then, frowning, he moves back up the foyer to the bedroom. His wife is still seated as we last saw her, her back to the door, her hands in her lap— slumped a little, but with an air of rigid stubbornness about her. The son-in-law regards her for a moment. Then he moves around the bed and sits down beside his wife. He puts his arm around her and pulls her to him. She rests her head on his chest. They sit silently for a moment.

Dissolve to: Interior, the shop. The full complement of working operators are there, all hunched over their machines, and the place is a picture of industry. The women chatter shrilly with each other as they work. A radio plays in the background. Occasionally, one of the operators lifts her head and bellows out: "Work! Work! Jessica! Gimme some work!" . . . The book-keeper, Jessica, scurries back and forth from her desk to the sorting table—where she picks up small cartons of materials, bringing them to the operators—and back to her desk.

Dissolve to: The old lady and her immediate neighbor, the Negro woman, both bent over their machines, sewing away. The motors hum. The two women move their materials under the plunging needles. The old lady hunches, intense and painfully concentrated, over her work. They sew in silent industry for a moment. Then . . .

OLD LADY (*Without daring to look up from her work*): I'm getting the feel back, you know?

NEGRO WOMAN (*Likewise without looking up*): Sure, you're gonna be all right, Mama.

OLD LADY: I used to be considered a very fast operator. I used to work on the lower East Side in those sweatshops, y'know. Six dollars a week. I quit in October 1916, because I got married and, in those days, y'know, it was a terrible disgrace for a married woman to work. So I quit. Not that we had the money. My husband was a house painter when we got married, which is seasonal work at best, and he had to borrow money to go to Atlantic City for three days. That was our honeymoon.

They lapse into silence. A woman's shrill voice from farther down the row of machines calls out: "Work! Hey, Jessica! Bring me some work!" The two women sew silently. Then . . .

OLD LADY: I got a feeling he's going to keep me on here. The boss, I mean. He seems like a nice enough man.

NEGRO WOMAN: He's nervous, but he's all right.

OLD LADY: I've been looking for almost four weeks now, y'know. My husband died a little more than a month ago.

NEGRO WOMAN: My husband died eighteen years ago.

OLD LADY: He was a very sick man all his life—lead poisoning, you know, from the paints. He had to quit the trade after a while, went into the retail grocery business. He was sixty-seven when he died, and I wonder he lived this long. In his last years, the circulation of the blood in his legs was so bad he could hardly walk to the corner.

NEGRO WOMAN: My big trouble is arthritis. I get terrible pains in my arms and in my shoulders sometimes.

OLD LADY: Oh, I been getting a lot of pains in my back, in between my shoulder blades.

NEGRO WOMAN: That's gall bladder.

OLD LADY: Is that what it is?

NEGRO WOMAN: I had that. When you get to our age, Missus Fanning, you gotta expect the bones to rebel.

OLD LADY: Well, now, you're not such an old woman.

NEGRO WOMAN: How old do you think I am?

OLD LADY: I don't know. Maybe forty, fifty.

NEGRO WOMAN: I'm sixty-eight years old.

For the first time, the old lady looks up. She pauses in her work.

OLD LADY: I wouldn't believe you were sixty-eight.

NEGRO WOMAN: I'm sixty-eight. I got more white hair than you have. But I dye it. You oughtta dye your hair too. Just go in the five-and-ten, pick up some kind of hair dye. Because most people don't like to hire old people with white hair. My children don't want me to work no more, but I'm gonna work until I die. How old do you think that old Greek woman over there is?

OLD LADY: How old?

NEGRO WOMAN: She's sixty-nine. She got a son who's a big doctor. She won't quit working either. I like working here. I come in here in the morning, punch the clock. I'm friends with all these women. You see that little Jewish lady down there? That's the funniest little woman I ever met. You get her to tell you some of her jokes during lunch sometime. She gets me laughing sometimes I can hardly stop. What do I wanna sit around my dirty old room for when I got that little Jewish woman there to tell me jokes all day? That's what I tell my children.

The old lady turns back to her sewing.

OLD LADY: Oh, I'd like to hear a couple of jokes.

At this moment there is a small burst of high-pitched laughter from farther down the rows of machines. Camera cuts to long shot of the rows of operators, singling out a group of three Puerto Rican girls in their twenties. One of them has apparently just said something that made the other two laugh. A fourth Puerto Rican girl, across the table and up from them, calls to them in Spanish: "What happened? What was so funny?" The Puerto Rican girl who made the others laugh answers in a quick patter of high-pitched Spanish. A sudden gust of laughter sweeps all the Puerto Rican girls at the machines. Another woman calls out: "What she say?" One of the Puerto Rican girls answers in broken English.

PUERTO RICAN GIRL: She say, t'ree week ago, she made a mistake, sewed the belts onna dress backward. Nobody found out. Yesterday, she went in to buy her little girl a dress inna store. They tried to sell her one-a these dresses . . . (*A wave of laughter rolls up and down the two rows of operators*) She says, the label onna dress say: "Made in California."

They absolutely roar at this.

Close-up: The old lady joining in the general laughter. She finishes the sleeve she has been working on. It is apparently the last of the bunch. She gathers together in front of her the two dozen other sleeves she has just finished and begins to tie them up with a black ribbon. She lifts her head up and—with magnificent professionalism—calls out.

OLD LADY: Work! Work! . . .

Camera closes down on the bundle of sleeves she has tied together with the black ribbon.

Dissolve to: The same bundle of sleeves. We pull back and see it is now being held by the boss. He is frowning down at them. At his elbow is standing one of the Puerto Rican girls. She is muttering in broken English.

PUERTO RICAN GIRL: So what I do? The whole bunch, same way . . .

BOSS (*Scowling*): All right, all right. Cut them open, resew the whole bunch . . .

PUERTO RICAN GIRL: Cut! I didn't do! I can't cut, sew, five o'clock the truckman . . . I gotta sew them on the blouse. Take two hours . . .

BOSS: All right, all right, cut them open, sew them up again . . .

The girl takes the bundle of sleeves and shuffles away. The boss turns, suddenly deeply weary. He goes to the desk.

BOSS (*To the bookkeeper*): The old lady come in today, she sewed all the sleeves for the left hand. She didn't make any rights. All lefts . . .

BOOKKEEPER: So what are you gonna do? It's half past four.

BOSS: Call up Raymond for me.

The bookkeeper picks up the phone receiver, dials. The boss looks up and through the pipe racks at the old lady, sitting hunched and intense over her machine, working with concentrated meticulousness. The boss's attention is called back to the phone by the bookkeeper. He takes the phone from her.

BOSS (*In a low voice*): Jerry? This is Sam. Listen. I can't give you the whole twenty dozen at five o'clock . . . All right, wait a minute, lemme . . . All right, wait a minute. I got fifteen dozen on the racks now . . . Jerry,

please. I just got a new operator in today. She sewed five dozen sleeves all left-handed. We're gonna have to cut the seams open, and resew them . . . Look, Jerry, I'm sorry, what do you want from me? I can get it for you by six . . . Jerry, I'll pay the extra freight fee myself . . . Jerry . . . Listen, Jerry, how about those fifty dozen faille sport suits? This doesn't change your mind, does it? . . . Jerry, it's an accident. It could happen to anyone . . . (*A fury begins to take hold of the boss*) Look, Jerry, you promised me the fifty dozen fai . . . Look, Jerry, you know what you can do with those fifty dozen failles? You think I'm gonna crawl on my knees to you? (*He's shouting now. Every head in the shop begins to look up*) You're a miserable human being, you hear that? I'd rather go bankrupt than ask you for another order! And don't come over to my house no more! You hear? I ain't gonna crawl to you! You hear me? I ain't gonna crawl to you! . . .*

He slams the receiver down, stands, his chest heaving, his face flushed. He looks down at the bookkeeper, his fury still high.

BOSS: Fire her! Fire her! Fire her!

He stands, the years of accumulated humiliation and resentment flooding out of him.

Fade out.

ACT III

Fade in: Interior of a subway car heading north to the Bronx during the rush hour—absolutely jam-packed. The camera manages to work its way through the dense crowd to settle on the old lady, seated in her black coat and hat, her hands folded in her lap, her old purse dangling from her wrist. She is staring bleakly straight ahead of herself, as if in another world. The train hurtles on.

Dissolve to: Interior of old lady's apartment—dark—empty. Night has fallen outside. The sound of a key being inserted into the lock. The bolts unlatch, and the door is pushed open. The old lady enters. She closes the door after herself, bolts it. She stands a moment in the dark foyer, then shuffles up the foyer to the living room. She unbuttons her coat, sits down by the table, places her purse on the table. For a moment she sits. Then she rises, goes into the kitchen, turns on the light.

It takes her a moment to remember what she came into the kitchen for. Then, collecting herself, she opens the refrigerator door, extracts a carton of milk, sets it on the cupboard shelf. She opens the cupboard door, reaches in, extracts the box of Rice Krispies and a bowl. She sets the bowl down, begins to open the box of cereal. It falls out of her hands to the floor, a number of the pebbles of cereal rolling out to the floor. She starts to bend to pick the box up, then suddenly straightens and stands breathing heavily, nervously wetting her lips. She moves out of the kitchen quickly now, goes to the table, sits down again, picks up the phone, and dials. There is an edge of desperation in her movements. She waits. Then . . .

OLD LADY: Frank? Who's this, Lillian? Lillian, dear, this is your mother-in-law, and I . . . oh, I'm sorry what? . . . Oh, I'm sorry . . . Who's this, the baby sitter? . . . This is Missus Fanning, dear—Mister Fanning's mother, is he in? . . . Is Missus Fanning in? . . . Well, do you expect them in? I mean, it's half past six. Did they eat their dinner already? . . . Oh, I see. Well, when do you . . . Oh, I see . . . No, dear, this is Mister Fanning's mother. Just tell him I called. It's not important.

She hangs up, leaving her hand still on the phone. Then she lifts the receiver again and dials another number. She places a smile on her face and waits. Then . . .

OLD LADY: Oh, Marie, dear, how are you . . . this is Mother . . . Oh, I'm glad to hear your voice . . . Oh, I'm fine . . . fine. How's Jack and the kids? . . . Well, I hope it's nothing serious . . . Oh, that's good . . . (*She is mustering up all the good humor she has in her*) Oh my, what a day I had. Oh, wait'll I tell you. Listen, I haven't taken you away from your dinner or anything . . . Oh, I went down to look for a job again . . . Yes, that's right, Annie was here this morning . . . how did you know? . . . Oh, is that right? Well, it cleared up, you know, and I didn't want to just sit around, so I went down to this job, and I got fired again . . . The stupidest thing, I sewed all left sleeves . . . Well, you know you have to sew sleeves for the right as well as the left unless your customers are one-armed people . . . (*She is beginning to laugh nervously*) Yes, it's comical, isn't it? . . . Yes, all left-handed . . . *She bursts into a short, almost hysterical laugh. Her lip begins to twitch, and she catches her laughter in its middle and breathes deeply to regain control of herself*) Well, how's Jack and the kids? . . . Well, that's fine. What are you doing with yourself tonight? . . . (*A deep weariness seems to have taken hold of her. She rests her head in the palm of her free hand. Her eyes are closed*) Oh, do you have a baby sitter? . . . Well, have a nice time, give my regards to your mother-in-law . . . No, no, I'm fine . . . No, I was just asking . . . No, no, listen, dear, I'm absolutely fine. I just come in the house, and I'm going to make myself some Rice Krispies, and I've got some rolls somewhere, and I think I've got a piece of fish in the refrigerator, and I'm going to make myself dinner and take a hot tub, and then I think I'll watch some television. What's tonight, Thursday?

252

. . . Well, Groucho Marx is on tonight . . . No, no, I just called to ask how everything was. How's Jack and the kids? . . . That's fine, have a nice time . . . Good-by, dear . . .

She hangs up, sits erectly in the chair now. Her face wears an expression of the most profound weariness. She rises now and shuffles with no purpose into the center of the dark room, her coat flapping loosely around her. Then she goes to the television set, turns it on. In a moment a jumble of lines appear, and the sound comes up. The lines clear up into Faye and Skitch Henderson engaging each other in very clever chitchat. The old lady goes back to a television-viewing chair, sits down stiffly—her hands resting on the armrests—and expressionlessly watches the show. Camera comes in for a close-up of the old lady, staring wide-eyed right through the television set, not hearing a word of the chitchat. She is breathing with some difficulty. Suddenly she rises and almost lurches back to the table. She takes the phone, dials with obvious trembling, waits . . .

OLD LADY: Annie? Annie, I wonder if I could spend the night at your house? I don't want to be alone . . . I'd appreciate that very much . . . All right, I'll wait here . . .

Dissolve to: Interior of the old lady's bedroom. The son-in-law, in his hat and jacket, is snapping the clasps of an old valise together. Having closed the valise, he picks it off the bed and goes into the living room. The old lady is there. She is seated in one of the straight-back chairs by the table, still in her coat and hat, and she is talking to the daughter—who can be seen through the kitchen doorway, reaching up into the pantry for some of her mother's personal groceries.

OLD LADY: . . . Well, the truth is, I'm getting old, and there's no point in saying it isn't true. (*To her son-in-law as he sets the valise down beside her*) Thank you, dear. I always have so much trouble with the clasp. . . . Did you hear the stupid thing I did today? I sewed all left-handed sleeves. That's the mark of a wandering mind, a sure sign of age, I'm sorry, George, to put you to all this inconvenience . . .

SON-IN-LAW: Don't be silly, Ma. Always glad to have you.

OLD LADY: Annie, dear, what are you looking for?

DAUGHTER: (*In the kitchen*): Your saccharin.

OLD LADY: It's on the lower shelf, dear. . . . This isn't going to be permanent, George. I'll just stay with you a little while till I get a room somewheres with some other old woman . . .

DAUGHTER: (*In the kitchen doorway*): Ma, you're gonna stay with us, so, for heaven's sakes, let's not have no more arguments.

OLD LADY: What'll we do with all my furniture? Annie, don't you want the china closet?

DAUGHTER: No, Ma, we haven't got any room for it . . .

OLD LADY: It's such a good-looking piece. What we have to do is to get Jack and Marie and Frank and Lillian and all of us together, and we'll divide among the three of you whatever you want. I've got that fine set of silver—well, it's not the best, of course, silver plate, y'know—it's older than you are, Annie. (*To her son-in-law*) It was a gift of the girls in my shop when I got married. It's an inexpensive set but I've shined it every year, and it sparkles. (*To her daughter in the kitchen*) Yes, that's what we'll have to do. We'll have to get all of us together one night and I'll apportion out whatever I've got. And whatever you don't want, well, we'll call a furniture dealer . . . (*To her son-in-law*) . . . although what would he pay me for these old things here? . . . (*To her *daughter*) Annie, take the china closet . . . It's such a fine piece . . .

DAUGHTER: Ma, where would we put it?

OLD LADY: Well, take that soft chair there. You always liked that chair . . .

DAUGHTER: Ma . . .

OLD LADY: There's nothing wrong with it. It's not torn or anything. The upholstery's fine. Your father swore by that chair. He said it was the only chair he could sit in.

DAUGHTER: Ma, let's not worry about it now. We'll get together sometime next week with Marie and Lillian.

OLD LADY: I want you to have the chair . . .

DAUGHTER: Ma, we got all modern furniture in our house . . .

OLD LADY: It's not an old chair. We just bought it about six years ago. No, seven . . .

DAUGHTER: Ma, what do we need the . . .

OLD LADY: Annie, I don't want to sell it to a dealer! It's my home. I don't want it to go piece by piece into a second-hand shop.

DAUGHTER: Ma . . .

SON-IN-LAW: Annie! we'll take the chair!

DAUGHTER: All right, Ma, the chair is ours.

OLD LADY: I know that Lillian likes those lace linens I've got in the cedar chest. And the carpets. Now these are good carpets, Annie. There's no sense just throwing them out. They're good broadloom. The first good money your father was making we bought them. When we almost bought that house in Passaic, New Jersey. You ought to remember that, Annie, you were about seven then. But we bought the grocery store instead. Oh, how we scraped in that store. In the heart of the depression. We used to sell bread for six cents a loaf. I remember my husband said: "Let's buy a grocery store. At least we'll always have food in the house." It seems to me my whole life has been hand-to-mouth. Did we ever not worry about the rent? I remember as a girl in Cork, eating boiled potatoes every day. I don't know what it all means, I really don't . . . (*She stares rather abstractedly at her son-in-law*) I'm sixty-six years old, and I don't know what the purpose of it all was.

SON-IN-LAW: Missus Fanning . . .

OLD LADY: An endless, endless struggle. And for what? For what? (*She is beginning to cry now*) Is this what it all comes to? An old woman parceling out the old furniture in her house . . . ?

She bows her head and stands, thirty years of repressed tears torturously working their way through her body in racking shudders.

DAUGHTER: Ma . . .

The old lady stands, her shoulders slumped, her head bowed, crying with a violent agony.

OLD LADY (*The words tumbling out between her sobs*): Oh, I don't care . . . I don't care . . .

Hold on the old lady, standing, crying.

Dissolve to: Film. Rain whipping through the streets of New York at night—same film we opened the show with—a frightening thunderstorm.

Dissolve to: The old lady's valise, now open, lying on a narrow single bed. We pull back to see the old lady—in a dress, but with her coat off—rummaging in the valise for something. The room she is in is obviously a little boy's room. There are a child's paintings and drawings and cutouts Scotch-taped to the wall, and toys and things on the floor. It is dark inside, and the rain whacks against the window pains. The old lady finally extracts from out of the valise a long woolen nightgown and, holding it in both arms, she shuffles to the one chair in the room and sits down. She sets the nightgown in her lap and bends to remove her shoes. This is something of an effort and costs her a few moments of quick breathing. She sits, expressionless, catching her breath, the white nightgown on her lap, her hands folded on it. Even after she regains her breath, she sits this way, now staring fixedly at the floor at her feet. Hold.

Dissolve to: The window of the child's bedroom. It is daylight now, and the rain has stopped. The cold morning sun shines thinly through the white chintz curtains. The camera pulls slowly back and finally comes to rest on the old lady sitting just as we saw her last, unmoving, wrapped in thought, the white nightgown on her lap, her hands folded. From some room off, the thin voice of a baby suddenly rises and abruptly falls. The old lady looks slowly up.

Then she bends and puts her shoes on. She rises, sets the nightgown on the chair from which she has just risen, moves with a slight edge of purpose down the room to the closet, opens the door, reaches in, and takes out her coat. She puts it on, stands a moment, looking about the room for something. She finds her hat and purse sitting on the chest of drawers. She picks them up. Then she turns to the door of the room and carefully opens it. She looks out onto the hallway. Across from her, the door to her daughter's and son-in-law's bedroom stands slightly ajar. She crosses to the door, looks in. Her daughter and son-in-law make two large bundles under their blankets. For a moment she stands and surveys them. Then the daughter turns in her bed so that she faces her mother. Her eyes are open; she has not been asleep. At the sight of her mother in the doorway, she leans upon one elbow.

OLD LADY (*In an intense whisper*): Annie, it just wasn't comfortable, you*

know? I just can't sleep anywheres but in my own bed, and that's the truth. I'm sorry, Annie, honest. You're a fine daughter, and it warms me to know that I'm welcome here. But what'll I do with myself, Annie, what'll I do? . . .

The daughter regards her mother for a moment.

DAUGHTER: Where are you going, Ma, with your coat on?

OLD LADY: I'm going out and look for a job. And, Annie, please don't tell me that everything's against me. I know it.

Well, I'll see you, dear. I didn't mean to wake you up. . . .

She turns and disappears from the doorway. The daughter starts quickly from the bed.

DAUGHTER: Ma . . .

She moves quickly across the room to the door of the hallway. She is in her pajamas. She looks down the hallway, which is fairly dark. Her mother is already at the front door, at the other end.

DAUGHTER: Ma . . .

OLD LADY: I'm leaving the valise with all my things. I'll pick them up tonight. And please don't start an argument with me, Annie, because I won't listen to you. I'm a woman of respect. I can take care of myself. I always have. And don't tell me it's raining because it stopped about an hour ago. And don't say you'll drive me home because I can get the bus two blocks away. Work is the meaning of my life. It's all I know what to do. I can't change my ways at this late time.

For a long moment the mother and daughter regard each other. Then the daughter pads quickly down to the old lady.

DAUGHTER (*Quietly*): When I'm your age, Ma. I hope I'm like you.

For a moment the two women stand

in the dark hallway. Then they quickly embrace and release each other. The old lady unbolts the door and disappears outside, closing the door after her. The daughter bolts it shut with a click. She turns and goes back up the dark foyer to her own bedroom. She goes in, shuffles to the bed, gets back under the covers. For a moment she just lies there. Then she nudges her sleeping husband, who grunts.

DAUGHTER: George, let's drop the kids at your sister's for a week or ten days and drive down to Virginia. You don't want to spend your one vacation a year sitting in New York, watching it rain.

The son-in-law, who hasn't heard a word, grunts once or twice more. The daughter pulls the blankets up over her shoulders, turns on her side, and closes her eyes.

Fade out.

FACE OF POVERTY

No one can communicate to you
The substance of poverty—
Can tell you either the shape,
    or the depth,
        or the breadth
Of poverty—
Until you have lived with her intimately.

No one can guide your fingers
Over the rims of her eye sockets,
Over her hollow cheeks—
Until perhaps one day
In your wife's once pretty face
You see the lines of poverty;
Until you feel
In her now skinny body,
The protruding bones,
The barely covered ribs,
The shrunken breasts of poverty.

Poverty can be a stranger
In a far-off land:
An alien face
Briefly glimpsed in a newsreel,
An empty rice bowl
In a skinny brown hand,
Until one bleak day
You look out the window—
And poverty is the squatter
In your own backyard.

Poverty wails in the night for milk,
Not knowing the price of a quart.

It is desperation in your teen-ager's face,
Wanting a new evening gown for the junior prom,
After going through school in rummage store clothes.
It is a glass of forgetfulness sold over the bar.

And poverty's voice is a jeer in the night—
    "You may bring another child
    Into the rat race that is your life;
    You may cut down on food
    To buy contraceptives;
    You may see your wife walk alone
    Down some back alley route

257

Reprinted by permission of Indiana University Press from Langston Hughes, ed., *New Negro Poets: U.S.A.* (Bloomington: Indiana University Press, 1964).

To a reluctant appointment
With an unsterile knife—
Or you may sleep alone."
And one morning shaving
You look in the mirror—
And never again will poverty be alien,
For the face of poverty is not over your shoulder,
The face of poverty is your own.
And hearing the break in your wife's voice
At the end of a bedtime story,
You realize that somewhere along the way
The stock ending in your own story went wrong.
And now you no longer ask
That you and your wife
Will live happily ever after—
But simply that you
And your wife
And your children
Will live.

—*Lucy Smith*

There are probably in fairly prosperous years no less than 10,000,000
persons in poverty, that is to say,
underfed, underclothed, and poorly
housed. *Robert Hunter*, Poverty

HAVE YOU SEEN MEN

Have you seen men handed refusals
    till they began to laugh
    at the notion of ever landing a job again—
Muttering with the laugh,
    "It's driving me nuts and the family too,"
Mumbling of hoodoos and jinx,
    fear of defeat creeping in their vitals—
Have you never seen this?
    or do you kid yourself
    with the fond soothing syrup of four words
    "Some folks won't work"?
Of course some folks won't work—
    they are sick or wornout or lazy
    or misled with the big idea
The idle poor should imitate the idle rich.

Have you seen women and kids
    step out and hustle for the family
    some in night life on the streets
    some fighting other women and kids
    for the leavings of fruit and vegetable markets
    of searching alleys and garbage dumps for scraps?
Have you seen them with savings gone
    furniture and keepsakes pawned
    and the pawntickets blow away in cold winds?
    by one letdown and another ending
    in what you might call slums—
To be named perhaps in case reports
    and tabulated and classified
    among those who have crossed over
    from the employables into the *un*employables?

Reprinted by permission of Harcourt, Brace & World from
Carl Sandburg, *The People, Yes* (New York: Harcourt,
Brace & World, 1964).

What is the saga of the employables?
    what are the breaks they get?
What are the dramas of personal fate
    spilled over from industrial transitions?
    what punishments handed bottom people
    who have wronged no man's house
    or things or person?

    Stocks are property, yes.
    Bonds are property, yes.
Machines, land, buildings, are property, yes.
    A job is property,
    no, nix, nah nah.

The rights of property are guarded
    by ten thousand laws and fortresses.
The right of a man to live by his work—
    what is this right?
    and why does it clamor?
    and who can hush it
    so it will stay hushed?
    and why does it speak
    and though put down speak again
    with strengths out of the earth?

    —Carl Sandburg

THE MAN WITH THE HOE

(Written after seeing Millet's world-famous painting)

God made man in His own image,
in the image of God made He him

Genesis

Bowed by the weight of centuries he leans
Upon his hoe and gazes on the ground,
The emptiness of ages in his face,
And on his back the burden of the world.
Who made him dead to rapture and despair,
A thing that grieves not and that never hopes,
Stolid and stunned, a brother to the ox?

The Man with the Hoe: Jean François Millet

Who loosened and let down this brutal jaw?
Whose was the hand that slanted back this brow?
Whose breath blew out the light within this brain?

Is this the Thing the Lord God made and gave
To have dominion over sea and land;
To trace the stars and search the heavens for power;
To feel the passion of Eternity?
Is this the dream He dreamed who shaped the suns
And marked their ways upon the ancient deep?
Down all the caverns of Hell to their last gulf
There is no shape more terrible than this—
More tongued with censure of the world's blind
    greed?
More filled with signs and portents for the soul—
More packt with danger to the universe.

What gulfs between him and the seraphim!
Slave of the wheel of labor, what to him
Are Plato and the swing of Pleiades?
What the long reaches of the peaks of song,
The rift of dawn, the redding of the rose?
Through this dread shape the suffering ages look;
Time's tragedy is in that aching stoop;
Through this dread shape humanity betrayed,
Plundered, profaned, and disinherited,
Cries protest to the Judges of the World,
A protest that is also prophecy.

O masters, lords, and rulers in all lands,
Is this the handiwork you give to God,
This monstrous thing distorted and soul-quenched?
How will you ever straighten up this shape;
Touch it again with immortality;
Give back the upward looking and the light;
Rebuilt in it the music and the dream;
Make right the immemorial infamies,
Perfidious wrongs, immedicable woes?

O masters, lords, and rulers in all lands,
How will the Future reckon with this man?
How answer his brute question in that hour
When whirlwinds of rebellion shake all shores?
How will it be with kingdoms and with kings—
When this dumb terror shall rise to judge the world,
After the silence of the centuries?

—*Edwin Markham*

MAN WITH A HOE, 1964

By Paul Jacobs

The park on the border of the Skid Row area in this California farm town is filled with men (and one or two women) sprawled out on the grass or sitting under the few trees. Some of them are sleeping, their mouths open, their stubbled faces pressed into the ground; others are merely staring off into space. Here and there a bottle is being passed around a group, each man taking a deep swig before handing it on to the next. I count about a hundred of these near-derelicts from where I sit on a bench at the edge of the park. Later, as I walk by, they look at me incuriously. No one hails me as "Sir," and no one tries to make a touch. In my dirty pants, torn sweatshirt, and straw workhat, an old beachbag in my hand, I look like just another farm worker living on Skid Row.

On my way through the park to find a cheap hotel or flophouse for a few nights, the eyeglass case I have in my shirt pocket begins to feel uncomfortable, so I stop to take it out and put it into the bag. As I do I am struck by the fact that very few of these people in the park seem to wear glasses; in fact, I can spot only three who are either wearing glasses or have eyeglass cases in their pockets. And yet, nearly everyone in the park is in the age group that would normally need glasses.

Just on the outskirts of the Skid Row area, I find a hotel where I can get a room for $2.00 a night. Most day-haul farm workers would spend only a dollar, or at most $1.50, but I have learned how terribly depressed I get in the dirty, gray flophouses that are the only homes so many farm workers know. Skid Row not only houses bums, outcasts, and voluntary exiles from society, but blurs at the edges to take in the old and the poor as well. For where else can a badly paid worker find a place to sleep for $2.00 or less?

I pay the $2.00 in advance—all rent in such "hotels" is paid in advance, either by the day, the week, or the month—and take the key to the room in which I will be staying for the next few days before going on to spend a couple of weeks in a migrant

Reprinted by permission of Cyrilly Abels and Paul Jacobs from *Commentary*, July 1964, pp. 26–29.

workers' camp in the San Joaquin Valley. The room is about what I expect: peeling walls, a window with a tattered shade overlooking a dark airshaft, a broken bureau with a plastic doily on top, one wooden chair, a closet built into a corner, and overhead, a light bulb swinging on a chain. There is no lamp by the bed—who reads in such a room at night?

My next stop is the farm labor office on the other side of the Skid Row area. Walking down a street past tong houses, Chinese shops and restaurants, Filipino barber shops and social clubs, and Mexican bars, I notice a small store with the word "Shoeshine" crudely lettered across the window, obviously, though, it isn't shines the three gaudily dressed Mexican women inside are selling. One of them catches my eye as I go by and shouts, "Hey, sport, come on in!"—waving her arm to show me the curtained recess at the back. Such girls service the Skid Row community, including fringe groups like the Filipinos. The most skilled of all the farm workers in Skid Row—they generally harvest asparagus, Brussels sprouts, and the early grape crop—many of these Filipinos have been in the area for more than twenty years without their families, and these women represent their only sexual contacts. Because they have no wives and the law once prohibited intermarriage, the Filipinos reportedly suffer from a high rate of venereal disease. Yet they tend to be neater and cleaner than their neighbors on Skid Row, and when they dress up in their big-brimmed hats, wide-seated pants, and heavily padded jackets, they remind one of sporty gangsters in a 1930s movie.

It is early afternoon by now, and the farm labor office—whose hours are from 5:00 A.M to 2:00 P.M.—is very quiet. Two men are sitting behind a counter (there are no chairs or benches on my side of the counter). I announce that I want to register for farm work, and wait while one of them checks to see if I have registered before at this office. Satisfied that my name isn't listed in any of his files, he motions me behind the counter to his partner's desk. "Can I see your social security card?" the man at the desk says. I take out my wallet, now thin and flabby without the thick bundle of credit cards I've left back home in San Francisco, and show him the social security card.

"Were you in the Army, Paul?" He uses my first name as a matter of course, even though I am at least ten years older than he is and he has never seen me before. I say that I was, giving him the little photostat of my Army discharge I carry with me on these trips. Then he asks me what kind of farm work I've done, and I tell enough of the right lies to get a green card from him with my new occupational title printed on it: "Farm hand, general."

"Is there much work?" I ask. "No," he answers, "the asparagus is about finished, but if you'll do stoop labor, you can work until the freeze in the fall. Be here tomorrow morning at 5:00 A.M. to get on the bus."

For the rest of the afternoon and evening, I walk around Skid Row, going from one dingy card room to another, where $2.00 will get you into a game of draw poker, lowball poker, or pan. The games are run by the house, which takes a chip from each pot in exchange for supplying the chairs and tables and a man to keep an eye on the betting. As for the players, they are a mixed group of Mexicans, Filipinos, Whites, and Negroes; and there are even a few young fellows who look as though they go to college and just come down to Skid Row for the cards.

I eat my dinner in one of the many grimy restaurants in the neighborhood. The floor is littered with napkins, the counter is greasy, and sugar is spilled around the rack holding the condiments. A pleasant Mexican waitress serves me watery tomato rice soup, fatty lamb stew with potatoes and rice, diced beets, and one slice of canned pineapple. The meal costs eighty-five cents, and I buy a nickel cigar on my way out. Again I wander the streets, indistinguishable from the other men shifting a frayed toothpick around in their mouths.

It is nightfall now. Skid Row is crowded; the bars are jammed with beer and sweet-wine drinkers; the drunks stagger into the street and collapse in the alleys. For many of these men, Skid Row is the end point of some personal tragedy—perhaps a divorce, or alcoholism, or unexpected unemployment. Then the police cars make their appearance. They cruise slowly around the area, circling it like keepers in a zoo. One of them pulls up to the corner where I'm standing talking with three asparagus cutters, and the officer behind the wheel looks at me. "Hello, there," he says. As I return the greeting, I notice him remarking to his partner, "That's a new face around here." He will keep my face in mind—just in case.

Back at the hotel three very old men and one middle-aged farm worker are sitting in a row in the lobby, dozing intermittently through a rerun of an "I Love Lucy" show on TV. I watch too for a while and then walk upstairs to my room. It is hot and stuffy. Undressing, I wonder what the temperature in the room gets to be during the summer when the valley becomes a furnace, made habitable for most of its residents only by air-conditioners.

The work day begins at night. At 4:00 A.M., wakened by the body noises of the man in the next room, I struggle out of my narrow, lumpy bed. As I wash, I can hear him washing; I brush my teeth, but he doesn't; and neither of us shaves. Outside it's still dark. In my dirty work clothes, I eat breakfast—a "short stack with bacon"—at the counter of a nearby all-night restaurant. After finishing the heavy pancakes soaked in thick syrup and drinking two mugs of coffee, I buy a box lunch from the Chinaman at the cash register to take with me out to the fields. For fifty-five cents I get three sandwiches of dry, thinly sliced roast beef with a piece of lettuce on soggy white bread, an orange, and a small Danish pastry.

Outside, crowds of men are heading toward the farm labor office where the contractors' buses pull in to pick up their loads of dayhaul workers. In the office, under a sign that says, "Do not spit, sit, or lie on the floor," I line up with about twenty-five other men, moving slowly toward the desk at which work is being assigned. Everybody is wearing some kind of hat or cap for protection against the hot sun, and the soiled, ragged clothes which are the day laborer's uniform and stigma. In my hand, I hold the green registration card that will get me on the bus if there is work to be had. The only jobs listed on the board today are cutting asparagus, and short-handled hoe work on tomatoes or beets. Asparagus is cut by crews and is a comparatively skilled job—much more desirable than such stoop labor as hoe work. But I've never done any asparagus cutting and so I have to take tomatoes or beets.

"Don't send anybody in who

won't work short-handle hoe!" one of the three men behind the counter of the employment office shouts angrily after one of the workers has refused the job. Because short-handle hoe work is back-breaking and pays badly, there is often difficulty in finding enough men to fill the contractors' quotas.

"Beets or tomatoes, Paul?" asks the young man at the desk. I choose tomatoes, even though they pay only $1.00 an hour as against $1.10 for beets. But beets, I know, are much harder to work.

By 5:15 A.M. the big yard next door is jammed with men waiting to be assigned to a contractor's bus. Only one or two of the huge California farms do their hiring directly; most of the others deal with the labor contractors who set a flat price for supplying the workers to handle a particular job. The contractor then pays the workers out of this flat fee, naturally keeping enough for himself to make a profit. Some of the contractors are decent employers, but some are known as chiselers, to be avoided if at all possible. Even so, the difference between the best and the worst is only a matter of small degree; most farm workers are subjected to conditions long banished from modern industry.

More than half the men in the loading yard are Mexicans. Somehow, their Spanish sounds more educated than the English of the whites and Negroes greeting their friends and talking about how they made out yesterday. One slightly tipsy Negro is jumping around playing a guitar very badly; the more everyone ignores him, the harder he strives to get their attention. The asparagus crews are the first to be assigned to buses; they all have cheap plastic goggles on their hats which they will later use to keep the heavy dust out of their eyes. Finally, from the back end of the yard I see a contractor coming for my group. He is recognizable immediately by his baseball cap, his leather jacket, his boots and, most of all, his assured manner. He stops to kibitz a bit with the man from the employment office, and it becomes obvious that the relationship between them is much different from the one each of them has with us. Even though we farm workers are formally the clients of the state employment service, the real clients are the contractors, for they are permanent while we are only temporary; we are dependent upon both of them; and besides, they are social equals and we are their social inferiors. It is to the contractor, who needs it least, and not to the worker, who needs it most, that the state gives the benefit of its publicly supported employment service: the state is the instrument that provides the contractors with a good income and the growers with a pool of extremely cheap labor.

We board an old bus, painted blue, with the name of the contractor stenciled on the outside. In front of me, two Mexicans are chatting in Spanish, and across from them another Mexican sits alone. There are also eight other men in the bus— three Negroes and five whites, including myself. We sit and doze in the chill dark air, and then, at 6:00 A.M., when the buses in front of us start leaving the lot, our driver, who is Mexican, comes back with six more workers—three young white men, a Negro, and two Mexicans. Only one of the group, I notice, is wearing glasses. A few minutes later, we swing out of the lot and drive out on the highway.

By this time it is daylight and I

can see the interior of the bus more clearly. On the dashboard is stenciled "Speed Limit 45 MPH," the maximum speed the state law allows farm buses to travel. I know these buses are supposed to be inspected by the state, but this one must have had its inspection a long time ago. The rear-view mirror is broken in half and the speedometer doesn't work at all. On the floor is a fire extinguisher, but it doesn't appear to be in very good working order either. Next to the driver is a large old-fashioned milk can filled with water. Once we get on the highway, the driver starts speeding, and we go barreling along until the contractor catches up to us in his pickup truck and signals the driver to stop. The driver gets out and I hear the contractor tell him in Spanish to slow down because the police are on the highway.

The driver gets back in the bus and begins going more slowly. But soon he is accelerating again, and in a few minutes we are moving at about the same speed as before. Some thirty-five minutes later, we turn off the highway and drive another three or four miles to a huge field with tomato plants growing in long straight furrows. Leaving our lunches on the seats, we file out of the bus, and the driver hands each of us a brand new hoe, about fifteen inches long with a head that is set back at an angle toward the handle.

In the field waiting for us is the contractor, talking with a stocky Nisei in his early forties. The Nisei tells us, in perfect English, to thin out the plants which are now about three inches high and growing close together. We are to chop out the row, leaving only one or two of the plants in each cluster, nipping off the weeds growing around them, and making sure that there is a space of from four to nine inches between the remaining plants. We station ourselves at every other furrow so that when we get to the end of the field, each of us can come back along the next row.

To chop at the tomato plants with a fifteen-inch hoe requires bending over almost double, and in only a few minutes, the sweat is pouring down my face. I soon fall behind almost all of the workers in the field: the end of the furrow seems a million miles away, and it takes me a half hour to get there. The bus driver, who is now acting as straw boss, keeps an impatient eye on me. He complains that I am not thinning the plants enough, and he tries to show me how to move my feet so that I can stay bent over. But the Nisei foreman tells me to take my time and do the job properly. As I get to the end of the row, the muscles in my back, thighs, and calves ache from the strain. Working my way back on the next furrow, I am acutely conscious of the straw boss watching and checking on me. By now, I am streaming sweat and in agony from the bending over. In the next furrow, an elderly man is working almost as slowly as I am, muttering to himself, "This here work's too hard, this here work's too hard."

"You ever done this kind of work before?" I ask him. "Sure," he answers, "I never done nothin' but farm work all my life, but this here's too hard. I'm too old to be bending over like this." Then, as I watch, he opens his pants and begins to urinate, never breaking the rhythm of his work, one hand hoeing, the other holding his organ with the urine dribbling through his fingers and down onto his pants.

And so the day moves on, with the sun rising in the sky and the heat rising in the field. The furrows extend into an eternity of tiny tomato plants and dirt, and the short-handled hoe is an instrument of torture. At last we take a break for lunch, after which a few of the men walk out into the field to defecate, scraps of newspaper stuck in their back pocket. Then hoeing again until shortly before four, when we quit and are driven a few miles to the labor camp, a small group of battered shacks in which crews are housed when they are working by the week. We line up at the contractor's office and are paid eight dollars for the day.

On the drive back to town the men talk more than they have all day, mostly about which bar serves the best beer for the money. In front of me, there is a discussion of how to beat the blood bank system. Selling blood is a good way to supplement your income. The only problem is that you can't give blood more than once every few months, and the date on which you sell the blood is marked on your fingers in ink that becomes visible under fluorescent light and won't wash off even with strong detergents. But one of the men has discovered that you can erase the ink by rubbing tobacco very, very hard over your fingers for a long time.

The bus stops on the street where the farm labor office is located, and we pile out. All around us, buses and trucks are pulling in to discharge their cargoes. Some of the men head for their rooms to wash off the dust and dirt; others make for a bar to get a beer or two first. Then there is the lamb-stew dinner again, and again the walk along the streets, the stopping on corners, the surveillance by the police, and maybe, if a couple of guys get together, the buying of a "jug" to knock off before bed. At 4:00 A.M., the work day will start again.

If you want to and have the strength to make it, you can go out to the fields six days a week and earn $48.00. Stoop labor is available in California for eight or nine months of the year, so you might, putting in six days a week, earn up to $1700—$600 more than the average wage of a farm worker in 1962. If you get sick, you earn nothing, and when the work season is over, you receive no unemployment insurance. Thus eventually you have to move on to another town, looking for another job which offers exactly the same conditions. And since you can never save enough to escape from Skid Row, it is easy to slip just a notch or two down to the bum level. At $1.00 an hour for back-breaking labor performed under the worst physical conditions, what possible incentive is there to work?

All this—when the government subsidizes crops and livestock, and when it has been estimated that doubling the wages of stoop labor might increase the retail price of tomatoes by a *penny* a can or a pound.

Hunger and malnutrition exist in this country, affecting millions of our fellow Americans and increasing in severity and extent from year to year.
Hunger U.S.A.
*Citizens Board of Inquiry into
Hunger & Malnutrition in the U.S.A.,*

LIFE IN HARLEM

By James Baldwin

There is a housing project standing now where the house in which we grew up once stood, and one of those stunted city trees is snarling where our doorway used to be. This is on the rehabilitated side of the avenue. The other side of the avenue—for progress takes time—has not been rehabilitated yet and it looks exactly as it looked in the days when we sat with our noses pressed against the windowpane, longing to be allowed to go "across the street." The grocery store which gave us credit is still there, and there can be no doubt that it is still giving credit. The people in the project certainly need it—far more, indeed, than they ever needed the project. The last time I passed by, the Jewish proprietor was still standing among his shelves, looking sadder and heavier but scarcely any older. Farther down the block stands the shoe-repair store in which our shoes were repaired until reparation became impossible and in which, then, we bought all our "new" ones. The Negro proprietor is still in the window, head down, working at the leather.

These two, I imagine, could tell a long tale if they would (perhaps they would be glad to if they could), having watched so many, for so long, struggling in the fishhooks, the barbed wire, of this avenue.

The avenue is elsewhere the renowned and elegant Fifth. The area I am describing, which, in today's gang parlance, would be called "the turf," is bounded by Lenox Avenue on the west, the Harlem River on the east, 135th Street on the north, and 130th Street on the south. We never lived beyond these boundaries; this is where we grew up. Walking along 145th Street—for example—familiar as it is, and similar, does not have the same impact because I do not know any of the people on the block. But when I turn east on 131st Street and Lenox Avenue, there is a first a soda-pop joint, then a shoeshine "parlor," then a grocery store, then a dry cleaners', then the houses. All along the street there are people who watched me grow up, people who grew up with me, people I watched grow up along with my brothers and sisters; and,

Reprinted by permission of The Dial Press from James Baldwin, *Nobody Knows My Name* (New York: The Dial Press, 1960).

sometimes in my arms, sometimes underfoot, sometimes at my shoulder —or on it—their children, a riot, a forest of children, who include my nieces and nephews.

When we reach the end of this long block, we find ourselves on wide, filthy, hostile Fifth Avenue, facing that project which hangs over the avenue like a monument to the folly, and the cowardice, of good intentions. All along the block, for anyone who knows it, are immense human gaps, like craters. These gaps are not created merely by those who have moved away, inevitably into some other

---

Such poverty as we have today in all our great cities degrades the poor, and infects with its degradation the whole neighborhood in which they live. And whatever can degrade a neighborhood can degrade a country and a continent and finally the whole civilized world which is only a large neighborhood.

George Bernard Shaw

ghetto; or by those who have risen, almost always into a greater capacity for self-loathing and self-delusion; or yet by those who, by whatever means —World War II, the Korean war, a policeman's gun or billy, a gang war, a brawl, madness, an overdose of heroin, or, simply, unnatural exhaustion—are dead. I am talking about those who are left, and I am talking principally about the young. What are they doing? Well, some, a minority, are fanatical churchgoers, members of the more extreme of the Holy Roller sects. Many, many more are "moslems," by affiliation or sympathy, that is to say that they are united by nothing more—and nothing less— than a hatred of the white world and all its works. They are present, for example, at every Buy Black street-corner meeting—meetings in which the speaker urges his hearers to cease trading with white men and establish a separate economy. Neither the speaker nor his hearers can possibly do this, of course, since Negroes do not own General Motors or RCA or the A & P, nor, indeed, do they own more than a wholly insufficient fraction of anything else in Harlem (those who *do* own anything are more interested in their profits than in their fellows). But these meetings nevertheless keep alive in the participators a certain pride of bitterness without which, however futile this bitterness may be, they could scarcely remain alive at all. Many have given up. They stay home and watch the TV screen, living on the earnings of their parents, cousins, brothers, or uncles, and only leave the house to go to the movies or to the nearest bar. "How're you making it?" one may ask, running into them along the block, or in the bar. "Oh, I'm TV-ing it"; with the saddest, sweetest, most shamefaced of smiles, and from a great distance.

This distance one is compelled to respect; anyone who has traveled so far will not easily be dragged again into the world. There are further retreats, of course, than the TV screen or the bar. There are those who are simply sitting on their stoops, "stoned," animated for a moment only, and hideously, by the approach of someone who may lend them the money for a "fix." Or by the approach of someone from whom they can purchase it, one of the shrewd ones, on the way to prison or just coming out.

And the others, who have avoided all of these deaths, get up in the morning and go downtown to meet "the man." They work in the white man's world all day and come home in the evening to this fetid block. They struggle to instill in their children some private sense of honor or dignity which will help the child to survive. This means, of course, that they must struggle, stolidly, incessantly, to keep this sense alive in themselves, in spite of the insults, the indifference, and the cruelty they are certain to encounter in their working day. They patiently browbeat the landlord into fixing the heat, the plaster, the plumbing; this demands prodigious patience; nor is patience usually enough. In trying to make their hovels habitable, they are perpetually throwing good money after bad. Such frustration, so long endured, is driving many strong, admirable men and women whose only crime is color to the very gates of paranoia.

One remembers them from another time—playing handball in the playground, going to church, wondering if they were going to be promoted at school. One remembers them going off to war—gladly, to escape this block. One remembers their return. Perhaps one remembers their wedding day. And one sees where the girl is now—vainly looking for salvation from some other embittered, trussed, and struggling boy—and sees the all-but-abandoned children in the streets.

Now I am perfectly aware that there are other slums in which white men are fighting for their lives, and mainly losing. I know that blood is also flowing through those streets and that the human damage there is incalculable. People are continually pointing out to me the wretchedness of white people in order to console me for the wretchedness of blacks. But an itemized account of the American failure does not console me and it should not console anyone else. That hundreds of thousands of white people are living, in effect, no better than the "niggers" is not a fact to be regarded with complacency. The social and moral bankruptcy suggested by this fact is of the bitterest, most terrifying kind.

The people, however, who believe that this democratic anguish has some consoling value are always pointing out that So-and-So, white, and So-and-So, black, rose from the slums into the big time. The existence—the public existence—of, say, Frank Sinatra and Sammy Davis, Jr. proves to them that America is still the land of opportunity and that inequalities vanish before the determined will. It proves nothing of the sort. The determined will is rare—at the moment, in this country, it is unspeakably rare—and the inequalities suffered by the many are in no way justified by the rise of a few. A few have always risen—in every country, every era, and in the teeth of regimes which can by no stretch of the imagination be thought of as free. Not all of these people, it is worth remembering, left the world better than they found it. The determined will is rare, but it is

not invariably benevolent. Furthermore, the American equation of success with the big time reveals an awful disrespect for human life and human achievement. This equation has placed our cities among the most dangerous in the world and has placed our youth among the most empty and most bewildered. The situation of our youth is not mysterious. Children have never been very good at listening to their elders, but they have never failed to imitate them. They must, they have no other models. That is exactly what our children are doing. They are imitating our immorality, our disrespect for the pain of others.

All other slum dwellers, when the bank account permits it, can move out of the slum and vanish altogether from the eye of persecution. No Negro in this country has ever made that much money and it will be a long time before any Negro does. The Negroes in Harlem, who have no money, spend what they have on such gimcracks as they are sold. These include "wider" TV screens, more "faithful" hi-fi sets, more "powerful" cars, all of which, of course, are obsolete long before they are paid for. Anyone who has ever struggled with poverty knows how extremely expensive it is to be poor; and if one is a member of a captive population, economically speaking, one's feet have simply been placed on the treadmill forever. One is victimized, economically, in a thousand ways—rent, for example, or car insurance. Go shopping one day in Harlem—for anything—and compare Harlem prices and quality with those downtown.

The people who have managed to get off this block have only got as far as a more respectable ghetto. This respectable ghetto does not even have the advantages of the disreputable one—friends, neighbors, a familiar church, and friendly tradesmen; and it is not, moreover, in the nature of any ghetto to remain respectable long. Every Sunday, people who have left the block take the lonely ride back, dragging their increasingly discontented children with them. They spend the day talking, not always with words, about the trouble they've seen and the trouble—one must watch their eyes as they watch their children —they are only too likely to see. For children do not like ghettos. It takes them nearly no time to discover exactly why they are there.

The projects in Harlem are hated. They are hated almost as much as policemen, and this is saying a great deal. And they are hated for the same reason: both reveal, unbearably, the real attitude of the white world, no matter how many liberal speeches are made, no matter how many lofty editorials are written, no matter how many civil-rights commissions are set up.

The projects are hideous, of course, there being a law, apparently respected throughout the world, that popular housing shall be as cheerless as a prison. They are lumped all over Harlem, colorless, bleak, high, and revolting. The wide windows look out on Harlem's invincible and indescribable squalor: the Park Avenue railroad tracks, around which, about forty years ago, the present dark community began; the unrehabilitated houses, bowed down, it would seem, under the great weight of frustration and bitterness they contain; the dark, the ominous schoolhouses from which the child may emerge maimed, blinded, hooked, or enraged for life; and the churches, churches, block upon block of churches, niched in the walls like cannon in the walls of a fortress. Even if the administration of the projects were not so insanely humiliating (for example: one must report raises in salary to the management, which will then eat up the profit by raising one's rent; the management has the right to know who is staying in your apartment; the management can ask you to leave, at their discretion), the projects would still be hated because they are an insult to the meanest intelligence.

Harlem got its first private project, Riverton—which is now, naturally, a slum—about twelve years ago because at that time Negroes were not allowed to live in Stuyvesant Town. Harlem watched Riverton go up, therefore, in the most violent bitterness of spirit, and hated it long before the builders arrived. They began hating it at about the time people began moving out of their condemned houses to make room for this additional proof of how thoroughly the white world despised them. And they had scarcely moved in, naturally, before they began smashing windows, defacing walls, urinating in the elevators, and fornicating in the playgrounds. Liberals, both white and black, were appalled at the spectacle. I was appalled by the liberal innocence —or cynicism, which comes out in practice as much the same thing. Other people were delighted to be able to point to proof positive that nothing could be done to better the lot of the colored people. They were, and are, right in one respect: that nothing can be done as long as they are treated like colored people. The people in Harlem know they are living there because white people do not think they are good enough to live anywhere else. No amount of "improvement" can sweeten this fact. Whatever money is now being earmarked to improve this, or any other ghetto, might as well be burnt. A ghetto can be improved in one way only: out of existence.

TO TOUSSAINT L'OUVERTURE

Toussaint, the most unhappy man of men!
Whether the whistling Rustic tend his plough
Within thy hearing, or thy head be now
Pillowed in some deep dungeon's earless den;—
O miserable Chieftain! where and when
Wilt thou find patience? Yet die not; do thou
Wear rather in thy bonds a cheerful brow:
Though fallen thyself, never to rise again,
Live, and take comfort. Thou hast left behind
Powers that will work for thee; air, earth, and skies;
There's not a breathing of the common wind
That will forget thee; thou hast great allies;
Thy friends are exultations, agonies,
And love, and man's unconquerable mind.

—*William Wordsworth*

MISTER TOUSSAN

By Ralph W. Ellison

Once upon a time
The goose drink wine
Monkey chew tobacco
And he spit white lime.
—Rhyme used as a prologue to Negro slave stories.

"I hope they all gits rotten and the worms git in 'em," the first boy said.

"I hopes a big wind storm comes and blows down all the trees," said the second boy.

"Me too," the first boy said. "And when ole Rogan comes out to see what happened I hope a tree falls on his head and kills him."

"Now jus' look a-yonder at them birds," the second boy said, "they eating all they want and when we asked him to let us git some off the ground he had to come calling us little nigguhs and chasing us home!"

"Doggonit," said the second boy, "I hope them birds got poison in they feet!"

The two small boys, Riley and Buster, sat on the floor of the porch, their bare feet resting upon the cool earth as they stared past the line on the paving where the sun consumed the shade, to a yard directly across the street. The grass in the yard was very green and a house stood against it, neat and white in the morning sun. A double row of trees stood alongside the house, heavy with cherries that showed deep red against the dark green of the leaves and dull dark brown of the branches. They were watching an old man who rocked himself in a chair as he stared back at them across the street.

"Just look at him," said Buster. "Ole Rogan's so scared we gonna git some his ole cherries he ain't even got sense enough to go in outa the sun!"

"Well, them birds is gitting their'n," said Riley.

"They mocking birds."

Reprinted by permission of William Agency and Ralph Ellison, 1941.

"I don't care what kinda birds they is, they sho in them trees."

"Yeah, ole Rogan don't see *them*. Man, I tell you white folks ain't got no sense."

They were silent now, watching the darting flight of the birds into the trees. Behind them they could hear the clatter of a sewing machine: Riley's mother was sewing for the white folks. It was quiet and as the woman worked, her voice rose above the whirring machine in song.

"Your mamma sho can sing, man," said Buster.

"She sings in the choir," said Riley, "and she sings all the leads in church."

"Shucks, I know it," said Buster. "You tryin' to brag?"

As they listened they heard the voice rise clear and liquid to float upon the morning air:

> *I got wings, you got wings,*
> *All God's chillun got a-wings*
> *When I git to heaven gonna put on my wings*
> *Gonna shout all ovah God's heaven.*
> *Heab'n, heab'n*
> *Everybody talkin' 'bout heab'n ain't going*
> *   there*
> *Heab'n, heab'n, Ah'm gonna fly all ovah God's*
> *   heab'n. . . .*

She sang as though the words possessed a deep and throbbing meaning for her, and the boys stared blankly at the earth, feeling the somber, mysterious calm of church. The street was quiet and even old Rogan had stopped rocking to listen. Finally the voice trailed off to a hum and became lost in the clatter of the busy machine.

"Wish I could sing like that," said Buster.

Riley was silent, looking down to the end of the porch where the sun had eaten a bright square into the shade, fixing a flitting butterfly in its brilliance.

"What would you do if you had wings?" he said.

"Shucks, I'd outfly an eagle, I wouldn't stop flying till I was a million, billion, trillion, zillion miles away from this ole town."

"Where'd you go, man?"

"Up north, maybe to Chicago."

"Man, if I had wings I wouldn't never settle down."

"Me, neither. Hecks, with wings you could go anywhere, even up to the sun if it wasn't too hot. . . ."

". . . I'd go to New York. . . ."

"Even around the stars. . . ."

"Or Dee-troit, Michigan. . . ."

"Hell, you could git some cheese off the moon and some milk from the Milkyway. . . ."

"Or anywhere else colored is free. . . ."

"I bet I'd loop-the-loop. . . ."

"And parachute. . . ."

"I'd land in Africa and git me some diamonds. . . ."

"Yeah, and them cannibals would eat the hell outa you too," said Riley.

"The heck they would, not fast as I'd fly away. . . ."

"Man, they'd catch you and stick soma them long spears in your behin'!" said Riley.

Buster laughed as Riley shook his head gravely: "Boy, you'd look like a black pin cushion when they got through with you," said Riley.

"Shucks, man, they couldn't catch me, them suckers is too lazy. The geography book says they 'bout the most lazy folks in the whole world," said Buster with disgust, "just black and lazy!"

"Aw naw, they ain't neither," exploded Riley.

"They is too! The geography book says they is!"

"Well, my ole man says they ain't!"

"How come they ain't, then?"

" 'Cause my ole man says that over there they got kings and diamonds and gold and ivory, and if they got all them things, all of 'em cain't be lazy," said Riley. "Ain't many colored folks over here got them things."

"Sho ain't, man. The white folks won't let 'em," said Buster.

It was good to think that all the Africans were not lazy. He tried to remember all he had heard of Africa as he watched a purple pigeon sail down into the street and scratch where a horse had passed. Then, as he remembered a story his teacher had told him, he saw a car rolling swiftly up the street and the pigeon stretching its wings and lifting easily into the air, skimming the top of the car in its slow, rocking flight. He watched it rise and disappear where the taut telephone wires cut the sky above the curb. Buster felt good. Riley scratched his initials in the soft earth with his big toe.

"Riley, you know all them African guys ain't really that lazy," he said.

"I know they ain't," said Riley, "I just tole you so."

"Yeah, but my teacher tole me, too. She tole us 'bout one of them African guys named Toussan what she said whipped Napoleon!"

Riley stopped scratching in the earth and looked up, his eyes rolling in disgust:

"Now how come you have to start lying?"

"Thass what she said."

"Boy, you oughta quit telling them things."

"I hope God may kill me."

"She said he was a *African?*"

"Cross my heart, man. . . ."

"Really?"

"Really, man. She said he come from a place named Hayti."

Riley looked hard at Buster and seeing the seriousness of the face felt the excitement of a story rise up within him.

"Buster, I'll bet a fat man you lyin'. What'd that teacher say?"

"Really, man, she said that Toussan and his men got up on one of them African mountains and shot down them peckerwood soldiers fass as they'd try to come up. . . ."

"Why good-God-a-mighty!" yelled Riley.

"Oh boy, they shot 'em down!" chanted Buster.

"Tell me about it, man!"

"And they throwed 'em off the mountain. . . ."

". . . Goool-leee! . . ."

". . . And Toussan drove 'em cross the sand. . . ."

"... Yeah! And what was they wearing, Buster? ..."

"Man, they had on red uniforms and blue hats all trimmed with gold, and they had some swords all shining what they called sweet blades of Damascus. ..."

"Sweet blades of Damascus! ..."

"... They really had 'em," chanted Buster.

"And what kinda guns?"

"Big, black cannon!"

"And where did ole what-you-call-'im run them guys? ..."

"His name was Toussan."

"Toussan! Just like Tarzan. ..."

"Not *Taar*-zan, dummy, *Toou*-zan!"

"Toussan! And where'd ole Toussan run 'em?"

"Down to the water, man. ..."

"... To the river water. ..."

"... Where some great big ole boats was waiting for 'em. ..."

"... Go on, Buster!"

"An' Toussan shot into them boats. ..."

"... He shot into em. ..."

"... Shot into them boats. ..."

"Jesus!! ..."

"With his great big cannons. ..."

"... Yeah! ..."

"... Made a-brass. ..."

"... Brass. ..."

"... An' his big black cannon balls started killin' them peckerwoods. ..."

"... Lawd, Lawd. ..."

"... Boy, till them peckerwoods hollowed *Please, Please, Mister Toussan, we'll be good!*"

"An' what'd Toussan tell em, Buster?"

"Boy, he said in his deep voice, *I oughta drown all a-you bastards.*"

"An' what'd the peckerwoods say?"

"They said, Please, Please, *Please, Mister Toussan.* ..."

"... We'll be good," broke in Riley.

"Thass right, man," said Buster excitedly. He clapped his hands and kicked his heels against the earth, his black face glowing in a burst of rhythmic joy.

"Boy!"

"And what'd ole Toussan say then?"

"He said in his big deep voice: *You all peckerwoods better be good, 'cause this is sweet Papa Toussan talking and my nigguhs is crazy 'bout white meat!*"

"Ho, ho, ho!" Riley bent double with laughter. The rhythm still throbbed within him and he wanted the story to go on and on. ...

"Buster, you know didn't no teacher tell you that lie," he said.

"Yes she did, man."

"She said there was really a guy like that what called hisself Sweet Papa Toussan?"

Riley's voice was unbelieving and there was a wistful expression in his eyes which Buster could not understand. Finally he dropped his head and grinned.

"Well," he said, "I bet thass what ole Toussan said. You know how grown folks is, they cain't tell a story right, 'cepting real old folks like grandma."

"They sho cain't," said Riley. "They don't know how to put the right stuff to it."

Riley stood, his legs spread wide and stuck his thumbs in the top of his trousers, swaggering sinisterly.

"Come on, watch me do it now, Buster. Now I bet ole Toussan looked down at them white folks standing just about like this and said in a soft easy voice: Ain't I done begged you white folks to quit messin' with me? . . ."

"Thass right, quit meszing with 'im," chanted Buster.

"But naw, you-all all had to come on anyway. . . ."

". . . Jus' 'cause they was black. . . ."

"Thass right," said Riley. "Then ole Toussan felt so damn bad and mad the tears come a-trickling down. . . ."

". . . He was really mad."

"And then, man, he said in his big bass voice: Goddamn you white folks, how come you-all cain't let us colored alone?"

". . . An' he was crying. . . ."

". . . An' Toussan tole them peckerwoods: I been beggin' you-all to quit bothering us. . . ."

". . . Beggin' on his bended knees! . . ."

"Then, man, Toussan got real mad and snatched off his hat and started stompin' up and down on it and the tears was tricklin' down and he said: You-all come tellin' me about Napoleon. . . ."

"They was tryin' to scare him, man. . . ."

"Said: I don't give a damn about Napoleon. . . ."

". . . Wasn', studyin' 'bout him. . . ."

". . . Toussan said: Napoleon ain't nothing but a man! Then Toussan pulled back his shining sword like this, and twirled it at them peckerwoods' throats so hard it z-z-z-zinged in the air!"

"Now keep on, finish it, man," said Buster. "What'd Toussan do then?"

"Then you know what he did, he said: I oughta beat the hell outa you peckerwoods!"

"Thass right, and he did it too," said Buster. He jumped to his feet and fenced violently with five desperate imaginary soldiers, running each through with his imaginary sword. Buster watched him from the porch, grinning.

"Toussan musta scared them white folks almost to death!"

"Yeah, thass 'bout the way it was," said Buster. The rhythm was dying now and he sat back upon the porch, breathing tiredly.

"It sho is a good story," said Riley.

"Hecks, man, all the stories my teacher tells us is good. She's a good ole teacher—but you know one thing?"

"Naw; what?"

"Ain't none of them stories in the books! Wonder why?"

"Hell, you know why, Ole Toussan was too hard on them white folks, thass why."

"Oh, he was a hard man!"

"He was mean. . . ."

"But a good mean!"

"Toussan was clean. . . ."

". . . He was a good, clean mean," said Riley.

"Aw, man, he was sooo-preme," said Buster.

"Riiiley!!"

The boys stopped short in their word play, their mouths wide.

"Riley, I say!" It was Riley's mother's voice.

"Ma'am?"

"She musta heard us cussin'," whispered Buster.

"Shut up, man. . . . What you want, Ma?"

"I says I wants you-all to go round in the backyard and play, you keeping up too much fuss out there. White folks says we tear up a neighborhood when we move in it and you-all out there jus' provin' them out true. Now git on round in the back."

"Aw, ma, we was jus' playing, ma. . . ."

"Boy, I said for you-all to go on."

"But, ma . . ."

"You hear me, boy!"

"Yessum, we going," said Riley. "Come on, Buster."

Buster followed slowly behind, feeling the dew upon his feet as he walked upon the shaded grass.

"What else did he do, man?" Buster said.

"Huh? Rogan?"

"Hecks, naw! I'm talkin' 'bout Toussan."

"Doggone if I know, man—but I'm gonna ask that teacher."

"He was a fightin' son-of-a-gun, wasn't he, man?"

"He didn't stand for no foolishness," said Riley reservedly. He thought of other things now, and as he moved along he slid his feet easily over the short-cut grass, dancing as he chanted:

> *Iron is iron,*
> *And tin is tin,*
> *And that's the way*
> *The story. . . .*

"Aw come on man," interrupted Buster. "Let's go play in the alley. . . ."

> *And that's the way. . . .*

"Maybe we can slip around and git some cherries," Buster went on.

> *. . . the story ends*, chanted Riley.

LET AMERICA BE AMERICA AGAIN

Let America be America again.
Let it be the dream it used to be.
Let it be the pioneer on the plain
Seeking a home where he himself is free.

(America never was America to me.)

Let America be the dream the dreamers dreamed—
Let it be that great strong land of love
Where never kings connive nor tyrants scheme
That any man be crushed by one above.

(It never was America to me.)

O, let my land be a land where Liberty
Is crowned with no false patriotic wreath,
But opportunity is real, and life is free,
Equality is in the air we breathe.

(There's never been equality for me,
Nor freedom in this "homeland of the free.")

Say who are you that mumbles in the dark?
And who are you that draws your veil across the stars?

I am the poor white, fooled and pushed apart,
I am the red man driven from the land.
I am the refugee clutching the hope I seek—
But finding only the same old stupid plan
Of dog eat dog, of mighty crush the weak.
I am the Negro, "problem" to you all.
I am the people, humble, hungry, mean—
Hungry yet today despite the dream.
Beaten yet today—O, Pioneers!
I am the man who never got ahead,
The poorest worker bartered through the years.

Yet I'm the one who dreamt our basic dream
In that Old World while still a serf of kings,
Who dreamt a dream so strong, so brave, so true,
That even yet its mighty daring sings
In every brick and stone, in every furrow turned
That's made America the land it has become.
O, I'm the man who sailed those early seas
In search of what I meant to be my home—

For I'm the one who left dark Ireland's shore,
And Poland's plain, and England's grassy lea,
And torn from Black Africa's strand I came
To build a "homeland of the free."

The free?
Who said the free? Not me?
Surely not me? The millions on relief today?
The millions who have nothing for our pay
For all the dreams we've dreamed
And all the songs we've sung
And all the homes we've held
And all the flags we've hung,
The millions who have nothing for our pay—
Except the dream we keep alive today.

O, let America be America again—
The land that never has been yet—
And yet must be—the land where every man is free.
The land that's mine—poor man's, Indians,
        Negro's, ME—
Who made America,
Whose sweat and blood, whose faith and pain,
Whose hand at the foundry, whose plow in the rain,
Must bring back our mighty dream again.

        O, yes,
        I say it plain,
        America never was America to me,
        And yet I swear this oath—
        America will be!

An ever-living seed,
Its dream
Lies deep in the heart of me.

We, the people, must redeem
Our land, the mines, the plants, the rivers,
The mountains and the endless plain—
All, all the stretch of these great green states—
And make America again.

        —*Langston Hughes*

DECLARATION OF INDEPENDENCE

When, in the Course of human events, it becomes necessary for one people to dissolve the political bands which have connected them with another, and to assume among the powers of the earth, the separate and equal station to which the Laws of Nature and of Nature's God entitle them, a decent respect to the opinions of mankind requires that they should declare the causes which impel them to the separation.

We hold these truths to be self-evident, that all men are created equal, that they are endowed by their Creator with certain unalienable Rights, that among these are Life, Liberty and the pursuit of Happiness. That to secure these rights, Governments are instituted among Men, deriving their just powers from the consent of the governed. That whenever any Form of Government becomes destructive of these ends, it is the Right of the People to alter or to abolish it, and to institute new Government, laying its foundation on such principles and organizing its powers in such form, as to them shall seem most likely to effect their Safety and Happiness. Prudence, indeed, will dictate that Governments long established should not be changed for light and transient causes; and accordingly all experience hath shewn, that mankind are more disposed to suffer, while evils are sufferable, than to right themselves by abolishing the forms to which they are accustomed. But when a long train of abuses and usurpations, pursuing invariably the same object, evidence a design to reduce them under absolute Despotism, it is their right, it is their duty, to throw off such Government, and to provide new Guards for their future security.

July 4, 1776

PROCLAMATION
TO THE GREAT WHITE FATHER AND ALL HIS PEOPLE

We, the native Americans, re-claim the land known as Alcatraz Island in the name of all American Indians by right of discovery.

We wish to be fair and honorable in our dealings with the Caucasian inhabitants of this land, and hereby offer the following treaty:

We will purchase said Alcatraz Island for twenty-four dollars (24) in glass beads and red cloth, a precedent set by the white man's purchase of a similar island about 300 years ago. We know that $24 in trade goods for these 16 acres is more than was paid when Manhattan Island was sold, but we know that land values have risen over the years. Our offer of $1.24 per acre is greater than the 47c per acre the white men are now paying the California Indians for their land.

We will give to the inhabitants of this island a portion of the land for their own to be held in trust by the American Indian Affairs and by the Bureau of Caucasian Affairs to hold in perpetuity—for as long as the sun shall rise and the rivers go down to the sea. We will further guide the inhabitants in the proper way of living. We will offer them our religion, our education, our life-ways, in order to help them achieve our level of civilization and thus raise them and all their white brothers up from their savage and unhappy state. We offer this treaty in good faith and wish to be fair and honorable in our dealings with all white men.

We feel that this so-called Alcatraz Island is more than suitable for an Indian Reservation, as determined by the white man's own standards. By this we mean that this place resembles most Indian reservations in that:

1. It is isolated from modern facilities, and without adequate means of transportation.
2. It has no fresh running water.
3. It has inadequate sanitation facilities.
4. There are no oil and mineral rights.
5. There is no industry and so unemployment is very great.
6. There are no health care facilities.
7. The soil is rocky and non-productive; and the land does not support game.
8. There are no educational facilities.
9. The population has always exceeded the land base.
10. The population has always been held as prisoners and kept dependent upon others.

Further, it would be fitting and symbolic that ships from all over the world, entering Golden Gate, would first see Indian land, and thus be reminded of the true history of this nation. This tiny island would be a symbol of the great lands once ruled by free and noble Indians.

—Indians of All Tribes

Red Power means we want power over our own lives. We do not wish to threaten anyone. We do not wish power over anyone. We are only half a million Indians. We simply want the power, the political and economic power, to run our own lives in our own way.

Vince Deloria, Jr.

A COMEBACK FOR THE VANISHING AMERICAN?

By James W. Hoffman

Recently a group of Mohawks formed a human roadblock on a bridge connecting New York State and the Province of Ontario in protest against paying customs duties on goods moving from the United States part of their reservation to the Canadian part.

Nationwide publicity was given to the presence of a handful of Indians at the antipoverty encampment in Washington, D.C.

Such developments have given rise to the term "Red Power," heard mostly from white men's lips. When I asked Indians about the expression, some had never heard it, and others showed displeasure at my mentioning it. The fact is that there is nothing like a Red Power Movement, with the connotations most Americans would infer from that term. The efforts of tribes and city Indians to unite for improving their lot has a different mood and different methods, and springs from a different heritage of leading ideas.

Obstructing traffic on a bridge is as far as Indians have gone, and even this act is bound to be deplored by most Red Men. Although the antipoverty demonstration was perfectly legal and rich in historic precedent, the Indians who took part were uncharacteristic of their race. The largest of the several Indian organizations, the National Congress of American Indians, had declined to participate, and had argued against the venture as involving a hazard of violence, as well as the likelihood of alienating the very forces it sought to persuade.

Indian participation in the encampment was sponsored by the Coalition of American Indian Citizens, a newer and smaller group. Headed by Mel Thom and based in Denver, this organization uses stronger (but not less dignified) language than the American Congress. But it, too, is constructive rather than disruptive, currently stressing community development on and off reservations.

Indians simply are not given to blatant, publicly conspicuous expres-

Reprinted by permission of *Presbyterian Life*, March 1, 1969.

sions of grievance. They don't question the right of any group to peaceable demonstration, but that isn't their style. Americans whose mental picture of Indians is distilled from TV bang-bang shows forget that any validity in such fiction derives from the period when Indians were fighting for their lands and lives against insurmountable odds.

The Indian way is typified by the young students in Chicago (and later another group in Los Angeles) who protested the antiquated—hence inadequate—living allowance granted them while they are pursuing heavy academic schedules. They elected a handful of spokesmen and sent them to the local office of the Bureau of Indian Affairs (BIA). Without raising their voices or fists, they presented their case forcefully, logically, and successfully, and won increased stipends. The Indian style in working for their cause was nutshelled by John Belindo, executive secretary of the National Congress. When I asked whether his organization could be considered "militant," he replied with a wry grin: "I think we are, but some other militants feel we don't make the grade. You see, we're building, not burning."

It is strange to reflect that Indians, who have as little cause as any group in our midst to love the United States, are unswervingly loyal. I remember an old man shaking his head in sorrow at reports from the Olympics of a few Americans expressing contempt for the national anthem and flag. "It's our country and a great country," he said. "We have wrongs to be righted, but what country hasn't?" In both world wars, Indians served in greater proportion than their numbers. They didn't have to be drafted; they volunteered. Indians are proud that in both wars tribal tongues used in military communications proved to be unbreakable codes. Commissioner Robert L. Bennett of the Bureau of Indian Affairs states that no Indian youth has been known to burn a draft card or trample the flag. "If Indian blood is ever spilt in the streets, it will be shed defending this country, not defaming it."

Race prejudice has a part in the picture of Indian life, but is spotty, inconsistent, and hard to evaluate. Seemingly, many Indians have never experienced it. Others have felt it to the degree of irritation, but found it a low hurdle, easy to step over or around. For some Indians in some places, prejudice is a crippling handicap, a contributing factor to unemployment, excessive drinking, and academic underachievement.

For generations there have been American families who make boast of the Indian in the family tree. And many Indians who move into the dominant society say they are more likely to be lionized than snubbed. Yet there are some white-only employers, and others who seem to think fair-employment policies apply only to blacks. Paradoxically, South Dakota, included on some people's lists of "anti-Indian states," has been sending Rosebud-Sioux Benjamin Reifel to the U.S. House of Representatives for nine years, and he is as popular among white voters as among red. Indian women have risen high in pursuits as varied as scholarship, beauty contests, and the creative arts; yet some mothers tell their daughters, "You have to be twice as well-dressed, charming, and intelligent to be the equal of a white girl when you're looking for a job."

All ethnic groups in our population—including the Anglo-American—have their deadbeats, slobs, and muggers. On the other hand, all have individuals and families whose quality of living would add to the pride of any nation. But the full range of human types in a race as small as the Indian is not always visible to the predominant group. Thus a landlord who has had an embittering experience with a slovenly Indian family is likely to conclude, "That's the way they are." And border towns which see too much of the sleazy underside of Indian life adopt "Stay away, Joe" as a community policy.

Racial bias is a tragic obstacle for some Indians, a blood-raising annoyance for others, and for still others, a thing they've only heard about. As a nationwide problem, it can hardly be ranked with the Indians' major troubles, which certainly include poverty, poor health, and inadequate education.

A white participant in Indian affairs told me that "BIA doesn't really stand for 'Bad Indian Administration,' though many Red Men seem to think so. The BIA would be an inevitable scapegoat even if it did a perfect job." And the Bureau is under the cloud of the period in our history when the word *politics* acquired its unsavory connotations in this country, years when graft, broken pledges, and devious dealings were almost standard practice. In those murky days, BIA agents both blundered and plundered. As a present-day Bureau agent told me, "If the BIA looks bad, it looked worse."

Though still not popular, the BIA is in better graces. Half of all its fourteen thousand employees are Indians willing to work for the Bureau. For several years Indians on reservations have been joking and gossiping with BIA agents who come around, where formerly these visitors were treated to a dignified chill and short answers.

It is probably not coincidence that the change has occurred during the service of Robert L. Bennett as commissioner. As the first Indian since 1871 to hold the highest Bureau post, he is called an Uncle Tomahawk by a few. But most take pride in him as a masterful driver in an antiquated machine.

During the political campaign last fall, the National Congress of American Indians and many tribal councils urged all three major candidates to retain Bennett in his post during the new Administration—the first time in history that Indians themselves have supported the retention of a commissioner.

Commissioner Bennett, an Oneida from Wisconsin, is a large weighty man who likes to talk standing or pacing, frequently using the small blackboard in his spacious office to illustrate his point. He is fluent in the polysyllabic jargon of bureaucracy, but also has the greater gift of simplicity and directness of homespun American speech.

The most bitter castigation of the Bureau I had heard was of its performance in education. Princeton University anthropologist Alfonso Ortiz, a Tewa Indian, calls BIA schools "a hundred years worth of failures." He ran away from one of them himself after seven years of tutelage. Presbyterian minister William Ng, speaking of student members of the Indian Welcome House in Los Angeles, says that the BIA "will continue to treat Indians as statistics, not as real people with real human needs."

I asked Robert Bennett about the boarding schools, backbone of the BIA system.

He described the situation of a century ago: only a quarter as many Indians as today, even more widely scattered over roadless wasteland. "And this was before school buses, remember." Sheer distance dictated that if youngsters were to go to school at all, they would have to live there all the time. "So we built boarding schools. Not nearly enough for all the children, but as many as we could with the money we had. Our critics don't seem to know that—we can do only what Congress tells us to do and is willing to pay for.

"Recently we've heard a lot about the psychological damage we do by taking children away from their parents for months at a time. Is this any worse than rich white people's sending their children off to boarding schools? In any case our system of schools grew up before the discoveries of modern educational psychology. And as you've probably seen, we've been building day schools, too, in places where there are enough children within bussing distance. We'd be happy to build more—enough for every Indian child to live at home and get his schooling— if the public would pay for the teachers, buildings, and buses it would take.

"Since I'm an Indian, I know another side of the problem the Bureau was up against—resistance to the white man's learning. Indian families are very close, and parents bitterly resented having their children taken away for a kind of teaching they couldn't see the need of. Parents would tell children to learn just enough to get by, and when they got home Mother and Dad would teach them the important things. And children would stay in school just long enough to keep their parents out of trouble with the law.

"Not until after World War II did Indian parents on any large scale willingly accept schooling for their children. I was present twenty-two years ago when a leader of the Navajos turned the tide for that people when he told them, 'Education is good food.

We should taste more of it.' Recently the popularity of education has accelerated, so that rather suddenly we're moved from a situation of hundreds of vacant desks to a clamor for more than we have available.

"We know all too well that Indian education has been substandard. But the BIA's not the only factor in making that situation, and we're doing everything in our power to improve it."

I told Commissioner Bennett that I had seen figures showing the sharp upturn in per capita enrollment, years spent in school, and students going on to college during the 1960's.

"Did you know," he asked me, "that we've received an increase of $752,000 in the amount we can spend on college scholarships? That brings it up to $3 million. And of course we're pressing for more."

At the same time he is proud that fellow Indians are seeking other sources of funds for higher education and for economic development on reservations. As an Indian, Bennett deplores paternalism and is as happy as any Red Man at the rise of Indian initiative and self-determination. "I'm proud as punch of our young people," he told me. "Without pickets, the commandeering of offices, or threats and violence, they're getting things done."

His idea of the place of the BIA is "not telling the Indian what he must do, but waiting for the Indian to decide what he wants to do, then helping him to do it by removing obstacles to his own solutions of his problems."

He asked me if I knew of the Rough Rock Demonstration School in Arizona, the only school operated completely by Indians. I told him I had read glowing praises in professional academic journals of this school's creative ventures in teaching methods and its aim of encouraging children from kindergarten through eighth grade to develop their inherited arts along with the learning of the Western World.

Bennett nodded. "I'm proud of what our people are doing at Rough Rock; they deserve all the recognition they receive. I only wish," he smiled, "that more people knew that school was built by the BIA, and we voluntarily turned it over to the local people to run."

As a right-thinking Red Man, Bennett wants to see the tribal languages and values preserved. He reminded me that his Bureau has turned its back on the old policy of forcibly washing the ancestral culture from a child's mind, and is now developing courses on the history and heritage of the race. But ruefully he admitted that it takes time for top policy to filter down to local situations, and did not deny the allegations that some schools may still forbid the use of tribal languages by the children. At the same time he felt that some culture enthusiasts are a bit excessive. "There's no point in teaching Pueblo culture to a Pueblo kid. He already knows that." But the child ought to learn the broad sweep of Indian contributions to world culture. Incidentally, one item of this contribution which white children could do with knowing is that more than half of all the crops which now feed American and European peoples were developed by the Indian, and were unknown to the white man before Columbus. The original American could claim to be the world's foremost pioneer in agriculture.

When we broached the subject of the Indian's predilection for firewater, Commissioner Bennett intimated that the white man hadn't much room to talk; then he blamed excessive drinking partly on the Federal prohibition of alcohol for reservation dwellers, which the Indians resented as unequal treatment. This was followed by spree-type drinking after partial repeal in 1953. Tribes are moving in on heavy drinking, he said, with AA groups and experts on treatment; the Apaches have employed a professional staff.

Of course he was aware of the common belief that suicide is especially prevalent among Indians. On his blackboard Bennett demonstrated the difficulty of proving this numerically as a nationwide phenomenon, while admitting that in a few places, figures kept over brief periods showed a high incidence of self-destruction, especially among young people.

Several prominent Indians had told me that they favored dismembering the BIA, and distributing its functions among other bureaus and departments (Health, Education and Welfare already handles Indian medical services). Robert Bennett said: "I don't think most Indians would want the BIA dismantled. But if they really do, they should take their request to Congress, and I believe Congress would grant it.

"Indian affairs are ready for a new turn," Bennett believes. "The BIA is changing roles from advocate of the government with Indians, to advocate of the Indians with the government. We want the tribes to control their own community matters; we tell them to take their ideas to Congress. Congress is now responsive to Indian wishes, and will listen to reasoned proposals. In a word, we feel that Indian hopes and expectations are higher now than they ever have been."

Indeed this seems to be true in every area of Indian life. On reservations, in cities, and on college campuses Indians are pressing for self-realization in their own distinctive ways. One of the newer organizations is the National Indian Youth Council, formed mainly by college students, but open to any Indian youth. One of the directors of the Council, Washington attorney Browning Pipestem (an Osage on his father's side and an Oto on his mother's), believes that many young Indians in higher education feel they must choose between dropping out of college, or ceasing to be themselves by adopting the ways of campus life around them. A co-ed told him that these students gradually "accept negative views of Indians, and become in many ways enemies of our own people."

To seek alternatives, Pipestem directed an institute of American Indian studies last summer, accredited for six hours by the University of Kansas. This summer he hopes to hold four such institutes in different colleges— "experiments in self-determination," he calls them. When one youth told his mother about last summer's sessions, she admitted she had dreaded the changes he might undergo in college, much as she wanted education for him. But now she held hope that "I'll still see me in you."

Maintaining individuality may be easier for students at the Navajo Community College at Many Farms, Arizona, opened last month. After two years with Indian classmates, students can go on to other colleges. Financed by the Office of Economic Opportunity (OEO), the Donner Foundation, and the Navajo Tribal Council, the school is the first college on a reservation and the first with an all-Indian Board of Regents.

Proponents of assimilation (joining the white culture) and of separatism (keeping clear of the white culture) are burying their hatchets in the realization that there are intermediate positions between these extremes. Individual Indians have been blazing their own trails through the lush growth of American society, finding what best suits their needs. As time goes on, more both-way communication between the red and white worlds seems inevitable.

Only one American in two hundred is an Indian. Nearing the end of my journeys among them, I began remembering examples of small groups whose influence on the thinking and doing of large populations was in high proportion to their numbers. The Christians in Asian countries came to mind, the Jews in Western nations.

In the American future, one thing seems certain: "We'll be seeing more of our copper-skinned compatriots— because there *are* more of them, with fifty percent of them under eighteen years of age. And as they're finally finding their voice, we'll be hearing more from them than at any time since the wardrums were stilled.

What will they have to say to us when we are ready to listen? What kinds of contribution will they add to the heterogeneous American culture? Everyone I asked mentioned the fields in which Indian giftedness is known: the arts, handicrafts, entertainment, sports; and perhaps government, for in some areas Indians increasingly participate in local and state politics.

But most seemed to feel that over the long range the Indian's deepest imprint would be made in the intangible realm of thought, feeling, and attitudes toward life and the world. And in these things perhaps no one can say anything really new. But a people coming out of another background may be able, by fresh modes of expression, to reawaken the wisdom that man has always known, and is always forgetting.

In his Washington office, John

Belindo of the National Congress of American Indians put it as well as anyone I'd talked with: "The Indian puts a premium on just being alive. He appreciates life more deeply and vividly than most other men. He can find beauty and harmony in the most commonplace things and everyday happenings.

"His value system is basically non-materialistic. He doesn't care much about material things—not nearly so much as about his friends and family. Of course he likes enough money to meet his needs as they come along, for food and clothing and 'hyacinths to feed the soul.' But he has little concept of accumulation of wealth or possessions—these things, he would say, make one not happy, but sad.

"A sense of sharing is strong in the Indian, but this doesn't diminish individuality. Just being an individual is an honor in itself. Sharing means you share yourself with others sharing themselves. It seems to me that in the white culture people sit in boxes and think about themselves. But Indians readily share thoughts and moods—

there's an instant rapport, an almost supernatural kind of communication."

Perhaps that's why, among themselves, Indians don't talk a great deal. They don't have to. In any case, as John Belindo summed it up, to an Indian his encounters with his inner self, with the selves of other men, and with God are the supremely important events of life to which everything else is subordinate.

The inheritor of defeat, the Indian remains a stranger in his homeland—America's prisoner of war. Despite three centuries of systematic effort to destroy or absorb the American Indian; he shows no sign of disappearing. His culture has been deeply and purposely eroded, yet it persists.

Citizens' Advocate Center,
Our Brother's Keeper:
The Indian in White America

THE CROSS OF CESAR CHAVEZ

Stan Steiner

In the bar the young man is drinking beer. He has been in the fields, on the picket lines, all morning, and he sweats with the bodily memory and fear, even now in the cool bar. Outside the sun is an inferno. "Here," he says, "it is peace." The People's Bar on the *huelga* side of town is a *huelguistas*' hangout. It is a poor man's sanctuary. But the young man is troubled. He is silent for a moment. "You know Cesar?" he asks timidly.

"A little."

"You will do me a favor?"

"Maybe."

"My father had a heart attack," the young man says. "I have to go home for a few days. I do not want to leave the strike, but I have to. Will you tell Cesar that for me? Tell Cesar I am sorry."

"You see him every day," I say to him. "Why don't you tell him yourself?"

"He is so tired," the young man says, with a deference I hear so often. "I do not want to take his time with my troubles."

So I promise to do as he asks. We drink our beers and shake hands and go our separate ways. Later when I tell Cesar Chavez what the young man has said of his father's heart attack, of his apology, he listens but says nothing.

"A leader who does not know how to listen does not know how to lead," he says.

Cesar Chavez has the eyes of the statue of a saint. His eyes are so large and full they look hollow. "We talk with our eyes," Eduardo Pérez has said. It is not true of everyone, but it is true of Chavez.

His eyes may become the eyes of a peon's with which he looks innocently at the visiting dignitaries and newsmen who swarm about his office. In an instant these eyes may turn to charcoal, fiery, then suddenly cold as stones when there is a crisis in the strike. He has special eyes for the making of decisions.

"No, I am not fiery," he insists. "I am not a speaker. I am a listener."

In the streets people come up to him; they come to his office and his home; they talk to him at meetings and probably in his dreams. Chavez does not turn them away, or turn a

Reprinted by permission of Harper & Row, Publishers from Stan Steiner, *La Raza: The Mexican Americans* (New York: Harper & Row, Publishers, 1970). Copyright © 1970 by Stan Steiner.

deaf ear to what they have to say. He listens because he believes it is they who lead him. It is his theory of leadership.

"People know what they want. And what they don't want," he says. "It's a case of staying with them and keeping your ears open and your eyes open.

"And they tell you! They don't tell you in so many words, but they tell you with their actions. They will not so much spell it out for you. They never have a clear way of doing that. They never write it down for you. They never hold your hand. It's never tangible, but if you listen to it, it comes.

"Once you begin to 'lead' the people, to force them, then you begin to make mistakes," he says. "Once you begin to feel you are really the 'leader,' then you begin to stop being a real leader. Then a reverse process starts. The 'leader' has less and less time for the people. He depends more on himself. He begins to play hunches, to play the long shots. He loses his touch with the people.

"It happens to most leaders. . . .

"Everything!" he says , with sudden force, "Everything in *huelga* of any importance has come from the farm workers. It is a gathering of bits and pieces of what the people want. I say, Everything! Every important decision, every important program in the strike has come from the people. It hasn't come in a resolution. It hasn't come in a well-documented report. But it comes the way the people express themselves. It comes sort of in *the way they make it appear*."

He smiles at that, knowing his thought is so clear it is cryptic. Chavez has a casual way of talking that makes his thoughts appear off-hand when he is being most intense. The listener may fool himself.

"Our function is to put it all together. We get our decision from the people. It comes so easily that if you don't watch out, you begin to think that you are the one, that you are the genius, that you are making all those wonderful ideas."

I ask him, "Why Cesar Chavez and why Delano? Aren't *you* making history?"

He laughs self-consciously. "It is dangerous to make statements like that. No, I think it is like many historical events; you have to be at the right place at the right moment. To the outside world we are making history. To us it is just a hard struggle. The *huelga* is the result of a lot of effort, frustration, tears, bloodshed, and sweat no one sees."

"But *you* are leading it," I say.

"Like a composer working night and day," he says. "If there is no orchestra, there is no music. No one hears it."

He is not humble. The romantic idea of the humble campesino fits him even less than most men. Rather, he voices the concept of innate, communal democracy of the barrio, and the age-old suspicions that the farm worker has of the leader—the *gobierno* —even if he is that leader.

Cesar Chavez was born to farm work. He grew to boyhood on the poor farm of his father, who clung to a few acres of desert in Yuma, Arizona. When the boy was ten, his father lost his land. In that inferno— —known as "the Sahara of the United States"—farming was dubious in the best of times, but in the Depression it was hopeless. The Chavez family became migrants. Wandering from town to town, they slept in their old jalopy, in tents, in deserted migrant camps. His father, with the obstinacy and pride of a small farmer, was not fitted for life on the road. The boy remembers fishing in irrigation ditches and picking weeds, mustard greens— "otherwise we would have starved." He vaguely remembers attending thirty or more schools by the eighth grade, when he had to drop out to work in the fields.

Estrada is his middle name: Cesar Estrada Chavez. In Spanish the word means a paved road, a highway or turnpike. Why did his parents give him so strange and prophetic a name?

In the worst of barrios in San Jose—the one they call Sal Si Puedes: Get Out If You Can—the family settled. The legend is that it was here that Fred Ross, an organizer for the Community Service Organization (CSO), "discovered" Cesar Chavez and hired him. The truth is more complex. Chavez had been a defiant youth, always attracting attention. One day when he was a boy he had refused to sit in the segregated Mexican section of a movie theater and was thrown into the street. The town was Delano. It was the year of 1943. He was seventeen.

His father had taught him years earlier the ways of protest and organization. The elder Chavez had become a union activist in 1939. "One of the old CIO unions began organizing workers in the dried-fruit industry, so my father and my uncle became members. Sometimes the men would meet at our house, and I remember seeing their picket signs and hearing them talk. They had a strike and my father and uncle picketed at night. It made a deep impression on me," Chavez reminisced in Eugene Nelson's book, *Huelga:* ". . . from that time on my father joined every agricultural union that came along. Often he was the first one to join, and when

I was nineteen, I joined the National Agricultural Workers' Union."

The strikes were all lost. The unions were defeated. Chavez learned the hard way how not to organize.

Catholicism offered a faith and a permanence in those gloomy days. Young Chavez met Father Donald McDonnell, a scholarly priest who spoke seven languages, who had a passion for labor history and a compassion for the farm workers. Night after night they discussed the doctrines of social justice and the Encyclicals of the Popes. "I began going to the bracero camps with him to help with Mass; to the city jail with him to talk to the prisoners—anything to be with him so that he could tell me more about the farm labor movement," Chavez says. It was Father McDonnell who introduced the young man to Fred Ross of the CSO.

"I was working in the fields when CSO came to San Jose," Chavez says. "I was in the orchards, apricots and peaches."

For ten years after that, Chavez was a community organizer up and down California. He registered voters, cajoled mayors, dealt with health laws, organized rent strikes, handled welfare problems, dealt with death and taxes. "I was learning a lot of things," he says. He became director of the National CSO. But he was restless to go back to the fields, to organize a union of farm workers.

Unhappy with the middle-class methods of the CSO, he was ill at ease. It was "unheard of" that they meet in a cheap hall, he says: "It had to [be] the best motel in town, very expensive, and it cut off all the farm workers who couldn't afford to be there. The reason given was, 'We have to build prestige.' The politicians have to know who we are; we can't take them to a dump. I was naïve

enough in the beginning to buy that. So we ended up just with farm workers who had gone to school or weren't farm workers any more.

"The officers of CSO were semiprofessionals or professionals," he says. "It became a problem communicating with the workers."

It was a conflict of styles of life, goals, attitudes, and even language, that has since divided the civil rights movement. Chavez says, "In most cases, the leadership had more to lose than the workers. They'd say, 'We should fight, but we should be moderate.' They felt that farm workers were outside the jurisdiction of the CSO. It was a 'labor' problem." He was thought to be too militant, he feels. His colleagues in the CSO do not agree with his version of history. Yet their side of the story complements his half of the conflict that has been so often repeated.

Mrs. Ursula Rios Gutierrez, a lady of distinguished gray hair and grace, worked with Cesar for three years in the National Office of the CSO. But she remembers his leaving differently. "He left for political reasons. He says we were not interested in farm workers. It's not true! One of our wealthy members offered $50,000 for Cesar to organize his farm workers.

"I was there when he came in and laid his keys on the desk and said, 'You probably read my letter of resignation. I am leaving. Here are the keys.' And I said, 'Yes, I know.' That was that.

"Like a boy," she says, hurt. "He walked out! We were good friends. His wife Helen and his children, I knew them like family." A motherly woman, she is still upset by what she feels is Chavez's lack of gratitude. His union's tactics upset her even more. She is a disapproving mother who is not ashamed to criticize in public what others hint at in private.

"What happened to Cesar? I don't know," says Mrs. Gutierrez. "I have a lot of respect for Cesar. He is doing good work. But I don't understand Cesar.

"Cesar has the image of a Mexican peasant. He has been built up that way in the newspapers. The union has built him up that way too, as one of the campesinos. If he ever betrays that image he is finished. Cesar knows that. That is what holds him.

"On the pilgrimage to Sacramento I saw it. The way they look at him. When they began shouting 'Viva Cesar!' that was too much. As though he was a saint, a god. He is not a saint, a god."

In "The Corrido of Cesar Chavez," the farm workers sang on the pilgrimage:

The seventeenth of March,
First Thursday morning of Lent,
Cesar walked from Delano,
Taking with him his faith.

When we arrive in Fresno,
All the people shout:
Long live Cesar Chavez,
And all who follow him.

Now we reach Stockton.
The mariachis sing to us:
Long live Cesar Chavez,
And the Virgin who guides him.

Where he came from and why does not seem to interest the farm workers. He came to them, giving up all he possessed, sacrificing everything. That is all they need to know.

Listen Señor Cesar Chavez,
Your name is honored;
On your breast you wear
The Virgin of Guadalupe.

The growers, who in the begin-ning talked of Chavez as an "outsider" with no roots in the vineyards, now recognize him as an adversary whose strength they have to respect. "Chavez's secret is that he has the utter loyalty of the Mexican workers," one grower says. "His appeal is primarily racial—and to some extent religious. They're not a trade union. They're a racial and religious organization."

"Our biggest mistake was to think Chavez was just another 'dumb Mex,'" another grower says.

"He is no saint, he is a devil," a Presbyterian churchman tells me.

In the fields of the San Joaquin Valley, they talk of Chavez as if he were a legend, the hero of a myth. A young farm worker seriously says to me, "You know, they offered Cesar one million dollars to sell us out. He told them where to go!" The tale of the bribe of betrayal is told in a dozen versions. In every tale the money varies—from $20,000 up to $2 million. And in every tale Cesar says no to betrayal. He is faithful to those who have faith. His independence is legendary. When he has made up his mind, not even the White House can change his mind. It has tried.

When, after long months of procrastination, the White House Conference on Mexican Americans was abandoned in the fall of 1967 as potentially too explosive, the high-level Cabinet hearings were scheduled instead in El Paso, Texas, and an invitation was sent to Chavez. He was to be an honored guest. The President was to attend, as was the Vice President, and several Cabinet members, and the invitation bore the prestige and pressure of the highest officials in the nation. He would surely come to be honoured.

Chavez said no. In silent protest at the barring of grassroots groups and militant leaders, such as Reies Tijerina, he stayed in Delano.

"Jesus was a troublemaker," he said to a friend. "Would they invite him?"

In the privacy of his office, Chavez later had reflective thoughts of his own. "What good do all these conferences do? Do they ever invite the farm workers in the field to attend? No! It's always the same people conferring with the same people. Everyone agrees: Let's unite. Everyone then speaks from his own narrow point of view, and everyone disagrees, and everyone goes home with the point of view they came with. Where is the unity? I think unity comes when people work together. It comes with hard work.

"So conferences don't solve the problems," Chavez says. He grins. "Maybe that's the point. If the conferences solved the problems, there would be no need to hold any more conferences. Then what would the 'experts' do?"

His sardonic words are reminiscent of his testimony before the Senate Subcommittee on Migratory Labor. Chavez began with the words: "This is a *'huelga'* button. Senator Williams, Senator Murphy, Congressman Hagen, we are meeting once again to discuss the problems of the farm worker and what might be done to correct these problems. Such meetings have been called for decades, and unfortunately, things have not changed very much in spite of them."

His patience with the problems of farm workers is one of his best-known traits. It is genuine. But Chavez has little patience with officious conferences and formal interviews. Once he led his *huelguistas* out of a meeting of a candidate he supported because he felt the officials were not "our kind of people."

Into his bare office—with its posters of Gandhi and Zapata, watched over by a statue of the Virgin of Guadalupe, where Chavez sits behind a modest, worn, old wooden desk—a delegation of dignitaries came not long ago. They were from one of the country's most influential and wealthiest foundations. Men of prominence, their mission to Delano was to invite him to serve on the Board of Directors of one of their multi-million-dollar projects. Chavez politely rejected the honor and whatever went with it.

"It's to help La Raza," the foundation men said.

"La Raza? Why be racist?" Chavez remembers telling his visitors. He smiles. "They were embarrassed. I told them, 'Our union has everyone in it—Mexicans, Filipinos, Blacks, Whites, Japanese, Chinese. Our belief is to help everyone, not just one race. Humanity is our belief.' " He laughs. "Their faces fell."

He retells the incident with a puckish delight, for within his gentle manner there is the muted and hidden anger of the boy on the road, in the migrant camps, in ragged clothes, hungry and unschooled and abused. It infuriates him, though he usually manages to hide his emotions, when he thinks the farm workers are being patronized. He resents the attitude of superiority of those who he feels offer pity, even in the form of desperately needed cash and good works.

But he subdues his wrath. He twits those who patronize him by patronizing them.

His disenchantment with the student activists is influenced by this feeling. In the beginning of the *huelga* the campus rebels and civil rights groups were welcomed in Delano; they were stalwarts on the picket lines and on the volunteer staff. When the union voted to join the AFL-CIO, many of the summer radicals withdrew, accusing Chavez of "selling out to the labor establishment," as one said.

"He used to call anyone who worked with politicians a 'political prostitute,' " says an old friend and former coworker. "I remember when he refused to go to a banquet honoring our Congressman. Now he goes to his own banquets. I can understand that. These things have to be done. What I don't understand is how *he* can do these things he never believed in."

Chavez says, "We were as pained as they were. We were pained that the students and others who felt this way had such little faith in the people. Every time they would bring up the merger, we would say, 'We don't think it's going to be that way,' or, 'It is the workers' choice.' But we very seldom told them what we felt. I personally felt pained to see how little trust they had in the people.

"I remember that some of the fellows that helped us in the beginning had a very strange picture of poor people," he says. "Like all farm workers were saints, you know."

The "idolizing of the poor" has the same effect as pitying them, Chavez says. "You can't help people if you feel sorry for them." He is realistic. "This kind of feeling doesn't carry you. After a little while it becomes old and there is no real basis for doing things that you're doing. There's got to be more than that."

In his mind he is still a farm worker. He sees and feels the world with the eyes of the campesino; whether it is in his gut or it is something nourished by a skillful organizer, he alone knows.

"For many years I was a farm worker, a migratory worker, and well, personally—and I'm being very frank —maybe it's just a matter of trying to even the score, you know," Chavez has said of his severe judgment of others and himself.

He has a hardness. It surprises some that this modest, soft-spoken, and mild-mannered man carries hatreds within him that are neither visible nor expected. Once, in a talk to the black militants of California SNCC, he sought to explain why he had become an organizer. He said offhandedly, "Of course, I had a lot of hatred for the cops." That casual remark, so rare in the reticent and careful words of Chavez, reveals his bitterness.

Chavez is an enigma to many. He is a different man to different people. "Who is Cesar?" says a union organizer who has been with him since the beginning of *huelga*. "He is so friendly and informal that everyone thinks they know him intimately. But no one knows him."

He is thought of as a man who grasps the infinite and remembers it in infinitesimal detail—the perfect organizer. Petty details are vital to Chavez; the most insignificant act and ordinary member is important. "When you come from the bottom up," he says, "you have to be very practical and very patient."

"From him we have learned," Lauro García, Jr., the village organizer of Guadalupe, Arizona, explains, "not only determination, dedication, and hard work, but unrelenting patience."

The patience is integral to his nature, to the farm workers. Chavez once said that he expected the *huelga* to "last for five years"; what urban union leader would calmly talk or think of striking for five years, on strike pay of $5 a week? Yet, when he is asked how long he thinks it will take to unionize the farm workers, Chavez says, "All my life."

Senator Murphy: How long have you been in this activity?

Chavez: Well, I have been a farm worker all my life.

At times, though, he becomes impatient with himself. He has that mundane dream of a public man: "Even when our work succeeds, I don't want to hang on forever," he tells Eugene Nelson. "What I would really like is to be alone somewhere—in Mexico, or in the mountains—and have time to read all the classics that there are in English and Spanish."

He is alone often. In the midst of a noisy meeting with everyone agitated and yelling, he seems quietly withdrawn, aloof, within himself.

The organizer is "an outsider," Chavez says. "If an organizer comes looking for appreciation, he might just as well stay home. He's not going to get any, especially out of a group that's never been organized or had any power before." He has to be willing to be lonely, to be nourished by his own beliefs. He came to Delano alone with his family. No organization supported him. Rarely does he ask a follower to do something he has not done, or does not do himself—whether it is working in the fields to organize, being jailed, or living on the $5 a week strike pay. He enacts his beliefs with his body.

His family lives in conspicuous poverty. A wife and eight children share a small, two-bedroom frame house in the barrio of Delano. In the era of affluent unionism, such a way of life is an anomaly for a union leader. But it is not martyrdom. The humility of his material goods is an aspect of his philosophy. He believes, as Gandhi did, that the leader of the poor has to live as the poor do, not for their sake, but for his own; the sanctity of his soul and peace of mind demand it of him.

"We will never have peace in the world until we have peace in ourselves," Chavez says. "How can we even begin to talk of peace in the world when we are not at peace with ourselves?" In this sense nonviolence is not a political tactic. Chavez talks of it as an act of purification of man. "It's what Gandhi was saying all those years. It's the most difficult thing."

Sacrifice is a principle. The poor cannot afford to suffer it, so the leader must suffer it for them.

"The poor have the biggest stake in peace," he says. "But they are the ones who can do the least because they are so busy scratching out a living to get something to eat."

I say to him one day, "If you do not win this strike soon you will have a long beard and I will be long dead."

He smiles. "That is not right."

"Why not?"

"*You* will have the long beard," he says, "and *I* will be dead."

He is not talking of the threats to his life. That is routine. He has no bodyguards. He has been hospitalized too often to talk of his illnesses. In his knowledge of himself there is only this: how many burdens of other men can one man bear before the accumulated pain becomes unbearable?

Lent is the fiesta of sacrifice, when the *penitentes* of New Mexico suffer the anguish of Christ; when the religious go on their knees to the shrine of San Juan in Texas; when in the provinces of Mexico, there are men who bodily are nailed to makeshift crosses, beside the ferris wheels of village fairs.

The sacrifice of Cesar Chavez began during Lent, in the chill spring of 1968. It was tragic and portentous.

302

He offered his body in a "Lenten Fast for Peace and Nonviolence" that lasted for twenty-five days. He sacrificed one-fifth of his flesh, thirty-five pounds, to "the pain and suffering of the farm workers." Except for a few ounces of bouillon and a few mouthfuls of unsweetened grapefruit juice ordered by his doctor, for twenty-five days he had nothing but water. He grew so weak he could hardly talk or walk.

He fasted because self-sacrifice was "the ultimate act of manliness," Chavez said. He fasted because "my heart was filled with grief when I saw the pain" of his people in the fields. He fasted for nonviolence.

An altar was built in the garage of the union's cooperative gas station, on the Forty Acres. Hundreds of farm workers came from the fields to pray every day. The altar, on the back of a truck, became a shrine.

Chavez sat in the unheated, unfinished garage and prayed and shivered. The Holy Mass that was celebrated every day for his sacrificial act became the scene of a pilgrimage. Women brought candles and offerings. The men knelt in the dirt by the hundreds, coming from the barrios, the remote country crossroads, the migrant camps.

On the fourth day of his fast, the land-grant leader of New Mexico, Reies Tijerina, came to pray. Chavez and Tijerina embraced.

In a rally of farm workers—though he was becoming weak—Chavez appealed for funds for the defense of the fiery land-grant leader

who had been arrested for kidnaping, murder, and insurrection. The poor campesinos contributed $500 and Chavez gave Tijerina a huge, red *huelga* flag, which Tijerina draped over his shoulders like a prayer shawl.

On the thirteenth day of his fast, Chavez, by now quite pale, was himself taken before Superior Court Justice Martin Baker to reply to charges of violation of court injunctions in the strike against Guimarra Vineyards. The growers had filed a complaint of twelve charges. Well over one thousand farm workers overflowed the courtroom in Bakersfield, its corridors, and the outside plaza. Judge Baker postponed the hearing, and Chavez returned to the altar in the garage.

On the twenty-fifth day, he broke his fast by breaking bread with the late Senator Robert Kennedy, who flew to Delano to be beside his friend.

Ten thousand farm workers and their families gathered before the altar in the cold March sun. Some say it was the largest meeting of farm workers in the history of the Southwest. Beneath the wooden cross that had been carried on the union's Pilgrimage to Sacramento, and the banner of the Virgin of Guadalupe, with rows of red flags of the *huelga* whirling in the wind, Robert Kennedy rose to say that by his sacrifice Cesar Chavez had told the world that "violence is no answer."

Three months later Robert Kennedy was dead. He had just celebrated his triumph in the presidential primary of California, where the votes of the campesinos and Chicanos had been the margin of victory. In his last words he had thanked Cesar Chavez.

"I have no taste for politics in my heart," Chavez told me after Kennedy's death. In his grief, he would say no more.

During his fast, Chavez had received a telegram: "I am deeply moved by your courage in fasting as your personal sacrifice for justice through non-violence. Your past and present commitment is eloquent testimony to the constructive power of non-violent action and the destructive impotence of violent reprisal. Your stand is a living example of the Gandhian tradition with its great force for social progress and its healing spiritual powers." The telegram was from the Reverend Martin Luther King. One month after he wrote these words, the Christian leader was assassinated. "Despite the tragic violence which took your husband," Chavez wrote to the Reverend King's widow, "there is much that is good about our nation." Now both King and Kennedy were dead. Who was to be next?

"Perhaps some of us will follow the path that Kennedy was made to follow," the Secretary of the Farm Workers Union, Antonio Orendain, declared in *El Malcriado*, "but we are ready for that journey, if it is necessary."

On the site of the fast of Cesar Chavez, they erected a huge cross made of telephone poles. The cross towered for thirty feet above the barren land, vines grew up on it and flowers were attached to it. Under this cross they held religious ceremonies, open air masses, and the sunrise service at Easter. Vandals tried twice to burn the cross to the ground. Its wood withstood the fires, and the charred symbol of nonviolence remained visible for miles.

The cross of Cesar Chavez was desecrated the week before the Fourth of July. It was cut by a power saw and fell in the dust and the weeds.

22 MILES

From 22 I see my first 8 weren't.
  Around the 9th, I was called "meskin."
    By the 10th, I knew and believed I was.
      I found out what it meant to know, to
        believe . . . before my 13th.

Through brown eyes, seeing only brown colors and
feeling only brown feelings . . . I saw . . . I felt . . . I
hated . . . I cried . . . I tried . . . I didn't understand
during these 4.
      I rested by just giving up.

While, on the side . . . I realized I BELIEVED in
  white as pretty,
 my being governor,
   blond blue eyed baby Jesus,
    cokes and hamburgers,
     equality for all regardless of race, creed, or
      color,
    Mr. Williams, our banker.
   I had to!
  That was all I had.
 Beans and Communism were bad.
 Past the weeds, atop the hill, I looked back.

Pretty people, combed and squeaky clean, on arrow-
like roads. Pregnant girls, ragged brats, swarthy
machos, rosary beads, and friends waddle clumsily
over and across hills, each other, mud, cold, and
woods on caliche ruts.

Reprinted by permission of Quinto Sol Publications from
Jose Angel Gutierrez, *El Grito* (Berkeley: Quinto Sol Publications, 1968).

At the 19th mile, I fought blindly at everything and
    anything.
  Not knowing, Not caring about WHY, WHEN, or
    FOR WHAT.
    I fought. And fought.
      By the 21st, I was tired and tired.

        But now . . .
I've been told that I am dangerous.
That is because I am good at not being a Mexican.
That is because I know now that I have been
    cheated.
That is because I hate circumstances and love
    choices.

      You know . . . chorizo tacos y tortillas ARE
        good, even at school.
    Speaking Spanish is a talent.
Being Mexican IS good as Rainbo bread.
And without looking back, I know that there are still
    too many . . .
    brown babies,
      pregnant girls,
        old 25 year-old women,
          drunks,
            who should have lived but didn't,
              on those caliche ruts.

        It is tragic that my problems during
          these past 21 miles
        were/are/might be . . .
          looking into blue eyes,
          wanting to touch a gringita,
        ashamed of being Mexican,
      believing I could not make it at college,
    pretending that I liked my side of town,

remembering the Alamo,
speaking Spanish in school bathrooms only,
and knowing that Mexico's prostitutes like Americans
    better.

At 22, my problems are still the same but now I
    know I am your problem.
That farm boys, Mexicans and Negro boys are in
    Vietnam is but one thing I think about:
        Crystal City, Texas 78839
        The migrant worker;
        The good gringo:

Staying Mexican enough;
Helping;
Looking at the world from the back of a truck.

The stoop labor with high school rings on their
     fingers;
The Anglo cemetery,
Joe the different Mexican,

                    Damn.
                    Damn.
                    Damn.

—*Jose Angel Gutierrez*

The worst crime the white man has committed has been to teach us to hate ourselves.   *Malcolm X*

La Familia: Jose Clemente Orozco.

THE NEW FEMINISM

By Lucy Komisar

A dozen women are variously seated in straight-backed chairs, settled on a couch, or sprawled on the floor of a comfortable apartment on Manhattan's West Side. They range in age from twenty-five to thirty-five, and include a magazine researcher, a lawyer, a housewife, an architect, a teacher, a secretary, and a graduate student in sociology.

They are white, middle-class, attractive. All but one have college degrees; several are married; a few are active in social causes. At first, they are hesitant. They don't really know what to talk about, and so they begin with why they came.

"I wanted to explore my feelings as a woman and find out what others think about the things that bother me." Slowly, they open up, trust growing. "I always felt so negative about being a woman; now I'm beginning to feel good about it."

They become more personal and revealing. "My mother never asked me what I was going to be when I grew up." "I never used to like to talk to girls. I always thought women were inferior—I never *liked* women." "I've been a secretary for three years; after that, you begin to think that's all you're good for." "I felt so trapped when my baby was born. I wanted to leave my husband and the child."

Repeated a hundred times in as many different rooms, these are the voices of women's liberation, a movement that encompasses high school students and grandmothers, and that is destined to eclipse the black civil rights struggle in the force of its resentment and the consequence of its demands.

Some of us have become feminists out of anger and frustration over job discrimination. When we left college, male students got aptitude tests, we got typing tests. In spite of federal law, most women still are trapped in low-paying, dead-end jobs and commonly earn less than men for the same work—sometimes on the theory that we are only "helping out," though 42 per cent of us support ourselves or families.

Reprinted by permission of Lucy Komisar from *Saturday Review*, February 21, 1970.

Others have discovered that the humanistic precepts of the radical movement do not always apply to women. At a peace rally in Washington last year, feminists were hooted and jeered off the speakers' platform, and white women working in civil rights or antipoverty programs are expected to defer to the black male ego. Many of us go out to salvage our own buffeted egos. However, most of the new feminists express only a general malaise they were never able to identify.

Nanette Rainone is twenty-seven, the wife of a newspaperman, the mother of a seven-month-old child, and a graduate of Queens College, where she studied English literature. She married while in graduate school, then quit before the year was out to become an office clerk at *Life* magazine. "I should have known the first day that I wasn't going to be promoted, but it took me eight months to find it out."

She spent the next five months idly at home, began doing volunteer public affairs interviews for WBAI radio, and now produces *Womankind*, a weekly program on the feminist movement.

"I always felt as though I was on a treadmill, an emotional treadmill. I thought it was neurotic, but it always focused on being a woman. Then I met another woman, who had two children. We talked about my pregnancy—my confusion about my pregnancy—and the problems she was having in caring for her children now that she was separated from her husband and wanted to work."

One evening Nanette Rainone's friend took her to a feminist meeting, and immediately she became part of the movement. "The child had been an escape. I was seeking a role I couldn't find on the outside," she says. "Then I became afraid my life would be overwhelmed, that I would never get out from under and do the things I had hoped to do.

"You struggle for several years after getting out of college. You know —what are you going to do with yourself? There's always the external discrimination, but somehow you feel you are talented and you should be able to project yourself. But you don't get a good job, you get a terrible job.

"I think I was typical of the average woman who is in the movement now, because the contradictions in the system existed in my life. My parents were interested in my education. I had more room to develop my potential than was required for the role I eventually was to assume.

"I don't put down the care of children. I just put down the fixated relationship that the mother has, the never-ending association, her urge that the child be something so that *she* can be something. People need objective projects. We all feel the need to actively participate in society, in something outside ourselves where we can learn and develop.

"The closest I've been able to come to what's wrong is that men have a greater sense of self than women have. Marriage is an aspect of men's lives, whereas it is the very center of most women's lives, the whole of their lives. It seemed to me that women felt they couldn't exist except in the eyes of men—that if a man wasn't looking at them or attending to them, then they just weren't there."

If women need more evidence, history books stand ready to assure us that we have seldom existed except as shadows of men. We have rarely been leaders of nations or industry or the great contributors to art and science, yet very few sociologists, political leaders, historians, and moral critics have ever stopped to ask why.

Now, all around the country, women are meeting in apartments and conference rooms and coffee shops to search out the answers.

The sessions begin with accounts of personal problems and incidents. For years, we women have believed that our anger and frustration and unhappiness were "our problems." Suddenly, we discover that we are telling *the same story*! Our complaints are not only common, they are practically universal.

It is an exhilarating experience. Women's doubts begin to disappear and are replaced by new strength and self-respect. We stop focusing on men, and begin to identify with other women and to analyze the roots of our oppression. The conclusions that are drawn challenge the legitimacy of the sex role system upon which our civilization is based.

At the center of the feminist critique is the recognition that women have been forced to accept an inferior role in society, and that we have come to believe in our own inferiority. Women are taught to be passive, dependent, submissive, not to pursue careers but to be taken care of and protected. Even those who seek outside work lack confidence and self-esteem. Most of us are forced into menial and unsatisfying jobs: More than three-quarters of us are clerks, sales personnel, or factory and service workers, and a fifth of the women with B.A. degrees are secretaries.

Self-hatred is endemic. Women—especially those who have "made it"—identify with men and mirror their contempt for women. The approval of women does not mean very much. We don't want to work for women or vote for them. We laugh, although with vague uneasiness, at jokes about women drivers, mothers-in-law, and dumb blondes.

We depend on our relationships with men for our very identities. Our husbands win us social status and determine how we will be regarded by the world. Failure for a woman is not being selected by a man.

We are trained in the interests of men to defer to them and serve them and entertain them. If we are educated and gracious, it is so we can please men and educate their children. That is the thread that runs through the life of the geisha, the party girl, the business executive's wife, and the First Lady of the United States.

Men define women, and until now most of us have accepted their definition without question. If we challenge men in the world outside the home, we are all too frequently derided as "aggressive" and "unfeminine"—by women as readily as by men.

A woman is expected to subordinate her job to the interests of her husband's work. She'll move to another city so he can take a promotion —but it rarely works the other way around. Men don't take women's work very seriously, and, as a result, neither do most women. We spend a lot of time worrying about men, while they devote most of theirs to worrying about their careers.

We are taught that getting and keeping a man is a woman's most important job; marriage, therefore, becomes our most important achievement. One suburban housewife says her father started giving her bridal pictures cut from newspapers when she was six. "He said that was what I would be when I grew up."

Most feminists do not object to marriage per se, but to the corollary that it is creative and fulfilling for an adult human being to spend her life doing housework, caring for children, and using her husband as a vicarious link to the outside world.

Most people would prefer just about any kind of work to that of a domestic servant; yet the mindless, endless, repetitious drudgery of housekeeping is the central occupation of more than fifty million women. People who would oppose institutions that portion out menial work on the basis of race see nothing wrong in a system that does the same thing on the basis of sex. (Should black and white roommates automatically assume the Negro best suited for housekeeping chores?) Even when they work at full-time jobs, wives must come home to "their" dusting and "their" laundry.

Some insist that housework is not much worse than the meaningless jobs most people have today, but there is a difference. Housewives are not paid for their work, and money is the mark of value in this society. It is also the key to independence and to the feeling of self-reliance that marks a free human being.

The justification for being a housewife is having children, and the justification for children is—well, a woman has a uterus, what else would it be for? Perhaps not all feminists agree that the uterus is a vestigial organ, but we are adamant and passionate in our denial of the old canard that biology is destiny.

Men have never been bound by their animal natures. They think and dream and create—and fly, clearly something nature had not intended, or it would have given men wings. However, we women are told that our chief function is to reproduce the species, prepare food, and sweep out the cave—er, house.

Psychologist Bruno Bettelheim states woman's functions succinctly: "We must start with the realization that, as much as women want to be good scientists or engineers, they want first and foremost to be womanly companions of men and to be mothers."

He gets no argument from Dr. Spock: "Biologically and temperamentally, I believe women were made to be concerned first and foremost with child care, husband care, and home care." Spock says some women have been "confused" by their education. (Freud was equally reactionary on the woman question, but he at least had the excuse of his Central European background.)

The species must reproduce, but this need not be the sole purpose of a woman's life. Men want children, too, yet no one expects them to choose between families and work. Children are in no way a substitute for personal development and creativity. If a talented man is forced into a senseless, menial job, it is deplored as a waste and a personal misfortune; yet, a woman's special skills, education, and interests are all too often deemed incidental and irrelevant, simply a focus for hobbies or volunteer work.

Women who say that raising a family is a fulfilling experience are rather like the peasant who never leaves his village. They have never had the opportunity to do anything else.

As a result, women are forced to live through their children and husbands, and they feel cheated and resentful when they realize that is not enough. When a woman says she gave her children everything, she is telling the truth—and that is the tragedy. Often when she reaches her late thirties, her children have grown up, gone to work or college, and left her in a bleak and premature old age. Middle-aged women who feel empty and useless are the mainstay of America's psychiatrists—who generally respond by telling them to "accept their role."

The freedom to choose whether or not to have children has always been illusory. A wife who is deliberately "barren"—a word that reinforces the worn-out metaphor of woman as Mother Earth—is considered neurotic or unnatural. Not only is motherhood not central to a woman's life, it may not be necessary or desirable. For the first time, some of us are admitting openly and without guilt that we do not want children. And the population crisis is making it even clearer that as a symbol for Americans motherhood ought to defer to apple pie.

The other half of the reproduction question is sex. The sexual revolution didn't liberate women at all; it only created a bear market for men. One of the most talked-about tracts in the movement is a pamphlet by Ann Koedt called "The Myth of the Vaginal Orgasm," which says most women don't have orgasms because most men won't accept the fact that the female orgasm is clitoral.

We are so used to putting men's needs first that we don't know how to ask for what *we* want, or else we share the common ignorance about our own physiology and think there is something wrong with us when we don't have orgasms "the right way." Freudian analysts contribute to the problem. The realization that past guilt and frustration have been unnecessary is not the least of the sentiments that draws women to women's liberation.

Feminists also protest the general male proclivity to regard us as decorative, amusing sex objects even in the world outside bed. We resent the sexual sell in advertising, the catcalls we get on the street, girlie magazines and pornography, bars that refuse to serve unescorted women on the assumption they are prostitutes, the not very subtle brainwashing by cosmetic companies, and the attitude of men who praise our knees in miniskirts, but refuse to act as if we had brains.

Even the supposedly humanistic worlds of rock music and radical politics are not very different. Young girls who join "the scene" or "the movement" are labeled "groupies" and are sexually exploited; the flashy porno-sheets such as *Screw* and *Kiss* are published by the self-appointed advocates of the new "free," anti-Establishment life-style. "*Plus ça change. . . .*"

We are angry about the powers men wield over us. The physical power—women who study karate do so as a defense against muggers, not lovers. And the social power—we resent the fact that men take the initiative with women, that women cannot ask for dates but must sit home waiting for the phone to ring.

That social conditioning began in childhood when fathers went out to work and mothers stayed home, images perpetuated in schoolbooks and games and on television. If we were bright students, we were told, "You're smart—for a girl," and then warned not to appear *too* smart in front of boys—"Or you won't have dates."

Those of us who persisted in reaching for a career were encouraged to be teachers or nurses so we would have "something to fall back on." My mother told me: "You're so bright, it's a pity you're not a boy. You could become president of a bank—or anything you wanted."

Ironically, and to our dismay, we discovered that playing the assigned role is precisely what elicits masculine contempt for our inferiority and narrow interests. *Tooth and Nail*, a newsletter published by women's liberation groups in the San Francisco area, acidly points out a few of the contradictions: "A smart woman never shows her brains; she allows the man to think himself clever. . . . Women's talk is all chatter; they don't understand things men are interested in."

It is my thesis that the core of the problem for women today is not sexual but a problem of identity—a stunting or evasion of growth that is perpetuated by the feminine mystique.

Betty Friedan
The Feminine Mystique

Or: "Don't worry your pretty little head about such matters. . . . A woman's brain is between her legs. . . . Women like to be protected and treated like little girls. . . . Women can't make decisions."

The feminist answer is to throw out the whole simplistic division of human characteristics into masculine and feminine, and to insist that there are no real differences between men and women other than those enforced by culture.

Men say women are not inferior, we are just different; yet somehow they have appropriated most of the qualities that society admires and have left us with the same distinctive features that were attributed to black people before the civil rights revolution.

Men, for example, are said to be strong, assertive, courageous, logical, constructive, creative, and independent. Women are weak, passive, irrational, overemotional, empty-headed, and lacking in strong superegos. (Thank Freud for the last.) Both blacks and women are contented, have their place, and know how to use wiles —flattery, and wide-eyed, open-mouthed ignorance—to get around "the man." It is obviously natural that men should be dominant and women submissive. Shuffle, baby, shuffle.

Our "sexist" system has hurt men as well as women, forcing them into molds that deny the value of sensitivity, tenderness, and sentiment. Men who are not aggressive worry about their virility just as strong women are frightened by talk about their being castrating females. The elimination of rigid sex-role definitions would liberate everyone. And that is the goal of the women's liberation movement.

Women's liberation groups, which have sprung up everywhere across the country, are taking names like Radical Women or the Women's Liberation Front or the Feminists. Most start as groups of ten or twelve; many, when they get too large for discussion, split in a form of mitosis. Sometimes they are tied to central organizations set up for action, or they maintain communications with each other or cosponsor newsletters with similar groups in their area.

Some are concerned with efforts to abolish abortion laws, a few have set up cooperative day-care centers, others challenge the stereotypes of woman's image, and many are organized for "consciousness-raising"—a kind of group therapy or encounter session that starts with the premise that there is something wrong with the system, not the women in the group.

The amorphousness and lack of central communication in the movement make it virtually impossible to catalogue the established groups, let alone the new ones that regularly appear; many of the "leaders" who have been quoted in newspapers or interviewed on television have been anointed only by the press.

The one organization with a constitution, board members, and chapters (some thirty-five) throughout the country is the National Organization for Women. Its founding in 1966 was precipitated by the ridicule that greeted the inclusion of sex in the prohibitions against job discrimination in the 1964 Civil Rights Act. (A staff member in the federal Equal Employment Opportunity Commission, which enforces the act, said it took pressure from NOW to get the EEOC to take that part of the law seriously.)

NOW members are not very different from women in other feminist groups, though they tend to include more professionals and older women. In general, they eschew "consciousness-raising" in favor of political action, and they are more likely to demonstrate for job equality and child-care centers than for the abolition of marriage or the traditional family unit.

NOW's president is Betty Friedan, who in 1963 published *The Feminine Mystique*, a challenge to the myth that a woman's place is either in a boudoir in a pink, frilly nightgown, on her hands and knees scrubbing the kitchen floor, or in a late model station wagon taking the kids to music lessons and Cub Scout meetings. (An article that previewed the theme of the book was turned down by every major women's magazine. "One was horrified and said I was obviously talking to and for a few neurotic women." When the book came out, two of these magazines published excerpts and several now have commissioned articles about the movement.)

Today, Betty Friedan says, the movement must gain political power by mobilizing the 51 percent of the electorate who are women, as well as seeking elected offices for themselves. "We have to break down the actual barriers that prevent women from being full people in society, and not only end explicit discrimination but build new institutions. Most women will continue to bear children, and unless we create child-care centers on a mass basis, it's all talk."

Women are beginning to read a good deal about their own place in history, about the determined struggles of the suffragettes, the isolation of Virginia Woolf, and the heroism of Rosa Luxemburg. The Congress to Unite Women, which drew some 500 participants from cities in the Northeast, called for woman's studies in high schools and colleges.

Present are all the accouterments of any social movement—feminist

magazines such as *No More Fun and Games* in Boston, *Up from Under* in New York, and *Aphra*, a literary magazine published in Baltimore. (Anne Sexton wrote in the dedication, "As long as it can be said about a woman writer, 'She writes like a man' and that woman takes it as a compliment, we are in trouble.")

There are feminist theaters in at least New York and Boston, buttons that read "Uppity Women Unite," feminist poems and songs, a feminist symbol (the biological sign for woman with an equal sign in the center), and, to denounce specific advertisements, gum stickers that state, "This ad insults women."

With a rising feminist consciousness, everything takes on a new significance—films, advertisements, offhand comments, little things that never seemed important before. A few women conclude that chivalry and flirting reduce women to mere sex objects for men. We stop feeling guilty about opening doors, and some of us experiment with paying our own way on dates.

Personal acts are matched by political ones. The National Organization for Women went to court to get a federal ruling barring segregated help-wanted ads in newspapers, and it regularly helps women file complaints before the EEOC and local human rights commissions.

A women's rights platform was adopted last year by the State Committee of the California Democratic Party, and the Women's Rights Committee of the New Democratic Coalition plans to make feminist demands an issue in New York politics. A women's caucus exists in the Democratic Policy Council, headed by Senator Fred Harris.

At Grinnell College in Iowa, students protested the appearance of a representative from *Playboy* magazine, and women from sixteen cities converged on Atlantic City to make it clear what they think of the Miss America Pageant. In New York, a group protested advertisements by toymakers that said "boys were born to build and learn" and "girls were born to be dancers."

Women's caucuses have been organized in the American Political Science, Psychological, and Sociological associations. At New York University, a group of law students won their fight to make women eligible for a series of coveted $10,000 scholarships.

Pro-abortion groups have organized around the country to repeal anti-abortion laws, challenge them in the courts, or openly defy them. In Bloomington, Indiana, New York City, and elsewhere, women's liberation groups have set up cooperative day-care centers, which are illegal under strict state rules that regulate child-care facilities.

Free child care is likely to become the most significant demand made by the movement, and one calculated to draw the support of millions of women who may not be interested in other feminist issues. About four million working mothers have children under six years of age, and only 2 per cent of these are in day-care centers.

Even Establishment institutions appear to reflect the new attitudes. Princeton, Williams, and Yale have begun to admit women students, though on an unequal quota basis—and not to the hallowed pine-paneled halls of their alumni clubhouses.

Nevertheless, most people have only a vague idea of the significance of the new movement. News commentators on year-end analysis shows ignored the question or sloughed it off uncomfortably. One said the whole idea frightened him.

Yet the women's movement promises to affect radically the life of virtually everyone in America. Only a small part of the population suffers because it is black, and most people have little contact with minorities. Women are 51 percent of the population, and chances are that every adult American either is one, is married to one, or has close social or business relations with many.

The feminist revolution will overturn the basic premises upon which these relations are built—stereotyped notions about the family and the roles of men and women, fallacies concerning masculinity and femininity, and the economic division of labor into paid work and homemaking.

If the 1960s belonged to the blacks, the next ten years are ours.

Youth must feel there is a possibility of change. *Robert Kennedy*

THE FORGOTTEN AMERICAN

By Peter Schrag

There is hardly a language to describe him, or even a set of social statistics. Just names: racist - bigot - redneck - ethnic - Irish - Italian - Pole - Hunkie - Yahoo. The lower middle class. A blank. The man under whose hat lies the great American desert. Who watches the tube, plays the horses, and keeps the niggers out of his union and his neighborhood. Who might vote for Wallace (but didn't). Who cheers when the cops beat up on demonstrators. Who is free, white, and twenty-one, has a job, a home, a family, and is up to his eyeballs in credit. In the guise of the working class—or the American yeoman or John Smith—he was once the hero of the civics book, the man that Andrew Jackson called "the bone and sinew of the country." Now he is "the forgotten man," perhaps the most alienated person in America.

Nothing quite fits, except perhaps omission and semi-invisibility. America is supposed to be divided between affluence and poverty, between slums and suburbs. John Kenneth Galbraith begins the foreword to *The*

Affluent Society with the phrase, "Since I sailed for Switzerland in the early summer of 1955 to begin work on this book . . ." But *between* slums and suburbs, between Scarsdale and Harlem, between Wellesley and Roxbury, between Shaker Heights and Hough, there are some eighty million people (depending on how you count them) who didn't sail for Switzerland in the summer of 1955, or at any other time, and who never expect to. Between slums and suburbs: South Boston and South San Francisco, Bell and Parma, Astoria, and Bay Ridge, Newark, Cicero, Downey, Daly City, Charlestown, Flatbush. Union halls, American Legion posts, neighborhood bars and bowling leagues, the Ukrainian Club and the Holy Name. Main Street. To try to describe all this is like trying to describe America itself. If you look for it, you find it everywhere: the rows of frame houses overlooking the belching steel mills in Bethlehem, Pennsylvania, two-family brick houses in Canarsie (where the most common slogan, even in the middle of a political campaign, is "curb your dog"); the

Fords and Chevies with a decal American flag on the rear window (usually a cut-out from the *Reader's Digest*, and displayed in counter-protest against peaceniks and "those bastards who carry Vietcong flags in demonstrations"); the bunting on the porch rail with the inscription, "Welcome Home, Pete." The gold star in the window.

When he was Under Secretary of Housing and Urban Development, Robert C. Wood tried a definition. It is not good, but it's the best we have:

He is a white employed male . . . earning between $5,000 and $10,000. He works regularly, steadily, dependably, wearing a blue collar or white collar. Yet the frontiers of his career expectations have been fixed since he reached the age of thirty-five, when he found that he had too many obligations, too much family, and too few skills to match opportunities with aspirations.

This definition of the "working American" involves almost 23-million American families.

The working American lives in the gray area fringes of a central city or in a close-in or very far-out cheaper suburban subdivision of a large metropolitan area. He is likely to own a home and a car, especially as his income begins to rise. Of those earning between $6,000 and $7,500, 70 per cent own their own homes and 94 per cent drive their own cars.

94 per cent have no education beyond high school and 43 per cent have only completed the eighth grade.

He does all the right things, obeys the law, goes to church and insists— usually—that his kids get a better education than he had. But the right things don't seem to be paying off.

While he is making more than he ever made—perhaps more than he'd ever dreamed—he's still struggling while a lot of others—"them" (on welfare, in demonstrations, in the ghettos) are getting most of the attention. "I'm working my ass off," a guy tells you on a stoop in South Boston. "My kids don't have a place to swim, my parks are full of glass, and I'm supposed to bleed for a bunch of people on relief." In New York a man who drives a Post Office trailer truck at night (4:00 P.M. to midnight) and a cab during the day (7:00 A.M. to 2:00 P.M.), and who hustles radios for his Post Office buddies on the side, is ready, as he says, to "knock somebody's ass." "The colored guys work when they feel like it. Sometimes they show up and sometimes they don't. One guy tore up all the time cards. I'd like to see a white guy do that and get away with it."

Nobody knows how many people in America moonlight (half of the eighteen million families in the $5,000 to $10,000 bracket have two or more wage earners) or how many have to hustle on the side. "I don't think anybody has a single job anymore," said Nicholas Kisburg, the research director for a Teamsters Union Council in New York. "All the cops are moonlighting, and the teachers; and there's a million guys who are hustling, guys with phony social-security numbers who are hiding part of what they make so they don't get kicked out of a housing project, or guys who work as guards at sports events and get free meals that they don't want to pay taxes on. Every one of them is cheating. They are underground people— *Untermenschen*. . . . We really have no systematic data on any of this. We have no ideas of the attitudes of the white worker. (We've been too busy studying the black worker.) And yet he's the source of most of the reaction in this country."

The reaction is directed at almost every visible target: at integration and welfare, taxes and sex education, at the rich and the poor, the foundations and students, at the "smart people in the suburbs." In New York State the legislature cuts the welfare budget; in Los Angeles, the voters reelect Yorty after a whispered racial campaign against the Negro favorite. In Minneapolis a police detective named Charles Stenvig, promising "to take the handcuffs off the police," wins by a margin stunning even to his supporters: in Massachusetts the voters mail tea bags to their representatives in protest against new taxes, and in state after state legislatures are passing bills to punish student demonstrators. ("We keep talking about permissiveness in training kids," said a Los Angeles labor official, "but we forget that these are our kids.")

And yet all these things are side manifestations of a malaise that lacks a language. Whatever law and order means, for example, to a man who feels his wife is unsafe on the street after dark or in the park at any time, or whose kids get shaken down in the school yard, it also means something like normality—the demand that everybody play it by the book, that cultural and social standards be somehow restored to their civics-book simplicity, that things shouldn't be as they are but as they were supposed to be. If there is a revolution in this country—a revolt in manners, standards of dress and obscenity, and, more importantly, in our official sense of what America is—there is also a counter-revolt. Sometimes it is inarticulate, and sometimes (perhaps most of the time) people are either too confused or apathetic—or simply too polite and too decent—to declare

themselves. In Astoria, Queens, a white working-class district of New York, people who make $7,000 or $8,000 a year (sometimes in two jobs) call themselves affluent, even though the Bureau of Labor Statistics regards an income of less than $9,500 in New York inadequate to a moderate standard of living. And in a similar neighborhood in Brooklyn a truck driver who earns $151 a week tells you he's doing well, living in a two-story frame house separated by a narrow driveway from similar houses, thousands of them in block after block. This year, for the first time, he will go on a cruise—he and his wife and two other couples—two weeks in the Caribbean. He went to work after World War II ($57 a week) and he has lived in the same house for twenty years, accumulating two television sets, wall-to-wall carpeting in a small living room, and a basement that he recently remodeled into a recreation room with the help of two moonlighting firemen. "We get fairly good salaries, and this is a good neighborhood, one of the few good ones left. We have no smoked Irishmen around."

Stability is what counts, stability in job and home and neighborhood, stability in the church and in friends.

Why are the times so dark
Men know each other not at all,
But governments quite clearly change
From bad to worse?
Days dead and gone were more
    worth while,
Now what holds sway? Deep gloom
    and boredom,
Justice and law nowhere to be found.
I know no more where I belong.

Eustache Deschamps
Fifteenth-century poet

319

At night you watch television and sometimes on a weekend you go to a nice place—maybe a downtown hotel —for dinner with another couple. (Or maybe your sister, or maybe bowling, or maybe, if you're defeated, a night at the track.) The wife has the necessary appliances, often still being paid off, and the money you save goes for your daughter's orthodontist, and later for her wedding. The smoked Irishmen—the colored (no one says black; few even say Negro)—represent change and instability, kids who cause trouble in school, who get treatment that your kids never got, that you never got. ("Those fucking kids," they tell you in South Boston, "raising hell, and not one of 'em paying his own way. Their fucking mothers are all on welfare.") The black kids mean a change in the rules, a double standard in grades and discipline, and—vaguely —a challenge to all you believed right. Law and order is the stability and predictability of established ways. Law and order is equal treatment—in school, in jobs, in the courts—even if you're cheating a little yourself. The Forgotten Man is Jackson's man. He is the vestigial American democrat of 1840: "They all know that their success depends upon their own industry and economy and that they must not expect to become suddenly rich by the fruits of their toil." He is also Franklin Roosevelt's man—the man whose vote (or whose father's vote) sustained the New Deal. . .

There are other considerations, other styles, other problems. A postman in a Charlestown (Boston) housing project: eight children and a ninth on the way. Last year, by working overtime, his income went over $7,000. This year, because he reported it, the Housing Authority is raising his rent from $78 to $106 a month, a catastrophe for a family that pays $2.20 a day for milk, has never had a vacation, and for which an excursion is "going out for ice cream." "You try and save for something better; we hope to get out of here to someplace where the kids can play, where there's no broken glass, and then something always comes along that knocks you right back. It's like being at the bottom of the well waiting for a guy to throw you a rope." The description becomes almost Chaplinesque. Life is humble but not simple; the terrors of insolent bureaucracies and contemptuous officials produce a demonology that loses little of its horror for being partly misunderstood. You want to get a sink fixed but don't want to offend the manager; want to get an eye operation that may (or may not) have been necessitated by a military injury five years earlier, "but the Veterans Administration says I signed away my benefits"; want to complain to someone about the teen-agers who run around breaking windows and harassing women but get no response either from the management or the police. "You're afraid to complain because if they don't get you during the day they'll get you at night." Automobiles, windows, children, all become hostages to the vague terrors of everyday life; everything is vulnerable. Liabilities that began long ago cannot possibly be liquidated: "I never learned anything in that school except how to fight. I got tired of being caned by the teachers so at sixteen I quit and joined the Marines. I still don't know anything."

American culture? Wealth is visible, and so, now, is poverty. Both have become intimidating clichés. But the rest? A vast, complex, and disregarded world that was once—in belief, and in fact—the American middle: Greyhound and Trailways bus terminals in little cities at midnight, each of them with its neon lights and its cardboard hamburgers; acres of tar-paper beach bungalows in places like Revere and Rockaway; the hair curlers in the supermarket on Saturday, and the little girls in the communion dresses the next morning; pinball machines and the *Daily News*, the *Reader's Digest* and Ed Sullivan; houses with tiny front lawns (or even large ones) adorned with statues of the Virgin or of Sambo welcomin' de folks home; Clint Eastwood or Julie Andrews at the Palace; the trotting tracks and the dog tracks—Aurora Downs, Connaught Park, Roosevelt, Yonkers, Rockingham, and forty others—where gray men come not for sport and beauty, but to read numbers, to study and dope. (If you win you have figured something, have in a small way controlled your world, have surmounted your impotence. If you lose, bad luck, shit. "I'll break his goddamned head.") Baseball is not the national pastime; racing is. For every man who goes to a major-league baseball game there are four who go to the track and probably four more who go to the candy store or the barbershop to make their bets. (Total track attendance in 1965: 62 million plus another 10 million who went to the dogs.)

There are places and styles, and attitudes. If there are neighborhoods of aspiration, suburban enclaves for the mobile young executive and the aspiring worker, there are also places of limited expectation and dead-end districts where mobility is finished. But even there you can often find, however vestigial, a sense of place, the roots of old ethnic loyalties, and a passionate, if often futile, battle against intrusion and change. "Everybody around here," you are told, "pays his own way." In this world the problems are not the ABM or air pollution (have they heard of Biafra?) or the inter-national population crisis; the problem is to get your street cleaned, your garbage collected, to get your husband home from Vietnam alive; to negotiate installment payments and to keep the schools orderly. Ask anyone in Scarsdale or Winnetka about the schools and they'll tell you about new programs, or about how many are getting into Harvard, or about the teachers; ask in Oakland or the North Side of Chicago, and they'll tell you that they have (or haven't) had trouble. Somewhere in his gut the man in those communities knows that mobility and choice in this society are limited. He cannot imagine any major change for the better; but he can imagine change for the worse. And yet for a decade he is the one who has been asked to carry the burden of social reform, to integrate his schools and his neighborhood, has been asked by comfortable people to pay the social debts due to the poor and the black. In Boston, in San Francisco, in Chicago (not to mention Newark or Oakland) he has been telling the reformers to go to hell. The Jewish schoolteachers of New York and the Irish parents of Dorchester have asked the same question: "What the hell did Lindsay (or the Beacon Hill Establishment) ever do for us?"

The ambiguities and changes in American life that occupy discussions in university seminars and policy debates in Washington, and that form the backbone of contemporary popular sociology, become increasingly the conditions of trauma and frustration in the middle. Although the New Frontier and Great Society contained some programs for those not already on the rolls of social pathology—federal aid for higher education, for example—the public priorities and the rhetoric contained little. The emphasis, properly, was on the poor, on the inner cities (e.g., Negroes) and the unemployed. But in Chicago a widow with three children who earns $7,000 a year can't get them college loans because she makes too much; the money is reserved for people on relief. New schools are built in the ghetto but not in the white working-class neighborhoods where they are just as dilapidated. In Newark the head of a white vigilante group (now a city councilman) runs, among other things, on a platform opposing pro-Negro discrimination. "When pools are being built in the Central Ward—don't they think white kids have got frustration? The white can't get a job; we have to hire Negroes first." The middle class, said Congressman Roman Pucinski of Illinois, who represents ·a lot of it, "is in revolt. Everyone has been generous in supporting anti-poverty. Now the middle-class American is disqualified from most of the programs."

The frustrated middle. The liberal wisdom about welfare, ghettos, student revolt, and Vietnam has only a marginal place, if any, for the values and life of the working man. It flies in the face of most of what he was taught to cherish and respect: hard work, order, authority, self-reliance. He fought, either alone or through labor organizations, to establish the precincts he now considers his own. Union seniority, the civil-service bureaucracy, and the petty professionalism established by the merit system in the public schools become sinecures of particular ethnic groups or of those who have learned to negotiate and master the system. A man who worked all his life to accumulate the points and grades and paraphernalia to become an assistant school principal (no matter how silly the requirements) is not likely to relinquish his position with equanimity. Nor is a dock worker whose only estate is his longshoreman's card. The job, the points, the credits become property:

Some men leave their sons money [wrote a union member to the *New York Times*], some large investments, some business connections, and some a profession. I have only one worthwhile thing to give: my trade. I hope to follow a centuries-old tradition and sponsor my sons for an apprenticeship. For this simple father's wish it is said that I discriminate against Negroes. Don't all of us discriminate? Which of us . . . will not choose a son over all others?

Suddenly the rules are changing—all the rules. If you protect your job for your own you may be called a bigot. At the same time it's perfectly acceptable to shout black power and to endorse it. What does it take to be a good American? *Give the black man a position because he is black, not because he necessarily works harder or does the job better.* What does it take to be a good American? Dress nicely, hold a job, be clean-cut, don't judge a man by the color of his skin or the country of his origin. What about the demands of Negroes, the long hair of the students, the dirty movies, the people who burn draft cards and American flags? Do you have to go out in the street with picket signs, do you have to burn the place down to get what you want? What does it take to be a good American? *This is a sick society, a racist society, we are fighting an imoral war.* ("I'm against the Vietnam war, too," says the truck driver in Brooklyn. "I see a good kid come home with half an arm and a leg in a brace up to here, and what's it all for? I was glad to see *my kid* flunk the Army physical. Still, somebody has to say no to these demonstrators and enforce the law.") What does it take to be a good American?

The conditions of trauma and frustration in the middle. What does it take to be a good American? Suddenly there are demands for Italian power and Polish power and Ukrainian power. In Cleveland the Poles demand a seat on the school board, and get it, and in Pittsburgh John Pankuch, the seventy-three-year-old president of the National Slovak Society demands "action, plenty of it to make up for lost time." Black power is supposed to be nothing but emulation of the ways in which other ethnic groups made it. But have they made it? In Reardon's Bar on East Eighth Street in South Boston, where the workmen come for their fish-chowder lunch and for their rye and ginger, they still identify themselves as Galway men and Kilkenny men; in the newsstand in Astoria you can buy *Il Progresso, El Tiempo*, the *Staats-Zeitung*, the *Irish World*, plus papers in Greek, Hungarian, and Polish. At the parish of Our Lady of Mount Carmel the priests hear confession in English, Italian, and Spanish and, nearby, the biggest attraction is not the stickball game, but the *bocce* court. Some of the poorest people in America are white, native, and have lived all of their lives in the same place as their fathers and grandfathers. The problems that were presumably solved in some distant past, in that prehistoric era before the textbooks were written—problems of assimilation, of upward mobility—now turn out to be very much unsolved. The melting pot and all: millions made it, millions moved to the affluent suburbs; several million—no one knows how many—did not. The median income in Irish South Boston is $5,100 a year but the community-action workers have a hard time convincing

the local citizens that any white man who is not stupid or irresponsible can be poor. Pride still keeps them from applying for income supplements or Medicaid, but it does not keep them from resenting those who do. In Pittsburgh, where the members of Polish-American organizations earn an estimated $5,000 to $6,000 (and some fall below the poverty line), the Poverty Programs are nonetheless directed primarily to Negroes, and almost everywhere the thing called urban backlash associates itself in some fashion with ethnic groups whose members have themselves only a precarious hold on the security of affluence. Almost everywhere in the old cities, tribal neighborhoods and their styles are under assault by masscult. The Italian grocery gives way to the supermarket, the ma-and-pa store and the walk-up are attacked by urban renewal. And almost everywhere, that assault tends to depersonalize and to alienate. It has always been this way, but with time the brave new world that replaces old patterns becomes increasingly bureaucratized, distant, and hard to control.

Yet beyond the problems of ethnic identity, beyond the problems of Poles and Irishmen left behind, there are others more pervasive and more dangerous. For every Greek or Hungarian there are a dozen American-Americans who are past ethnic consciousness and who are as alienated, as confused, and as angry as the rest. The obvious manifestations are the same everywhere—race, taxes, welfare, students—but the threat seems invariably more cultural and psychological than economic or social. What upset the police at the Chicago convention most was not so much the politics of the demonstrators as their manners and their hair. (The barbershops in their neighborhoods don't advertise Beatle Cuts but the

Flat Top and the Chicago Box.) The affront comes from middle-class people—and their children—who had been cast in the role of social exemplars (and from those cast as unfortunates worthy of public charity) who offend all the things on which working class identity is built: "hippies [said a San Francisco longshoreman] who fart around the streets and don't work"; welfare recipients who strike and march for better treatment; "all those [said a California labor official] who challenge the precepts that these people live on." If ethnic groups are beginning to organize to get theirs, so are others: police and firemen ("The cop is the new nigger"); schoolteachers; lower-middle-class housewives fighting sex education and bussing; small property owners who have no ethnic communion but a passionate interest in lower taxes, more policemen, and stiffer penalties for criminals. In San Francisco the Teamsters, who had never been known for such interests before, recently demonstrated in support of the police and law enforcement and, on another occasion, joined a group called Mothers Support Neighborhood Schools at a school-board meeting to oppose—with their presence and later, apparently, with their fists—a proposal to integrate the schools through bussing. ("These people," someone said at the meeting, "do not look like mothers.")

Which is not to say that all is frustration and anger, that anybody is ready "to burn the country down." They are not even ready to elect standard model demagogues. "A lot of labor people who thought of voting for Wallace were ashamed of themselves when they realized what they were about to do," said Morris Iushewitz, an officer of New York's Central Labor Council. Because of a massive last-minute union campaign, and per-

haps for other reasons, the blue-collar vote for Wallace fell far below the figures predicted by the early polls last fall. Any number of people, moreover, who are not doing well by any set of official statistics, who are earning well below the national mean ($8,000 a year), or who hold two jobs to stay above it, think of themselves as affluent, and often use that word. It is almost as if not to be affluent is to be un-American. People who can't use the word tend to be angry; people who come too close to those who can't become frightened. The definition of affluence is generally pinned to what comes in, not to the quality of life as it's lived. The $8,000 son of a man who never earned more than $4,500 may, for that reason alone, believe that he's "doing all right." If life is not all right, if he can't get his curbs fixed, or his streets patrolled, if the highways are crowded and the beaches polluted, if the schools are ineffectual he is still able to call himself affluent, feels, perhaps, a social compulsion to do so. His anger, if he is angry, is not that of the wage earner resenting management—and certainly not that of the socialist ideologue asking for redistribution of wealth—but that of the consumer, the taxpayer, and the family man. (Inflation and taxes are wiping out most of the wage gains made in labor contracts signed during the past three years.) Thus he will vote for a Louise Day Hicks in Boston who promises to hold the color line in the schools or for a Charles Stenvig calling for law enforcement in Minneapolis but reject a George Wallace who seems to threaten his pocketbook. The danger is that he will identify with the politics of the Birchers and other middle-class reactionaries (who often pretend to speak for him) even though his income and style of life are far removed from theirs; that taxes, for example, will be identified with welfare rather than war, and that he will blame his limited means on the small slice of the poor rather than the fat slice of the rich.

If you sit and talk to people like Marjorie Lemlow, who heads Mothers Support Neighborhood Schools in San Francisco, or Joe Owens, a house painter who is president of a community-action organization in Boston, you quickly discover that the roots of reaction and the roots of reform are often identical, and that the response to particular situations is more often contingent on the politics of the politicians and leaders who appear to care than on the conditions of life or the ideology of the victims. Mrs. Lemlow wants to return the schools to some virtuous past; she worries about disintegration of the family and she speaks vaguely about something that she can't bring herself to call a conspiracy against Americanism. She has been accused of leading a bunch of Birchers, and she sometimes talks Birch language. But whatever the form, her sense of things comes from a small-town vision of national virtues, and her unhappiness from the assaults of urban sophistication. It just so happens that a lot of reactionaries now sing that tune, and that the liberals are indifferent.

Joe Owens—probably because of his experience as a Head Start parent, and because of his association with an effective community-action program —talks a different language. He knows, somehow, that no simple past can be restored. In his world the villains are not conspirators but bureaucrats and politicians, and he is beginning to discover that in a struggle with officials the black man in the ghetto and the working man (black or white) have the same problems. "Every time you ask for something from the politicians they treat you like a beggar, like you ought to be grateful for what you have. They try to make you feel ashamed."

The imponderables are youth and tradition and change. The civics book and the institution it celebrates—however passé—still hold the world together. The revolt is in their name, not against them. And there is simple decency, the language and practice of the folksy cliché, the small town, the Boy Scout virtues, the neighborhood charity, the obligation to support the church, the rhetoric of open opportunity: "They can keep Wallace and they can keep Alabama. We didn't fight a dictator for four years so we could elect one over here." What happens when all that becomes Mickey Mouse? Is there an urban ethic to replace the values of the small town? Is there a coherent public philosophy, a consistent set of beliefs to replace family, home, and hard work? What happens when the hang-ups of upper-middle-class kids are in fashion and those of blue-collar kids are not? What happens when Doing Your Own Thing becomes not the slogan of the solitary deviant but the norm? Is it possible that as the institutions and beliefs of tradition are fashionably denigrated a blue-collar generation gap will open to the Right as well as to the Left? (There is statistical evidence, for example, that Wallace's greatest support within the unions came from people who are between twenty-one and twenty-nine, those, that is, who have the most tenuous association with the liberalism of labor.) Most are politically silent; although SDS has been trying to organize blue-collar high-school students, there are no Mario Savios or Mark Rudds—either of the Right or the Left—among them. At the same time the union leaders, some of them old hands from the Thirties, aren't sure that the kids are following them either. Who speaks for the son of the longshoreman or the Detroit auto worker? What happens if he doesn't get to college? What, indeed, happens when he does?

Vaguely but unmistakably the hopes that a youth-worshiping nation historically invested in its young are becoming threats. We have never been unequivocal about the symbolic patricide of Americanization and upward mobility, but if at one time mobility meant rejection of older (or European) styles it was, at least, done in the name of America. Now the labels are blurred and the objectives indistinct. Just at the moment when a tradition-bound Italian father is persuaded that he should send his sons to college—that education is the only future—the college blows up. At the moment when a parsimonious taxpayer begins to shell out for what he considers an extravagant state university system the students go on strike. Marijuana, sexual liberation, dress styles, draft resistance, even the rhetoric of change become monsters and demons in a world that appears to turn old virtues upside down. The paranoia that fastened on Communism twenty years ago (and sometimes still does) is increasingly directed to vague conspiracies undermining the schools, the family, order and discipline. "They're feeding the kids this generation-gap business," says a Chicago housewife who grinds out a campaign against sex education on a duplicating machine in her living room. "The kids are told to make their own decisions. They're all mixed up by situation ethics and open-ended questions. They're alienating children from their own parents." They? The churches, the schools, even the YMCA and the Girl Scouts, are implicated. But a major share of the villainy is now also attributed to "the social science centers," to the apostles

of sensitivity training, and to what one California lady, with some embarrassment, called "nude therapy." People with sane minds are being altered by psychological methods." The current major campaign of the John Birch Society is not directed against Communists in government or the Supreme Court, but against sex education.

(There is, of course, also sympathy with the young, especially in poorer areas where kids have no place to play. "Everybody's got to have a hobby," a South Boston adolescent told a youth worker. "Ours is throwing rocks." If people will join reactionary organizations to protect their children, they will also support others: community-action agencies which help kids get jobs; Head Start parent groups, Boys Clubs. "Getting this place cleaned up" sometimes refers to a fear of young hoods; sometimes it points to the day when there is a park or a playground or when the existing park can be used. "I want to see them grow up to have a little fun.")

Beneath it all there is a more fundamental ambivalence, not only about the young, but about institutions—the schools, the churches, the Establishment—and about the future itself. In the major cities of the East (though perhaps not in the West) there is a sense that time is against you, that one is living "in one of the few decent neighborhoods left," that "if I can get $125 a week upstate (or downstate) I'll move." The institutions that were supposed to mediate social change and which, more than ever, are becoming priesthoods of information and conglomerates of social engineers, are increasingly suspect. To attack the Ford Foundation (as Wright Patman has done) is not only to fan the embers of historic populism against concentrations of wealth and power, but also to arouse those who feel that they are trapped by an alliance of upper-class Wasps and lower-class Negroes. If the foundations have done anything for the blue-collar worker he doesn't seem to be aware of it. At the same time the distrust of professional educators that characterizes the black militants is becoming increasingly prevalent among a minority of lower-middle-class whites who are beginning to discover that the schools aren't working for them either. ("Are all those new programs just a cover-up for failure?") And if the Catholic Church is under attack from its liberal members (on birth control, for example) it is also alienating the traditionalists who liked their minor saints (even if they didn't actually exist) and were perfectly content with the Latin Mass. For the alienated Catholic liberal there are other places to go; for the lower-middle-class parishioner in Chicago or Boston there are none.

Perhaps, in some measure, it has always been this way. Perhaps none of this is new. And perhaps it is also true that the American lower middle has never had it so good. And yet surely there is a difference, and that is that the common man has lost his visibility and, somehow, his claim on public attention. There are old liberals and socialists—men like Michael Harrington—who believe that a new alliance can be forged for progressive social action:

From Marx to Mills, the Left has regarded the middle class as a stratum of hypocritical, vacillating rear-guarders. There was often sound reason for this contempt. But is it not possible that a new class is coming into being? It is not the old middle class of small property owners and entrepreneurs, nor the new middle class of managers. It is composed of scientists, technicians, teachers, and professionals in the public sector of the society. By education and work experience it is predisposed toward planning. It could be an ally of the poor and the organized workers—or their sophisticated enemy. In other words, an unprecedented social and political variable seems to be taking shape in America.

The American worker, even when he waits on a table or holds open a door, is not servile; he does not carry himself like an inferior. The openness, frankness, and democratic manner which Tocqueville described in the last century persists to this very day. They have been a source of rudeness, contemptuous ignorance, violence —and of a creative self-confidence among great masses of people. It was in this latter spirit that the CIO was organized and the black freedom movement marched.

There are recent indications that the white lower middle class is coming back on the roster of public priorities. Pucinski tells you that liberals in Congress are privately discussing the pressure from the middle class. There are proposals now to increase personal income-tax exemptions from $600 to $1,000 (or $1,200) for each dependent, to protect all Americans with a national insurance system covering catastrophic medical expenses, and to put a floor under all incomes. Yet these things by themselves are insufficient. Nothing is sufficient without a national sense of restoration. What Pucinski means by the middle class has, in some measure, always been represented. A physician earning $75,000 a year is also a working man but he is hardly a victim of the welfare

American Gothic: Wood

. . . taking a new step, uttering a new
word is what people fear most.
Feodor Dostoevsky

system. Nor, by and large, are the stockholders of the Standard Oil Company or U.S. Steel. The fact that American ideals have often been corrupted in the cause of self-aggrandizement does not make them any less important for the cause of social reform and justice. "As a movement with the conviction that there is more to people than greed and fear," Harrington said, "the Left must . . . also speak in the name of the historic idealism of the United States."

The issue, finally, is not *the program* but the vision, the angle of view.

A huge constituency may be coming up for grabs, and there is considerable evidence that its political mobility is more sensitive than anyone can imagine, that all the sociological determinants are not as significant as the simple facts of concern and leadership. When Robert Kennedy was killed last year, thousands of working-class people who had expected to vote for him—if not hundreds of thousands —shifted their loyalties to Wallace. A man who can change from a progressive democrat into a bigot overnight deserves attention.

Who is the slayer, who the victim? Speak.   *Sophocles*

CHANT FOR ALL THE PEOPLE ON EARTH

Not to forget not to ever forget so long as you live so
long as you love so long as you breathe eat wash
walk think see feel read touch laugh not to forget not
to ever forget so long as you know the meaning of
freedom of what lonely nights are to torn lovers so
long as you retain the soul heart of a man so long as
you resemble man in any way in any shape not to
forget not to ever forget for many have already
forgotten many have always planned to forget fire fear
death murder injustice hunger gas graves for they
have already forgotten and want you to forget but do
not forget our beloved species not to forget not to
ever forget for as long as you live carry it with you let
us see it recognize it in each other's face and eyes
taste it with each bite of bread each time we shake
hands or use words for as long as we live not to forget
what happened to 6 million Jews to living beings who
looked just as we look men people children girls
women young old good bad evil profound foolish vain
happy unhappy sane insane mean grand joyous all
dead gone buried burned not to forget not to ever
forget for as long as you live for the earth will never
be the same again for each shred of sand cries with
their cries and our lungs are full of their dying sounds
for god was killed in each of them for in order to live
as men we must not forget for if they are forgotten O
if they are forgotten forget me also destroy me also
burn my books my memory and may everything I
have ever said or done or written may it be destroyed
to nothing may I become less than nothing for then I
do not want even one memory of me left alive on cold
killing earth for life would have no honor for to be
called a man would be an insult—

—*Leslie Woolf Hedley*

Reprinted by permission of Leslie Woolf Hedley and International Publishers from Walter Lowenfels, ed., *Poets of Today* (New York: International Publishers, 1964).

MILITARISM

OVERPOPULATION

POLLUTION

LINES NOT TO CROSS

All that is necessary for the forces of evil
to win in the world is for enough good men
to do nothing.
Edmund Burke

Man has lost the capacity
to foresee and to forestall.
He will end by destroying
the earth.
Albert Schweitzer

Technology has lengthened our lives and
provided us with material comforts that we
desire above everything else. But recently,
man has begun to realize that he faces
his own destruction unless he changes his
priorities; from war to peace, from a
growth-oriented, exploitive system to one
focused on stability and conservation.

Laocoon.

MILITARISM IN AMERICA

By Donald McDonald

Is the United States a militarized society? Two quick—and contradictory—answers can be given to this question. The "yes" answer is usually based on a few pieces of evidence; military expenditures and the Vietnam war are the ones most often cited. The "no" answer rests on the fact that a civilian is Commander-in-Chief of our armed forces and that another civilian, the Secretary of Defense, exercises direct authority over the administration of these forces. The "yes" proceeds from insufficient evidence; the "no" evades the issue because it assumes that civilians really do control our armed forces and that the mere fact of civilian control—constitutional and/or actual —proves that the control is not leading to a militarization of American society.

Neither of the answers, of course, is satisfactory. I suspect that what must be done is to treat this question as a genuine query. That means we must let our answer develop out of an understanding of the meaning of the key term, "a militarized society," and out of an examination and critical analysis of the contemporary American experience to determine whether our experience fits the definition of such a society.

I

The following seem to be major characteristics of a militarized society:

1. *A militarized society is an authoritarian society.* Free expression is a threat, dissent cannot be tolerated, and disobedience is met with swift repression.

2. *In a militarized society, stability is a cardinal virtue.* Questions of social justice and human rights, when they are not altogether ignored, are viewed with sour suspicion because they cannot be entertained, even abstractly, without at least implying that in certain circumstances stability is not a virtue but a vice.

3. *The militarized society is a fearful society.* The ultimate justification for a militarized society is that it is surrounded by enemies. In such an atmosphere, human trust withers, paranoia becomes a national disease, and it is never possible to have too many weapons.

4. *The militarized society is a self-righteous society.* It regards its motives as the purest, its values as unquestionable, its ideals as unsurpassable. When it wages war or intervenes in the affairs of another people, it is sure that it does so only to protect these qualities or enable others to enjoy them.

5. *In a militarized society, the military is not a means to an end, it is the end itself.* Whatever is good for the military is good for society. Military logic is the national philosophy.

6. *A militarized society gives to the military the highest priority in claims on the national resources.* In practice, the military consumes the lion's share of the government's revenues from taxes on the people; a substantial part of what is left over is spent to placate a restless people and to repress those who will not be placated.

7. *A militarized society has an unchallengeable claim on the lives of its young men.* Conscription into military service becomes a natural—and, in time, almost an unnoticed—part of the political and social landscape.

8. *In a militarized society, the military are beyond effective criticism and control.* The institutions that ordinarily exercise such critical con-

Reprinted by permission of *The Center Magazine*, January 1970, (Santa Barbara: Center for the Study of Democratic Institutions, 1970).

trol—legislative bodies, courts, press, universities, churches—are silenced, ignored, or drawn into acquiescence.

9. *In a militarized society, deception is accepted as a normal fact of life.* Foreign and domestic espionage, sabotage, subversion, and other paramilitary activities are carefully cultivated within the military; these have the twofold effect of keeping the enemy off balance and one's own citizens ignorant and therefore unable to ask critical questions.

10. *A militarized society perceives most political problems as military problems and the militarized solution is, therefore, the only realistic solution.* The options confronting such a society in a world community are determined and defined by the military. Civilian policymakers who consider other options do so at the risk of being labeled "soft-headed" if not "disloyal."

11. *In a militarized society, the economy is dependent on the military.* The military constitutes the single biggest "industry" and its dissolution would be as catastrophic for the nation as the dismantling of the single industry in a one-industry town.

12. *The militarized society is a sterile society.* Because it turns human and material resources into instruments of death and consequently neglects problems concerned with the quality of life, and because, in the process, it either suppresses or buys off with enormous rewards of money, prestige, and power the possibility of divergent views and voices, the militarized society deprives itself of the life-quickening energies of its artists and its philosophers, its critics and saints, its youth with their idealism, and its elders with their wisdom and experience. The result is sterility, emptiness, barrenness.

13. *The militarized society is a barbaric society.* The barbarian is not necessarily covered with blood, nor does he have to wear a military uniform. In a technologized military society, it is possible for decent people to perform tasks at drawing boards and in laboratories that will insure the death of hundreds of thousands of people halfway around the world; it is possible for pilots and technicians, pressing buttons and switching on computers, to complete the killing process without seeing the faces of those they are killing. Militarization inevitably makes one indifferent about taking human life. A technologized militarization simply makes it easier and less painful to cultivate that indifference.

II

If the above is an accurate profile of a militarized society, the question is: To what extent is it matched by the contemporary American experience? . . .

If the budget of the Pentagon were reduced from 80 billion dollars to 20 billion it would still be over twice as large as that of any other agency of government.

William O. Douglas,
Points of Rebellion

WHEN GOD DECIDED TO INVENT

when god decided to invent
everything he took one
breath bigger than a circustent
and everything began

when man determined to destroy
himself he picked the was
of shall and finding only why
smashed it into because

       —e. e. cummings

Reprinted by permission of Harcourt, Brace & World from e. e. cummings, *Poems: 1923–1954* (New York: Harcourt, Brace & World, 1944).

Guernica by Pablo Picasso.

THE FIDDLE AND THE DRUM

And so once again
My dear Johnny, my dear friend
And so once again
You are fightin' us all
And when I ask you why
You raise your sticks and cry, and I fall
Oh, my friend
How did you come
To trade the fiddle for the drum

You say I have turned
Like the enemies you've earned
But I can remember
All the good things you are
And so I ask you please
Can I help you find the peace and the star
Oh, my friend
What time is this
To trade the handshake for the fist

And so once again
Of America my friend
And so once again
You are fighting us all
And when we ask you why
You raise your sticks and cry and we fall
Oh, my friend
How did you come
To trade the fiddle for the drum

You say we have turned
Like the enemies you've earned
But we can remember
All the good things you are
And so we ask you please
Can we help you find the peace and the star
Oh, my friend
We have all come
To fear the beating of your drum.

—Joni Mitchell

Reprinted by permission of Harry Fox Agency and Siquomb
Publishing Corporation.

BY THE WATERS OF BABYLON

By Stephen Vincent Benét

The north and the west and the south are good hunting ground, but it is forbidden to go east. It is forbidden to go to any of the Dead Places except to search for metal and then he who touches the metal must be a priest or the son of a priest. Afterwards, both the man and the metal must be purified. These are the rules and the laws; they are well made. It is forbidden to cross the great river and look upon the place that was the Place of the Gods—this is most strictly forbidden. We do not even say its name though we know its name. It is there that spirits live, and demons—it is there that there are the ashes of the Great Burning. These things are forbidden—they have been forbidden since the beginning of time.

My father is a priest; I am the son of a priest. I have been in the Dead Places near us, with my father—at first, I was afraid. When my father went into the house to search for the metal, I stood by the door and my heart felt small and weak. It was a dead man's house, a spirit house. It did not have the smell of man, though there were old bones in a corner. But it is not fitting that a priest's son should show fear. I looked at the bones in the shadow and kept my voice still.

Then my father came out with the metal—a good, strong piece. He looked at me with both eyes but I had not run away. He gave me the metal to hold— I took it and did not die. So he knew that I was truly his son and would be a priest in my time. That was when I was very young—nevertheless, my brothers would not have done it, though they are good hunters. After that, they gave me the good piece of meat and the warm corner by the fire. My father watched over me—he was glad that I should be a priest. But when I boasted or wept without a reason, he punished me more strictly than my brothers. That was right.

After a time, I myself was allowed to go into the dead houses and search for metal. So I learned the ways of those houses—and if I saw bones, I was no longer afraid. The bones are light and old—sometimes they will fall into dust if you touch them. But that is a great sin.

I was taught the chants and the spells—I was taught how to stop the running

Reprinted by permission of Brandt & Brandt from Stephen Vincent Benét, *Selected Works of Stephen Vincent Benét*.

of blood from a wound and many secrets. A priest must know many secrets—that was what my father said.

If the hunters think we do all things by chants and spells, they may believe so—it does not hurt them. I was taught how to read in the old books and how to make the old writings—that was hard and took a long time. My knowledge made me happy—it was like a fire in my heart. Most of all, I liked to hear of the Old Days and the stories of the gods. I asked myself many questions that I could not answer, but it was good to ask them. At night, I would lie awake and listen to the wind—it seemed to me that it was the voice of the gods as they flew through the air.

We are not ignorant like the Forest People—our women spin wool on the wheel, our priests wear a white robe. We do not eat grubs from the tree, we have not forgotten the old writings, although they are hard to understand. Nevertheless, my knowledge and my lack of knowledge burned in me—I wished to know more. When I was a man at last, I came to my father and said, "It is time for me to go on my journey. Give me your leave."

He looked at me for a long time, stroking his beard, then he said at last, "Yes. It is time." That night, in the house of the priesthood, I asked for and received purification. My body hurt but my spirit was a cool stone. It was my father himself who questioned me about my dreams.

He bade me look into the smoke of the fire and see—I saw and told what I saw. It was what I have always seen—a river, and, beyond it, a great Dead Place and in it the gods walking. I have always thought about that. His eyes were stern when I told him—he was no longer my father but a priest. He said, "This is a strong dream."

"It is mine," I said, while the smoke waved and my head felt light. They were singing the Star song in the outer chamber and it was like the buzzing of bees in my head.

He asked me how the gods were dressed and I told him how they were dressed. We know how they were dressed from the book, but I saw them as if they were before me. When I had finished, he threw the sticks three times and studied them as they fell.

"This is a very strong dream," he said. "It may eat you up."

"I am not afraid," I said and looked at him with both eyes. My voice sounded thin in my ears but that was because of the smoke.

He touched me on the breast and the forehead. He gave me the bow and the three arrows.

"Take them," he said. "It is forbidden to travel east. It is forbidden to cross the river. It is forbidden to go to the Place of the Gods. All these things are forbidden."

"All these things are forbidden," I said, but it was my voice that spoke and not my spirit. He looked at me again.

"My son," he said. "Once I had young dreams. If your dreams do not eat you up, you may be a great priest. If they eat you, you are still my son. Now go on your journey."

I went fasting, as is the law. My body hurt but not my heart. When the dawn came, I was out of sight of the village. I prayed and purified myself, waiting for a sign. The sign was an eagle. It flew east.

Sometimes signs are sent by bad spirits. I waited again on the flat rock, fasting, taking no food. I was very still—I could feel the sky above me and the earth beneath. I waited till the sun was beginning to sink. Then three deer passed in the valley going east—they did not mind me or see me. There was a white fawn with them—a very great sign.

I followed them, at a distance, waiting for what would happen. My heart was troubled about going east, yet I knew that I must go. My head hummed with my fasting—I did not even see the panther spring upon the white fawn. But, before I knew it, the bow was in my hand. I shouted and the panther lifted his head from the fawn. It is not easy to kill a panther with one arrow but the arrow went through his eye and into his brain. He died as he tried to spring—he rolled over, tearing at the ground. Then I knew I was meant to go east—I knew that was my journey. When the night came, I made my fire and roasted meat.

It is eight suns' journey to the east and a man passes by many Dead Places. The Forest People are afraid of them but I am not. Once I made my fire on the edge of a Dead Place at night and, next morning, in the dead house, I found a good knife, little rusted. That was small to what came afterward but it made my heart feel big. Always when I looked for game, it was in front of my arrow, and twice I passed hunting parties of the Forest People without their knowing. So I knew my magic was strong and my journey clean, in spite of the law.

Toward the setting of the eighth sun, I came to the banks of the great river. It was half-a-day's journey after I had left the god-road—we do not use the god-roads now for they are falling apart into great blocks of stone, and the forest is safer going. A long way off, I had seen the water through trees but the trees were thick. At last, I came out upon an open place at the top of a cliff. There was the great river below, like a giant in the sun. It is very long, very wide. It could eat all the streams we know and still be thirsty. Its name is Ou-dis-sun, the Sacred, the Long. No man of my tribe had seen it, not even my father, the priest. It was magic and I prayed.

Then I raised my eyes and looked south. It was there, the Place of the Gods.

How can I tell what it was like—you do not know. It was there, in the red light, and they were too big to be houses. It was there with the red light upon it, mighty and ruined. I knew that in another moment the gods would see me. I covered my eyes with my hand; and crept back into the forest.

Surely, that was enough to do, and live. Surely it was enough to spend the night upon the cliff. The Forest People themselves do not come near. Yet, all through the night, I knew that I should have to cross the river and walk in the places of the gods, although the gods ate me up. My magic did not help me at all and yet there was a fire in my bowels, a fire in my mind. When the sun rose, I thought, "My journey has been clean. Now I will go home from my journey." But, even as I thought so, I knew I could not. If I went to the Place of the Gods, I would surely die, but, if I did not go, I could never be at peace with my spirit again. It is better to lose one's life than one's spirit, if one is a priest and the son of a priest.

Nevertheless, as I made the raft, the tears ran out of my eyes. The Forest People could have killed me without fight, if they had come upon me then, but they did not come. When the raft was made, I said the sayings for the dead and painted myself for death. My heart was cold as a frog and my knees like water, but the burning in my mind would not let me have peace. As I pushed the raft from the shore, I began my death song—I had the right. It was a fine song.

"I am John, son of John," I sang. "My people are the Hill People. They are the men.
I go into the Dead Places but I am not slain.
I take the metal from the Dead Places but I am not blasted.
I travel upon the god-roads and am not afraid. E-yah! I have killed the panther, I have killed the fawn!
E-yah! I have come to the great river. No man has come there before.
It is forbidden to go east, but I have gone, forbidden to go on the great river, but I am there.
Open your hearts, you spirits, and hear my song.
Now I go to the Place of the Gods, I shall not return.
My body is painted for death and my limbs weak, but my heart is big as I go to the Place of the Gods!"

All the same, when I came to the Place of the Gods, I was afraid, afraid. The current of the great river is very strong—it gripped my raft with its hands. That was magic, for the river itself is wide and calm. I could feel evil spirits about me, in the bright morning; I could feel their breath on my neck as I was swept down the stream. Never have I been so much alone—I tried to think of my knowledge, but it was a squirrel's heap of winter nuts. There was no strength in my knowledge any more and I felt small and naked as a new-hatched bird—alone upon the great river, the servant of the gods.

Yet, after a while, my eyes were opened and I saw. I saw both banks of the river—I saw that once there had been god-roads across it, though now they were broken and fallen like broken vines. Very great they were, and wonderful and broken—broken in the time of the Great Burning when the fire fell out of the sky. And always the current took me nearer to the Place of the Gods, and the huge ruins rose before my eyes.

I do not know the customs of rivers—we are the People of the Hills. I tried to guide my raft with the pole but it spun around. I thought the river meant to take me past the Place of the Gods and out into the Bitter Water of the legends. I grew angry then—my heart felt strong. I said aloud, "I am a priest and the son of a priest!" The gods heard me—they showed me how to paddle with the pole on one side of the raft. The current changed itself—I drew near to the Place of the Gods.

When I was very near, my raft struck and turned over. I can swim in our lakes—I swam to the shore. There was a great spike of rusted metal sticking out into the river—I hauled myself up upon it and sat there, panting. I had saved my bow and two arrows and the knife I found in the Dead Place but that was all. My raft went whirling downstream toward the Bitter Water. I looked after it, and thought if it had trod me under, at least I would be safely dead. Nevertheless, when I had dried my bowstring and re-strung it, I walked forward to the Place of the Gods.

It felt like ground underfoot; it did not burn me. It is not true what some of the tales say, that the ground there burns forever, for I have been there. Here and there were the marks and stains of the Great Burning, on the ruins, that is true. But they were old marks and old stains. It is not true either, what some of our priests say, that it is an island covered with fogs and enchantments. It is not. It is a great Dead Place—greater than any Dead Place we know. Everywhere in it there are god-roads, though most are cracked and broken. Everywhere there are the ruins of the high towers of the gods.

How shall I tell what I saw? I went carefully, my strung bow in my hand, my skin ready for danger. There should have been the wailings of spirits and the shrieks of demons, but there were not. It was very silent and sunny where I had landed—the wind and the rain and the birds that drop seeds had done their work—the grass grew in the cracks of the broken stone. It is a fair island—no wonder the gods built there. If I had come there, a god, I also would have built.

How shall I tell what I saw? The towers are not all broken—here and there one still stands, like a great tree in a forest, and the birds nest high. But the towers themselves look blind, for the gods are gone. I saw a fish-hawk, catching fish in the river. I saw a little dance of white butterflies over a great heap of broken stones and columns. I went there and looked about me—there was a carved stone with cut-letters, broken in half. I can read letters but I could not understand these. They said UBTREAS. There was also the shattered image of a man or a god. It had been made of white stone and he wore his hair tied back like a woman's. His name was ASHING, as I read on the cracked half of a stone. I thought it wise to pray to ASHING, though I do not know that god.

How shall I tell what I saw? There was no smell of man left, on stone or metal. Nor were there many trees in that wilderness of stone. There are many pigeons, nesting and dropping in the towers—the gods must have loved them, or, perhaps, they used them for sacrifices. There are wild cats that roam the god-roads, green-eyed, unafraid of man. At night they wail like demons but they are not demons. The wild dogs are more dangerous, for they hunt in a pack, but them I did not meet till later. Everywhere there are the carved stones, carved with magical numbers or words.

I went north—I did not try to hide myself. When a god or a demon saw me, then I would die, but meanwhile I was no longer afraid. My hunger for knowledge burned in me—there was so much that I could not understand. After a while, I knew that my belly was hungry. I could have hunted for my meat, but I did not hunt. It is known that the gods did not hunt as we do—they got their food from enchanted boxes and jars. Sometimes these are still found in the Dead Places—once, when I was a child and foolish, I opened such a jar and tasted it and found the food sweet. But my father found out and punished me for it strictly, for, often, that food is death. Now, though, I had long gone past what was forbidden, and I entered the likeliest towers, looking for the food of the gods.

A renewal of faith in common human nature, in its potentialities in general, and in its power in particular to respond to reason and truth, is a surer bulwark against totalitarianism than a demonstration of material success or a devout worship of special legal and political forms. *John Dewey*

I found it at last in the ruins of a great temple in the mid-city. A mighty temple it must have been, for the roof was painted like the sky at night with its stars—that much I could see, though the colors were faint and dim. It went down into great caves and tunnels—perhaps they kept their slaves there. But when I started to climb down, I heard the squeaking of rats, so I did not go—rats are unclean, and there must have been many tribes of them, from the squeaking. But near there, I found food, in the heart of a ruin, behind a door that still opened. I ate only the fruits from the jars—they had a very sweet taste. There was drink, too, in bottles of glass—the drink of the gods was strong and made my head swim. After I had eaten and drunk, I slept on the top of a stone, my bow at my side.

When I woke, the sun was low. Looking down from where I lay, I saw a dog sitting on his haunches. His tongue was hanging out of his mouth; he looked as if he were laughing. He was a big dog, with a gray-brown coat, as big as a wolf. I sprang up and shouted at him but he did not move—he just sat there as if he were laughing. I did not like that. When I reached for a stone to throw, he moved swiftly out of the way of the stone. He was not afraid of me; he looked at me as if I were meat. No doubt I could have killed him with an arrow, but I did not know if there were others. Moreover, night was falling.

I looked about me—not far away there was a great, broken god-road, leading north. The towers were high enough, but not so high, and while many of the dead-houses were wrecked, there were some that stood. I went toward this god-road, keeping to the heights of the ruins, while the dog followed. When I had reached the god-road, I saw that there were others behind him. If I had slept later, they would have come upon me asleep and torn out my throat. As it was, they were sure enough of me; they did not hurry. When I went into the dead-house, they kept watch at the entrance—doubtless they thought they would have a fine hunt. But a dog cannot open a door and I knew, from the books, that the gods did not like to live on the ground but on high.

I had just found a door I could open when the dogs decided to rush. Ha! They were surprised when I shut the door in their faces—it was a good door, of strong metal. I could hear their foolish baying beyond it but I did not stop to answer them. I was in darkness—I found stairs and climbed. There were many stairs, turning around till my head was dizzy. At the top was another door—I found the knob and opened it. I was in a long small chamber—on one side of it was a bronze door that could not be opened, for it had no handle. Perhaps there was a magic word to open it but I did not have the word. I turned to the door in the opposite side of the wall. The lock of it was broken and I opened it and went in.

Within, there was a place of great riches. The god who lived there must have been a powerful god. The first room was a small ante-room—I waited there for some time, telling the spirits of the place that I came in peace and not as a robber. When it seemed to me that they had had time to hear me, I went on. Ah, what riches! Few, even, of the windows had been broken—it was all as it had been. The great windows that looked over the city had not been broken at all though they were dusty and streaked with many years. There were coverings on the floors, the colors not greatly faded, and the chairs were soft and deep. There were pictures upon the walls, very strange, very wonderful—I remember one of a bunch of flowers in a jar—if you came close to it, you could see nothing but bits of color, but if you stood away from it, the flowers might have been picked yesterday. It made my heart feel strange to look at this picture—and to look at the figure of a bird, in some hard clay, on a table and see it so like our birds. Everywhere there were books and writings, many in tongues that I could not read. The god who lived there must have been a wise god and full of knowledge. I felt I had a right there, as I sought knowledge also.

Nevertheless, it was strange. There was a washing-place but no water— perhaps the gods washed in air. There was a cooking place but no wood, and though there was a machine to cook food, there was no place to put fire in it. Nor were there candles or lamps—there were things that looked like lamps but they had neither oil nor wick. All these things were magic, but I touched them and lived—the magic had gone out of them. Let me tell one thing to show. In the washing-place, a thing said "Hot" but it was not hot to the touch—another thing said "Cold" but it was not cold. This must have been a strong magic but the magic was gone. I do not understand—they had ways—I wish that I knew.

It was close and dry and dusty in their house of the gods. I have said the magic was gone but that is not true—it had gone from the magic things but it had not gone from the place. I felt the spirits about me, weighing upon me. Nor had I ever slept in a Dead Place before—and yet, tonight, I must sleep there. When I thought of it, my tongue felt dry in my throat, in spite of my wish for knowledge. Almost I would have gone down again and faced the dogs, but I did not.

I had not gone through all the rooms when the darkness fell. When it fell, I went back to the big room looking over the city and made fire. There was a place to make fire and a box with wood in it, though I do not think they cooked there. I wrapped myself in a floor-covering and slept in front of the fire—I was very tired.

Now I tell what is very strong magic. I woke in the midst of the night. When I woke, the fire had gone out and I was cold. It seemed to me that all around me there were whisperings and voices. I closed my eyes to shut them out. Some will say that I slept again, but I do not think that I slept. I could feel the spirits drawing my spirit out of my body as a fish is drawn on a line.

Why should I lie about it? I am a priest and the son of a priest. If there are spirits, as they say, in the small Dead Places near us, what spirits must there not be in that great Place of the Gods? And would not they wish to speak? After such long years? I know that I felt myself drawn as a fish is drawn on a line. I had stepped out of my body—I could see my body asleep in front of the cold fire, but it was not I. I was drawn to look out upon the city of the gods.

It should have been dark, for it was night, but it was not dark. Everywhere there were lights—lines of lights—circles and blurs of light—ten thousand torches would not have been the same. The sky itself was alight—you could barely see the stars for the glow in the sky. I thought to myself "This is strong magic" and trembled. There was a roaring in my ears like the rushing of rivers. Then my eyes grew used to the light and my ears to the sound. I knew that I was seeing the city as it had been when the gods were alive.

That was a sight indeed—yes, that was a sight: I could not have seen it in the body—my body would have died. Everywhere went the gods, on foot and in chariots—there were gods beyond number and counting and their chariots blocked the streets. They had turned night to day for their pleasure—they did not sleep with the sun. The noise of their coming and going was the noise of many waters. It was magic what they could do—it 'was magic what they did.

I looked out of another window—the great vines of their bridges were mended and the god-roads went east and west. Restless, restless, were the gods and always in motion! They burrowed tunnels under rivers—they flew in the air. With unbelievable tools they did giant works—no part of the earth was safe from them, for, if they wished for a thing, they summoned it from the other side of the world. And always, as they labored and rested, as they feasted and made love, there was a drum in their ears—the pulse of the giant city, beating and beating like a man's heart.

Were they happy? What is happiness to the gods? They were great, they were mighty, they were wonderful and terrible. As I looked upon them and their magic, I felt like a child—but a little more, it seemed to me, and they would pull down the moon from the sky. I saw them with wisdom beyond wisdom and knowledge beyond knowledge. And yet not all they did was well done—even I could see that—and yet their wisdom could not but grow until all was peace.

Then I saw their fate come upon them and that was terrible past speech. It came upon them as they walked the streets of their city. I have been in the fights with the Forest People—I have seen men die. But this was not like that. When gods war with gods, they use weapons we do not know. It was fire falling out of the sky and a mist that poisoned. It was the time of the Great Burning and the Destruction. They ran about like ants in the streets of their city—poor gods, poor gods! Then the towers began to fall. A few escaped—yes, a few. The legends tell it. But, even after the city had become a Dead Place, for many years the poison was still in the ground. I saw it happen, I saw the last of them die. It was darkness over the broken city and I wept.

All this, I saw. I saw it as I have told it, though not in the body. When I woke in the morning, I was hungry, but I did not think first of my hunger for my heart was perplexed and confused. I knew the reason for the Dead Places but I did not see why it had happened. It seemed to me it should not have happened, with all the magic they had. I went through the house looking for an answer. There was so much in the house I could not understand—and yet I am a priest and the son of a priest. It was like being on one side of the great river, at night, with no light to show the way.

Then I saw the dead god. He was sitting in his chair, by the window, in a room I had not entered before and, for the first moment, I thought that he was alive. Then I saw the skin on the back of his hand—it was like dry leather. The room was shut, hot and dry—no doubt that had kept him as he was. At first I was afraid to approach him—then the fear left me. He was sitting looking out over the city—he was dressed in the clothes of the gods. His age was neither young nor old—I could not tell his age. But there was wisdom in his face and great sadness. You could see that he would have not run away. He had sat at his window, watching his city die—then he himself had died. But it is better to lose one's life than one's spirit—and you could see from the face that his spirit had not been lost. I knew, that, if I touched him, he would fall into dust—and yet, there was something unconquered in the face.

That is all of my story, for then I knew he was a man—I knew then that they had been men, neither gods nor demons. It is a great knowledge, hard to tell and believe. They were men—they went a dark road, but they were men.

I had no fear after that—I had no fear going home, though twice I fought off the dogs and once I was hunted for two days by the Forest People. When I saw my father again, I prayed and was purified. He touched my lips and my breast, he said, "You went away a boy. You come back a man and a priest." I said, "Father, they were men! I have been in the Place of the Gods and seen it! Now slay me, if it is the law—but still I know they were men."

He looked at me out of both eyes. He said, "The law is not always the same shape—you have done what you have done. I could not have done it my time, but you come after me. Tell!"

I told and he listened. After that, I wished to tell all the people but he showed me otherwise. He said, "Truth is a hard deer to hunt. If you eat too much truth at once, you may die of the truth. It was not idly that our fathers forbade the Dead Places." He was right—it is better the truth should come little by little. I have learned that, being a priest. Perhaps, in the old days, they ate knowledge too fast.

Nevertheless, we make a beginning. It is not for the metal alone we go the Dead Places now—there are the books and the writings. They are hard to learn. And the magic tools are broken—but we can look at them and wonder. At least, we make a beginning. And, when I am chief priest we shall go beyond the great river. We shall go to the Place of the Gods—the place newyork—not one man but a company. We shall look for the images of the gods and find the god ASHING and the others—the gods LICOLN and BILTMORE and MOSES. But they were men who built the city, not gods or demons. They were men. I remember the dead man's face. They were men who were here before us. We must build again.

346

THE DANGERS OF A MILITARY-INDUSTRIAL COMPLEX

By D. D. Eisenhower

First, I should like to express my gratitude to the radio and television networks for the opportunities they have given me over the years to bring reports and messages to our nation. My special thanks go to them for the opportunity of addressing you this evening.

Three days from now, after half a century in the service of our country, I shall lay down the responsibilities of office as, in traditional and solemn ceremony, the authority of the Presidency is vested in my successor.

This evening I come to you with a message of leave-taking and farewell, and to share a few final thoughts with you, my countrymen.

Like every other citizen, I wish the new President, and all who will labor with him, Godspeed. I pray that the coming years will be blessed with peace and prosperity for all.

Our people expect their President and the Congress to find essential agreement on issues of great moment, the wise resolution of which will better shape the future of the nation.

My own relations with the Congress, which began on a remote and tenuous basis when, long ago, a member of the Senate appointed me to West Point, have since ranged to the intimate during the war and immediate postwar period, and, finally, to the mutually interdependent during these past eight years.

In this final relationship, the Congress and the Administration have, on most vital issues, co-operated well to serve the national good rather than mere partisanship, and so have assured that the business of the nation should go forward. So, my official relationship with the Congress ends in a feeling, on my part, of gratitude that we have been able to do so much together.

II

We now stand 10 years past the midpoint of a century that has witnessed four major wars among great nations. Three of these involved our own country. Despite these holocausts, America is today the strongest, the most influential and most productive nation in the world. Understandably proud of this pre-eminence, we yet realize that America's leadership and prestige depend, not merely upon our unmatched material progress, riches and military strength, but on how we use our power in the interest of world peace and human betterment.

III

Throughout America's adventure in free Government, our basic purposes have been to keep the peace; to foster progress in human achievement, and to enhance liberty, dignity and integrity among people and among nations. To strive for less would be unworthy of a free and religious people. Any failure traceable to arrogance or our lack of comprehension or readiness to sacrifice, would inflict upon us grievous hurt both at home and abroad.

Progress toward these noble goals is persistently threatened by the conflict now engulfing the world. It commands our whole attention, absorbs our very beings. We face a hostile ideology—global in scope, atheistic in character, ruthless in purpose and insidious in method. Unhappily, the danger it poses promises to be of indefinite duration. To meet it successfully there is called for, not so much the emotional and transitory sacrifices of crisis, but rather those which enable us to carry forward steadily, surely and without complaint the burdens of a prolonged and complex struggle—with liberty the stake. Only thus shall we remain, despite every provocation, on our charted course toward permanent peace and human betterment.

Crises there will continue to be. In meeting them, whether foreign or domestic, great or small, there is a recurring temptation to feel that some spectacular and costly action could become the miraculous solution to all current difficulties. A huge increase in newer elements of our defenses; development of unrealistic programs to cure every ill in agriculture; a dramatic expansion in basic and applied research—these and many other possibilities, each possibly promising in itself, may be suggested as the only way to the road we wish to travel.

But each proposal must be weighed in the light of a broader consideration: The need to maintain balance in and among national programs—balance between the private and the public economy; balance between cost and hoped-for advantages; balance between the clearly necessary and the comfortably desirable; balance between our essential requirements as a nation and the duties imposed by the nation upon the individual; balance between actions of the moment and the national welfare of the future. Good judgment seeks balance and progress; lack of it eventually finds imbalance and frustration.

The record of many decades stands as proof that our people and their Government have, in the main,

understood these truths and have responded to them well, in the face of stress and threat. But threats, new in kind or degree, constantly arise. Of these, I mention two only.

IV

A vital element in keeping the peace is our military establishment. Our arms must be mighty, ready for instant action, so that no potential aggressor may be tempted to risk his own destruction.

Our military organization today bears little relation to that known by any of my predecessors in peacetime, or indeed by the fighting men of World War II or Korea.

Until the latest of our world conflicts, the United States had no armaments industry. American makers of plowshares could, with time and as required, make swords as well. But now we can no longer risk emergency improvisation of national defense; we have been compelled to create a permanent armaments industry of vast proportions. Added to this, 3.5 million men and women are directly engaged in the defense establishment. We annually spend on military security alone more than the net income of all United States corporations.

This conjunction of an immense military establishment and a large arms industry is new in the American experience. The total influence—economic, political, even spiritual—is felt in every city, every statehouse, every office of the Federal Government. We recognize the imperative need for this development. Yet we must not fail to comprehend its grave implications. Our toil, resources and livelihood are all involved; so is the very structure of our society.

In the councils of Government, we must guard against the acquisition

If a nation expects to be ignorant and free, it expects what never was and never will be. *Thomas Jefferson*

of unwarranted influence, whether sought or unsought, by the military-industrial complex. The potential for the disastrous rise of misplaced power exists and will persist.

We must never let the weight of this combination endanger our liberties or democratic processes. We should take nothing for granted. Only an alert and knowledgeable citizenry can compel the proper meshing of the huge industrial and military machinery of defense with our peaceful methods and goals, so that security and liberty may prosper together.

Akin to, and largely responsible for the sweeping changes in our industrial-military posture, has been the technological revolution during recent decades.

In this revolution, research has become central; it also becomes more formalized, complex and costly. A steadily increasing share is conducted for, by, or at the direction of the Federal Government.

Today, the solitary inventor, tinkering in his shop, has been overshadowed by task forces of scientists in laboratories and testing fields. In the same fashion, the free university, historically the fountainhead of free ideas and scientific discovery, has experienced a revolution in the conduct of research. Partly because of the huge costs involved, a Government contract becomes virtually a substitute for intellectual curiosity. For every blackboard there are now hundreds of new electronic computers.

The prospect of domination of the nation's scholars by federal employ-ment, project allocations, and the power of money is ever present—and is gravely to be regarded.

Yet, in holding scientific research and discovery in respect, as we should, we must also be alert to the equal and opposite danger that public policy could itself become the captive of a scientific-technological elite.

It is the task of statesmanship to mold, to balance and to integrate these and other forces, new and old, within the principles of our democratic system—ever aiming toward the supreme goals of our free society.

V

Another factor in maintaining balance involves the element of time. As we peer into society's future, we—you and I, and our Government—must avoid the impulse to live only for today, plundering, for our own ease and convenience, the precious resources of tomorrow. We cannot mortgage the material assets of our grandchildren without risking the loss also of their political and spiritual heritage. We want democracy to survive for all generations to come, not to become the insolvent phantom of tomorrow.

VI

Down the long lane of the history yet to be written, America knows that this world of ours, ever growing smaller, must avoid becoming a community of dreadful fear and hate, and be, instead, a proud confederation of mutual trust and respect.

Such a confederation must be one of equals. The weakest must come to the conference table with the same confidence as do we, protected as we are by our moral, economic and military strength. That table, though scarred by many past frustrations, cannot be abandoned for the certain agony of the battlefield.

Disarmament, with mutual honor and confidence, is a continuing imperative. Together we must learn how to compose differences, not with arms, but with intellect and decent purpose. Because this need is so sharp and apparent, I confess that I lay down my official responsibilities in this field with a definite sense of disappointment. As one who has witnessed the horror and the lingering sadness of war—as one who knows that another war could utterly destroy this civilization which has been so slowly and painfully built over thousands of years—I wish I could say tonight that a lasting peace is in sight.

Happily, I can say that war has been avoided. Steady progress toward our ultimate goal has been made. But —so much remains to be done. As a private citizen, I shall never cease to do what little I can to help the world advance along that road.

VII

So—in this, my last "good night" to you as your President—I thank you for the many opportunities you have given me for public service in war and in peace. I trust that, in that service, you find some things worthy; as for the rest of it, I know you will find ways to improve performance in the future. You and I—my fellow citizens—need to be strong in our faith that all nations, under God, will reach the goal of peace with justice. May we be ever unswerving in devotion to principle, confident but humble with power, diligent in pursuit of the nation's great goals.

To all the peoples of the world, I once more give expression to America's prayerful and continuing aspiration:

We pray that peoples of all faiths, all races, all nations, may have their great human needs satisfied; that those now denied opportunity shall come to enjoy it to the full; that all who yearn for freedom may experience its spiritual blessings; that those who have freedom will understand, also, its heavy responsibilities; that all who are insensitive to the needs of others will learn charity; that the scourges of poverty, disease and ignorance will be made to disappear from the earth, and that, in the goodness of time, all peoples will come to live together in a peace guaranteed by the binding force of mutual respect and love.

Now, on Friday noon I am to become a private citizen. I am proud to do so. I look forward to it.

The world has never had a good definition of the word liberty, and the American people, just now, are much in want of one.   *A. Lincoln*

THE CONQUERORS

It seems vainglorious and proud
Of Atom-man to boast aloud
    His prowess homicidal
When one remembers how for years,
With their rude stones and humble spears,
Our sires, at wiping out their peers,
    Were almost never idle.

Despite his under-fissioned art
The Hittite made a splendid start
    Toward smiting lesser nations;
While Tamerlane, it's widely known,
Without a bomb to call his own
    Destroyed whole populations.

Nor did the ancient Persian need
Uranium to kill his Mede,
    The Viking earl, his foeman.
The Greeks got excellent results
With swords and engined catapults.
    A chariot served the Roman.

Mere cannon garnered quite a yield
On Waterloo's tempestuous field.
    At Hastings and at Flodden
Stout countrymen, with just a bow
And arrow, laid their thousands low.
    And Gettysburg was sodden.

Though doubtless now our shrewd machines
Can blow the world to smithereens
    More tidily and so on,
Let's give our ancestors their due.
Their ways were coarse, their weapons few.
But ah! how wondrously they slew
    With what they had to go on.

    —Phyllis McGinley

Reprinted by permission of The Viking Press from Phyllis McGinley, *Times Three* (New York: The Viking Press, 1959).

THE DUAL CRISIS IN SCIENCE AND SOCIETY

By Barry Commoner

There is ample, tragic evidence of a deep crisis in the human condition. We struggle to live and to create in the shadow of death and destruction. More than two-thirds of the world population is either undernourished or on the verge of starvation. Even in the wealthiest nation in human history —the United States of 1968—many citizens are still struggling to emerge from poverty and win a just share of the nation's wealth. Spurred by such want, in the last fifty years the world has been shaken by a series of revolutions that have drastically changed the economic, social, and political structure of most of its nations—the USSR, China, India, nearly all of Africa and the Middle East, and most of Latin America. In that period of time the world has endured two great wars; in the last decade this nation has undertaken two major wars in the Far East, and one of them, in Vietnam, continues its desperate course. In the last half century the world has been in constant turmoil, which year by year has spread, become more complex, and vastly more dangerous.

The achievements of science and technology contrast vividly with the quality of life: we can nourish a man in the supreme isolation of outer space, but we cannot adequately feed the children of Calcutta or of Harlem. We hope to analyze life on other planets, but we have not yet learned to understand our own neighbors. We are attempting to live on the moon, but cannot yet live peacefully on the earth.

This is a terrible and frightening paradox: in the world of nature man exhibits—apparently—a magnificent competence; but in his own world, in human society, man appears to be a gross incompetent. The usual explanation of this paradox is that we are competent in the realm of science because no value judgments are demanded, and that we are tragically incompetent in dealing with each other because this does require adjustment between personal values and the social good—an adjustment of which we are frequently incapable.

I should like to propose another explanation: that the contrast between our technological competence and our

Reprinted by permission of Jossey-Bass, Publishers from G. Kerry Smith, ed., *Stress and Campus Response* (San Francisco: Jossey-Bass, Publishers, 1968), pp. 15–26.

ethical ineptitude is only apparent. We are tragically blind, I believe, not only about our fellow men, but also about important aspects of nature; we are dangerously incompetent not only in our relations with each other, but also in our relations to the natural world; our survival is threatened not only by a growing social crisis, but also by a technological crisis. And I believe that we must understand the deep connections between these crises if we are to learn how human values can guide the power of science and technology toward the improvement of the human condition and, indeed, if we are to survive these recent acquisitions of power.

There is an insidious logic that implies that men must adapt to machines, not machines to men; that production, speed, novelty, progress at any price must come first, and people second; that mechanization may be pushed as far as human endurance will allow. *Stewart L. Udall*

One of the striking features of

modern life is a deep and widespread faith in the efficacy of science and in the usefulness of technological progress. But there is now at least one good reason to question this faith: the phenomenon that has just begun to capture the public attention that it merits—environmental pollution. The rapid deterioration of the environment in which we live has become a chief determinant of the quality of our lives. We all know the dismal list: air pollution; pollution of water by urban and industrial wastes and by runoff of farmland fertilizer; multiple hazards of widespread dissemination of insecticides, herbicides, and fungicides; radiation hazards from fallout due to nuclear testing; and—for the future, if we make the catastrophic blunder— the consequences for the biology of man, beast, and plant of the massive nuclear, chemical, and biological weapons of modern war. These issues exemplify a general fault in the large-scale application of modern science to technology. We used to be told that nuclear testing was perfectly harmless. Only now, long after the damage has been done, we know differently. In October 1956, President Eisenhower had this to say about nuclear testing: "The continuance of the present rate of H-bomb testing, by the most sober and responsible scientific judgment, does not imperil the health of man." In October 1964, eight years later, President Johnson, in connection with the nuclear test-ban treaty, said:

This treaty has halted the steady, menacing increase of radioactive fallout. The deadly products of atomic explosions were poisoning our soil and our food and the milk our children drank and the air we all breathe. Radioactive deposits were being formed in increasing quantity in the teeth and bones of young Americans. Radioactive poisons were beginning to threaten the safety of people throughout the world. They were a growing menace to the health of every unborn child.

Clearly, in 1956 the government thought that there was no harm associated with nuclear tests; but we exploded the bombs *before* we knew the biological and medical consequences.

This pattern is characteristic of many other accomplishments of modern science and technology. We produced power plants and automobiles, which envelop our cities in smog— before anyone understood its harmful effects on health. We synthesized and disseminated new insecticides—before anyone learned that they also kill birds and might be harmful to people. We produced synthetic detergents and put billions of pounds into our surface waters—before we realized that they would not be degraded in disposal systems and would pollute our water supplies. We are now, in Vietnam, spraying herbicides on an unprecedented scale—with no knowledge of their long-term effects on the life of that unhappy land. We are fully prepared to conduct a nuclear war—even though its effects on life, soil, and the weather may destroy our civilization.

Clearly we have compiled a record of serious failures in recent encounters with the environment. This record shows that we do not yet understand the environment well enough to make new large-scale intrusions on it with a reasonable expectation of accurately predicting the consequences.

This failure raises two important questions about the relations between science and technology and human values. First, what are the relative roles of science and human desires in the resolution of the important issues generated by our failures in the environment? Next, what are the causes of these failures, and how do they illuminate the dual crisis in technology and human affairs?

How can we resolve the grave public issues generated by our assaults on the environment? Sometimes it is suggested that since scientists and engineers have made the bombs, insecticides, and autos, they ought to be responsible for deciding how to deal with the resultant hazards. More cogently, it is argued that scientists and technologists are the only people who can resolve these issues. Here is the rationale of this position: scientists have the relevant technical facts essential to understanding the major public issues generated by new technology. Since scientists are trained to analyze the complex forces at work in such issues, they have an ability for rational thought that frees them, to some degree, of the emotions that encumber the ordinary citizen's views of these calamitous issues. And because the scientist is now in a particularly favorable position to be heard when he speaks—by government executives, congressional committees, the press, and the people at large—he has important opportunities to influence these social decisions.

There is a basic flaw in this position. Resolving the social issues imposed on us by modern scientific progress requires a decision based not on scientific laws, but on value judgments. What scientific procedure can determine, for example, whether the benefits of nuclear testing to the national interest outweigh the hazards of fallout? How can scientific method determine who is right—the proponents of urban superhighways or those who complain about the resultant smog? What scientific principle can

tell us how to make the choice—which may be forced upon us by the insecticide problem—between the shade of the elm tree and the song of the robin? Certainly, science can validly describe the information to be gained from a nuclear experiment, the economic value of a highway, the medical hazard of radioactive contamination or of smog. However, the choice of the balance point between benefit and hazard is a value judgment; it is based on ideals of social good, or morality, or religion—but not on science. And if this balance is a social and moral judgment, it ought to be decided, not by scientists and technologists alone, but by *all* citizens.

How can a citizen make such judgments? These issues require a confrontation between human values and rather complex scientific data: the ecology of strontium-90 and herbicides, the chemistry of smog, the interactions between urban waste and runoff of farmland fertilizer. But most citizens are poorly prepared to understand such scientific matters. The solution demands of the scientist a new duty. I believe that scientists, as the custodians of the technical knowledge relevant to these public issues, have an obligation to bring this information before their fellow citizens in understandable terms. By this means scientists can place the decisions for the grave issues they have helped to create in the proper hands—an informed citizenry.

This duty is now recognized by many scientists in the United States. There is a growing movement among them to inform the public about the scientific basis of major social issues such as military and domestic aspects of nuclear power and environmental contamination. To the academic community in St. Louis, it is a source of pride that scientists and citizens in our own city have pioneered in this important work. And, at my own university, we have begun in some courses to teach science not simply as a discipline sufficient unto itself, but as the substance of the new political, social, and moral issues that trouble the modern world.

Nowhere is the urgency of this new task more clearly seen than in the matter of nuclear war. The scientific facts now available tell us that the entire system of nuclear war is incapable of fulfilling the prime purpose of national defense—preservation of our society. Our present military system's reliance on nuclear power is therefore futile. But the horrible face of nuclear war can be described only in scientific terms; it can be pictured only in the language of megatonnage and roentgens. The scientist has an obligation to help his fellow citizens penetrate the technological mask that hides the self-destructiveness of nuclear war. If he fails in his duty, the scientist will have deprived humanity of the right to sit in judgment on its own fate.

For these reasons I believe that the new duty of the scientist to inform his fellow men is the key to the humane use of the new powers of science. By this act the scientist can open the momentous issues of the modern world to the judgment of humanity. And it is only this judgment that has the strength to direct the enormous power of science toward the welfare of man.

How can we account for our recent failures in the environment, and what can we learn from such an inquiry about the relationship between science and technology and human values? These failures reveal a fundamental difficulty in the area of basic research on which we must rely for knowledge about the biological systems that are at risk in the environment. Biology has become a flourishing and well-supported science in the United States; it is producing a wealth of new knowledge, and is training many scientists skilled in its new methodology. But modern biological research is now dominated by the conviction that the most fruitful way to understand life is to discover a specific molecular event that can be identified as "the mechanism" of a particular biological process. The complexities of soil biology or the delicate balance of the nitrogen cycle in a river, which are not reducible to simple molecular mechanisms, are now often regarded as uninteresting relics of some ancient craft. In the pure glow of molecular biology, the biology of sewage is a dull and distasteful study hardly worth the attention of a "modern" biologist.

It is not surprising, then, that in contrast to the rapid increase in our knowledge of the molecular features of life, research on environmental biology has been slow. For example, the fundamental biology of soil nitrogen is still so poorly understood that we cannot, even today, draw up a reliable balance sheet to describe the fate of the huge tonnage of nitrogen fertilizer added yearly to the soil—much of which runs off the soil and contaminates the water.

For these reasons I believe that if we are to succeed as inhabitants of a world increasingly transformed by technology, we must reassess our attitudes toward the natural world on which our technology intrudes. Primitive people always see man as a dependent part of nature, a frail reed in a harsh world, governed by immutable processes that must be obeyed if he is to survive. The knowledge of nature primitive peoples achieve is remarkable. The African bushman survives in one of the most stringent habitats on earth; food is scarce, water even more so, and extremes of weather come rapidly. In this environment the bushman survives because he has an incredibly intimate understanding of the environment in which he lives. A bushman can, for example, return after many months and miles of travel to find a single underground tuber, noted in his previous wanderings, when he needs it for his water supply.

We claim to have escaped from such dependence on the environment. Where the bushman must squeeze water from a searched-out tuber, we get ours by the turn of a tap. Instead of trackless wastes, we have the grid of city streets; instead of seeking the sun's heat when we need it, or shunning it when it is too strong, we warm ourselves and cool ourselves with man-made machines. All this tends to foster the idea that we have made our own environment and no longer depend on the one provided by nature. In the eager search for the benefits of modern science and technology we have become enticed into a nearly fatal illusion: that we have at last escaped from the dependence of man on the balance of nature.

The truth is tragically different. We have become not less dependent on the balance of nature but more dependent on it. Modern technology has so stressed the web of processes in the living environment at its most vulnerable points that there is little leeway left in the system. Unless we begin to match our technological power with a deeper understanding of the balance of nature, we run the risk of destroying this planet as a place suitable for human habitation. Despite our vaunted mastery of nature, we in the "advanced" countries are far less competent inhabitants of our environment than the bushmen are of theirs.

We are brilliantly successful at managing those processes that can be confined to a laboratory or a factory, but this success dwindles at the doorstep.

Perhaps *the* basic inadequacy of modern science is its neglect of systems and processes that are intrinsically complex. Certainly this failing is evident in our environmental problems. The systems at risk in environmental pollution are natural and, because they are natural, complex. For this reason they are not readily approached by the atomistic methodology characteristic of modern biological research. Water pollutants stress the total ecological web that ties together the numerous organisms that inhabit lakes and rivers; their effects on the whole natural system are not adequately described by laboratory studies of pure cultures of separate organisms. Smog attacks the self-protective mechanism of the human lung; its noxious effects on man are not accountable by an influence on a single enzyme or even a single tissue. If, for the sake of analytical detail, molecular constituents are isolated from the smashed remains of a cell, or single organisms are separated from their natural neighbors, what is lost is the network of interrelationships that crucially determines the properties of the natural whole. Therefore any new basic knowledge that is expected to elucidate environmental biology, and guide our efforts to understand and control pollution, must be relevant to the entire natural biological systems in which these problems exist.

Nor is our neglect of complex systems limited to environmental biology. A further neglect is quickly revealed, for example, by a brief inquiry into the state of modern computer science. Shortly before he died, Norbert Wiener, the mathematician who did so much to develop cybernetics, the science of designing computers, warned us about the problem. He cited, as a parable, experience with computers that had been programmed to play checkers. Engineers built into the electronic circuits a correct understanding of the rules of checkers, and also a way of judging (from a stored record of its opponents' moves) what moves were most likely to beat the human opponents. The first results of the checker tournaments between the computer and its human programmers were that the machine started out playing an accurate but uninspired game that was easy to beat. But after about ten or twenty hours of practice, the machine got the hang of it, and from then on the machine always won. Wiener concluded that it had become technically possible to build automatic machines to carry out very complex activities that elude the comprehension of their operators and that "most definitely escape from the complete effective control of the man who has made them."

Recently this difficulty has become painfully evident to the specialists who are attempting to manage the operation of the current generation of electronic computers. They are extraordinarily frustrated men. They have at their disposal beautifully designed machines, capable, in theory, of complex interdigitation of numerous mathematical operations. However, the operators have not yet learned how to operate these machines at their full capacity for complex computations without encountering inexplicable errors. A spectacular example of a similar difficulty is the New England power blackout of November 1965, in which a complex powerline network, designed to effect an even distribution of generating capacity over an 80,000 square mile area, failed. Instead of providing outside power to a local

Canadian power system that had suffered a relay failure, the network acted in reverse and caused every connected power system to shut down. And a frightening potential catastrophe is the possibility that the complex, computer-guided missile systems—which can in minutes thrust us into the last World War—are equally susceptible to such failures.

There is, I believe, a common cause for our failures in situations as diverse as a power network and fallout. A power network or a computer is a machine of enormous internal complexity. What the failures tell us is that it has now become possible to construct machines that are so internally complicated as to overreach our present capability to understand complex systems. Our inability to understand the fallout problem or environmental pollution has a similar source, except that here the complete system involved is not made by man, but by nature.

It is not a coincidence, I believe, that the scientific and technological problems that affect the human condition involve inherently complex systems. Life, as we live it, is rarely encompassed by a single academic discipline. Real problems that affect our lives and impinge on what we value rarely fit into the neat categories that appear in the college catalogue: medieval history, nuclear physics, or molecular biology. For example, to encompass in our minds the terrifying deterioration of our cities we need to know not only the principles of economics, architecture, and social planning, but also the chemistry of airsheds, the biology of water systems, and the ecology of the domestic rat and the cockroach. In a word, we need to understand science and technology that is *relevant* to the human condition.

However, we in the university

community have been brought up in a different tradition. We have a justified pride in our intellectual independence, and know—for we often have to battle to maintain it—how essential this independence is to the search for truth. But academic people may sometimes tend to translate intellectual independence into a kind of mandatory disinterest in all problems that do not arise in their own minds—an approach that may in some cases cut them off from their students and from the real and urgent needs of society—such as a habitable environment.

We university scientists have a clear obligation to the society that supports us. Supported by that society, we have gained a deep knowledge of nature; our universities are the custodians of this knowledge. And as the custodians of knowledge won at social expense, we have the solemn duty to make that knowledge useful to society. We have no right, I believe, to retreat behind the walls of our laboratories, if—as it must—our knowledge of the world can, help improve that world as a place for human habitation.

If we accept this duty, how can we make it jibe with the principle of academic freedom, so firmly associated with the life of learning, which holds that every scholar should be free to pursue the studies that interest him and free to express whatever conclusions the evidence and the powers of his mind may generate? Does not such protection give him immunity from the students' appeal for relevance and from the demands of society for service to its needs? Is not this protection essential to the intellectual independence of the university and the justification for its freedom from political restraints?

There are no simple answers to these questions, but a useful guide has been given by a man who has contributed much to the making of the modern American university—Alexander Meiklejohn. According to Meiklejohn, academic freedom is not a special immunity from social responsibility, but, on the contrary, a basic part of the duty the university and the scholar owe to society. The university, he believes, is an institution established by society to fill its own need for knowledge about the nature of the world and man. For no society can long endure unless it takes into account the laws of nature and the aspirations of man. The scholar's search for the truth is thus not merely an obligation to himself, to his profession, or to the university, but a duty to society. And in this search open discourse is essential, for no scholar's work is complete or faultless; and the truth—whether it relates to the mechanism of biological inheritance, to the medical effects of fallout, or to the political origins of the war in Vietnam—can emerge only from the interaction, open and unconstrained, among the views of the separate scholars that make up the academic community. The scholar's duty is not to truth for its own sake, but to truth for society's sake. As Meiklejohn says, our final responsibility as scholars and teachers is not to the truth, but to the people who need the truth.

The scholar's work, therefore, must be devoted not only to the truth, but to human needs; the scholar's duty becomes, thereby, inevitably coupled to social issues. But if we accept relevance to social need as an important criterion for the choice of a field of inquiry, we, and the society that supports us, must recognize, as a necessary consequence, that scholars will become concerned not only with social needs, but with social goals. We cannot ask a physician, a biochemist, or a historian to dedicate his inquiring mind to society's needs without at the same time expecting him to be equally inquisitive about what those needs are, and what he thinks they ought to be. He will be motivated in his work not only by a concern for the truth about nature and man, but by an equally strong sense of engagement in the problems of society. And if society expects the scholar to honor a duty toward the development of socially significant knowledge, society must equally honor his freedom openly to express a concern with social goals. Those whom we serve should see in our zeal for this freedom not the selfish exercise of privilege, but a response to these solemn obligations.

The academic world is now emerging from a long period of silence, a silence that has obscured the true purpose of the university, and has weakened its service to society. We now hear many new voices in the universities. Some speak in the traditional well-modulated language of the scholar, some in the sharper tones of dissent, and some in a new language that is concerned less with transmitting ideas than feelings. But behind nearly all the voices is a mutual concern with the quality of life. Among our students this concern is often reduced to its most elementary level—a demand for the right to life itself. And this is natural, for our students represent the first generation of human beings who have grown to adulthood under the constant threat of instant annihila-

tion. Our own generation—yours and mine—is often criticized because we have, with our own minds and hands, created the weapon of total human destruction; we invented the first nuclear bomb, and worse, we have built and deployed for instant release enough of them to ensure the destruction of humanity. But an even greater sin is that our generation has become numb to the frightful meaning of what we have done. We can speak, with relative calm, of the choice between a war that kills fifty million people or one that kills a hundred million; the very effort to apply logic to a situation that is in its entirety totally inhumane, is, in effect, a confession of our own inhumanity.

The newer generation, our students, have a different way of sensing these things. If nuclear death threatens our generation with an earlier end to an already in part fulfilled life, it threatens theirs with the total loss of a life yet to be fulfilled. They, far better than we, can sense the total inhumanity of the civilization that we share. If they fail to suggest a reasonable way out they have at least defined what it is that we must try to escape. We need the sharpness of their definition of the issues; they need from us the competence and steady purpose that is the gift of experience. Together we can, I believe, secure for all of us what is so gravely threatened by the dual crisis in science and in society—a technology that serves the life of man and a society that cherishes the right to life.

MAN'S CONCERN MUST BE LIFE, NOT DEATH

By George Wald

All of you know that in the last couple of years there has been student unrest breaking at times into violence in many parts of the world: in England, Germany, Italy, Spain, Mexico and, needless to say, in many parts of this country. There has been a great deal of discussion as to what it all means.

Perfectly clearly, it means something different in Mexico from what it does in France, and something different in France from what it does in Tokyo, and something different in Tokyo from what it does in this country. Yet unless we are to assume that students have gone crazy all over the world, or that they have just decided that it's the thing to do, there must be some common meaning.

I don't need to go so far afield to look for that meaning. I am a teacher, and at Harvard, I have a class of about 350 students—men and women—most of them freshmen and sophomores. Over these past few years I have felt increasingly that something is terribly wrong—and this year ever so much more than last. Something has gone sour, in teaching and in learning. It's almost as though there were a widespread feeling that education has become irrelevant.

A lecture is much more of a dialogue than many of you probably appreciate. As you lecture, you keep watching the faces, and information keeps coming back to you all the time. I began to feel, particularly this year, that I was missing much of what was coming back. I tried asking the students, but they didn't or couldn't help me very much.

But I think I know what's the matter, even a little better than they do. I think that this whole generation of students is beset with a profound uneasiness. I don't think that they have yet quite defined its source. I think I understand the reasons for their uneasiness even better than they do. What is more, I share their uneasiness.

What's bothering these students? Some of them tell you it's the Vietnam war. I think the Vietnam war is the most shameful episode in the whole of American history.

The concept of war crimes is an

American invention. We've committed many war crimes in Vietnam, but I'll tell you something interesting about that. We were committing war crimes in World War II, even before the Nuremburg trials were held and the principle of war crimes started. The saturation bombing of German cities was a war crime, and if we had lost the war, some of our leaders might have had to answer for it.

I've gone through all of that history lately, and I find that there's a gimmick in it. It isn't written out, but I think we established it by precedent. That gimmick is that if one can allege that one is repelling or retaliating for an aggression—after that everything goes.

And you see, we are living in a world in which all wars are wars of defense. All War Departments are now Defense Departments. This is all part of the double talk of our time. The aggressor is always on the other side.

And I suppose this is why our ex-Secretary of State, Dean Rusk—a man in whom repetition takes the place of reason and stubbornness takes the place of character—went to such pains to insist, as he still insists, that in Vietnam we are repelling an aggression. And if that's what we are doing—so runs the doctrine—anything goes.

If the concept of war crimes is ever to mean anything, they will have to be defined as categories of acts, regardless of provocation. But that isn't so now.

I think we've lost that war, as a lot of other people think, too. The Vietnamese have a secret weapon. It's their willingness to die beyond our willingness to kill. In effect, they've been saying, you can kill us, but you'll have to kill a lot of us, you may have to kill all of us. And thank heavens, we are not yet ready to do that.

Yet we have come a long way—far enough to sicken many Americans, far enough even to sicken our fighting men, far enough so that our national symbols have gone sour. How many of you can sing about "the rockets' red glare, bombs bursting in air" without thinking, those are our bombs and our rockets bursting over South Vietnamese villages?

When those words were written, we were a people struggling for freedom against oppression. Now we are supporting real or thinly disguised military dictatorships all over the world, helping them to control and repress peoples struggling for their freedom.

But that Vietnam war, shameful and terrible as it is, seems to me only an immediate incident in a much larger and more stubborn situation.

Part of my trouble with students is that almost all the students I teach were born since World War II. Just after World War II, a series of new and abnormal procedures came into American life. We regarded them at the time as temporary aberrations. We thought we would get back to normal American life some day.

But those procedures have stayed with us now for more than 20 years, and those students of mine have never known anything else. They think those things are normal. They think we've always had a Pentagon, that we have always had a big army and that we always had a draft. But those are all new things in American life, and I think that they are incompatible with what America meant before.

How many of you realize that just before World War II, the entire American army, including the Air Force, numbered 139,000 men? Then World War II started, but we weren't yet in it; and seeing that there was great trouble in the world, we doubled this army to 268,000 men. Then in World War II, it got to be eight million.

And then World War II came to an end, and we prepared to go back to a peacetime army somewhat as the American army had always been before. And indeed in 1950—you think about 1950, our international commitments, the cold war, the Truman Doctrine and all the rest of it—in 1950 we got down to 600,000 men.

Now we have 3.5 million men under arms: about 600,000 in Vietnam, about 300,000 more in "support areas" elsewhere in the Pacific, about 250,000 in Germany. And there are a lot at home. Some months ago we were told that 300,000 National Guardsmen and 200,000 reservists had been specially trained for riot duty in the cities.

I say the Vietnam war is just an immediate incident, because so long as we keep that big army, it will always find things to do. If the Vietnam war stopped tomorrow, with that big a military establishment, the chances are that we would be in another such adventure abroad or at home before you knew it.

As for the draft: Don't reform the draft—get rid of it.

A peacetime draft is the most un-American thing I know. All the time I was growing up, I was told about oppressive Central European countries and Russia, where young men were forced into the army, and I was told what they did about it. They chopped off a finger, or shot off a couple of toes; or better still, if they could manage it, they came to this country. And we understood that, and sympathized, and were glad to welcome them.

Now, by present estimates, 4000 to 6000 Americans of draft age have left this country for Canada, another 2000 or 3000 have gone to Europe and it looks as though many more are preparing to emigrate.

A few months ago, I received a letter from the *Harvard Alumni Bulletin* posing a series of questions that students might ask a professor involving what to do about the draft. I was asked to write what I would tell those students. All I had to say to those students was this: If any of them had decided to evade the draft and asked my help, I would help him in any way I could.

I would feel as I suppose members of the underground railway felt in pre-Civil War days, helping runaway slaves to get to Canada. It wasn't altogether a popular position then, but what do you think of it now?

A bill to stop the draft was recently introduced in the Senate (S. 503), sponsored by a group of Senators that ran the gamut from McGovern and Hatfield to Barry Goldwater. I hope it goes through; but any time I find that Barry Goldwater and I are in agreement, that makes one take another look.

And indeed, there are choices in getting rid of the draft. I think that when we get rid of the draft, we must also cut back the size of the armed forces. It seems to me that in peacetime a total of one million men is surely enough. If there is an argument for American military forces of more than one million men in peacetime, I should like to hear that argument debated.

There is another thing being said closely connected with this: that to keep an adequate volunteer army, one would have to raise the pay considerably. That's said so positively and often that people believe it. I don't think it is true.

The great bulk of our present

armed forces are genuine volunteers. Among first-term enlistments, 49 percent are true volunteers. Another 30 percent are so-called "reluctant volunteers," persons who volunteer under pressure of the draft. Only 21 percent are draftees. All re-enlistments, of course, are true volunteers.

So the great majority of our present armed forces are true volunteers. Whole services are composed entirely of volunteers: the Air Force, for example, the submarine service, the Marines. That seems like proof to me that present pay rates are adequate.

One must add that an act of Congress in 1967 raised the base pay throughout the services in three installments, the third installment still to come, on April 1, 1969. So it is hard to understand why we are being told that to maintain adequate armed services on a volunteer basis will require large increases in pay; they will cost an extra $17 billion per year. It seems plain to me that we can get all the armed forces we need as volunteers, and at present rates of pay.

But there is something ever so much bigger and more important than the draft. The bigger thing, of course, is what ex-President Eisenhower warned us of, calling it the military-industrial complex. I am sad to say that we must begin to think of it now as the military-industrial-labor union complex.

What happened under the plea of the cold war was not alone that we built up the first big peacetime army in our history, but we institutionalized it. We built, I suppose, the biggest government building in our history to run it, and we institutionalized it.

I don't think we can live with the present military establishment and its $80-100 billion a year budget and keep America anything like we have known it in the past. It is corrupting the life of the whole country. It is buying up everything in sight: industries, banks, investors, universities, and lately it seems also to have bought up the labor unions.

The Defense Department is always broke; but some of the things they do with that $80 billion a year would make Buck Rogers envious. For example: the Rocky Mountain Arsenal on the outskirts of Denver was manufacturing a deadly nerve poison on such a scale that there was a problem of waste disposal. Nothing daunted, they dug a tunnel two miles deep under Denver, into which they have injected so much poisoned water that beginning a couple of years ago Denver began to experience a series of earth tremors of increasing severity.

Now there is a grave fear of a major earthquake. An interesting debate is in progress as to whether Denver will be safer if that lake of poisoned water is removed or left in place. (*New York Times*, July 4, 1968; *Science*, Sept. 27, 1968.)

Perhaps you have read also of those 6000 sheep that suddenly died in Skull Valley, Utah, killed by another nerve poison—a strange and, I believe, still unexplained accident, since the nearest testing seems to have been 30 miles away.

As for Vietnam, the expenditure of fire power has been frightening. Some of you may still remember Khesanh, a hamlet just south of the Demilitarized Zone, where a force of U.S. Marines was beleaguered for a time. During that period, we dropped on the perimeter of Khesanh more explosives than fell on Japan throughout World War II, and more than fell on the whole of Europe during the years 1942 and 1943.

One of the officers there was quoted as having said afterward, "It looks like the world caught smallpox and died." (*New York Times*, March 28, 1968.)

The only point of government is to safeguard and foster life. Our government has become preoccupied with death, with the business of killing and being killed. So-called defense now absorbs 60 percent of the national budget, and about 12 percent of the gross national product.

A lively debate is beginning again on whether or not we should deploy antiballistic missiles, the ABM. I don't have to talk about them; everyone else here is doing that. But I should like to mention a curious circumstance.

In September, 1967, or about 1½ years ago, we had a meeting of MIT and Harvard people, including experts on these matters, to talk about whether anything could be done to block the Sentinel system, the deployment of ABMs. Everyone present thought them undesirable, but a few of the most knowledgeable persons took what seemed to be the practical view: "Why fight about a dead issue? It has been decided, the funds have been appropriated. Let's go on from there."

Well, fortunately, it's not a dead issue.

An ABM is a nuclear weapon. It takes a nuclear weapon to stop a nuclear weapon. And our concern must be with the whole issue of nuclear weapons.

There is an entire semantics ready to deal with the sort of thing I am about to say. It involves such phrases as "those are the facts of life." No— these are the facts of death. I don't accept them, and I advise you not to accept them.

We are under repeated pressures to accept things that are presented to us as settled-decisions that have been made. Always there is the thought: Let's go on from there! But this time we don't see how to go on. We will have to stick with those issues.

We are told that the United States and Russia between them have by now stockpiled in nuclear weapons approximately the explosive power of 15 tons of TNT for every man, woman and child on earth. And now it is suggested that we must make more. All very regrettable, of course, but those are "the facts of life."

We really would like to disarm, but our new Secretary of Defense has made the ingenious proposal that one must be practical. Now is the time to greatly increase our nuclear armaments so that we can disarm from a position of strength.

I think all of you know there is no

365

adequate defense against massive nuclear attack. It is both easier and cheaper to circumvent any known nuclear defense system than to provide it. It's all pretty crazy. At the very moment we talk of deploying ABMs, we are also building the MIRV, the weapon to circumvent ABMs.

So far as I know, with everything working as well as can be hoped and all foreseeable precautions taken, the most conservative estimates of Americans killed in a major nuclear attack run to about 50 million. We have become callous to gruesome statistics, and this seems at first to be only another gruesome statistic. You think, Bang!—and next morning, if you're still there, you read in the newspapers that 50 million people were killed.

But that isn't the way it happens. When we killed close to 200,000 people with those first little old-fashioned uranium bombs that we dropped on Hiroshima and Nagasaki, about the same number of persons were maimed, blinded, burned, poisoned and otherwise doomed. A lot of them took a long time to die.

That's the way it would be. Not a bang, and a certain number of corpses to bury, but a nation filled with millions of helpless, maimed, tortured and doomed survivors huddled with their families in shelters, with guns ready to fight off their neighbors, trying to get some uncontaminated food and water.

A few months ago, Sen. Richard Russell of Georgia ended a speech in the Senate with the words: "If we have to start over again with another Adam and Eve, I want them to be Americans, and I want them on this continent and not in Europe." That was a United States Senator holding

a patriotic speech. Well, here is a Nobel laureate who thinks that those words are criminally insane.

How real is the threat of full-scale nuclear war? I have my own very inexpert idea, but realizing how little I know and fearful that I may be a little paranoid on this subject, I take every opportunity to ask reputed experts. I asked that question of a very distinguished professor of government at Harvard about a month ago.

I asked him what sort of odds he would lay on the possibility of full-scale nuclear war within the foreseeable future. "Oh," he said comfortably, "I think I can give you a pretty good answer to that question. I estimate the probability of full-scale nuclear war, provided that the situation remains about as it is now, at 2 percent per year." Anybody can do the simple calculation that shows that 2 percent per year means that the chance of having that full-scale nuclear war by 1990 is about one in three, and by 2000 it is about 50-50.

I think I know what is bothering the students. I think that what we are up against is a generation that is by no means sure that it has a future.

I am growing old, and my future, so to speak, is already behind me. But there are those students of mine who are in my mind always; there are my children, two of them now 7 and 9, whose future is infinitely more precious to me than my own. So it isn't just their generation; it's mine, too. We're all in it together.

Are we to have a chance to live? We don't ask for prosperity, or security; only for a reasonable chance to live, to work out our destiny in peace and decency, not to go down in history as the apocalyptic generation.

And it isn't only nuclear war. Another overwhelming threat is in the population explosion. That has not yet even begun to come under control.

There is every indication that the world population will double before the year 2000, and there is a widespread expectation of famine on an unprecedented scale in many parts of the world. The experts tend to differ only in their estimates of when those famines will begin. Some think by 1980; others think they can be staved off until 1990; very few expect that they will not occur by the year 2000.

That is the problem. Unless we can be surer than we now are that this generation has a future, nothing else matters. It's not good enough to give it tender, loving care, to supply it with breakfast foods, to buy it expensive educations. Those things don't mean anything unless this generation has a future. And we're not sure that it does.

I don't think that there are problems of youth, or students problems. All the real problems I know are grownup problems.

Perhaps you will think me altogether absurd, or "academic," or hopelessly innocent—that is, until you think of the alternatives—if I say as I do to you now: We have to get rid of those nuclear weapons. There is nothing worth having that can be obtained by nuclear war: nothing material or ideological, no tradition that it can defend. It is utterly self-defeating.

Those atom bombs represent an unusable weapon. The only use for an atom bomb is to keep somebody else from using it. It can give us no protection, but only the doubtful satisfaction of retaliation. Nuclear weapons offer us nothing but a balance of terror, and a balance of terror is still terror.

We have to get rid of those atomic weapons, here and everywhere. We cannot live with them.

I think we've reached a point of great decision, not just for our Nation, not only for all humanity, but for life upon the Earth. I tell my students, with a feeling of pride that I hope they will share, that the carbon, nitrogen and oxygen that make up 99 percent of our living substance were cooked in the deep interiors of earlier generations of dying stars.

Gathered up from the ends of the universe over billions of years, eventually they came to form in part the substance of our sun, its planets and ourselves. Three billion years ago, life arose upon the Earth. It seems to be the only life in the solar system. Many a star has since been born and died.

About two million years ago, man appeared. He has become the dominant species on the Earth. All other living things, animal and plant, live by his sufferance. He is the custodian of life on Earth. It's a big responsibility.

The thought that we're in competition with Russians or with Chinese is all a mistake, and trivial. Only mutual destruction lies that way. We are one species, with a world to win. There's life all over this universe, but we are the only men.

Our business is with life, not death. Our challenge is to give what account we can of what becomes of life in the solar system, this corner of the universe that is our home, and, most of all, what becomes of men— all men of all nations, colors and creeds.

It has become one world, a world for all men. It is only such a world that now can offer us life and the chance to go on.

WORLD POPULATION: A BATTLE LOST?

By Paul R. Ehrlich

The facts of human population growth are simple. The people of the Earth make up a closed population, one to which there is no immigration and from which there is no emigration. It can be readily shown that the Earth's human population will remain essentially closed—that no substantial movement of people to other planets is likely and that no substantial movement to other solar systems is possible. Now, a closed population will grow if the birth rate exceeds the death rate, and will shrink in size if the death rate is greater than the birth rate. Over the past half-century or so a massive increase in man's understanding and utilization of death control has resulted in a rapid rise in the rate of growth of the human population. So, we have a closed, growing population. And, intriguing as the prospect may be to certain irresponsible politicians, economists, and religious leaders, we will not achieve an infinite population size. Sooner or later the growth of the human population must stop.

On the "later" side it has been possible to compute when physical limitations, notably the problem of dissipating the heat produced by human metabolic processes, will put an end to growth in the solar system. We are forever barred from exporting a significant part of our population to the stars, so the theoretical maximum for the solar system coincides closely with the extreme possible numerical peak for Homo sapiens, estimated by some to be one billion billion people. This peak would be reached at the current growth rate, in far under 1500 years. Indeed, if we are confined in large part to the planet Earth (and there is every reason to believe we will be), the end will be reached in less than 1000 years. For those interested in such long-range thinking there is one more cheery datum—the rate of increase of the population is itself accelerating!

On the "sooner" side we must face considerably less certainty. A fantastic world effort over the next decade at changing the attitude of people toward family size and developing, promoting, and distributing birth control technology might conceivably arrest population growth at two to three times its present level—if nothing untoward intervenes. On the other hand, it is quite within our power to reduce the population size to zero tomorrow, should we opt for thermonuclear war. But, later or sooner, one thing is certain. The human population will stop growing. This halt must come through either a decrease in the birthrate, or an increase in the death rate, or both. A corollary of this is that in the birthrate is automatically an agent for eventually increasing the death rate.

Since we need have only an academic interest in theoretical limits on the size of the human population, I am going to examine the very real crisis we face this instant. It is shockingly apparent that in the battle to feed humanity our side has been routed. In 1966 the population of the world increased by some 70 million people and there was no compensatory increase in food production. Indeed in areas such as Africa and Latin America there has actually been a decrease in food production over the past two years. According to the United Nations Food and Agriculture Organization, advances in food production made in developing nations between 1955 and 1965 have been wiped out by agricultural disasters in 1965 and 1966. All this means that last year, on the average, each person on earth had 2 percent less to eat. The reduction is, of course, not uniformly distributed. Starvation already is a fact in many countries. Only 10 countries, including the United States, grew more food than they consumed—all other populous countries, including Russia, China, and India imported more than they exported.

Agricultural experts state that a tripling of the food supply of the world

will be necessary in the next 30 years or so, if the 6 or 7 billion people who may be alive in the year 2000 are to be adequately fed. Theoretically such an increase might be possible, but it is becoming increasingly clear that it is totally impossible in practice. A few months ago I would have told you that *if* we had ideal conditions of research, development and international cooperation we might triple our food production by then—if we started immediately. I would then have examined the possibility of meeting such assumptions. You would have been treated to the history of the unsuccessful attempts of the International Whaling Commission to control the hunting of whales, as a sample of the kind of international cooperation we can anticipate. I would have explained why the idea that our food supply can be dramatically increased by harvesting the sea is a gigantic hoax. Then I would have told you about some of the unhappy physical and social barriers in the way of attempting to produce much more food on the land.

All of this, however, now seems to me to be beside the point. There is not going to be any massive tooling up to meet the food crisis. There is not going to be any sudden increase in international cooperation. Even if there were a miraculous change in human attitudes and behavior in this area, *it is already too late to prevent a drastic rise in the death rate through starvation*. In a massively documented book, William and Paul Paddock predict that the time of famines will be upon us full-scale in 1975. The U.S. Department of Agriculture estimates that America can continue to feed the developing countries until 1984. Which estimate is more correct will depend in part on the validity of the assumptions on which they are based, and in part on such things as the weather. My guess is that the Paddocks are more likely correct, but in the long run it makes no difference. Millions of people are going to starve to death and soon. There is nothing that can be done to prevent it. They will die because of shortsighted governmental attitudes. They will die because some religious organizations have blocked attempts over the years to get governmental and United Nations action under way to control human birthrates. They will die because scientists have managed to per-suade many influential people that a technological rabbit can always be pulled out of the hat to save mankind at the last moment. They will die because many people, like myself, who recognized the essential role of over-population in the increasing woes of Homo sapiens, could not bring them-selves to leave the comforts of their daily routine to do something about it. Their blood will be distributed over many hands.

But then, what good can a parti-tioning of guilt do? Perhaps some people will recognize their culpability

"Quit worrying about overpopulation . . . with everything nature provides, we'll live forever."

and mend their ways—too late. What's done is done, to coin a phrase. We must look to the survivors, if there are to be any. We must assume that the "time of famines" will not lead to thermonuclear Armageddon, and that man will get another chance, no matter how ill-deserved. What I'd like to consider now is what we can do today that would improve the probability of man's making the most of a second chance should he be lucky enough to get one.

Of course, the most important thing that we must do is to educate people and change many of their attitudes. We must, for example, alert people to the possible environmental consequences of attempting continually to increase food production. They must be made aware of subtle biological properties of our environment which, if ignored, may lead to very unsubtle future calamities. For instance, one of the basic facts of population biology is that the simpler an ecological system (or ecosystem) is, the more unstable it is. A complex forest, consisting of a great variety of plants and animals, will persist year in and year out with no interference from man. The system contains many elements, and changes in different ones often cancel one another out. Suppose one kind of predator eating small rodents, say foxes, suffers a population decline. There may be a compensatory increase in the population of another predator, perhaps wildcats. Such compensation may not be possible in a simpler system. Similarly, no plant-eating animal feeds on all kinds of plants, and the chance of a population explosion of a herbivore completely defoliating a mixed woodland is virtually nil.

Man, however, is a simplifier of complex ecosystems, and a creator of simple ecosystems. For instance, he persists in creating systems which consist almost entirely of uniform stands of a single grass—wheat fields and corn fields are familiar examples. Any farmer can testify to the instability of these ecosystems. Without human protection such an ecosystem rapidly disappears.

Plans for increasing food production invariably involve large-scale efforts at environmental modification. And the more we have manipulated our environment, the more we have been required to manipulate it. The more we have used synthetic pesticides, the less we have been able to do without them. The more we have deforested land, the more flood control dams we have had to build. The more farmland we have subdivided, the more pressure we have created to increase the yield on the land remaining under cultivation and to farm marginal land. This trend has been enhanced by an unhappy historical factor. The Earth has come largely under the control of a culture which traditionally sees man's proper role as dominating nature, rather than living in harmony with it. It is a culture which equates "growth" and

Rubber wheeled vehicles of all sorts are claiming an ever greater proportion of the earth's surface. The residential developer's rule of thumb is to set aside a minimum of *twenty-five* percent of all available land for roads and parking. In downtown Los Angeles approximately *sixty-six* percent of all available land is devoted to the automobile.

Chermayeff & Alexander,
Community & Privacy

"progress" and considers both as self-evidently desirable. It is a culture which all too often considers "undeveloped" land to be "wasted" land. Unquestionably people's attitudes toward their physical environment need changing if we are to make the grade—attitudes which unfortunately are among the most basic in Western culture. And, unfortunately, the state of our physical environment is just part of the problem.

Perhaps more important than recent changes in our physical environment are those in our psychic environment. Unhappily, we cannot be sure of these latter changes—although riots, the hippie movement, and increased drug usage are hardly cheery signs. We can't even be sure of how much of an individual's reaction to these environmental changes will be hereditarily conditioned and how much it will be a function of his culture.

Man clearly has gone a long way toward adapting to urban environments and despoiled landscapes. We badly need to understand the effects of this adjustment, especially in terms of group behavior, and to be able to predict the effects of further changes in man's perceptual environment. It is important to note that our perceptual systems have evolved primarily to react to stimuli representing a sudden change in our environment—a line's charge, a flaring fire, a child's cry. Long-term changes often are not noticed. We tend not to perceive a friend's aging, or the slowing of our reflexes. If the transition from the Los Angeles of 1927 to that of 1967 had occurred overnight Angelenos surely would have rebelled. But a gradual 40-year transition has permitted southern Californians actually to convince themselves that the Los

Angeles basin of 1967 is a suitable habitat for Homo sapiens.

It is clear that man's present physical and psychic environment is far from optimum, and that permitting today's trends to continue is likely to lead to further rapid deterioration. We also know that we will have a dramatic increase in the death rate in the near future, an increase we can do nothing about. What then should be our course of action?

I think our first move must be to convince all those we can that the planet Earth must be viewed as a space ship of limited carrying capacity. It must be made crystal clear that population growth must stop, and we must arrive at a consensus as to what the ideal size of the human crew of the Earth should be. When we have determined the size of the crew, then we can attempt to design an environment in which that crew will be maintained in some sort of optimum state. The sociopolitical problems raised by such an approach are, of course, colossal. People within cultures have different ideas on how close they want to live to their neighbors, and cross-cultural differences in feelings about crowding are obvious. The only way I can think of for achieving a consensus is for people to start voicing opinions. So here goes.

I think that 150 million people—rather than our present population of 200 million—would be an optimum number to live comfortably in the United States. Such a number is clearly enough to maintain our highly technological society. It is also a small enough number that, when properly distributed and accommodated, it should be possible for individuals to find as much solitude and breathing space as they desire. With a population stabilized at such a level we could concentrate on improving the quality of human life at home and abroad. And, what a pleasure it would be to work toward an attainable goal instead of fighting the miserable rearguard action to which runaway population condemns us.

After all, what do we gain from packing more and more people into the United States? Those encouraging population growth in the hope of keeping our economy expanding must realize the consequences of such advocacy. Some men would doubtless accumulate considerable wealth, and would be able to retreat from riot-torn cities to the increasingly smoggy countryside in order to live. If thermonuclear war does not solve their children's problems permanently, what kind of a world will those children inherit? Will their heritage include social disorder and unemployment on an unprecedented scale? Will they have to wear smog masks as a matter of routine? Will they enjoy mock steaks made from processed grass or seaweed? Will they have to be satisfied with camping under plastic trees planted in concrete? Will they accept regimentation and governmental control at a level previously unheard of? Will they fight willingly in small wars and prepare diligently for the big one? Above all, will they be able to retain their sanity in a world gone mad?

Let's suppose that we decide to limit the population of the United States and of the world. How could such limitation be accomplished? Some biologists feel that compulsory family regulation will be necessary to retard population growth. It is a dismal prospect—except when viewed as an alternative to Armageddon. I would like to suggest four less drastic steps which might do the job in the United States. I suggest them in the full knowledge that they are socially unpalatable and politically unrealistic.

The first step would be to establish a Federal Population Commission with a large budget for propaganda which supports reproductive responsibility. This Commission would be charged with making clear the connection between rising population and lowering quality of life. It would also be charged with the evaluation of environmental tinkering by other governmental agencies—with protecting us from projects such as the FAA's supersonic transports or from the results of the Army Engineers' well-known "beaver complex" (which some predict will only be satiated when every gutter in the country has a dam thrown across it). Commission members should be distinguished citizens, as free as possible from political or bureaucratic meddling.

The second step would be to change our tax laws so that they discourage rather than encourage reproduction. Those who impose the burden of children on society should, whenever they are able, be made to pay for the privilege. Our income tax system should eliminate all deductions for children and replace them with a graduated scale of increases. Luxury taxes should be placed on diapers, baby bottles, and baby foods. It must be made clear to our population that it is socially irresponsible to have large families. Creation of such a climate of opinion has played a large role in Japan's successful dealing with her population problem.

Third, we should pass federal laws which make instruction in birth control methods mandatory in all public schools. Federal legislation should also forbid state laws which limit the right of any woman to have an abortion which is approved by her physician.

Fourth, we should change the pattern of federal support of biomedical research so that the majority of it goes into the broad areas of population regulation, environmental sciences, behavioral sciences, and related areas, rather than into shortsighted programs on death control. It is absurd to be preoccupied with the medical quality of life until and unless the problem of the quantity of life is solved. In this context we must do away with nonsense about how important it is for "smart" people to have large families in order to keep Homo sapiens from being selected for stupidity. It is far from established that the less intelligent portion of our population is out-reproducing the more intelligent. Even if a reproductive disparity did exist, the worst consequence over a period of a few generations only would be a slight lowering of average intelligence — a slight and "reversible" lowering. *Quantity is the first problem.* If we can lick that one perhaps we will buy the time for scientists in fields such as biochemical genetics to solve some of the problems of quality. If we don't solve the quantity problem the quality problem will no longer bother us.

All of these steps might produce the desired result of a reversal of today's population growth trend. If they should fail, however, we would then be faced with some form of compulsory birth regulation. We might, for instance, institute a system which would make "positive" action necessary before reproduction is possible. This might be the addition of a temporary sterilant to staple food, or to the water supply. An antidote would have to be taken to permit reproduction. Even with the antidote freely available, the result of such a program would be a drastic reduction in birthrates. If this

374

reduction were not sufficient, the government could dole out the antidote in the proper quantities. If we wished to stabilize the American population at its present level, each married couple could be permitted enough antidote to produce two offspring. Then each couple who wished could be given a chance in a lottery for enough antidote for a third child — the odds carefully computed to produce the desired constancy of population size. At the moment, the chances of winning would have to be adjusted to about two out of five, assuming that all couples wanted to play the game.

An attempt to institute such a system is interesting to contemplate, especially when one considers the attitude of the general public toward such a relatively simple thing as fluoridation. I would not like to be the first elected official seriously to suggest that a sterility agent be added to our reservoirs. Perhaps it might seem that we can start such a program by treating the wheat we ship India, or fish meal we ship to South America. Or can we? As you doubtless realize, the solution does not lie in the direction. For one thing, saying that the population explosion is a problem of underdeveloped countries is like telling a fellow passenger "your end of the boat is sinking." For another, it is naive to think that Indians or Brazilians are any more anxious to be fed fertility-destroying chemicals with their daily bread than are Americans. Other people already are suspicious of our motives. Consider what their attitude would be toward an attempt to sterilize them en masse.

If we can solve the population problem at home then we will be in a position to make an all-out effort to halt the growth of the world's population. Perhaps we can shorten the time of famines and lay the groundwork for avoiding a second round of population-food crises. Our program should be tough-minded. We should remember that seemingly charitable gestures such as our grain exports to India have actually harmed rather than helped Indians in the long run. I think that we should:

1. Announce that we will no longer ship food to countries where dispassionate analysis indicates that the food-population unbalance is hopeless.

2. Announce that we will no longer give aid to any country with an increasing population until that country convinces us that it is doing everything within its power to limit its population.

3. Make available to all interested countries massive aid in the technology of birth control.

4. Make available to all interested countries massive aid for increasing yield on land already under cultivation. The most important export in this area should be trained technicians, not fertilizer. We need to establish centers in the country where technicians can be trained not only in agronomy, but also in ecology and sociology. Many of the barriers to increased yields are sociological, and all increase should be made in a man-ner which minimizes environmental deterioration.

5. Accept the fact that if we can use our power to further military goals, then it can be used for the good of mankind as well. Extreme political and economic pressure should be brought on any country impeding a solution to the world's most pressing problem. A good place to start would be closing our diplomatic channels to the Vatican until that organization brings its policies into line with the desires of the majority of American Catholics. Much of the world will be horrified at our stand, but as a nation we're clearly willing to go against world opinion on other issues—why not on the most important issue?

Well, perhaps if we get on the ball and set a good example the United States can lead the way in focusing the world's attention on the cause of its major sickness rather than upon the symptoms. Perhaps we can shift our efforts from the long-term pain-depressing activities to the excising of the cancer. The operation will require many brutal and callous decisions. The pain will be intense, but the disease is so far advanced that only with radical surgery does the patient have any chance of survival.

THE FUTURE IS A CRUEL HOAX

By Stephanie Mills

Traditionally, commencement exercises are the occasion for fatuous comments on the future of the graduates present. This future is generally painted in glowing terms, characterized as long and happy. My depressing comment on that rosy future, that infinite future, is that it is a hoax. Our days as a race on this planet are, at this moment, numbered, and the reason for our finite, unrosy future is that we are breeding ourselves out of existence. Within the next ten years, we will witness widespread famines, and possible global plagues raging through famine-weakened populations. Soon we may have to ask ourselves grisly questions like, "Will I be willing to shoot my neighbor if he tries to steal my last loaf of bread? Will I be forced to become a cannibal?'

The hideous fact that we are reproducing so rapidly that it is conceivable that our means of sustenance will be grossly inadequate within ten years was foreseen nearly two centuries ago. In 1798, Thomas Robert Malthus, in his "Essay on the Principle of Population," said, "Population, when unchecked, increases in a geometrical ratio. Subsistence increases only in an arithmetical ratio." We have had nearly two hundred years to think over the consequences of that projection, yet at the turn of the century, people were arrested in New York for distributing birth control information, and only last year, Pope Paul the Sixth issued an encyclical which forbade the members of his flock to use contraceptives. At this point in our history as a race, Dr. Paul Ehrlich of Stanford has observed, "Anyone . . . who stands in the way of measures to bring down the birth rate is automatically working for a rise in the death rate."

So—we have had at least a two hundred years' warning, yet in 1969, still, virtually nothing is being done by anyone with enough power to substantially affect the situation. Mind you, I said affect, not eliminate. One of the more depressing aspects of the problem is that we cannot escape unscathed. Dr. Ehrlich and others say that immediate action must be taken simply to minimize the consequences. And *if* this action is taken, which it

Full text of valedictory address entitled "The Future is a Cruel Hoax" delivered by Senior Class Representative Stephanie Mills of Phoenix, Arizona, at Mills College commencement exercises Sunday, June 1.

probably won't be, the psychological damage that we will all suffer is great. One of the suggestions for reducing the range of the disaster is the involuntary sterilization of any person who has produced more than two children. This may sound grossly inhumane, and perhaps it is to an extent, since our identities as men and women are so conditioned by our reproductive functions. I am terribly saddened by the fact that the most humane thing for me to do is to have no children at all. But the piper is finally demanding payment.

As an ex-potential parent, I have asked myself what kind of world my children would grow up in. And the answer was, "Not very pretty, not very clean. Sad, in fact." Because, you see, if the population continues to grow, the facilities to accommodate that population must grow, too. Thus we have more highways and fewer trees, more electricity and fewer undammed rivers, more cities and less clean air.

Reprinted by permission of San Francisco Chronicle.

Mankind has spread across the face of the earth like a great unthinking, unfeeling cancer. We have horribly disfigured this planet, ungrateful and shortsighted animals that we are. Our frontier spirit involves no reverence for any forms of life other than our own, and now we are even threatening ourselves with the ultimate disrespect of suicide. Perhaps we are unconsciously expiating our guilt, but it is just this quality—unconsciousness—that we must fight in ourselves. Rather than blindly walking into the abyss, we must take warning and try to extricate ourselves from it before it is really too late.

Too often, members of the so-called real world, that is the non-academic world, by some people's definition, are willing to dismiss the warnings and insights of the unreal, academic world. This often made distinction and subsequent dismissal is a result of practicing a peculiar brand of pragmatism. It is the kind of pragmatism which says, "Let's be realistic —it just isn't profitable to develop an electric automobile." This kind of pragmatism is false, nearsighted, and a very shallow form of self-delusion. One of the advantages of a college education is escaping this kind of pragmatism for four years, being free of the small reality of earning a living. From this freedom comes a long-range perspective, which is a desperate necessity. For four years I have been spared the reality of car payments and refrigerators, and in these four years, I have had more and more to come to grips with the awesome reality of human survival on this planet. Coping with this reality has not been a privilege, and certainly not a luxury. It is a very disheartening responsibility.

One of the reasons that it is so disheartening is the knowledge that it would be easier for me to leave this ivory tower to earn a living as a cocktail waitress than to earn a living as a crusader, of sorts, for human survival. If I had enough time, I'd try to get rich, become a philanthropist, and endow a foundation. But I have less than ten years, and so for that matter, do you. This business of impending extinction is something that the so-called real and unreal worlds share. I can't eat a dollar bill, and Howard Hughes can't eat my diploma. The real and unreal worlds both have to become pragmatic on a grand scale, or you and I should believe that the famine can and will happen if for no other reason than that we still may be able to do something. And doing something to save the human race has always been a fond dream of idealists both over and under thirty.

Too many cars, too many factories, too much detergent, too much pesticide, multiplying contrails, inadequate sewage treatment plants, too little water, too much carbon dioxide —all can be traced easily to *too many people.   Paul R. Ehrlich*

THE DAWN OF MAN Man first walked the earth at least 1,000,000 years ago. Yet population was so slow that by the time of Christ, there were only about 200,000,000 living people—a mere 6 per cent of today's total. By 1,000 A.D., world population had reached about 300,000,000.

THE SURVIVAL OF MAN During most of man's history, famine and pestilence threatened the very survival of the human race. Until modern times, high fertility was man's best safeguard against extinction. Families needed to be nearly as large as possible, just to make up for all those who died of starvation and disease. Anyone who lived beyond the age of 25 was considered old—and lucky.

THE MARCH OF MAN This graph shows only about 1/10 of 1 per cent of man's history. Before Christ, some 50,000 successive generations of men had lived and reproduced their kind. But only 100 generations separate us from the beginning of the Christian era! Yet population has grown as much in the last three generations—just since 1900—as in all the ones before, down through the whole history of mankind.

STRIDES AGAINST HUNGER AND DISEASE By 1600, starvation had been greatly reduced by improved agriculture and food transport by ships. The straight, gradual slope of the population curve begins to curl upward slightly as the rate of growth increases.

By 1800, the early phases of modern medicine began to cut the death rate further—sharply decreasing the awful toll of epidemic diseases like the plague and the Black Death. More people lived longer to have more children—and more of the babies survived.

LONGER LIVES—MORE PEOPLE In the decades after 1900, modern medicine, sanitation and public health dramatically cut death rates in nation after nation. While some people in Europe and America began to practice contraception, birth rates remained high throughout most of the world. The tempo of population growth accelerated swiftly—the "Population Explosion" was underway.

THE ARITHMETIC OF CRISIS The "Population Explosion" has just really started: It took more than a million years for humanity to reach its first 3,000,000,000 population (in 1960). But unless world birth rates are drastically curbed, it will add its second 3,000,000,000 within 35 years—an interval less than 1/28,000th as long!

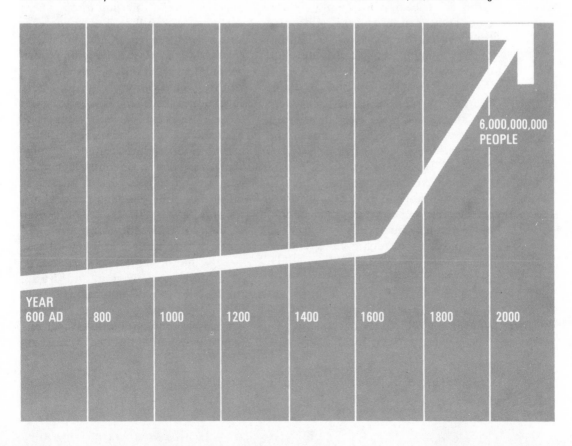

6,000,000,000 PEOPLE

YEAR
600 AD   800   1000   1200   1400   1600   1800   2000

WE MUST STOP POLLUTION NOW

By Genevieve Millet Landau

From sea to shining sea, America has become a land where more and more beautiful lakes and rivers are no longer safe to swim in or fit to fish in. Throughout our country, trees, plants, and flowers have been stunted or are disappearing; fruit and vegetable farms have been wiped out. In our cities and for miles and miles into the countryside, the very air is bad to breathe—not merely unpleasant, but dangerously toxic.

The by-products of industry discharged into the air, water, and land are killing off wild life, destroying commercial crops, and threatening the well-being, even the survival, of mankind. In many cases, the very substances developed to increase the productivity of the land have noxious side effects which more than cancel out their benefits. Most shocking of all is the fact that such pollution is not a necessary concomitant of a highly developed industrial society. We need not give up our technological advances, our material comforts, to restore our world to its natural purity. The most common, most dangerous pollutants can be eliminated, and fairly quickly, but only if industry and government assume the responsibility to do so—that is, if enough concerned citizens demand that this be done.

What then can be done?

Consider the automobile, our major source of air pollution. There are some 83 million passenger cars and 17 million trucks and busses on the roads today. Although, they burn 70 billion gallons of gasoline a year, emitting 66 million tons of deadly carbon monoxide gas and discharging, as well, 18 million tons of dangerous hydrocarbons that cause the irritating and disease-producing photochemical smog. In rush hours on busy highways the amount of carbon monoxide in the air reaches dangerous levels. Drivers become drowsy (the first sign of carbon monoxide poisoning) and accidents increase.

But motor vehicles do not have to be a source of pollution, and during the last few years, automobile manufacturers have begun to work hard to reduce the contaminants discharged from the exhaust pipes of cars. Man-

Reprinted by permission of *Parents' Magazine,* November 1969.

ufacturers claim that last year's and this year's engines meet the recently adopted Federal standards for the emission of hydrocarbons. But "Everything they've done today could have been done ten years ago," a government official remarked when automobile manufacturers put exhaust control devices on car engines. However, such measures are not enough. With the increasing number of cars on the road (every year nearly three million more vehicles are added to those already in use), the reduction in contaminants will be canceled out by the increase in cars. Perhaps it is not too much to hope that citizens will soon demand, and manufacturers will produce, pollution-free automobiles powered by steam or electricity. As a start in this direction, the California Highway Patrol is already testing two different kinds of steam-powered cars. If these cars prove to be satisfactory (and there is good reason to think they will), the California legislature has ordered its purchasing agents to buy 700 of them every year.

Industry ranks second only to cars as a source of air pollution. From the stacks of factories, 17 million tons of dust and dirt pour forth each year. Staten Island, New York (an area with very little industry), is covered with smoke from the New Jersey industrial complex across the bay. The prevailing western wind carries a heavy load of contaminants, polluting the air over the northern portion of Staten Island. The deaths from respiratory cancer in this area are considerably greater than they are only a few miles away, where the air is cleaner.

Yet industrial plants can greatly decrease the pollutants they pour into the air by complying with regulations concerning the kind of fuel burned and the manner of burning it.

In Los Angeles, for example, since the steel mills, oil refineries, and backyard incinerators have begun to burn clean fuel, these so-called stationary offenders are no longer contributing to local air pollution.

Another group of stationary offenders are the nation's power plants, which provide our electric current. In addition to producing electricity, these plants annually spew out 20 million tons of sulphur oxides, gases, and dust, which scatter light, reduce visibility, damage plant life, corrode and destroy steel and stone.

Similarly, the fuel burned to heat homes and offices discharges some 8 million tons of grime and noxious gases into the air each year.

In the United States, the air is dirtiest in New York City, with Chicago, Philadelphia, and Los Angeles runners-up. But there is hardly any place, really, where the air is clean. In Montana's still underpopulated countryside, lumber mills blanket the hills and valleys with black smog. In central and southern Florida, citrus crops have been severely damaged, causing some growers to relocate. Throughout New Jersey, pollution damage to vegetation affects at least 36 commercial crops.

Day by day, the cost of air pollution increases, not only in dollars and cents but also in the loss of health and well-being. Most people have heard of the great air pollution disasters—the times when certain weather conditions have prevented the dissipation of heavy outpouring of gases, causing acute illness and many deaths. During the five-day black fog in London in 1952, there were 4,000 more deaths than could normally be expected for that period. Londoners underwent another such experience in 1962, and here in the United States, New Yorkers suffered similar disasters in 1953, in 1962, and again a couple of years ago

when, during a smog-bound Thanksgiving weekend, the death rate went up almost ten percent. These are extraordinary conditions. More terrible, even, are the insidious effects of continued exposure to pollutants in the air.

Emphysema, a lung disease which was uncommon less than a generation ago, is now the fastest-growing of all causes of death; the increase has been seventeen-fold since 1950. Deaths from emphysema are twice as high in areas of heavy air pollution as they are elsewhere, and studies have shown that emphysema patients improve when protected from air pollution.

Chronic bronchitis, asthma, and lung cancer are all on the increase, and all of them are sometimes caused, and always aggravated, by air pollution. The death rate for lung cancer in large metropolitan areas is double the rural rate, with full allowance made for differences in smoking habits. Even the common cold is greater in air-polluted areas.

Though the substitution of atomic power for conventional fuel has been suggested as a way of cutting down pollution, this, too, is hazardous. In fact, Supreme Court Justices William O. Douglas and Hugo L. Black stated that nuclear power "represents the greatest pollution threat of all to our environment." A year ago there were already 15 commercial nuclear power plants in the United States, producing about one percent of our electrical output, and the government has been promoting a plan whereby 25 percent of our electricity would be generated by atomic power by 1980. Unfortunately, the by-product of such a process is the creation of radioactive material. Such material cannot just be dumped into the atmosphere. It has to be safely contained, and that raises great problems.

Three years ago, in Michigan, a failure in safeguards which led to a fuel melt-down in a Fermi reactor came perilously close to becoming a nuclear runaway. Though an explosion was averted, the fact that safeguards, supposed to be foolproof, failed, is extremely frightening. Now the Atomic Energy Commission is expressing misgivings about the planned increase in nuclear plants.

Like the air, our waterways are also being poisoned. According to Dr. John J. Hanlon, Deputy Administrator of the Government's consumer Protection and Environmental Health Services, "One out of every two Americans is served by a drinking water supply that either does not measure up to Federal standards or is of unknown quality." Our rivers, lakes, bays, and streams are used as dumping grounds for human and industrial wastes that contaminate our wells and the land around them. Fertilizers developed to increase crop yields are washed from from the fields to contaminate rivers and river banks. Plants and factories release dirty, chemically-loaded water into rivers and lakes. Sewage, insuf-

ficiently treated, is discharged into our waterways.

But it is perfectly possible to remove or sterilize industrial wastes, and to transform sewage-filled water into clean water. In the southern California town of Santee, for example, children can now go swimming in a once contaminated lake that today is as clean as a high mountain stream. The water in this lake has been "reclaimed" through a fairly complicated process.

It's true that complete water purification is expensive, and though some communities allocate sufficient funds to do it, many do not. Huge quantities of sewage and industrial wastes are discharged into the Mississippi and Missouri rivers. But when asked about plans to clean up a polluted area, an official declared, "When the Federal people show us that additional treatment is necessary to maintain the river's quality, we'll do it—but not until then."

Having clean water is not a luxury; it's a necessity. Though it's true that typhoid and other serious water-borne diseases of the past have been controlled, new ones have appeared. Not long ago, 18,000 residents of a single community were stricken with gastroenteritis. Babies were among the worst sufferers. The bacteria that caused the infection were transmitted through the general water supply. A few years ago clams taken from polluted Raritan Bay caused an outbreak of infectious hepatitis in New Jersey. And about 75,000 acres of New York State's shoreline is teeming with clams that cannot be eaten because the shallow waters in which they live are polluted. "Two-thirds of the food that mankind takes from the sea live in shallow waters where pollution is greatest," notes Robert Boardman of the National Audubon Society. In many once rich waters there are now no fish at all. Lake Erie, for example, has become an overheated chemical tank in which nothing lives but a huge jungle of seaweed through which boats move only with difficulty.

Every day billions of gallons of hot waste water are discharged, primarily by power plants, into lakes, bays, and rivers. The dangers of thermal pollution, as it is called, have only recently been recognized. It has been discovered that an increase in temperature of only a few degrees is enough to kill many species of fish. And the fish are threatened by even a smaller rise in temperature because the warmth of the water causes fish eggs to hatch prematurely and the fish to be spawned at a season when there is not any food for them to eat.

Not even seaweed flourishes in the oil-befouled waters of the Santa Barbara Channel in California, scene of one of our worst water pollution catastrophes. Drilling operations to pump the oil beneath the seas off American shores have been going on for many years. Two years ago, Santa Barbara officials, fearing that oil rigs would pollute local waters, persuaded the government to create a two-mile buffer zone off-shore where drilling could not take place. Last year, when oil slick appeared along the shoreline, Santa Barbara requested the Department of Interior to avert potential disaster by extending the buffer area. But the government did not do so, assuring the community, as their county supervisor put it, "that we had nothing to fear." Suddenly, one day last January, an underwater oil well blew out and thousands of gallons of oil and natural gas poured out and kept on pouring without pause for 11 days. By the end of that time, 200,000 gallons of oil had spouted into the sea, contaminating several hundred miles

of channel water and 40 miles of beachfront land. Fish and shellfish perished in great numbers. Sea elephants, fur seals, and the rare sea otter were gravely imperiled. Many sea birds, their feathers matted with oil, unable to fly or to swim, were drowned. As Michael Neushul, University of California botanist, observed, the disaster "could lead to a drastic ecological imbalance." Even so, after the leak was sealed, drilling was resumed. Senator Cranston of California bitterly pointed out that both the United States government and the oil company involved stand to make millions of dollars through continued drilling.

Another monstrous water pollution disaster occurred in the Rhine River this past summer when chemical insecticides released into the river spread over 200 miles in Western Germany and the Netherlands. After six days, 100 tons of dead fish had been washed up; all of the fish in the area, and many river ducks as well, had been killed. The destruction of fish alone was estimated at more than half-a-million dollars. The same kind of insecticide that poisoned the fish was held responsible for sterilizing up to one-half of the heron population of Britain and for causing one species of gull to lay eggs without shells. Although Dutch authorities claimed that the chemicals weren't harmful to people, French conservationists charged that a partial study made in southwestern France, testing the effect of similar chemicals, had disclosed 75 cases of poisoning in human beings, four of them fatal.

The scale of the Rhine disaster was mammoth; similar smaller catastrophes occur frequently.

Not long ago, the United States Food and Drug Administration seized about 28,000 pounds of frozen salmon that had been caught in Lake Michigan. The fish contained more DDT than was safe for people to eat. DDT is not only highly toxic to the insects it is designed to destroy, but to all forms of life. Insecticides such as DDT and its chemical relatives remain in the environment year after year. An orchard is sprayed with an insecticide and soon the rain washes the chemical off the leaves and carries it into underground streams, spreading it widely throughout the land. DDT has now journeyed to the ends of the earth; traces have been found in the fat of seals which have never left the Antarctic. DDT permeates the algae growing in rivers; fish feed on the algae and are poisoned; birds feed on the fish and die. A diet of DDT-contaminated fish is held responsible for the destruction of the great bald eagle in areas around Lake Michigan where once this bird was common. Today only one nest is left and the single pair of surviving eagles have produced no young in the past five years.

Elm trees on a college campus were sprayed with DDT and the following spring the robins began to die. In a year or two they were all gone. The robins had eaten earthworms which had eaten the sprayed elm leaves.

Man, too, carries poisonous insecticides in his body fat. The amount is small thus far, but dangerous. If the use of this kind of insecticide continues, the quantities in our bodies will increase. Even now, according to Dr. William B. Deichmann of the University of Miami School of Medicine, a research study made of some persons who had liver cancer, leukemia, and high blood pressure at the time of death revealed that they had two to three times more DDT and related insecticides in their bodies than persons who died accidentally.

Air, water, and land are dangerously polluted, not because of ignorance—we know what the pollutants are and we can eliminate them—but because of our disregard for life, a disregard motivated in all too many cases by the desire to make money.

Controversy over DDT and similar chemicals has been going on for two decades, but only within the last year has major action been taken to curb their use. This year, Michigan became the first state to ban the sale of DDT, and more than half-a-dozen other states are considering legislation to outlaw its use. In April, Sweden became the first country to halt the use of DDT and similar insecticides.

There are other ways to control the damage done by insects. A number of chemical formulas contain pyrethrins, the only generally available insecticides that can legally be labeled "non-toxic to humans and pets." Industry is also working to develop selective chemicals which affect only the target insects. Moreover, insects can be controlled without the use of chemical killers at all. Synthetic hormones to prevent the reproduction of certain insects, sterilization of male insects, and the introduction of bacteria or viruses to infect only certain insects are approaches to insect control now being developed.

Pollution can be stopped; our environment can be made clean again. And at last a beginning has been made. Laws requiring higher standards for the condition of air and water have been passed, and a new government agency dealing with all aspects of pollution has been formed.

Walter J. Hickel, United States Secretary of the Interior, recently announced that the Federal Government is proceeding to "prosecute those who pollute." The accused polluters, including several very large industrial manufacturers, have been summoned to appear before the Federal Water Pollution Control Administration where they will be given firm deadlines to clean up the discharges their plants produce or face prosecution by the Justice Department. One local government after another has responded to the public clamor for improved pollution control. Incinerators have been banned in some communities and upgraded in others. In some places, high sulphur coal and low-grade fuel oil, both major sources of pollution, have been outlawed altogether.

How have these improvements been brought about? California was the first state to require smog-control devices on automobiles. This paved the way for the eventual passage of a law ordering manufacturers to place them on all cars. The impetus for this law began with one woman in Los Angeles whose allergic child suffered terribly from air pollution. She induced half a dozen friends and neighbors to join her in forming an organization to present their demand for cleaner air first to their local government, then to the state, and then to the Federal Government. They studied the causes of pollution and learned of the measures needed to combat it. They testified at public hearings, wrote letters to political figures, organized demonstrations. Gradually, the organization grew so large that it was able to swing political weight.

In Washington, D.C., the Kenilworth Dump, where garbage was burned, was until last year one of the biggest sources of air pollution in the area. Then a child was burned while playing there, and public opinion was so aroused that the burning ceased. Now the garbage is compressed, placed in the dump at regular intervals, and covered with soil. In time, this former eyesore will become a public park.

There are many organizations active in the fight against air pollution that can be called on for encouragement, literature, and advice. Such organizations include the Izaak Walton League of America, the League of Women Voters, the National Audubon Society, the Sierra Club, the Garden Club of America, the National Tuberculosis and Respiratory Disease Association.

The American Littoral Society, which is concerned with the nation's shoreline, is involved in the battle against water pollution. More than 200 of its members man an "alert corps," which keeps track of industrial or community activities that might degrade the quality of the water in any region. Not long ago they learned of a plan to dredge lower Chesapeake Bay, which would pollute a fishing area. The alert corps volunteered its services to the community; members attended public hearings and testified in court. In this manner, they have twice prevented the dredging operation from being started, and may well be successful in stopping it altogether.

Any person who wishes to fight pollution should not hesitate to attend and participate in public hearings. Under a recent change in the Federal Air Quality Act, clean air standards are being set for one region of the country after the other. The legal limits for dust, dirt, and gases will be set following public hearings. How clean will the air be in your community? That may depend upon you —and other interested citizens. The industrial groups that are largely responsible for pollution are always represented at such hearings. It is up to private citizens to give the opposing view if they are to prevail.

The laws regulating the use of incinerators and requiring industrial plants to install control devices may not be enforced unless all of us make it our business to see that they are enforced. Any time black smoke is observed pouring from a factory or apartment house, a complaint should be made to the community's pollution control agency.

The diseases brought about by pollution can be conquered. The waters of our lakes and rivers can be clean again, our land fertile, our air fragrant. All this lies within our grasp. The technology that has polluted our environment can as well—and better —be used to repurify it.

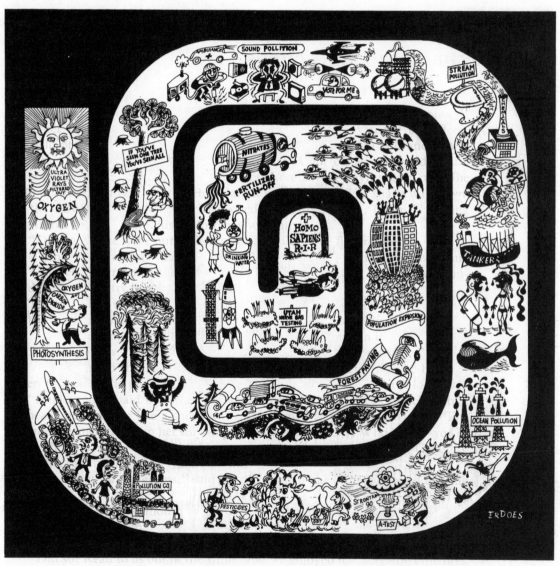

Reprinted by permission. Copyright © 1969 by The New York Times Company.

NOISE: THE GATHERING CRISIS

By Mark O. Hatfield

There is a bumper sticker now circulating which says: "Eliminate Pollution Before Pollution Eliminates You." Immediately we will think of studies which threaten a lack of water by 1980 and conjure up the words of California scientists stating that within 50 years their state will be uninhabitable for any form of life. Or we hold our breath for a moment remembering that 142 million tons of smoke and noxious fumes are dumped into the atmosphere each year. Momentarily we feel brief panic and then for one reason or another, we forget the threatening words of the bumper sticker and go about our daily duties in a comfortable shield of self-deception and false security. Unfortunately such an attitude has now brought us to a situation in which the rapidly deteriorating quality of our environment is the most hazardous challenge to not only our health and well-being but to our very lives and those of our children and grandchildren.

Environmental pollution may not pose the immediate destruction that nuclear war does, but I might remind you that the effects are the same and just as lasting. And I might remind you that destruction at the hands of our environment is as immediate as your and my lifetime. And finally, I might remind you that lack of inhabitable land, lack of food, lack of good water to drink and good air to breathe are the very conditions under which men become desperate and resort to any and all means to preserve their survival. It is with these thoughts in mind that I state my firm conviction that pollution—all forms of pollution; air, water, and noise pollution, overpopulation, land and soil pollution— is the most challenging and the most crucial problem facing the man of the 20th century. And it is with these thoughts in mind that I firmly believe that if we do not meet this problem with all the creativity and ingenuity of our age, then within a very short time nothing else will matter, for there will be nothing else to worry about.

Your concern with environmental pollution has brought you here today

Delivered before the Noise Abatement Council of America, October 8, 1969.

in order to form an effective citizen's group to combat this onslaught on our planet before it is indeed too late. Your special concern is with the assault of noise pollution on our society and in your recognition of noise as a pollutant you have established yourself as somewhat pioneers in combating the effects of noise on our society. It was therefore an honor to be invited to speak at this organizational meeting of the Noise Abatement Council of America. Had such groups been instrumental in educating the public to appreciate the inevitable results of uncontrolled air and water pollution and in effecting remedial action to combat these problems even ten years ago then we would not be faced with the present national crises in these areas. Today let us pledge ourselves to the task of preventing noise becoming another uncontrolled threat to our existence.

The effects of noise, although long a problem, have only begun to receive the well-founded concerns of government, health, industrial and community organizations. We are already far behind the rest of the world in appreciating the scope of the problem. For our backwardness in the field of noise abatement the United States is now the noisest country on this planet, and frankly, I hate to think that we are now carrying this lack of respect for civilized standards to other planetary bodies. Basically, noise pollution is reaching crisis proportions in the United States and I think that it is time that all of us wake up to this fact.

We should be concerned with noise as a problem because for over a century noise exposure of sufficient intensity and duration has been recognized to produce sensori-neural hearing loss. But in spite of this knowledge, an over-exposure to excessive noise is the major cause of hearing loss in the United States today. In fact it is estimated that 10-20 million people in the United States have some degree of hearing impairment.

Everyone realizes that if he is exposed to a very loud noise such as an explosion he may very likely wind up deaf—at least temporarily. What is not so apparent is that the effect of noise is cumulative; it produces as Dr. Leo Beranek, whose work in acoustics is international in scope, an acoustic fatigue." Repeated moderate noise builds up to produce the same effect as would a single loud noise. And even more important is the fact that repeated noise is the only type, short of a shattering explosion, that produces *permanent* hearing loss. The importance of this is readily seen when one is considering the harmful effects of exposure to daily occupational noise.

Another matter of some concern is that the noise level of the United States is increasing at an astonishing rate. Over the past 25 years the average increase in noise level has been at one decibel per year. When one considers that damage to the ears can occur at sustained exposures to the ranges around 85 decibels and over, and given our present noise levels, it will not be too many years before noise levels in the United States become lethal. To quote Dr. Vern O. Knudsen, physicist and former Chancellor of the University of California, "If the noise we make keeps increasing at the present rate, it will be as deadly in thirty years in some of our downtown cities as were the ancient Chinese tortures for executing condemned prisoners."

We know of course that the most pronounced physical effect of noise is damage to the ear. Exposure to intense noise over varying durations causes partial and in some cases permanent hearing loss due to actual cell damage in the organ of the Corti located within the cochlea of the inner ear.

But noise has much farther reaching effects than just hearing damage. As Paul E. Sabine stated even back as far as the March 1944 issue of the *American Journal of Public Health*: "There is a wealth of reliable data from medical sources in support of the statement that sustained exposure to noise is a contributing factor in impaired hearing, chronic fatigue that lowers bodily resistance, neurasthenia, increased blood pressure, and decreased working and mental efficiency and that noise should rightfully be classified as an occupational hazard along with gases, fumes, dust, toxic liquids, and bacteria." To put this into, if nothing else, economic perspective, the total cost to industry in compensation payments, lost production and decreased efficiency due to noise is estimated at well over $4 billion per year. In relation to business a World Health Organization report states that before 1939 office noise was costing United States business $2 million per day through inefficient work. Today that figure is $4 billion. The psychological and physiological effects of noise are difficult to assess but the correlation between noise and such things as sleep disturbances, hypertension due to the constant response of hormonal and neurological mechanisms to noise stress, interference with basic communication, the loss in efficient performance and even damage to property must be counted as a very real and a very enormous threat to our well-being, not to mention the economic repercussions.

The effects of noise cannot be fully appreciated until we have more thorough studies in the field. One effect which needs to be especially explored by sociologists and criminologists is referred to in a recent *Fortune* magazine article. As related by *Fortune*: In the Bronx borough of New York City one evening last spring, four boys were at play, shouting and racing in and out of an apartment building. Suddenly from a second-floor window came the crack of a pistol. One of the boys sprawled dead on the pavement. The victim happened to be Roy Innis, Jr., thirteen, son of a prominent Negro leader, but there was no political implication in the tragedy. The killer, also a Negro, confessed to police that he was a nightworker who had lost control of himself because the noise from the boys prevented him from sleeping. This incident is extreme but worthy of our careful attention due to the implications it has on the worsening human problems which we are now experiencing in our cities.

Until recently the most authoritative voices about noise have come from within the industrial occupations due to the mere fact that noise has been a problem much longer in this area than in any other. Industrial management has become increasingly concerned with the adverse effects of noise on those persons who work under constant exposure to intense levels of noise—and I might add with due reason.

According to Dr. Glorig, director of the Callier Hearing and Speech Center in Dallas, Texas: "Industrial noise is now the most important single cause of hearing loss." Despite numerous research, training and regulatory programs now underway in some industries and in various Federal agencies, and despite the great strides accomplished in responsible noise abatement efforts in the occupational field, there is still need for a vast amount of education in the field of occupational noise. For instance, B. F. Goodrich estimates that the total market for acoustical goods and products will reach $875 million by 1970, which if one takes into account all that this comprises is a very paltry sum.

Another example of the need for increased emphasis placed on occupational noise is the fact that permanent hearing loss caused by excessive exposure to noise is now a recognized occupation hazard and is compensable in only 35 states. I am always reminded of the basic lack of awareness in this field, by an unfortunately true story which occurred when one of my aids was touring a textile factory in the South. When he commented on the high level of noise to which the workers were subjected, the manager hastened to assure him that immediate efforts were being made to correct the unpleasant conditions. "Next week the factory is playing country-western music over the loudspeakers at a level which will block out the noise of the factory."

The noise of our industries is put into further perspective when one considers them in light of "safe" noise levels. There are differences of opinion about permissible occupational noise levels. The American Academy of Ophthalmology and Otolarynaology states that our present knowledge of the relation of noise exposure and hearing loss is much too limited to propose safe amounts of exposure. However, the Academy recommends noise-exposure control and tests of hearing if there is habitual exposure to continuous noise at 85 decibels at a frequency of 300–1200 cycles per second. Noise is measured in a dimensionless unit called the decibel which is used to describe the levels of acoustical pressure, power and intensity.

The decibel expresses a logarithmic ratio between two sounds. In other words, the difference between a noise with a decibel rating of 60 and that with a rating of 70 is a relative increase of 10 times the lower level. The frequency of noise expressed in cycles per second is useful for rating noise hazards since some frequencies are more likely to cause hearing damage than others, with high pitched sounds more annoying than low pitched sounds. The British Medical Society recommends hearing conservation measures when noise exceeds 85 decibels in the 250–4000 cycles per second range.

The United States Air Force recommends ear defenders when personnel are exposed to 85 decibels in the 300–4800 frequency range. The American Standards Association has suggested permissible daily quotas of exposure to noise which they suggest should protect the worker from hearing loss. Over an eight hour working day they suggest a limit of 85 decibels at any frequency range above 700 cycles per second. In the Walsh-Healey Public Contracts Act the Federal government has adopted 90 decibels at any frequency range as a permissible safe occupational noise level.

Only recently has there been concern about the entire realm of urban and community noise although millions of Americans are affected each day by the repercussions of this type of noise. As Dougherty and Welsh commented in "Community Noise and Hearing Loss:"

"The saving quality heretofore has been that community noise has been a short-term exposure as compared to an 8 hour day period in industry. As the power use of both home and street increase, steps must be taken to limit the noise output. Otherwise, total timed exposure will exceed industrial standards that actually rely on regular audiograms to prevent severe hearing loss."

Indeed the din in the cities at times far exceeds the noise levels considered "safe" for an occupational situation. A noise level of 100 decibels was once recorded on the Avenue of the Americas in New York City where the Transit Authority was building the extension of the 6th Avenue subway. Construction is perhaps the most irritating source of noise to the urbanite and the problem is intensified when once we realize that there are virtually no legal controls on the amount of noise that can emanate from a construction site. In the absence of any forms of control the consequences are logical—existing knowledge for noise control is not even applied.

Noise control costs money, and it is not reasonable to ask sympathetic construction firms to invest in noise control only to let unsympathetic firms underbid them on jobs by avoiding the noise control costs. Air compressors, pneumatic drills, power saws, concrete mixers and other machines involved in the construction or demolition of buildings are permitted in some urban areas between 7 a.m. and 6 p.m., six days a week and at night with special permit. Combined with the poor soundproofing in modern apartments, the sounds of congested traffic which can reach upwards of 90 decibels, and the multitudinous other sounds of "civilized living," the city dweller is caught in the midst of a cacophonic catastrophe.

Europe and such countries as Russia and Japan have for some time had strictly enforced noise abatement laws, including zoning and construction measures and national councils like the Swiss Anti-Noise Commission which deals with the basic medical, acoustic and technical questions of road, rail and water traffic; aircraft noise, noise in industry, building construction, homes, etc.; and legal questions.

The United States by contrast has few laws regarding noise abatement and even those that it has are barely enforced. For example, New York City is one of the cities that has strict noise laws against horn-blowing and even has a legal noise limit for the city of 88 decibels at 150 feet. If you have ever been to New York, I am sure that these laws will come as surprising news.

The final assault on the nation's well-being due to noise and the one which brings you here today is that of aircraft noise. Of all the fields of noise abatement that of air transportation has received the most attention by industry and government due to the obvious severity of the problem. The possible adverse effects of aircraft noise have been recognized for several years. In 1952 the Dolittle Report pointed out that "positive efforts should be continued by both government and industry to reduce or control aircraft noise nuisance to people on the ground and that substantial reduction of such noise is practicable."

Such firms as Pratt and Whitney, General Electric and Boeing have been involved for some years in the research and development of a "quiet" engine. According to sources within the field, we are five years away from a prototype which when operational will only reduce the perceived noise level at takeoff and landing by 10 percent. The problem in this area is not so much a matter of money as lack of available technology. The sound of a jet taking off is approximately 130 decibels which is also the estimated maximum noise bearable to human ears. A reduction of 10 percent will barely scratch the surface of the noise problem in this area unless there is a major technological breakthrough.

Therefore in combating aircraft noise we also need to pursue abatement efforts in the aspects of aircraft operations and apply methods of compatible landuse around the airports. In the realm of flight patterns, airport design and placement, guaranteed buffer zones, adequate soundproofing of buildings in and around airports, extension of runways, legal controls, and so on, joint action will have to be taken by the Federal government, the airlines, and the community. With over 98 percent of our airports owned by some level of state government, it will be primarily up to the local government and the airport operators of the same to effect noise abatement controls. In addition airport operators should share the responsibility of enforcing the new Federal Aviation Agency noise standards to be announced this month and closely coordinating local efforts with such programs as the Aircraft Noise Alleviation Program established under the F.A.A. in 1961.

For examples of innovative noise control efforts I recommend such programs as that taken in the Los Angeles area in which community efforts and pilot programs have been established to abate noise at the Los Angeles International Airport. The Port of New York Authority has also carried out extensions costing several million dollars to the three runway at New York's Kennedy International Airport solely out of noise abatement considerations. Dulles International Airport in Washington is a good example of how zoning laws and design can be effectively employed to control noise levels emanating from aircraft.

But despite these examples, the fact remains that there is much left to do before we can successfully cope with aircraft noise. Your recognition of this fact has brought you here today. There are many questions which must be answered before actual work can even begin. The most important of these is funding of noise abatement efforts. Who is responsible? Should we ever obtain an operational "quiet" engine, the estimated cost of retrofitting our four engine commercial jets has been upwards of $300 million. This is perhaps the most touchy issue which will face you in your efforts to combat jet noise for the costs are formidable and the responsibility ill-defined.

Another problem of considerable concern is that of the sonic boom. Until recently the shock waves from the sonic boom was confined to occasional military flights scheduled to fly over unpopulated areas of the United States. However, since President Nixon's request for $96 million for the current fiscal year ending June 30, 1970 in order to finance the start of construction of two SST prototype aircraft it now appears that within the next 10 years we will be subjected to the sound of commercial sonic booms. I am opposed to the development of this aircraft. Aside from the obvious criticism of low cost-benefit considerations, I find it difficult to justify the vast noise disturbance of this aircraft in light of the small domestic value derived. The plane has no defense value, will cost the government a total of $1.29 billion, out of a total development cost of $1.51 billion, and its flights have been estimated to disturb 20 million groundlings every time the SST flies from coast to coast.

The repercussions of the noise problem have just begun to be understood and much has been done to alleviate the noise onslaught on our environment. For instance, New York City has a law requiring walls sound-

393

Before and after shot of Middle Fork, Lost Man Creek.

Reprinted by permission. From *The Last Redwoods*, Sierra Club, pp. 74–75. James Rose.

"Visitors to the area sometimes express concern over appearance of the land immediately after logging . . . . It takes big equipment to move the heavy logs over steep country. The ground does get scuffed. Like a corn field just after harvest, it presents a ruffled picture."

Arcata Redwood Company Folder

proof enough to reduce any airborne noise passing through by 45 decibels. Some construction companies have proved that buildings can be constructed quietly, by muffling blasting by special steel mesh blankets, welding instead of using the horrendous racket of riveting or bolting. New machines have been offered on the market which have a vast reduction in decibel rating over their old predecessors such as a new compressor which reduces the decibel level from 110 to 85 decibels and a new paving breaker that has had its sound reduced by 2/3.

New York, California, New Jersey, Minnesota, and other states have voted or have pending various legislation on noise abatement particularly in the realm of vehicular noise. Numerous local ordinances deal with specific noise problems of their area offering such things as prevention of transistor playing in public areas, zoning laws, etc. Some states have legislation which prohibits vehicles on its public highways that exceed certain established noise levels for that particular vehicle.

All of these are good beginnings but they cannot be assessed as anything more than just beginnings. What is needed are guaranteed standards for the man on the street, on his job, or in his home. In this category I would like to mention the Walsh-Healey Public Contracts Act which was signed into effect by Secretary of Labor Shultz on May 17, 1969. This Act provides for a limit of on-the-job noise levels at 90 decibels at any frequency. This regulation only applies to firms that have a $10,000 or better contract with the Federal government during the course of one year. The Walsh-Healey Act is a step in the right direction but again it is only a beginning. It only affects certain segments of workers and sets as a standard

a noise level which is of debatable safety for an occupational level.

The real question at hand in the consideration of the noise level of our society is whether we are going to preserve the basic amenities of civilized life in the onslaught of technological advance.

As one noted figure in the noise abatement field, William H. Ferry, once said: "We have been neither interested nor successful in controlling noise because we have been neither interested nor successful in coping with technology."

Some 60 years ago Robert Koch, a bacteriologist and Nobel Laureate predicted: "The day will come when man will have to fight merciless noise as the worst enemy to his health."

That day is not so far away. The problem must be faced now before it is beyond our control. So I offer a few suggestions from my meager knowledge of the problem of what may prevent a continuation of the insult of noise on the future sensibilities of our nation. The problem of our "cacophonic republic" requires education, public awareness, increased research and greater application of economical acoustical materials, and a great deal of cooperation and coalition of effort between industry, business, government, health officials and community groups in order to find and carry out solutions to local, regional and national noise problems.

We need a uniform noise control standard for all industrial and office workers . . . a Walsh-Healey Public Contracts Act of more encompassing and more rigorous standards.

We need to educate consumer demand that will call for quieter jobs and products in order to make it desirable for industry to compete to produce both at less cost.

We need the City Code level to

handle such noise sources as garbage collection, construction, loudspeakers, and motor vehicles. We need a regional approach to the research and development of programs directed toward the alleviation of the noises that plague particular areas of the United States. Lastly we need the full cooperation of the Federal government in assisting, coordinating and financing these efforts to provide a quieter environment.

As Dr. William H. Stewart of the Public Health Service once stated: "Those things within man's power to control which impact upon an individual in a negative way, which infringes upon his integrity, and interrupt his pursuit of fulfillment, are hazards to the public health."

Noise can and must be controlled as a danger to the public health and economy, but above all else we must commit ourselves to the control of the noise in our society on the basis of civilized standards.

DANGER

By Anthony Wolff

By the time we got to America the Beautiful, Europe was already the worse for wear. London was shadowed by smog in the 13th century. Paris, already ancient, was a textbook of urban problems. The common cures for overpopulation were war and pestilence. The European wilderness was extinct, and the tamed, subdivided earth and its fruits were rationed in favor of the rich. For the rest, those who would or could, those who dared, it was time to get out.

So we came here, some to extend and renew the depleted homeland, some to escape it, but eventually turning our backs on Europe, dedicated, the myth says, to a fresh start in a New World. We tapped a continental cornucopia. Of earth, air, fuel and water we had enough and more, for ourselves and a biblical progression of generations.

The idea of a New World flowered in the American earth into a vision of a New Eden. The hugeness of the landscape concealed our rapacity: as much as we wasted, there was always another virgin forest, hillside, river just ahead. We appropriated God's blessing and even His purpose for our prodigal exploitation of Creation. When faith began to fail, we adapted from Darwin a social theory that extended the *imprimatur* of science to our exploitation of our fellowman as well. We were rolling westward with the endless frontier, on a crusade consecrated to our Manifest Destiny.

But then, hardly a century ago, the American landscape seemed equal to our relatively limited power to destroy. That was before 50 million buffalo had been slaughtered in an orgy of waste, until there was not a wild one left; before the Indian nations had been humbled or exterminated; before three billion passenger pigeons had been dragged from the skies. That was before mountains from the Appalachians to the Sierras had been denuded of their timber and disemboweled into the streams and rivers; and before 25 million Americans in 1850 had become 180 million in 1960, on the way to 300 million by the time this century turns. Most of us were working too hard and having too much fun to count the price of success.

We built a transcontinental empire and reached beyond, transmuting the earth's resources into a glittering mail-order catalogue of the Good Life. We made our destiny manifest; we reached the frontier; now we are turned back on ourselves to live in our rich, ravished landscape. By all the standards we have set, we are a success.

Does our genius mock us? Do we begin to suspect that our success is more than we can sustain, or perhaps even survive? The evidence has long been accumulating in the reports of specialists—biologists, hydrologists, agronomists, geologists, demographers and the rest—who analyze the cause and effect of the death of Lake Erie, the desiccation of the Southwest, the pollution of the air—all the side effects of our success. Those who synthesize this isolated data, the ecologists who study the whole complex relationship between living things and the environment, draw grisly conclusions.

But we ignore the musty statistics and doomsday pronouncements of scientists; we are preoccupied with fighting for or enjoying our share of the riches. We do not want to consider the idea that the source of supply may be drying up. It takes the undeniable, unimpeachable evidence of our own senses to make us pause.

On a summer day, venturing into the shadeless urban outdoors beyond the air-conditioning, we may wonder that the air stinks. We tune out our minds against the metropolitan din, contract our pores against the atmosphere, take shallow breaths, and go about our business. But we wonder.

It is such relatively minor irritations that may well end up making conservationists of us all. We do not weep for vital topsoil, millennia in the making, eroded away; we mourn at a distance the extinction of another animal species; we shrug off the subtle symptoms that imply our own eventual degradation or destruction. We might even suffer the effects of air pollution deep in our own lungs if our sense of smell were not offended in the process. But let our nostrils suggest to us that our self-proclaimed well-being is fragile, that the limits of our comfort are very close indeed, and we get edgy, nervous. We begin to sense in a very personal way that our material wealth has been charged against the natural resources of our environment, and that the price may be unacceptable, our credit is not unlimited.

Pursued to the limit, this new awareness may cause us to make some radical connections. We may begin to see that our reckless exploitation of our environment is Siamese twin to our exploitation of men. Our enslavement of Africans to support a one-crop cotton economy was intrinsic to the exhaustion of the earth in the same cause. The systematic impoverishment of the Appalachian landscape for timber and coal is inseparable from the impoverishment of the region's people. Much of the pathology of modern American life may prove susceptible to this kind of ecological insight. Even our easy-come-easy-go credit-card morality is genetically related to our buy-now-pay-never attitude toward the earth itself.

But even without pushing self-analysis this far, a rapidly increasing number of Americans are finding both personal and philosophical reasons for joining the once-derided conservation movement. So far, it is an odd, unstructured mix: garden-club ladies, card-carrying National Rifle Association gunmen, bird watchers, anglers, boaters and bathers, old-line conservationists and neophyte nature lovers —a Noah's Ark of disparate shipmates. Even the amorphous American youth movement, looking beyond Vietnam for issues, may refocus on America's imperialism toward nature in place of imperialism overseas. The growing commitment to communal living in remote areas is one evidence of the search for a new kind of relationship between people and the environment, people and people. There are more than enough good conservation battles to go around.

The fight to preserve the American wilderness is one—a rearguard action that has been losing ground for three hundred years. Now, there is so little wilderness left that we guard the remnants like fragile souvenirs of the past. But those who naively insist that the precedence of wilderness over economics is self-justifying are doomed to witness the disappearance of the wilderness. We still hear, from industries that have grown rich from feeding off the land, that even these besieged islands of virgin land are a luxury the richest nation on earth cannot afford. We are accustomed to drawing on Creation for capital. Over the last several years, Gov. Ronald Reagan and the California lumber industry blunted a Federal move to sequester enough remaining redwood forest to insure the survival of the species. Trees that were tall when Columbus discovered America are still felled to make cheap lawn furniture.

By definition, wilderness is hard to justify in hard-cash terms. Its true values are not described by the language of the marketplace or weighed in mercantile scales.

Even the recreation value of true wilderness is limited. As it has become more circumscribed and remote, the wilderness has become reserved for the few who seek it with single-minded persistence.

But we need the wilderness as a personal, as well as a scientific reference if we ever hope to discover what we are. There is as much mystery for man in an acre of living wilderness than in all of mortuary space. For whatever else we may be, we are wild creatures, under the veneer of civilization. There are tides in us that answer to the moon. If we have anything like a racial memory or a soul, its natural context is wilderness.

Most of the remaining wilderness, outside of a few specially designated national park areas, has survived only because it was too forbidding or remote or resource-poor to be easily developed. Now, the easy pickings are gone, and the developers and the conservationists are fighting over the remnants. The battle lines were clearly drawn this year in the Florida Everglades, where massive development has been delayed, but not forestalled.

Hell's Canyon, where the Snake River cuts along the Seven Devils range on the Idaho-Oregon border, is even more remote than the Everglades. The land was christened for its inhospitality, which makes it all the more appealing to those hungry for wilderness experience. The canyon's abrupt, forbidding landscape—including the deepest chasm in North America, deeper even than the Grand Canyon—seemed secure until public and private power companies began to fight over which would harness the wild Snake with a power dam, and drown the gorge. The Supreme Court ruled that no dam could be built in Hell's Canyon until alternative sites, alternative sources of power, and the need for additional power in the area had been considered. Both of Idaho's senators have cosponsored a bill to forbid the destruction of the gorge. Conservationists will not relax until the Snake is given Federal protection as a wild river.

Meanwhile, the recent high bidding for drilling rights on Alaska's oil-rich North Slope has dramatized the defense of America's last truly vast wilderness. Northern Alaska's Arctic climate and grim topography conceal the vulnerability of the environment. Under a thin layer of topsoil, the ground is permanently frozen. A minor disturbance of the topsoil will expose the permafrost to thawing and erosion. The dry cold inhibits the natural restoration of the environment once it has been injured. Even organic refuse persists wherever it falls, in the perpetual deep freeze.

Not even the most quixotic conservationist dreams that the Alaskan oil reserves will be left in the ground. A year and a half after the first well came in, airlines serving the oil country were booked 5,000 flights ahead. But a concerted effort is being made, with the support of the Interior Department headed by former Alaska Governor Walter Hickel, to cushion the effect of inevitable development on the irreplaceable wilderness.

Closer to home for most Americans, in the urban areas where 70 percent of the population crowds together on one percent of the land, the preservation of wilderness is a long-gone issue. In the entire Northeast, the single full-fledged national park is an island preserve in northern Maine. Neighborhood groups and a few corporations in New York City scratch in the rubble of vacant lots to plant vest-pocket oases, while the Sierra Club takes arms against the intrusion of a semiprivate croquet field in Central Park. Any open space larger than a window box is desperately coveted to provide even minimal recreation for the maximum number of people.

In recent years, attention has focused on urban waterfronts as the most neglected inner-city resource for recreation. Before rail and air transport altered the flow of our lives, we were a nation of seaports, river ports, lake ports. Boston, New York, Philadelphia, Charleston, Savannah, Jacksonville on the East Coast; San Francisco and Seattle on the West; New Orleans, St. Louis, Chicago, Cleveland, Detroit, Buffalo in between: all are waterfront towns. But for the most part, their waterfronts are decaying with age and disuse, or strangled by surrounding urban growth, or zoned for commercial use; in one way or another, they have become unavailable to millions of city people physically and spiritually starved for open space and contact with nature.

Some cities are beginning to re-establish recreation alongside commerce as the best use of their waterfronts. In Boston and Savannah, crumbling commercial buildings have been restored to useful life. A plan for the renovation of lower Manhattan reorients that part of the city outward toward its original focus, the magnificant harbor. And Peter Seeger sails the sloop *Clearwater* in the polluted Hudson to inspire a cleanup.

Until this year, historic old New Orleans was shadowed by long-standing plans to build a superhighway between the French Quarter and its Mississippi riverfront. A citizens' group fought the plan all the way to Washington, and forced the last-minute discovery of a better route on the other side of the river.

The San Francisco area has been fighting hard for its waterfront, perhaps because San Francisco Bay is so much to lose, and because so much of it has already been lost. In the century since California joined the Union, the surface area of the bay has shrunk by about one-third, through filling and diking. According to the U.S. Army Corps of Engineers, ever helpful in such matters, more than half the remaining bay is similarly "susceptible of reclamation." Private interests and local governments claim ownership of almost half the bay, and these are the very landlords who have been most anxious in the past to convert shallow water into real estate. Proposals have already been filed to fill ten percent of what is left for private development, while of the bay's 276-mile shoreline, only an estimated ten miles are open to the public for recreation.

San Francisco Bay was doomed to contract into a river until a committee of citizens determined to save it. They engineered the creation of a San Francisco Bay Conservation and Development Commission, with the power to control garbage dumping, filling and development around the bay until a thorough study could be made.

The commission's report was unequivocal: "The most important uses of the bay are those providing substantial public benefits and treating the bay as a body of water, not as real estate." The commission, its life and powers newly extended by the California legislature, now has a chance to implement the specific recommendations of its report. For the first time since 1850, there are plans to enlarge the bay, not diminish it.

Between the extremes of the city and the wilderness, America has a whole catalogue of environmental problems to solve, from imbalances in the ecology of suburban backyards to interstate and national crises like air and water pollution.

But pursuing any one of our problems to its source will bring us up against a common root: population. America has clung to the belief that continued population growth can fuel a perpetual gravy train. Not long ago, we held a public celebration to herald the birth of the two-hundred-millionth American, whose own offspring already figure prominently in the rosy forecasts of corporate annual reports. Looking at a mid-19th century America of 25 million people, the Scottish essayist Thomas Carlyle predicted: "You won't have any trouble in your country as long as you have few people and much land, but when you have many people and little land, your trials will begin." As we worry about the social and psychological chaos of our cities, as we probe the whole complex pathology of American life, we may conclude that our trials are indeed beginning. We may begin to question whether we have outgrown the power of our democratic insitutions to cope. And we may wonder what will happen to the quality of our lives, and to our precious liberty, early in the next century, when we will be twice as many Americans, in twice as many houses, with twice as many automobiles on twice as many highways, and twice as many. . . . How much of America will be beautiful then? There are no New Edens.

WASTELAND

By Marya Mannes

Cans. Beer cans. Glinting on the verges of a million miles of roadways, lying in scrub, grass, dirt, leaves, sand, mud, but never hidden. Piel's, Rheingold, Ballantine, Schaefer, Schlitz, shining in the sun or picked by moon or the beams of headlights at night; washed by rain or flattened by wheels, but never dulled, never buried, never destroyed. Here is the mark of savages, the testament of wasters, the stain of prosperity.

Who are these men who defile the grassy borders of our roads and lanes, who pollute our ponds, who spoil the purity of our ocean beaches with the empty vessels of their thirst? Who are the men who make these vessels in millions and then say, "Drink—and discard"? What society is this that can afford to cast away a million tons of metal and to make of wild and fruitful land a garbage heap?

What manner of men and women need thirty feet of steel and two hundred horsepower to take them, singly, to their small destinations? Who demand that what they eat is wrapped so that forests are cut down to make the paper that is thrown away, and what they smoke and chew is sealed so that the sealers can be tossed in gutters and caught in twigs and grass?

What kind of men can afford to make the streets of their towns and cities hideous with neon at night, and their roadways hideous with signs by day, wasting beauty; who leave the carcasses of cars to rot in heaps; who spill their trash into ravines and make smoking mountains of refuse for the town's rats? What manner of men choke off the life in rivers, streams and lakes with the waste of their produce, making poison of water?

Who is as rich as that? Slowly the wasters and despoilers are impoverishing our land, our nature, and our beauty, so that there will not be one beach, one hill, one lane, one meadow, one forest free from the debris of man and the stigma of his improvidence.

Who is so rich that he can squander forever the wealth of earth and water for the trivial needs of vanity or the compulsive demands of greed;

or so prosperous in land that he can sacrifice nature for unnatural desires? The earth we abuse and the living things we kill will, in the end, take their revenge; for in exploiting their presence we are diminishing our future.

And what will we leave behind us when we are long dead? Temples? Amphora? Sunken treasure?

Or mountains of twisted, rusted steel, canyons of plastic containers, and a million miles of shores garlanded, not with the lovely wrack of the sea, but with the cans and bottles and light-bulbs and boxes of a people conserved their convenience at the expense of their heritage, and whose ephemeral prosperity was built on waste.

POLLUTION

If you visit American city,
You will find it very pretty.
Just two things of which you must beware:
Don't drink the water and don't breathe the air.
Pollution, pollution,
They got smog and sewage and mud,
Turn on your tap and get hot and cold running crud.

See the halibuts and the sturgeons
Being wiped out by detergents.
Fish got to swim and birds got to fly
But they don't last long if they try.
Pollution, pollution,
You can use the latest toothpaste,
And then rinse your mouth with industrial waste.

Just go out for a breath of air,
And you'll be ready for Medicare.
The city streets are really quite a thrill,
If the hoods don't get you, the monoxide will.

Pollution, pollution,
Wear a gas mask and a veil.
Then you can breathe, long as you don't inhale.

Lots of things there that you can drink,
But stay away from the kitchen sink.
Throw out your breakfast garbage, and I've got a
      hunch
That the folks downstream will drink it for lunch.

So go to the city, see the crazy people there.
Like lambs to the slaughter
They're drinking the water
And breathing the air.

　　　— *Tom　Lehrer*

Reprinted by permission of Tom Lehrer, 1965.

THE GLOBAL DIMENSIONS OF HEALTH

By Albert Rosenfeld

April 22 has been designated Environment Day, or Earth Day, featuring simultaneous teach-ins at thousands of college campuses across the nation. What's it all about? Another one of those incomprehensible Happenings on the other side of The Generation Gap? Another excuse for the youngsters to make a lot of noise? Anything but.

To be sure, some of the more activist students can be expected to take advantage of the event to engineer disruptions and take-overs. But that is not what Earth Day is about. Nor should the more bizarre sidelights, if they do occur, divert us from what Earth Day *is* about. It signifies an almost explosive public awakening to the fact that man's well-being depends on the well-being of the planet he lives on, and includes the well-being of the other creatures who share it with him. Earth Day also symbolizes the coming-into-its-own of the science of ecology—the study that embraces all living organisms in the context of their total natural environments.

If the world ecology has an abstract ring to it, with only the remotest relevance to our everyday personal lives, consider the following:

Air pollution is on the rise almost everywhere, even in what were considered safely rural areas. In Los Angeles, on half the days of the year, school children are being advised *not to exercise*, for fear they will breathe too deeply of the smog-laden air.

Waters everywhere are becoming dangerously polluted. In one dramatic instance last summer, the Cuyahoga River in Ohio got so full of oily wastes that *the waters caught on fire* and burned for several days.

Noise pollution is a growing medical and psychiatric concern as a discordant crescendo of hyped-up sound assaults our ears and nervous systems. We have all read about the sonic boom. But even an ordinary subway train operates at a decibel level above the threshold where deafness begins. Many common noises, scientists are discovering, can do damage to an embryo developing in what used to be considered the safety of the womb.

Reprinted by permission of *Family Health*, April, 1970.

Pesticide residues are almost universally present in living organisms. We have all seen pictures of the corpses of birds and fish killed by insecticides, but few of us realize that the flesh of the average American could never pass the standards set by inspectors for the marketplace; it contains pesticide residues far beyond the maximum permissible concentration. For the same reason, the milk that infants drink from their mothers' breasts would be pronounced unfit for sale by a commercial dairy. A recent protest poster showed an expectant mother's breast in profile, with the label: "Caution—keep out of reach of children."

Though we smile at such sardonic humor, no one really thinks the situation is funny. Fortunately, an understanding of its seriousness has been spreading rapidly from the scientific community to the consumer—with the college student acting as a catalyst—to the halls where high policy is made. The new awareness is attested to by the sudden spurt of political interest at every level, from municipal to federal, and especially by the emphasis given it in the President's State of the Union message.

The awakening comes none too soon. Back in the seventeenth century, when the poet John Donne wrote "No man is an Island, entire of it self," it required a leap of creative insight to recognize man's interdependence with his surroundings. But today, in the latter part of the twentieth century, this basic concept has to be incorporated into the common understanding of the human race; otherwise, we go the way of the dinosaur.

We are very much in the position of astronauts on an Apollo mission. In a space capsule, if the crew members use up their supplies too quickly, if they foul their life-support system, all of them die—no matter which one might have been responsible.

On the spacecraft we call Earth, man is both pilot and passenger. All his life-support systems are contained in the thin envelope of air and water known as the biosphere. It stretches above the ground no more than 400 feet, and under the water only 500 feet. As Spaceship Earth sweeps through the void in its majestic solar orbit, its 3.5-billion-man crew is using up its resources at an extravagant rate and fouling its life-support systems with a remarkable lack of regard for consequences. It is easy to forget that the frail and tenuous biosphere is all that separates us from the inhospitable cold and vacuum of the cosmos.

To put it another way, ecologists are telling us that we all live in the same fish bowl. Any disturbance anywhere in the bowl is felt everywhere else in the bowl. Poisons, a drop at a time here and there, gradually diffuse, and no creature anywhere in the bowl is immune. On Earth today, whatever anyone does happens to everyone else as well—whether they like it or not, whether they know it or not. Under these circumstances, health takes on global dimensions.

Take DDT as one example. Blown by the winds and borne by the waters, this persistent pesticide has been found in a variety of living creatures as far afield as Antarctica and the Galápagos Islands. Even where it is present in seemingly insignificant quantities, it can build up to formidable concentrations as it goes through the complexities of the food chain. In one study at Big Bear Lake in California, the DDT in the water amounted to no more than two tenths of one part per million. But in the plankton that floated on the water, the concentration had built up to 77 parts per million; in the goldfish that ate the plankton, to 200 parts per million; and in the pelicans that ate the goldfish, to 1,700 parts per million.

In our human fish bowl, we Americans alone use some 25 trillion gallons of water every year. Virtually all of it has already been used, perhaps more than once, by some other person, creature, or industry. The waters that run through the continents are full of diverse dumpings, from the subtlest of chemical pollutants to outright garbage. Even the oceans are not limitless in their capacity to absorb it all. In Lake Erie, all life has died except for a strange mutant carp that thrives on contaminants.

Even the sparkling lakes of Switzerland and the fabled fjords of Norway are clouded and awash with junk, and the Rhine is recognized as "the sewer of Europe." A man who takes excellent care of himself and goes only to the best doctors and surgeons can still get hepatitis from polluted clams in New York or acute gastroenteritis from the drinking water in Cleveland. If he lives in any one of many smog-bound cities, a mere change in weather may bring on wheezing or aggravate whatever respiratory troubles already afflict him.

As a matter of fact, on an individual basis neither men nor families can ensure good health for themselves, no matter how carefully they follow any given regimen of diet and exercise, no matter how extensive—or how expensive—are the medical facilities they can call upon.

Each of our bodies and minds is constantly assailed by the ingredients we collectively add to the world. Noise and stress, for instance—noise enough to put a continuing overload on a man's cardiovascular system and increase his chances of heart attack; stress enough to drive un-

stable personalities (or even stable ones) to violence. The list is long. Radiation—from bomb tests, power plants, radioactive wastes. Pesticides are herbicides. Food additions, preservatives, and colorants. Drugs and detergents. Belchings into the atmosphere of all manner of gases and particle-filled wastes from automobiles and smokestacks—in such volume, some scientists believe, as to change drastically the nature of the biosphere. Depending on circumstances, the temperature of the earth could either (1) go up, melting the polar ice caps and inundating coastal cities and plains, or (2) go down, bringing on a new Ice Age.

The basic unit of ecology is a very large one, the "ecosystem." An ecosystem takes in everything necessary to maintain in stable balance a given chain of life—in other words, a natural community, taken in its entirety. Ecosystems vary in size and scope from region to region, and the whole earth consists of one vast interrelated ecosystem. One of the key elements in our global ecosystem is the presence of green plants.

Through the process of photosynthesis, green plants are the only things on earth capable of utilizing the sun's energy to turn raw, inorganic elements into living matter. They absorb the carbon dioxide that we breathe out, and we stay alive on the oxygen they exhale. Greenery is indispensable to our own existence. Yet, in this nation alone, we eliminate more than a million acres of greenery and trees every year by paving them over, mostly for highways, partly for home and industrial use. In so doing, we create the means to pollute the air and use up its oxygen, while at the same time destroying the means to renew the atmosphere's oxygen supply.

Some 70 percent of the earth's oxygen is manufactured by phytoplankton, the tiny plants that float on the surfaces of the seas. The sheer extent of the oceans would therefore seem to ensure perpetual oxygen renewal. But we certainly cannot count on that. A few accidents could upset the balance. If the *Torrey Canyon*, the tanker that spilled its huge cargo of oil along the British coast in 1967, had dumped a cargo of herbicides instead, it might have wiped out all the phytoplankton in the North Sea. Even without such a mishap, it takes the accumulation of only one milligram of DDT in a thousand quarts of sea water to diminish its oxygen-producing capacity by a fourth.

In any ecosystem's complexly woven web of life, even small tamperings can produce large and unlooked-for consequences. Nor is a highly developed industrial setting necessary to set in motion a chain of events that can endanger the health of an entire population.

Out in the coral reefs of the Pacific, for instance, certain sea creatures were collected in great quantities because of a profitable market in their lovely shells. Some of these creatures were voracious eaters of the starfish known as Crown of Thorns. As the predators have diminished in numbers, the starfish have proliferated and are now eating up the coral reefs at an alarming rate. The fish that lived in the coral reefs have been moving elsewhere. The islanders have thus lost not only their main source of food, but also their principal barrier against the mighty buffetings of the sea itself.

In sections of South Africa, the hippopotamus once wallowed in clumsy splendor on the riverbanks. Because the hippos were considered to be a useless nuisance, they were shot wholesale. Then came the medical backlash: schistosomiasis, a wracking and debilitating disease of the liver and intestines. It turned out that, with the hippos gone, there was nothing to stir up the river silt and the area became an ideal breeding grounds for the worm that causes schistosomiasis. No one would have predicted—no one but an ecologist, that is—that declaring open season on hippos would bring on an epidemic. But it did.

Even under pastoral conditions, then, the chain of life is readily interfered with. The interference rate goes up sharply as soon as industrialization and urbanization set in. In a recent report, Dr. Warren Winkelstein, Jr., head of the epidemiology division of the School of Public Health at the University of California, Berkeley, declared that environment was "the most important determinant" of health.

To support his assertion, Dr. Winkelstein offered the results of a 10-year study in Buffalo, N.Y., comparing the health of people living in polluted, industrialized neighborhoods, with the health of those living in relatively pollution-free areas. By every measurement known to medicine, the first group suffered from much poorer health and a higher overall death rate. The mere improvement—even the perfection—of medical services and facilities will never do much for them, in Winkelstein's view, unless something is also done about the environment.

One thing that might be done about the environment, says Dr. Walter Modell, a Cornell University pharmacologist, is to develop drugs that would help "make an intolerable environment tolerable." By this he does not mean to offer everyone chemical blues-chasers to make them forget their troubles, as in *Brave New World*. He is referring to drugs that really do things to toxic materials in the human body. Writing in *Medical World News*, Dr. Modell says research has already turned up various drugs that can, in certain instances, (1) step up the production of poison-destroying enzymes, (2) permit the body to excrete poisons more rapidly, (3) directly suppress the effects of poisons, or (4) combine with the poisonous substances in ways that render them no longer poisonous.

In brief, Dr. Modell suggests that an intensive research program might well provide an armamentarium of drugs that could combat pollution internally. Though it would be convenient to have such drugs at hand, few people relish the prospect as a way of life. (Remember the famous E. B. White story where everyone in the world must get "Tri-D shots" at regular 21-day intervals "to counteract the lethal effect of food"?)

Besides, very few medical scientists—probably not even Dr. Modell himself—would regard such a program, however ingeniously executed, as anything more than an interim solution for the complexities of environmental medicine. In fact, we cannot blindly count on medicine, science, or technology—as many people naively do—to come up with any definitive solutions, though they may provide us indispensable tools for the task. Over the long pull, radical therapy must be administered to the

---

Somehow we've got to change from a growth-oriented, exploitative system to one focused on stability and conservation. *Paul R. Ehrlich*

---

sick environment itself. It is time to clean the fish bowl.

Happily, recognition of this pressing need is spreading around the world of medicine, and there now exists a National Institute of Environmental Health Sciences, located at Research Triangle Park, N.C. "The importance of each physician's and scientist's stake in environmental health," says its director, Dr. Paul Kotin, "is an almost academic consideration. As a citizen, as a unit of a waste-producing society, and as one who insists on progress, each shares in all of society's responsibilities for environmental contamination."

The point that Dr. Kotin makes for the benefit of doctors and scientists really applies to all of us: much of the existing pollution comes about simply because each of us demands a high technological standard of living. Each of us wants houses, cars, electricity, highways, slick packaging, fashionable clothes, food of any kind in all seasons, and every variety of gadgetry. There are more of us all the time, and each individual, especially if he has classified himself until now as a have-not, is insisting on a more plentiful share of worldly goods.

It is all too easy to wax fat (or aspire to) while self-righteously denouncing all those profit-hungry industrialists and all those stupid government bureaucrats. Industry and government should certainly be assigned their share of the blame. But the true villain of the piece, if there is one, is none other than the victim: the consumer. Especially the American consumer. The United States, with only 5.7 percent of the world's population, uses up about 40 percent of the world's resources.

According to Sen. Gaylord Nelson (D-Wis.)—who discovered ecology before it was in vogue and who is a vocal encourager of Earth Day— every year Americans junk seven million cars, 100 million tires, 28 million tons of paper, 28 *billion* bottles, and 48 billion cans. It costs nearly $3 billion a year just to collect it, and getting rid of it is a task of staggering proportions. *Time* magazine has estimated that the garbage and trash discarded by Californians alone would make a wall 30 feet high and 100 feet wide stretching all the way from Oregon to the Mexican border.

The Lord may have created the earth for man to have dominion over, but He surely had in mind a custodianship of nature's glories and harmonies rather than their conversion into a global garbage dump. "We've already run out of earth," says Martin Litton, a director of the Sierra Club, "and nothing we can do will keep humankind in existence for as long as another two centuries."

Not all conservationists share quite so pessimistic a view. Dr. Barry Commoner, biologist and pioneer in the new ecological renaissance, believes that "we are in a period of grace. We have . . . perhaps a generation . . . to save the environment from . . . the violence we have done to it."

To reverse the consequences of our own past follies will be costly— in time, in energy, in patience, and in hard cash. But to fail to make the necessary commitments, would be costlier still—in human health, in human lives, even in hard cash. And it would also be a dirty trick to play on our children, and on theirs. They can only inherit what we leave them.

On a planetary scale, there are no longer haves and have-nots. We all make it, or none of us does. Our family becomes the whole human family, and our health is inseparable from the earth's.

411

OUR EFFLUENT SOCIETY

By Eric B. Outwater

From now to the turn of the century the five boroughs of New York City will generate enough bottles, cans, paper and other solid waste to cover Central Park with a plateau the height of the Empire State Building.

No means for the disposal of most of it, short of shipping by train for deposit elsewhere, has as yet been conceived. It is no longer just a problem of "Keeping America Beautiful" by depositing trash in a litter basket; at a cost of from 60 to 90 cents to pick up one item of litter that has not been placed in the basket, we are now generating waste at the staggering rate of almost five pounds per day per person, and "where to put it" is growing into a crisis of monumental proportions.

Waste collection and disposal now cost the American public $6 billion per year, and the price keeps escalating. The word "disposal" is an unfortunate choice of words; "deposit" would be more apt, as more than 80 per cent of the solid waste in the United States goes into the ground pretty much in the form we discard it. The alternate methods of disposal are also far from ideal. The most common is to dump into an open pit, where combustion takes place which pollutes the air. Then leaching by rain pollutes the water table, and vermin infestation adds another unpleasant dimension to the problem.

The unsavory sight of such an area during its use and the uncertain qualities of its future use as a site for home building or as a recreational area leave only one redeeming feature— it's cheap. When waste is placed into the ground, there remains a residue from all methods of disposal that should be treated by a technique called sanitary land fill. By use of mechanical equipment the waste is not only compacted to reduce its volume, but is also daily covered by a layer of soil so that any burning is inhibited and exposure of the waste is at a minimum. By burying them we tend to forget the fact that many items of solid waste are virtually indestructible even after their deposit in the ground. A plastic bottle buried today will be in virtually the same condition ten or even a hundred centuries later.

Although most people believe that municipal incineration takes care of the problem, this is far from the case. The poor design of incinerators has made this technique not only costly but also a major contributor to air pollution. In New Jersey, of 32 incinerators built, only eleven are still operated. Uncontrolled incineration of the familiar open-burning or on-site type leaves bulky debris, and results in such self-defeating chaos as the 300,000 tons of solid matter that are discharged in the air of New York City every year, with the resultant vast cost of removal through cleaning and sweeping. As the composition of waste includes more and more fire-resistant items, such as glass and metal, these add to the residue that must be removed from the incinerator and deposited elsewhere.

A much-touted system of re-use and reclamation to recover part of the cost is known as "composting." This system does produce something of value to the farmer. But, unfortunately, the cost of production and the fact that our largest waste-generating areas are far from agricultural areas has made composting in most areas

Reprinted by permission of *National Review*, February 24, 1970.

uneconomical when compared to its more efficient chemical equivalent.

Ideally, waste should be reclaimed and cycled into a re-use pattern such as the system built in the space capsules. Some effort has been made with the aluminum beer can, but economies of re-use and a trend in consumer demand has resulted in almost all consumer packaging being on a one-trip, single-service basis. Even with waste paper: as recently as fifteen years ago over 60 per cent was salvaged, but today, due to the economics of the paper industry, only 10 to 20 per cent is recycled. Regrettably, manual sorting is the only way known to separate plastic, aluminum and glass from waste. Ideally, manual sorting should be done in the home or at the point of initial disposal. To accomplish this, a vast consumer education program would be necessary, as well as a system of economic incentives for recycling.

The crisis in disposal is also complicated by the arbitrary political boundaries between communities. Where one area has high population density, another might have land available for disposal. Getting two

communities to agree on a mutually acceptable arrangement has often proved impossible. Compounding the difficulty is the fact that physical boundaries of watersheds, airsheds and disposal areas are not likely to coincide.

This points up the competition for sites between the community need for living space, and the community need for a deposit area or disposal site. The inability of local governments and private groups to solve their own problems and the unwillingness of industry to acknowledge its role in the disposal crisis have raised the possibility of massive intervention of the Federal Government.

There are, of course, many sources of pollution other than solid waste that affect our environment. As the number of automobiles soars and the level of air pollution increases, the ability of the atmosphere to cleanse itself of exhaust falls farther and farther behind. Additionally, there is oil pollution in the ocean, pollution of water through dumping raw sewage and industrial waste, and even noise pollution.

It is interesting to note that many

of the proponents of conservation talk in such phrases as "clean air," "pure water" and "litter free." These are, of course, no longer realistic goals for a conservationist—he can now only strive to keep the levels of waste and pollution below the community's threshold of non-acceptability. These levels of tolerance are closely related to what a community is willing to pay, in relation to what it is willing to put up with. This is normally the conditioning of people already hardened through continued exposure to varying degrees of pollution. A ghetto family is likely to be resigned to dirty streets, but draws the line at rat infestation.

In most areas we are willing to accept the fact that if things don't get worse, we can put up with them. But, of course, the situation everywhere will get worse, in geometrical proportion, in the near future. New York City is facing the problem of having no more deposit sites within seven years, at the present rate of generation, without resorting to using trains to ship the material to some distant site.

The hope has been often expressed that technological breakthroughs will come to alleviate the problem. These are usually a matter of incentives, which do not appear as yet to exist. A survey of the hundred largest manufacturers in the United States shows little or no involvement in the development of any methods to alleviate the waste problem, even that generated by the use of their own products. Rarely has clear-cut acknowledgement been made of their responsibility for adding to our pollution and waste-disposal problems. This is understandable, since the aims of the package manufacturer and the conservationist not only fail to coincide, but conflict. The conserva-

tionist would like to see packaging homogeneous, easily degradable and uniform in size. The packager strives to achieve marketability through more types of packages and combinations of materials that are the strongest possible.

What will it take to make industry assume its responsibility in this area? Perhaps a Ralph Nader or Rachel Carson will come along and act as a catalyst, or some new breakthrough in reduction and energy exchange may be developed. What is much more likely is belated governmental recognition of the problem, followed by severe and strict federal and state legislation and interference at every level.

The following excerpt from a bill introduced in the New York State Senate by Senator Seymour in February 1968 was one of at least seventeen acts introduced in as many state legislatures concerned with ultimate disposal of packaging materials: "To prescribe regulations governing the design and composition of disposable containers manufactured or sold within the state, to facilitate reclamation of waste materials contained therein or to aid the decomposition or other disposal thereof."

When we consider that pollution problems result not only from such tangible items as old cars and furniture, ships, packages, smoke and building rubble, but also from heat, noise, waste water, invisible odorless gas, and crop fertilizers, and affect health, crops and even the supply of oxygen in our atmosphere, we realize the staggering opportunities for the well-meaning government bureau to involve itself in every level of our existence.

Effective voluntary limitation of much waste generation would be possible if the economic advantages were fully understood and translated into tangible financial savings. Lower maintenance costs to home owners, the easing of discomfort and the reduction of doctor bills for asthma sufferers could be proven if, for instance, the sulfur content of fuel oil used for heating were lowered. The marketing convenience of one-way packages for beverages would not be as attractive if the disposal costs were reflected in tax savings by bottlers who furnish returnable deposit bottles.

Federal legislation enacted in a time of acute crisis, by necessity, is normally overly restrictive when applied nationally, regardless of degree of the crisis in a particular area. Waste and pollution problems vary markedly by area. Local ordinances could reflect the needs of particular communities and would tend to be more equitable. To pass worthwhile local ordinances and to encourage community cooperation, there must be an accurate source of unbiased information. Until recently no public service organization existed on a national level that could supply the necessary unbiased and accurate information on which a local community could base its planning, and which could factually mediate between political groups.

A new non-profit organization has been organized called FORCE, the Foundation for Responsible Conservation of our Environment, which will be programming a data bank to give up-to-date answers to such questions as cost and efficiency of various disposal methods, as they apply to a particular area. Also under study will be the level of public tolerance for waste and pollution. More important,

FORCE will provide information assistance, such as accurate data regarding the addition or deletion of various sources of waste and pollution on a national level. Thus, if a soft-drink bottler switches to a particular package, this fact will be programmed and related to its effect on the disposal facilities of a specified community in that bottler's distribution area, so that long range planning and local legislation can be geared to fact, as it applies to that area. This will eliminate guesswork, or the costly and lengthy undertaking of a private study by a consulting firm on an area-by-area basis.

It must be apparent that James Reston's recent statement in the *New York Times* that "the old optimistic illusion that we can do anything we want is giving way to doubt, even to a new pessimism" is again confirmed by our seeming plunge into a conflicting chaos of cause and effect in the constant changes in our human environment. We should take heart however from the fact that modern man can adjust and thrive in an atmosphere of environmental pollution, crowding, dietary deficiency, monotony and ugliness, at the same time heeding the warning of René Dubos in his book *So Human an Animal* that "all too often the wisdom of the body is a short-sighted wisdom" and "evaluated over the entire lifespan, the homeostatic mechanisms through which adaption is achieved often fail in the long run because they result in delayed pathological effects."

We must hope that man's massive interventions will not, in William Faulkner's words, "turn the earth into a howling waste, from which he would be the first to vanish."

WHAT YOU CAN DO ABOUT POLLUTION

By A. R. Roalman

"Look at that smoke!" The group was standing in front of a floor-to-ceiling window in their new offices. About 200 feet away a large stack disgorged thick, black smoke. Someone in the group commented on the ugliness of the smoke and how it was polluting the air. But, like most big-city residents, they had learned to accept polluting smokestacks as part of their lives.

The stack did become part of life for the people in the new office building. About 30 times a day, for short periods of from one to three minutes, the carbon-black smoke came out in thick swirls.

But nobody did anything except watch and complain to one another. Nobody did anything, that is, until one man, an amateur photographer, brought his camera to the office one day and had it ready each time the black smoke began to come out. He took about 20 photographs that showed black, ugly smoke against an otherwise bright background. He sent them to a local newspaper. He was

determined to do *something* about the offensive smoke.

Nothing happened during the next two weeks.

Then he decided on a new approach and called city hall. He asked if there was a smoke-abatement office. Not only was there a smoke-abatement office but an official there was anxious to hear about the problem. "We don't have the manpower to spot all of the offenses that occur," said the official. "We are very much dependent upon calls from people like you."

That afternoon, an inspector from the smoke-abatement office visited the building with the polluting smokestack. A few weeks afterwards, the black, thick smoke stopped pouring out of the building.

Worth noting is that one person— an ordinary citizen—was the key to stopping the pollution. It demonstrated an important point: While pollution is a giant problem, it is not so large that individuals cannot do something to combat it.

One suburbanite, disturbed from

Reprinted by permission of the American Medical Association from *Today's Health*, March 1969.

"<u>Now</u> maybe they'll be moved to do something about water pollution!"

his weekend sleep by gas-powered model airplanes and power mowers that were operated during relatively early morning hours, sat down and calmly wrote a well-thought-out letter to his village's governing board. He encouraged adoption of an ordinance that would stop "noise pollution of our town" (a suburban area of about 20,000 people) by banning such noise makers before 10 a.m.

The letter, signed by the heads of 30 different households in the area before it was mailed to the village board, was considered by the village fathers and, ultimately, passed, without serious opposition, into law. Apparently, a number of residents had been awakened by the roar of power mowers and model airplanes. Now the town remains relatively hushed so that people can rest, especially on weekends.

The fact is, many individuals *have* done some impressive things to combat pollution. They are not all Rachel Carsons capable of writing society-rocking books. Most are citizens who have wondered if they could do something, and they found that the power of the individual still is great, even in our king-size society. Here are seven more cases of people who became concerned about the pollution that is befouling our waters, land, and skies and chose to do something about it.

In the fall of 1968, President Johnson signed a bill establishing a tract of land in northern New Jersey as Great Swamp National Wildlife Refuge Wilderness. The signing seemed to crown with victory a long struggle by area conservationist groups to save the swamp from the Port of New York Authority, which wanted the land for a jetport.

The future of Great Swamp, however, was as dismal as its mid-November foliage, for a township was determined to continue dumping trash and garbage on the northern property of the swamp. Seepage from the dump was poisoning the swamp.

Mrs. Helen Fenske—secretary of the North Jersey Conservation Federation, which raised nearly a million dollars to preserve the swamp—found it "ironic" that communities that were so eager to save the swamp from developers were now so complacent over the pollution threat.

Soon Mrs. Fenske was circulating petitions to stop dumping that would hurt Great Swamp and her work led to a telephone campaign. She and her friends also encouraged public hearings which received newspaper and television publicity. Public feeling was aroused to the point where the dumping stopped in December.

The Flat River in Michigan today offers good fishing because of John Fravel, a fisherman who in 1965 became upset about pollution. He became upset because fish he had caught in the Flat were contaminated with petroleum.

When he and his wife, Mary, ate the fish, both became ill. "The experience almost made us move to Florida," says Fravel. They were long-time residents of Michigan, but pollution of their favorite stream was the last straw.

"Why not call the head of the conservation department?" Mary asked. "Surely, they could do something."

The head of the department, Dr. Howard Tanner, was interested in Fravel's report and asked for a letter. A few days after the letter went in the mail, Fravel had a call from a representative of the states water resources commission. The water resources man said that he would begin working on the problem, trying to find the sources of the polluting oil.

But the commission's man was not able to track down the oil source as easily as he had expected. Finally the water resources commission found, with the help of Fravel and other fishermen in the area, two sources of pollution. One company was dumping phosphates which caused excessive weed growth in the river, and another was allowing machine oil to drain into the Flat. Both companies, when they saw the damage they were doing to a good fishing stream, invested about $100,000 each in units that prevented further pollution. Chalk up another victory—after two years—for a man who decided to do something about pollution.

Harry Martin works for a company that has a factory on the Mississippi River. One day his supervisor ordered him to dump waste cyanide into a drain pipe. He told his supervisor that that act would kill a lot of fish.

His supervisor ordered him to do it anyway, so he did. But then he went to the telephone and called John Warren, outdoors editor of the Moline, Illinois, *Daily Dispatch*. The resultant story caused considerable embarrassment to Martin's employer, and stopped his foreman from ever again ordering anybody to do what he had ordered Martin to do.

One of the more unusual fights against pollution was led by Arthur Glowka of Stamford, Connecticut. A long-time fighter against pollution of the Hudson River, he discovered that the still-valid federal River and Harbor Act of 1888 had a section specifying that half of all fines collected from persons convicted of polluting the river would be paid to the person who reported the violation.

"This is bounty hunting at its best," according to Glowka, who says that such a provision has stimulated people in his area to report violations.

He also discovered, recently, that the Federal Refuse Act of 1899 has the same provisions for any navigable water in the United States. He says that it had been difficult to get the U.S. attorney in the area to act on pollution reports, but there now is an indictment against a large railroad accused of pouring oil continuously into the Hudson River. Fines for convictions under the 1888 and 1899 laws are a minimum of $250 and a maximum of $2500, so informants can make from $125 to $1250 by reporting concrete evidence of pollution action *that results in a conviction.**

James Robey, outdoor writer for the Dayton *Journal Herald*, says Pete Gam, a local resident, has led a relentless effort to clean the waters of Ohio. Unlike many people who take only isolated actions to halt pollution, Gram has been working at it for more than 30 years. When he sees evidence that an industry or municipality has dumped pollutants in a stream, he calls the press. "Only in the past two years, since others are becoming aware of the problem of pollution, has his work begun to produce results," says Robey.

Gram has written or telephoned to congressmen, county trustees, game protectors, and, especially, outdoors writers. He has found the latter group

*U.S. attorneys have the responsibility for prosecution under the Federal Refuse Act of 1899, which applies to any navigable water in the country. Informants must have a specific pollution situation, such as oil or raw sewage pouring out of a pipe into a river. With firm evidence, the next step is a letter to the area's U.S. attorney. Informants should identify the place where the pollution is occurring; include supporting documents, such as a statement from a local conservation officer; and lay claim to the cash bounty. If the U.S. attorney doesn't act on the matter, he can be sued.

to be valuable contacts, since they are able to gather facts and prepare articles that catch the attention of the public.

As a result of Gram's recent efforts, state officials have designated the Mad River—one of the few Ohio waterways that will support trout—as water worthy of higher pollution-control standards than previously had been assigned to it. But Gram still isn't satisfied. Now he wants the higher standards enforced, and he has the support of two biology professors who have written testimonials supporting his efforts to clean up the River.

The Izaac Walton League of America reports that Clarence Stuebe of Peoria, Illinois, has been effective in a continuing battle to clean up the Illinois River. Stuebe provided a great deal of the raw information used by former state senator Clyde Trager in his successful legislative efforts to obtain passage of present state water-pollution laws.

Stuebe also has talked before several citizens groups in an effort to get them interested in pollution legislation. Among the people contacted by Stuebe have been those manning Peoria newspapers and radio and television stations. He also encouraged his employer, Caterpiller Tractor Co., to stop practices that caused pollution and to encourage other industries to stop theirs.

A fishing-lure manufacturer and fish-hatchery operator named William Gressard became incensed when he saw the city of Akron, Ohio, dumping sludge into the Cuyahoga River. The sludge came from the city's water-treatment plant and contained impurities removed from the city's water, plus other chemicals used in the treatment of water. Tests showed that the sludge killed plants necessary to support fish in the river.

He wrote letters to conservation groups and to city officials. He also contacted the state health department and the *Record-Courier*, a newspaper serving Ravenna and Kent, Ohio.

Fighting with Akron city officials, Gressard found an ammunition-packed legal precedent. Akron had been found guilty of damaging the property of a farm below the site of the water-treatment plant and was paying damages to the farm owner.

To dramatize his fight, Gressard also began to fish below the dam that was part of the water-treatment plant. According to an Akron ordinance, people were forbidden to fish within 1000 feet of the dam. Gressard maintained that the river was a navigable waterway and not city property. Therefore, city officials could not prohibit anyone from fishing there.

Local newspapers became interested in the fight of one man against a polluting city. His fight eventually led to the city of Akron building sludge basins to stop the pollution.

"What can one man do?" asked a subsequent editorial in the *Record-Courier*.

"This question is an oft-repeated one in matters relating to public issues. All too frequently this cynical approach is used to excuse failure to express opinions on public matters. Indeed, it many times is presented as an excuse to explain failure to go to the polls.

"What can one man do? William Gressard, Twin Lakes sportsman, fishing-lure manufacturer, and fish-hatchery operator, has proved what one man can do. His 'one-man' campaign to halt pollution of the Cuyahoga River and to improve fishing is achieving results. To be sure, his campaign has won support of other citizens and organizations but it has clearly demonstrated that there is plenty that one man can do."

What can you do to stop pollution in you location?

There are a great many forces involved in pollution. Some of them are gigantic and can only be stopped by other gigantic forces. But there also are many one-man-sized problems that will be stopped only when some one person recognizes them, calls the attention of the proper officials to them, and then tries to alert others to the corrective action that needs to be taken.

Don Cullimore, executive director of the Outdoor Writers Association of America (OWAA), offers these guides to individual action that can stop pollution:

1. Be aware of the problem. Take the time to read about pollution of water, land, and air. Read magazine and newspaper articles related to the different forms of pollution.

2. When you see a problem, call it to the attention of the outdoors editor of a newspaper in your area. If you don't know the name of an outdoor editor near your home, write to OWAA, Guitar Building, Columbia, Missouri. A complete list of all outdoors editors is maintained there. For the name of the outdoors editor nearest you, send a stamped, addressed envelope.

3. Local conservation groups are interested in stopping pollution. You can get the name of one near you through your telephone directory or by writing to The Izaac Walton League of America, 1326 Waukegan Road, Glenview, Illinois, 60025.

4. Call city hall or the county building if you see examples of air pollution. Keep a record of your calls, names of officials with whom you talk, and results of your calls. When possible, take photographs (have the processor date them) and find other witnesses to the violations. Then if you don't get corrective action, call your local newspaper. You don't have to call the outdoors editor on smoke problems. The city editor will do. Describe the problem and the action you have taken. Tell him that you have kept a diary of your efforts, have witnesses (if you do), and have photographs. There are few good newspapermen who will not leap at such a story and, with such evidence, bring major criticism down on city officials and pollution offenders.

5. Be aware of the important role of the individual in combating pollution:

Have your car's exhaust and other operating systems checked periodically to make sure that they are not spewing unusually large amounts of unburned smoke into the atmosphere.

In the same way, check your home heating system, your power mower, your outboard motor, your son's motorbike, or any other family item that burns fuel for heat or power.

Refrain from open-trash and incinerator burning when some other form of disposal is available. When boating, don't throw trash overboard.

6. Finally, cooperate with public health officials by taking the time to know local rules and regulations concerning air, water, and land pollution and by observing them. Also, don't be reluctant to report violations of local laws. Authorities often must depend upon reports from responsible citizens. Only with such information can they begin to combat the many contributions to pollution.

Adam and Eve, Ltd.

AN ECOLOGICAL FABLE BY W. B. PARK

From there on it was easy. In no time he had banged out a frame, worked up tires, a little upholstery and a rearview mirror.

Soon Adam was wheeling Eve around the place, but before he really had the feel of the thing he zonked a couple of animals. After that the landlord grew sort of unhappy and suggested they find lodging elsewhere so they moved to Detroit.

Adam really liked Detroit. He got together a bunch of guys and began turning out fantastic numbers of cars. He was an overnight success and was quickly accepted as a community leader.

What with working day and night and weekends, however, it was no surprise to anyone when Eve ran off with a Baptist preacher, and was last seen managing a small apple jelly stand at Bloomers Ferry, Idaho.

Not too many years ago there was a couple who liked to be called Adam and Eve.
They lived together in this place full of fruit flowers birds trees and animals and they danced a lot and ate a lot and took naps. There was no traffic no war and no neon signs. It was a very good scene.

However, Adam's head was full of ideas and ambition and he was always tinkering and fooling with things and one day he suddenly put together an internal combustion engine.

Wow, he said. I did it — I put together this — ah— internal combustion engine.

continued

Things really came up shiny for Adam. He enlarged his Detroit operation and branched into other industry, business and finance. Stacking up success after success, he continued to amaze astound delight and titillate the world with his discoveries inventions and displays of remarkable talent and genius. He invented the cigarette and gunpowder. And the pencil eraser. He gave the world flying machines duck callers and alphabet soup.

Acclamation flowed in from all sides. He was voted Mr. VIP by the Junior Chamber of Commerce. He was made a full colonel in the National Guard. He was given a lifetime subscription to TV Guide. He dated film stars, and important columnists wrote in-depth studies of him entitled What Makes Adam Run? Twice he appeared on the Johnny Carson show.

Years passed and pressures began to mount on Adam. He felt obliged to come up with ever greater triumphs. So he built larger cities planes stadiums missiles and Disneylands. He covered the planet with outdoor billboards four lane highways and drive-in restaurants. He conceived the quantum theory, solved the mystery of Stonehenge, and perfected the inner spring mattress in the same afternoon. But his public grew ever more demanding. More, they screamed, more. So Adam gave them computers parking meters TV commercials napalm paper plates shuffleboard yoga and artificial grass and finally people began to notice something:

There weren't any trees left.

Or flowers birds and butterflies bears seashells frogs fish meadows mountain streams marshes or gentle summer rains... or rainbows.

There was a lot of pavement buildings traffic signals noise litter garbage exhaust fumes vapor trails and crowded jumbled nerve jangling confusion.

Things are getting out of hand, people fretted. It's a shame they would say. But finally everyone sort of got used to the litter and noise and all the rest... That's progress, they said. That's the price we pay.

And no one really seemed to mind.

Whatever happened to Adam? He was cooled by a large bus when he stopped at a roadside stand one day... for a jar of apple jelly.

APPLE JELLY
DDT CONTENT
LESS THAN
3%

The Peaceable Kingdom: Edward Hicks.

ALL WATCHED OVER BY MACHINES OF LOVING GRACE

I like to think (and
the sooner the better!)
of a cybernetic meadow
where mammals and computers
live together in mutually
programming harmony
like pure water
touching clear sky.

I like to think
    (right now please!)
of a cybernetic forest
filled with pines and electronics
where deer stroll peacefully
past computers
as if they were flowers
with spinning blossoms.

I like to think
    (it has to be!)
of a cybernetic ecology
where we are free of our labors
and joined back to nature,
returned to our mammal
brothers and sisters,
and all watched over
by machines of loving grace.

—*Richard Brautigan*

Reprinted by permission of Delacorte Press from Richard Brautigan, *The Pill Versus the Springhill Mine Disaster* (New York: Delacorte Press, 1968).